Emotion
Interdisciplinary Perspectives

Emotion
Interdisciplinary Perspectives

Edited by

Robert D. Kavanaugh
Betty Zimmerberg
Steven Fein
Williams College

LEA LAWRENCE ERLBAUM ASSOCIATES, PUBLISHERS
1996   Mahwah, New Jersey

Lawrence Erlbaum Associates, Inc., Publishers
10 Industrial Avenue
Mahwah, New Jersey 07430

Library of Congress Cataloging-in-Publication Data

Emotion : interdisciplinary perspectives / edited by Robert D.
Kavanaugh, Betty Zimmerberg, Steven Fein.
   p.   cm.
   Papers originally presented at the 3rd G. Stanley Hall Symposium
held at Williams College in 1993.
   Includes bibliographical references and index.
   ISBN 0-8058-1527-9 (alk. paper). — ISBN 0-8058-2028-0 (pbk. :
alk. paper)
   1. Emotions—Congresses. I. Kavanaugh, Robert D. II. Zimmerberg,
Betty. III. Fein, Steven. IV. G. Stanley Hall Symposium
(3rd : 1993 : Williams College)
BF531.E495 1996
152.4—dc20
                                                        95-13757
                                                          CIP

Books published by Lawrence Erlbaum Associates are printed on acid-free paper,
and their bindings are chosen for strength and durability

Printed in the United States of America
10 9 8 7 6 5 4 3 2 1

Contents

Foreword

Robert D. Kavanaugh
Betty Zimmerberg
Steven Fein
Williams College

This book celebrates the third in a series of symposia sponsored by the psychology department of Williams College honoring the memory of G. Stanley Hall, who graduated from Williams in 1867.

Hall was an enthusiastic student at Williams, drawn particularly to philosophy and political economics, whose wide-ranging extracurricular interests included participation in the college's choral group, chess club, theological society, and art association. He also served as editor of a quarterly magazine, and in his senior year was elected to Phi Beta Kappa. Hall seems to have been thwarted only on the baseball field, where his ambition to make the varsity team went unfulfilled.

The promise that Hall demonstrated as an undergraduate blossomed shortly after he left Williams to become the first recipient of a psychology PhD in the United States under the auspices of William James. This was but one of many firsts in Hall's distinguished career. He founded the first officially recognized psychological laboratory in the United States, became the first president of the American Psychological Association, and was the editor of the first psychology journal in America. As a scholar, Hall demonstrated a wide range of interests that took him to Europe to study with Wundt and led him to launch the child-study movement in America with the newly devised questionnaire method. Hall was known also for his keen interest in bringing contemporary issues to the fore, perhaps best demonstrated by his 1909 invitation to Freud, Jung, and other leaders of the emerging European psychoanalytic movement to speak at Clark University in Worcester, Massachusetts.

The purpose of Williams College's G. Stanley Hall symposia is to honor Hall's seminal contribution to psychology by bringing a group of eminent scholars to Williamstown to address topics of enduring interest to the field. The subject of the first symposium, held in 1986, was memory (see Solomon, Goethals, Kelley, & Stephens, 1988). The second symposium, held in 1989, addressed the topic of the self (see Strauss & Goethals, 1991). In the fall of 1993, we convened the third symposium to discuss contemporary perspectives on emotion. As in the previous symposia, our goal was to select scholars who represented diverse approaches and invite them to seek common ground among their differing viewpoints. Consequently, our participants included neuroscientists, developmentalists, social and personality psychologists, and clinical psychologists. In addition to delivering individual papers, participants joined in a series of round table discussions at the end of each of the two days of the symposium. These discussions, moderated by the editors of this volume, were interesting and far ranging. We think both the participants and the audience learned a great deal from these round tables, and we are grateful to our speakers for their frank and thoughtful contributions to these discussions.

The emotion symposium opened with a keynote address by Nico Frijda. Over the next two days papers were presented, in order, by Jaak Panksepp, Joseph Campos, Leslie Brody, E. Tory Higgins, Leslie Greenberg, Carol Magai, Nancy Stein, Robert Robinson, Marian Sigman, Michael Davis, and Dolf Zillmann. The participants' presentations form the basis for the current chapters that, in some instances, are coauthored with colleagues. In addition to thanking our participants and their coauthors for the thoughtful papers found in this volume, we would like to express our gratitude, first and foremost, to Francis C. Oakley, former president of Williams College, for both his financial support of the symposium and his gracious welcoming remarks to the participants on the opening night. We are also indebted to the Division of Neuroscience and Behavioral Science of the National Institute of Mental Health and the Essel Foundation for grant support that was vital to the symposium. In addition, we want to thank John H. Brooks of the Sterling and Francine Clark Art Institute for providing a comfortable and exceptionally beautiful setting for our presentations and round table discussions. We also express thanks to our colleagues in the psychology department at Williams for their helpful suggestions about the organization of the symposium as well as their support throughout the three days of the conference.

We turned the countless details of travel and local arrangements over to Judy O'Neil, who was as competent as she was cheerful in handling her many chores. Our departmental secretary, Mary Swift, found time in her busy schedule to assist Judy with the daily management of the conference. Mary has also been an invaluable resource in the preparation of this volume and we are very grateful for all of her efforts. We also want to thank C. J. Gillig, technical assistant to the psychology department, for his assistance with a number of conference details, and Cheryl Stanton, who graciously volunteered time during her senior year at Williams to help with a host of day-to-day arrangements. Finally, we are indebted to the editorial staff at Lawrence Erlbaum Associates, and, in particular, to Judith Amsel and Kathleen Dolan for their thoroughly professional assistance in the preparation of this volume.

REFERENCES

Solomon, P. R., Goethals, G. R., Kelley, C. M., & Stephens, B. (Eds.). (1988). *Memory: Interdisciplinary approaches*. New York: Springer-Verlag.

Strauss, J., & Goethals, G. R. (Eds.). (1991). *The self: Interdisciplinary approaches*. New York: Springer-Verlag.

Preface

Emotion is central to much of what intrigues psychologists. Research on a variety of social issues, including self-esteem, interpersonal relationships, and psychopathology, intersects with the study of emotion. So, too, does emotion influence traditionally cognitive enterprises, such as the study of memory, reasoning, and decision making. Furthermore, because emotions have physiological as well as behavioral characteristics, they should be of interest to a wide spectrum of investigators involved in research on the neuroanatomical and neurochemical bases of behavior.

It is ironic then that, historically, emotion not only failed to play a central role in mainstream scientific psychology, but that it was virtually absent from the field until the 1960s (Izard, 1991); this despite the fact that allied disciplines have long highlighted the importance of emotion. It is difficult to name a major philosopher, from Aristotle to Dewey, who did not underscore the importance of emotion, and equally difficult to ignore developments in psychoanalysis and behavioral medicine that have long brought the centrality of emotion into sharp relief (Plutchik, 1962). Furthermore, even a casual perusal of the arts—theater, music, and writing—points to the central role of emotion in the quest to understand the human condition.

Psychology's extended absence from the debate and discussion about emotion must be puzzling to those outside the field but, as always, the view from within is quite different. It seems highly improbable that the study of emotion simply failed to interest psychologists. Certainly, the subfields of developmental and clinical psychology have long wrestled with complex issues, such as the attachment between parent and child, that fall well within the rubric of emotion. It is more likely that emotion assumed a relegated position within psychology because it did not appear to conform easily to the emphasis on objective, behavioral principles that dominated the field throughout the first half of the century. As a result, emotion constructs were thought to be confusing and to possess little explanatory power (Duffy, 1962). When emotion did appear in the pre-1960 literature, it was often limited to, or subsumed under, topics and constructs that could be easily operationalized, such as drives, motivation, and physiology (Izard, 1991). Emotion per se, particularly as it applied to the study of cognitive and social phenomena, rarely attracted the full force of psychological research.

Since roughly 1960, however, emotion has become a topic of considerable importance to psychologists. Particularly over the last 15 years, we have witnessed a dramatic growth in the number of influential books and monographs on emotion (cf. Lazarus, 1991). There is no doubt that the renewed interest in emotion we see today is attributable to many different factors. Psychology is broader in focus, and more open to a variety of reliable methods and approaches to empirical questions, than it was 40-odd years ago. Scientific rigor is no longer confused with, or restricted to, particular methods or overarching philosophical dispositions. Equally important is the broadening of perspective on issues central to the field. One example seems particularly telling—the emergence of cognitive science as a major force in psychology. It is both striking and sobering that a discipline that once stepped gingerly around the topic of mind has spawned a cognitive "revolution" that forced a rethinking of some very fundamental ideas about human cognition. Now not only do we speak freely about the capacities of the mind, and how it emerges during childhood, but we attribute mentalistic capabilities—and, yes, minds—to animals and possibly machines (cf. Whiten, 1991). As cognitive scientists began to explore these uncharted waters they found colleagues of very different persuasions intrigued rather than repelled by their inquiry into the machinations of the mind. They were joined by neuroscientists searching for the biological bases of mental capacities, by developmentalists examining the origins of the child's "theory of mind," and by social psychologists looking at the complex interrelationship between cognitive and social processes (cf. Bartsch & Wellman, 1995; Tomaz & Graeff, 1993; Wyer & Srull, 1994).

The study of emotion did not benefit directly from progress in cognitive science, but it did profit from the same broadening of perspective that recognized the legitimacy of inquiries into the workings of the mind.

Emotion emerged from the shadows as psychology's lens widened, and the restricted focus on traditional topics (e.g., perception, learning, intelligence) gradually waned. Emotion was no longer seen in opposition to the "hard side" of psychology and began to assume a more pivotal role in the field. One of the earliest testimonials to the centrality of emotion issued from no less a learning theorist than Mowrer (1960), who argued that emotion played a critical and even indispensable role in the learning process. Mowrer's view was part of an emerging zeitgeist that would eventually discard, or at least broaden substantially, the positivism of S–R psychology. One of the by-products of this larger conceptualization of psychological phenomena was a healthy respect for the study of emotion. Emotion research began to appear as a centerpiece in a number of subfields within psychology. Just as importantly, it served as a link between subfields, as indicated by journals such as *Cognition and Emotion* and *Motivation and Emotion*.

G. STANLEY HALL SYMPOSIUM ON EMOTION

The principal goal of our symposium was to encourage further discussion of the links between subfields in psychology that address the topic of emotion. Toward that end, we asked 12 distinguished scholars in the emotion field, who represented a variety of different theoretical perspectives, to illuminate the breadth of their current work on emotion. The chapters that follow illustrate the diversity of their approaches, but also highlight some common themes.

Nico Frijda opened the conference with a provocative paper urging psychologists to focus on the role of emotions in passionate and socially consequential behavior. Frijda argued that every emotion, even those that might be disparaged as mere feelings, contains the "action readiness" that can translate into socially consequential behavior. How this process comes about is complex, in Frijda's view, and amounts to an analysis of a neglected feature of emotions—their power or intensity. According to Frijda, what are most fundamental to any powerful emotion are the deeply rooted concerns that motivate it. Concerns, of course, must translate into action, and Frijda believes that the added stimulus comes from several important sources: an appraisal of the degree to which events can be controlled, the individual's sense of how vivid and pressing the events are, and a cluster of peripheral factors such as mood state and arousal. Finally, Frijda addressed the role that beliefs play in both motivating and sustaining intense emotions. He drew attention to the way in which beliefs dispose people to act, and to the self-perpetuating role that beliefs play in evaluating new information about relevant events.

BIOLOGICAL SUBSTRATES OF EMOTION

Two of the conference participants, Jaak Panksepp and Michael Davis, spoke about the biological and neural substrates of emotion. Panksepp began his presentation with an impassioned exploration of the role of behavioral neuroscience in the scientific study of emotion, explaining how animal models are critical for a comprehensive understanding of the fundamental mechanisms underlying human emotions. Panksepp then provided an overview of the subcortical structures involved in emotive circuits with particular attention to the PANIC system, which mediates separation stress, and presented a series of studies from his laboratory detailing the anatomical connections underlying the emotions of loneliness and grief, which can be quantified by measuring distress vocalizations following social isolation. His series of neurochemical studies examining the role of peptide neurotransmitters, such as the opioids, prolactin and oxcytocin, in separation distress point to some possible neurochemical mechanisms of human sadness and related emotions. Early childhood autism is suggested to be partially caused by excessive endogenous activity in the fetal brain's opioid systems; experimental studies involving the treatment of autism with naltrexone that support this hypothesis are presented here. Finally, a new imaging technique that can map neural activity across the surface of the cortex in real time is described, and may provide a powerful tool to study responses to emotion-provoking stimuli in humans.

Using a well-characterized animal model developed in his laboratory, Michael Davis described an elegant series of studies examining the neural mechanisms of fear. This paradigm, the fear-potentiated startle response, provides a rich experimental environment in which Davis has been able to trace the pathways underlying conditioned fear responses. In particular, pathways within the amygdala are characterized for their contribution to the different components of the conditioned response. Extending the experimental paradigm from the animal laboratory, this chapter also presents a series of studies in which almost identical procedures are used to investigate fear-potentiated startle in psychiatric and nonpsychiatric populations. Because experiences associated with the emotion of fear are intimately involved in the development of anxiety, this model system can now be used to ask parallel questions in animals and humans to better understand abnormal conditioning of emotions. This chapter also relates a series of new studies on the neurochemical systems mediating this pathway. These studies suggest a critical role for glutamate in conditioned fear responses, both in the amygdala and brainstem, and will undoubtedly prove to be valuable in the development of new treatments for anxiety disorders.

DEVELOPMENT AND EMOTION

Several conference participants adopted developmental perspectives on emotion, none more explicitly than Joe Campos and his colleagues who sought to apply broad epigenetic principles to an understanding of emotional development in infancy. The two principles that guide their work are that (a) intraperson changes set the stage for subsequent developmental achievements, and (b) each developmental change profoundly influences the person–environment relationship. Data from a series of clever experiments involving a moving room apparatus lead Campos and his colleagues to conclude that the first epigenetic principle is demonstrated in the acquisition of motor skills (crawling/creeping) that lead to emotional changes (fear of heights) of great adaptive value. The second principle is illustrated in a subsequent study which revealed that the onset of locomotion produced major changes in *both* infants and parents. With the onset of creeping or crawling, parents reported marked changes in the quality and intensity of the infant's attachment behaviors and in their own relationship with the infant. The authors conclude by suggesting that their epigenetic analysis of fear of heights should also apply to other physical milestones (e.g., reaching and walking), and that these, too, should be viewed as developmental phenomena that will create far-reaching changes in the person–environment relationship.

Leslie Brody and Carol Magai also discussed developmental issues in their papers. Brody addressed the complex question of the relationship between gender, emotional expression, and family relationships. She considered gender differences in a number of different emotions, but is particularly interested in shame and guilt among a sample of young adult males and females. Participants in her study, and their siblings, made independent judgments about family functioning and their own emotional expressiveness. Brody found that the quality of parent–child boundaries relates both to the intensity and frequency of expressed affect, but often in complex ways. For example, for sons the presence of an intrusive father may relate to intense positive and negative interpersonal emotions, but for daughters an intrusive father may relate to less interpersonal sadness, shame, and anger. She also found the concept of *boundaries*—the degree of individuation/separation that her subjects experienced—to be a particularly useful theoretical tool. Brody's large data base, combined with her thoughtful analysis, allowed her to speculate about the intricate relationships between emotional expression and family relationships for both women and men. In the end, she posited a systemic model of emotion expression that intertwines individual differences in child temperament, parental responses to their children's emotions, and the developmental consequences of the parents' own boundary relationships.

Carol Magai combined developmental and personality psychology perspectives to examine the central role that emotions play in human personality from infancy through adulthood. Magai reviewed the history of trait theory approaches to the study of personality, and she observed that these approaches have not addressed adequately "the *why*, the *wherefore*, and the *ontogeny* of human personality" (p. 174). As a counterpoint, Magai offered a compelling theory of personality that addresses these questions by examining issues of motivation, domains of influence, interactions of person and situation, individual differences, and continuity and discontinuity. She argued that emotions are at the core of personality and are the primary sources of motivation, and that the critical emotions around which an individual's personality traits are organized have profound influence on his or her thoughts, perceptions, and behaviors. Magai reinterpreted the current five-factor and two- or three-factor models of personality within the framework of discrete emotions theory. She specified five higher order emotion traits which map onto the five factors that emerge in current factor-analytic studies and presented a thorough and compelling examination of a particular personality pattern—that organized around anger and hostility—to illustrate how her functionalist framework can address the why, wherefore, and ontogeny of personality.

EMOTION AND SOCIAL–COGNITIVE PROCESSES

Nancy Stein, E. Tory Higgins, and Dolf Zillmann presented papers that spoke to the role of social–cognitive processes in emotion. Stein and her colleagues, Maria Liwag and Elizabeth Wade, advanced a model of emotional understanding that emphasizes the role of goals and appraisals in the processes of experiencing and remembering emotional events. They argued that happiness, anger, sadness, and fear map onto a particular pattern of goal–outcome relationships and beliefs concerning the probability of reinstating or maintaining a goal. Thus, critical to an individual's emotional experience of an event are (a) whether or not the individual thinks that the event has caused the success or failure of important goals, and (b) the individual's beliefs about his or her ability "to reinstate a failed or attained goal or to prevent specific goal states from occurring" (p. 93). Stein and colleagues' method of analyzing the content and structure of on-line thinking and memory representations provides data that offer fascinating illustrations of children's and adults' value judgments, implicit theories of action and causality, perceptions of agency, expectations about the world, and strategies for attaining goals and avoiding unwanted outcomes. These data challenge several assumptions of current models of emotional understanding, and provide a methodological as well as a theoretical model for future research to follow.

E. Tory Higgins proposed that "distinct self-regulatory systems underlie different emotional experiences" (p. 233). These self-regulatory systems
stem from discrepancies between individuals' perceptions of their actual
self and their ideal (representations of hopes, wishes, and aspirations)
and ought (representations of duty, obligations, and responsibilities)
selves. Higgins' chapter emphasizes the distinction between a self-regulatory system that focuses on the maximization of pleasure—emphasizing
ideal self-guides—and a self-regulatory system that focuses on the minimization of pain—emphasizing *ought* self-guides. Higgins challenges
theories that propose that intensity or arousal is a critical attribute of
emotions and asserts instead that outcome focus—an important component of self-regulatory systems—is a more critical property of emotions.

Perhaps the most impressive aspect of Higgins' chapter is the breadth
and sophistication of the methodological approaches used in this research.
With data collected from hundreds of subjects using measures, manipulations, and hypotheses spanning across clinical, cognitive, developmental,
personality, and social psychology, Higgins and his colleagues have illustrated both relatively stable individual differences and context-dependent
situational variables that cause either the ideal or the ought self-regulatory
system to determine an individual's emotional experience.

Zillmann examined the nature of emotions by focusing on transitions
between emotional experiences; here, excitation transfer theory represents
an interdisciplinary approach to the study of emotion that combines
neuroscientific, cognitive, health, and social psychological perspectives.
Zillmann proposed to integrate neuroendocrinologically mediated autonomic activity with higher order social–cognitive processes such as causal
attribution, interpersonal perception, and social validation, and he posited
that it is only through such an integration that one can predict and
understand the sequential processes in emotional experiences and responses. At the heart of Zillmann's research is the interaction between
cognitive elaboration and autonomic activity. He identified a number of
variables that determine how, and to what extent, these processes interact,
and discussed a large body of research that contributes to our understanding of complex relationships such as those between sexual arousal
and aggression, frustration and anger, and fear and euphoria.

EMOTION AND PATHOLOGY

Three of the conference presenters—Marian Sigman, Robert Robinson,
and Leslie Greenberg—discussed the role of emotions in the lives of
individuals who are confronted with physical or emotional problems that
compromise either the production or understanding of emotion expres-

sion. Marian Sigman and her colleague Lisa Capps compared the emotional development of children with autism to that of normally developing children, with the goal of understanding the emotional isolation or "aloneness" that is characteristic of individuals with autism. Capps and Sigman documented that, contrary to stereotype, children with autism are not completely devoid of social skills. For example, children with autism are as responsive and playful as normally developing children, though somewhat more passive, in interactive games such as rolling a ball from one person to another. What is different about children with autism is that they are less likely to initiate social interactions and share positive emotional experiences with caregivers by making eye contact, showing favored toys, or looking to the caregiver during moments of uncertainty. To account for these differences, Capps and Sigman proposed that what is absent in autism is central "coherence," a quality that manifests itself in the need to integrate and contextualize disparate information into a connected whole. Coherence forms the basis for the emotional exchanges that are manifest in turn taking, empathy, shared communication, and narrative. In the view of Capps and Sigman, without central coherence children with autism struggle to achieve what appears so effortless in the emotional development of normal children.

Robinson's research is focused on the "natural experiments" provided by humans who have brain lesions subsequent to strokes or have suffered traumatic head injuries. By examining the deficits exhibited by these patients, and investigating the behavior of rats with similarly placed lesions, Robinson has been able to study the cerebral basis of mood disorders. One of his most important findings is that patients with major depressive disorder are more likely to have left-hemisphere lesions than right-hemisphere lesions, with the frontal cortex and basal ganglia of the left hemisphere implicated particularly in major depression. Through a series of imaging studies Robinson has also moved closer to an understanding of the biological mechanism of depression. For example, receptor-binding studies revealed differences between the right and left hemispheres' regulation of serotonin receptors in response to injury. As Robinson notes, the study of the neural bases of emotions is still in its infancy, but his chapter advances our knowledge of how limbic structures regulate mood and suggests important new directions for this field.

Greenberg addressed the question of how emotions, particularly those surrounding painful psychic experiences, can become helpful growth experiences for the individual. Beginning with the assumption that emotions/feelings are adaptive, Greenberg speculated about the origins of maladaptive emotions and the thoughts and actions that sustain them. At the root of many emotional problems is the maladaptive response of avoiding feelings, of failing to trust feelings, and, eventually, the splitting off of painful feelings in an effort to protect the self from becoming overwhelmed. Thus, Greenberg believes that successful therapeutic intervention allows clients to experience emotions that had previously been disallowed. If clients are unaware of primary feeling, therapists should assist them in acknowledging and symbolizing these previously disallowed feelings. Allowing and accepting feelings is, however, not the only therapeutic goal. People must also learn to change the way in which they cope with internal experiences; thus, in therapy people are encouraged to explore and differentiate the processes that produce bad feelings so that the thoughts and behavior that generate these feelings can be uncovered.

CONCLUSION

The 12 chapters presented here represent a range of approaches to the topic of emotion. We trust that readers of this volume will appreciate the diversity of questions and methods presented by scholars who represent distinctly different subfields, but we also hope that they will note the common ground that emerges in these discussions. As we noted earlier, emotion seems to be an ideal candidate for the cross pollination of ideas that can emerge from interdisciplinary research efforts. We recognize that such undertakings are not easy, and that not everyone would be sanguine about the potential benefits. We also acknowledge that links between subfields are difficult to forge and not entirely without cost. Nonetheless, we believe that the chapters herein represent the beginning of a dialogue about possible intersections in the study of emotion from scholars who embrace sharply different perspectives on this complex topic. We also believe it is fitting that an enterprise such as this should honor the memory of G. Stanley Hall.

—*Robert D. Kavanaugh*
—*Betty Zimmerberg*
—*Steven Fein*

REFERENCES

Bartsch, K., & Wellman, H. M. (1995). *Children talk about the mind.* New York: Oxford University Press.
Duffy, E. (1962). *Activation and behavior.* New York: Wiley.
Izard, C. E. (1991). *The psychology of emotions.* New York: Plenum.
Lazarus, R. S. (1991). *Emotion and adaption.* New York: Oxford University Press.
Mowrer, O. H. (1960). *Learning theory and behavior.* New York: Wiley.

Plutchik, R. (1962). *The emotions: Facts, theories, and a new model.* New York: Random House.

Tomaz, C., & Graeff, F. G. (1993). Emotion and memory. *Behavioural Brain Research, 58,* 1–210.

Whiten, A. (Ed.). (1991). *Natural theories of mind: Evolution, development, and simulation of everyday mindreading.* Oxford, England: Blackwell.

Wyer, R. S., & Srull, T. K. (Eds.). (1994). *Handbook of social cognition* (2nd ed.). Hillsdale, NJ: Lawrence Erlbaum Associates.

Passions: Emotion and Socially Consequential Behavior[1]

Nico H. Frijda
Amsterdam University

At the present time, Western Europe is again the close neighbor to one of the great atrocities of human history—to extremes of cruelty and other violence, the willful neglect of human dignity, and the blinding passions of the interests of one group at the cost of the lives of another. We are, moreover, close neighbors to events that may, at any moment, burst into still more widespread destruction. Not only in Europe but elsewhere too, one is at the risk of outbursts caused by the passion of self-righteousness in particular faiths. Nationalism, too, seems to be rampant wherever you go, exploding into violence on many an occasion.[1]

Much of this behavior is driven by emotions. This chapter, in fact, is a first, tentative effort to see clearly into an issue with which I think the psychology of emotion should preoccupy itself: that of the role of emotions in behavior having social consequence. Although vital systematic information is lacking, and what is to follow is groping and incomplete, I feel that psychology has an obligation to form its views about the subject.

Of course, we know that grand-scale violence is not primarily precipitated by emotions, let alone by the emotions of the individuals perpetrating that violence. Such violence is caused by political, religious, and economical conflicts or strivings. To a large extent it is based on strategic considerations regarding gains or the avoidance of losses, in line with

[1]I am much indebted to Batja Mesquita for her careful comments and for adding relevant information.

Clausewitz' (1832/1987) dictum that war is the continuation of negotiations by other means. It is effectuated through social organization and obedience to its rules, and the individual usually comes to violence through such rules and through opportunity and circumstance. Somewhere on the road from the political, religious, or economic strivings to the shootings, the rapes, and the murders, however, emotions enter the game and seem to play a major role.

Serbian–Bosnian women and children could recently be seen on newsreels blocking the progress of a United Nations relief transport to Sarajevo with angry shouts and faces, carrying banners covered with angry texts. Such ferocious anger was dominant in the discussions in the Serbian, Croatian, and Serbian–Bosnian parliaments, and so forth. Of course, reports abound of fears for the Chetniks—the Serbian militiamen—at the hands of the Bosnian and Croatian sides, and for the Usthashas—the Croatian militiamen—at that of the Serbians. We speak of the hatred between formerly peaceful neighbors in the mixed villages and of the pride and pathos with which one expressed devoted nationalism for the ground upon which one had lived for 300 years. Pride is felt for the grandeur of Stefan Dusan and his Great Serbia in the 14th century and the honorable defeat at the Blackbird field in 1389. Of course, we also heard of the joy in plundering and carrying TV sets off to one's home country, the arrogance with which U.N. personnel was turned away from the roadblocks and U.N. negotiators were turned down by representatives of the forces they dealt with, and how the major players, such as generals, talked about the situation, their enemies, and their plans (Glenny, 1992).

I take my examples from Yugoslavia; of course, I need not do that. Films and interviews provide ample evidence of the enthusiasm of Nazi skinheads setting out to burn Turkish homes in Germany, the lynch mobs in the pre-Civil Rights American South, the fierce, cruel hatreds and desire for revenge flaring in the Colombian Violencia in the 1940s (Pearce, 1990), and the massacres in the Palestinian camps of Sabra and Chatila in 1982 Lebanon (Fisk, 1991).

Prosocial behavior brings up the same problem. Why and when do pity or indignation lead to actual, effortful behavior, and to taking risks? What was the role of emotions in making people hide Jews during the great persecutions, or in risking their skin today in Somalia or Bosnia? Not all love makes the individual traverse fires; not all pity and sympathy makes us lift a finger, let alone spend time and money or voluntarily face dangers. We all grieve for the Bosnian or Somali children, but who takes one into his or her home? We all are disturbed by environmental pollution, but who drives his or her car a mile less, or agrees with taxing gasoline more heavily? The problem is familiar from the study of the relations between attitudes and behavior—here I want to discuss it from a different angle. What is the role of emotions in those relations, and what is it about emotions (if it is emotions) that makes one take such actions as those mentioned?

Much of what I have just discussed is not solid proof on the role of emotion in socially consequential behavior—neither of its magnitude nor of its place in the chains of events. However, I take it as sufficient evidence to affirm that this role is considerable. This, then, is the topic of this chapter: What is the contribution of emotion to socially consequential behavior? I try to approach the problem by examining two somewhat more modest questions. First, under what conditions might emotions lead to socially consequential behavior? Second, what, in general, might be the role of emotions in the shaping of such behavior? What can the psychology of emotion contribute to understanding such behavior?

The problem of the role of emotions in socially consequential behavior is not posed by destructive behavior and emotions only. It is posed also by positive emotions, such as love. Both Tristan and Isolde and Abélard and Heloïse defied hardships and rejection. That, of course, may merely be fiction, but the sacrifices of the Fathers of the Desert such as St. Anthony were not; love of God was involved, according to their testimony (Regnault, 1990). The same problem exists with regard to explaining some behaviors motivated by grief, such the one that brought the Roman emperor Hadrian to the construction of the city of Antinoopolis, in memory of his dead friend Antinoous (Yourcenar, 1951).

In discussing this question, it may be useful to use a special word to designate those motivational states that do not merely lead to impulsive behaviors of short duration, as do fits of anger or upsurges of love but, rather, to emotionally charged goals and planned activities over a longer time span. I will use the word *passion* for the impulses towards such goals, and *passionate emotions* for emotions that show persistence over time, power of drastic actions, and neglect of consequences. To some extent, the questions that I posed earlier boil down to this: Under what circumstances do passions arise, and when do passionate emotions, and what is it that accounts for their power and duration?

THE RELATIONSHIP BETWEEN EMOTIONS AND BEHAVIOR

The emergence of passions is in many ways merely a special case of the emergence of emotional behavior. Emotional goals are but extensions of the aims of more impulsive short-lived emotional behaviors—aims such as fleeing from threat or hurting one's opponent. Passions exemplify the general problem of understanding the relationship between emotions and behavior.

That relationship is an intimate one. Emotions are always and necessarily linked to behavior or, at least, to changes in behavioral readiness. That is to say: Change in action readiness is a major, if not *the* major, aspect of the response to emotionally significant events, and one that is directly elicited by such events of any strength. Emotionally significant events may elicit physiological changes, and they may elicit feelings, but unless they imply or involve changes in the readiness for relationships with something in the environment (or the actual implementation of such changes) they are of no consequence for either the individual or for others.

The relationship between emotions and behavior has been seen as a loose one only fairly recently. Emotion was viewed as appraisal-based behavioral impulse in Aristotle's (trans. 1941) *Rhetoric* and was defined as appraisal-linked modification of the power of acting by Spinoza (1677/1989). It became a sort of minimal movement in Berkeley, and mere feeling, a sort of sensation, no earlier than in the analytical psychology of Hume (1739/1969) and, later, Wundt (1902). It came to be almost identical to autonomic upset (or autonomic upset combined with cognitions) only in the present century. With these latter shifts the connection of emotion with behavior became extrinsic, arbitrary, and incomprehensible. During the last decades, the view on emotion is changing again. It was never presented in such a way in psychoanalytic thought, and emotions came to be seen as explicitly motivational in the works of Sartre (1948), Arnold (1960), Tomkins (1962), Izard (1977), and Lazarus (1966). It still deserves, however, to be emphasized that change in readiness for action is central in emotion.

What is meant by the assertion that action readiness is central in emotion? It means that changes in action readiness are among the phenomena that are elicited directly by the emotional stimulus constellation as appraised, independently of autonomic change, and largely independently of conscious emotional feeling, and that these changes in readiness, under appropriate circumstances, lead to actual action. In fact, emotional experience—conscious feeling—is often inseparable from the preparation of response. For instance, the experience of an insult as "intolerable" refers to a call for action. At a more basic and general level, the experiences of pleasure and pain, or pleasantness and unpleasantness, are intrinsically and unavoidably tied to approach and avoidance or, rather, to the continuation and the termination of interaction (Arnold, 1960).

States of emotional action readiness share a characteristic that more or less defines them as "emotional": that which I have elsewhere called *control precedence* (Frijda, 1986). The action readiness that we consider "emotional" tends to control actual dealings with the environment and it also tends to control cognitive activity. Readiness for a particular kind of relational change (for disrupting the relationship with a particular object, for instance, or for avoidance, hostile dealings, or approach) tends to let behavior reach the goal for which it is ready, ignoring the calls for attention or action relevant to other issues, usurping attention for pertinent information, resuming goal-related overt and cognitive activity after interruption, and tending to push aside obstacles on the way. When angry, you tend to forget the damages of retaliation. When afraid, you tend to abandon your duties, and the same happens when you are in love. This notion of control precedence tries to locate the imperative character of emotions in the emotion process, and to specify what that imperative character consists of: the emotions' power to guide attention, to distract and interrupt and, first and foremost, their character of impulse. It is important to note that control precedence in emotion does not only fall to readiness for action, but also to unreadiness, in its various forms: to anxiety paralysis, to the apathy of grief and the abandonment of striving in despair, the passive call for help in grief, pain, and anguish, the breakdown of focused action in diffuse excitement. All of these are as difficult to resist or overcome as the impulses for flight or attack.

Control precedence of the current state of action readiness is an elementary aspect of the dynamics of action and of the relations of the individual to his or her environment. The process of assuming control over action and cognitive activity results from a basic mechanism that is not derived from something else, such as goal priority calculations or prior reinforcement. The impulses of emotions just tend to do it—about its mechanics one can only speculate. My theory is that control precedence is a direct outflow of the system detecting concern relevance, or, which amounts to the same, a direct, hardwired consequence of affect signals (pleasures and pains) of any strength. Watch a baby's hunger distress or the writhing in response to physical pain: such things absorb the individual's attention and processing resources to a degree that takes considerable force to restrain or overcome. Watch their mental equivalent, anguish, as it occurs in all the variants of separation distress such as grief, jealousy, guilt emotion, or deprivation under addiction. There, too, nothing counts but the experience at hand. How could this be so? A possible hypothesis may suppose control precedence to be one of the properties of the activation of elementary behavior systems or circuits, like those for anger, anxiety, or desire, as conceived by Panksepp (1982) and Gray (1982). A hypothesis concerning a mechanistic basis for either is not hard to find: So many neurochemical agents with widespread neurotransmitting or neuromodulatory functions are involved in emotions (Panksepp, 1993).

The upshot of this is that the occurrence of overpowering action impulses forms part of the very nature of emotions. They are not, I think, socially constructed excuses, as Averill (1982) has argued, or a result of culturally adopted metaphors as Lakoff and Koveckses (1983) will have it. Cultures may choose one metaphor or another, such as that of a fire consuming or of a pot containing, but all they do is try to find an image for a property that is there. That property, control precedence, often takes the form of behavioral impulse that crashes through obstacles, throws decency to the wind, and does not care about tomorrow. Emotions, at heart, are of a passionate nature.

It may be objected that so many emotions are mere feelings, without any pressures for action or for action abandonment; examples are nostalgia, religious awe, aesthetic admiration, and the varieties of nonsexual love. For one thing, however, emotions such as these do involve control precedence. Nostalgia of any strength, for instance, is not something one just feels; it makes one put down one's knitting and stare out of the window. For another thing, the emotional life is of course stamped by two dies, the excitatory one and the inhibitory, regulatory one. Many emotions are reduced to "feelings," and are forced to remain inside the mind as nothing but feelings, due to regulatory processes. In fact, all emotions are controlled to some degree, except under brain damage or mass intoxication (Frijda, 1986), and culture may powerfully contribute to such control. We in the West, in particular, *mirabile dictu*, live in "civilized societies," in the sense of Elias (1969): Civilization and affect control are nearly synonymous. As a consequence, Western reflection tends to condemn emotion's passionate nature, to deny it, to consider it a secondary product of cultural perversions, as opposed to the more traditional views. We hardly know the violent nature of emotions any more, until phenomena such as those mentioned previously remind us of the fact that this, and not motionless feeling state, is and was emotion's unadulterated nature.

The passionate nature of many emotions is most evident in the emotions called *desires*. Desire is not a popular emotion category in current psychology, although it was one of the three basic emotions for Spinoza (1677/1989), and is one of the four basic emotion circuits for Panksepp (1982). By desire I mean the action tendency towards possessing and consuming a given object or arriving at a given end state. States of desire have all of the major characteristics of other emotions: They involve appraisal (of the goal object as being fit for satisfaction), action readiness change, and control precedence. Desires are impulses; they merely differ from other emotions in that they are not elicited by an emotional event other than that of meeting a fit object or the thought of it. The only reason to discuss them separately is the important role they play in the emotional turmoil of war, and in causing what I labeled socially relevant behavior.

Causation of aggression is a case in point. Much aggression has nonemotional sources, such as the striving for political gain. Many other instances have emotional sources in the reactions to unpleasant events, like the anger evoked by frustration or insult. In addition, however, it appears that there is much aggression that indeed is emotional, yet is not elicited by adverse events. Much extreme cruelty and wanton destruction appears to be instigated by sheer pleasure, the expectation of sheer personal satisfaction. What the concerns are from which such pleasure stems is not always clear. Desire for social prestige is a likely source, as is the desire for power, mentioned as the explanation of cruelty by Schopenhauer (1819) and Bain (1876), and the competence motive (White, 1959), in a perverted variant. Subduing others makes the ego grow, and submitting them to torture may do so still more. This applies quite emphatically to rape, which is motivated to a large extent by a desire to humiliate, to show power, and to inflate the ego to obtain the pleasures of satisfying those concerns (Brownmiller, 1976). That desire for prestige and power may not—and quite clearly often *is* not—the individual's desire for his or her own personal prestige or power, but for that of the group. Serbian and Croatian rapists were reported to have said to their Bosnian victims that each Bosnian woman should bear a Serbian (or Croatian) child, and in this fashion no Bosnian man would ever want them again (Mesquita, personal communication, July 1993).

EMOTIONAL INTENSITY

The preceding is a reminder that producing behavior with social consequences and control precedence belongs to the very nature of emotions. It does not, however, resolve the main problems posed: to understand the passionate nature of many emotions and the emergence of passions, the magnitude of the consequences that these may entail, and the time spans over which those consequences are pursued. I refer to the aspects of the emotions responsible for consequences of great magnitude as the "power" of emotions, taking the term from Spinoza (1677/1989). I have argued that emotions, by their nature, may have great power, and this fact makes it comprehensible that emotions *can* run to extremes. It indicates that emotions are, so to speak, ready to run to extremes and need little encouragement to actually do so. But this does not always happen. They do, however, need *some* encouragement, and the question remains: What it is that gives them such encouragement?

Thus, on what does the power of emotions depend? One's first hunch might be that it depends on the emotion's intensity, but this would not involve a meaningful hypothesis because it is not at all clear how the notions of emotional intensity and emotional power are different. The notion of *intensity* covers a number of aspects of emotions that may vary in magnitude more or less independently (Frijda, Ortony, Sonnemans, &

Clore, 1992; Sonnemans, 1991). What I call the "power" of an emotion refers to several of these aspects, but not necessarily to all of them. It refers to drastic action impulse, long emotion duration, large changes in beliefs and in the conduct of life, and recurrence of the event in thought. What one calls intensity refers to these same aspects, along with some others. The notion of intensity may also be taken to refer to the intensity of subjective feeling (Frijda et al., 1992; Sonnemans, 1991), but felt intensity itself may well be merely awareness of the aspects mentioned earlier. To take intensity as a causal factor for power is thus not satisfactory. It is better to turn directly to the determinants of intensity in its various guises.

Peculiarly enough, modern psychology has been almost silent on this issue. Emotional intensity has scarcely been a subject of research, or even of consideration, although numerous studies have used the magnitude of some emotional response variable to measure the effect of some variable or manipulation. Intensity as such, however, has largely remained out of focus. I only know of the analysis by Ortony, Clore, and Collins (1988) and of our own studies (Frijda et al., 1992; Sonnemans, 1991), as the first systematic discussions since that given by Spinoza, in 1677, in the fourth book of *Ethics*. True enough, Spinoza does give a highly detailed and plausible account of what determines the power of emotions (Frijda, in press), and it was used as a source of hypotheses for our own work.

What gives an emotion its intensity, or determines the intensity of its various aspects? Hypotheses can be derived from process theories of emotion. In our view, emotions are caused by the interaction of a number of factors, and emerge in a process involving of a number of steps (Frijda, 1986). Figure 1.1 illustrates that process and its conditions. Emotional

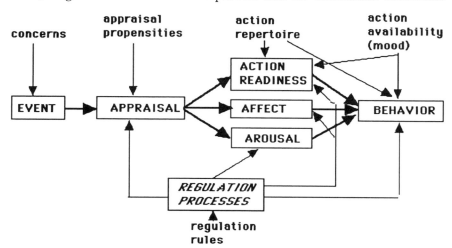

FIG. 1.1. The emotion process and its conditions.

Intensity=f (Concerns, Event, Appraisal, Action repertoire, Regulation, Mood)

FIG. 1.2.   Factors influencing emotional intensity.

intensity can therefore also be assumed to be caused by an interaction of many factors, since each of the elements in the causation of emotion may vary in magnitude. The determination of emotional intensity can be summarized as a joint function, as shown in Fig. 1.2; the one presented here is a slight modification of one described earlier (Frijda et al., 1992; Sonnemans, 1991).

Understanding how emotions and their intensity emerge amounts to specifying the precise nature of each of the factors in Fig. 1.2. What is it about the concerns, the nature of the events, and so on that contributes to intensity? Understanding the power of emotions amounts to a particular set of such specifications. Variables that affect, say, the intensity of autonomic response, or even the intensity of feeling, may not affect the variables subsumed under "power."

CONCERNS AND EVENTS

Motivation forms the basis for emotions, according to most current emotion theories (e.g., Frijda, 1986; Lazarus, 1991; Oatley, 1992; Ortony et al., 1988; Scherer, 1984). Emotions result from the individual's goals, motives, values, or, as I will say, from his or her concerns. They emerge when an event or object is appraised as favoring, harming, or threatening one or several of one's concerns. It is a plausible assumption that the stronger or more important the concern(s) to which an event or object is relevant, the more intense the emotion. *Concern strength* may be conceptualized as the degree to which the concern is unsatisfied (as operationalized, for instance, by time of deprivation), or by how serious the consequences are when the concern is not satisfied (when you do not get food, you die; when you do not find a mate, that may merely be unpleasant), or as the number of events and behaviors that depend on the concern's satisfaction. (High self-esteem presumably potentiates all encounters and one's confidence in all of one's actions; the high value of one's religion may be based on the fact that it affects our sense of identity, and thus the stability of all our judgments and rules of conduct.)

Emotional intensity also depends on the degree of relevance of the event that elicits the emotion; that is, on the magnitude of the satisfaction offered, or the seriousness of the threat. Presumably, intense pain causes more emotion than weak pain, and pain that announces serious illness causes more emotion than equally intense pain that does not. The major variable, however, that probably links concerns to emotional intensity is the number of different concerns that a given event calls into play, or that a particular issue of concern represents. One's attachments are so emotionally important, one may suppose, because so many concerns simultaneously seek satisfaction there: personal proximity, sex, succor, company, and intimacy, among others. Jealousy is often so emotionally trenchant because the provoking event implies a threat to erotic satisfactions, self-esteem, one's control over someone else, as well as to one's relationship as such, all at the same time (Buunk & Bringle, 1987).

There is indeed empirical evidence for the important role of concerns in determining emotional intensity. In a self-report emotion recall study, subjects were asked to rank a number of concerns as to their felt importance, and to indicate for each reported emotion incident which concerns were relevant in that event, and to what degree. Felt emotional intensity correlated .40 with the number of concerns that the subjects had checked as relevant to the incident, .49 with the highest of each of the products of concern strength and relevance, and .44 with the sum of the strength/relevance products. Together, these variables led to a multiple correlation of .55 between the various concern measures and overall felt intensity.

The powerful and central concerns that underlie socially consequential behavior are, to a large extent, of an intangible, and, in a sense, subtle nature. Sure enough, violent action may be called forth by straightforward threat to one's life, one's family, or one's economic security, but it is unclear how often these concerns are the decisive ones for undertaking or participating in riskful action.

As the preceding example illustrated, at least as important are concerns like social prestige and self-esteem, with the contingent emotions of pride and shame (Scheff, 1994), sense of belonging to and acceptance by the group (Baumeister & Leary, 1995), sense of individual or group identity (Tajfel, 1981), freedom in determining one's fate (Brehm, 1972), and sense of competence (White, 1959). Being treated uncivilly, for instance, is a potent element in the intensity of the anger evoked by interrogations or by being corrected by people in positions of power (Mikula, Petri, & Tanzer, 1990); presumably, the uncivility negates a person's position of being socially esteemed. Being shamed is generally one of the most powerful sources of rage and revenge (Scheff, 1994).

Similarly, unfairness or injustice in receiving harm or not receiving reward provides a major or even necessary contribution for events of those kinds to evoke anger (Tedeschi & Nesler, 1993)—norm violation adds insult to injury. What is it that so enraged the Krajina Serbs when they were ordered to give up the Cyrillic script? What is it in one's right to write one's language that makes it worth risking death? It is not the frustration as such, but the infringement on their self-determination or the inferior power position in comparison to others. What is it that made so many Serbians take up arms against their Croatian or Bosnian neighbors? Well, probably not in the least place because they felt a sense of belonging to the Serbian group, and did not want, or could not afford, to lose that feeling (and it is the same, of course, for members of the other groups). What brings people to perform extreme acts of cruelty? As I said earlier, the sense that one is able to do so, exertion of one's competence, may be one of the reasons. One is able to fully subdue someone else; one is able to flaunt the most basic of human taboos, and criminals sometimes say so openly (Leyton, 1989).

Incidentally, the importance of these more "subtle" concerns applies not only to emotions, but to the conditions that lead to many socially consequential actions without involving emotion as well. The motives for partaking in armed resistance, for instance, and the motives for partaking in risky altruistic behavior in large measure consist of the sense that one cannot afford not to partake—with regard to self-esteem as much as with regard to the esteem and acceptance given by others. It may not be emotion that stirs one to action, but then it is anticipation of the emotions like shame, guilt, and loss of self-esteem that would arise if one did not go into action.

Interestingly, the concerns that appear to be decisive as the source for socially relevant action quite often seem to form the background rather than the foreground for emotional impact. They do not follow directly from the event; they are not the most clearly visible concerns; still, they seem to be decisive for the intensity of impact. When someone has killed one of your kin, the foreground concern is the attachment, and the foreground meaning is the personal loss. However, the emotional impact that moves into action comes from these background concerns such as social status or the desire to be in control. The impact may even come entirely from these background concerns: The anger, hatred, and desire for revenge can be violent, regardless of whether the person killed was liked or not. All of this is, of course, old hat and obvious, but it may merit repetition in this analysis of the power of emotions. It may also merit continued scrutiny in understanding how such power arises in response to particular emotion events.

I think that, in fact, our understanding of the impact of issues of concern is rudimentary and ad hoc. I have mentioned the centrality of patriotism, the concern for national prominence, and the respect for one's religion and made some guesses about the background of these concerns in one's sense of identity, but I am not sure how satisfactory that explanation is, and why it is so heavy in those contexts.

A word should be said, at this point, about the provenance of the individuals' concerns that determine the emotions influencing socially relevant behavior. Individuals and groups may well differ in the strength or prominence of certain of their concerns. Self-esteem and honor do not mean in one culture what they mean in another, and the desire for power may not be equally strong in everyone. The latter point is of importance because one individual's emotions and actions may well exert considerable influence on those of others. Sessile, Arkan, and Mládic were three notable personalities in recent Serbian violence. All three are unusual individuals, one of them an acknowledged criminal, and have been quite influential in allowing Serbian violence attain the magnitude and scale that it had (Glenny, 1992).

It is, moreover, a plausible assumption that the strength or prominence of an individual's concerns is strongly influenced by his or her immediate social surroundings; the same applies to one's appraisals.[2] One tends to covet what one sees others coveting or attaining; one tends to follow in the interests of one's close comrades, particularly when one is exposed to risks together with them. Considering the fact that most of the socially relevant behavior discussed in this chapter is performed by groups rather than individuals, the importance of this social origin of concern strength and prominence (and perhaps even of some concerns as such) can probably hardly be overrated. When group status is invoked as a motive, as in the aforementioned example of rape, this appears quite evident. In many group situations, however, the motivational forces go much further, are much more pervasive. There is what Rabbie and Lodewijkx (1987) have called the group enhancement of norms and motives, and such enhancement is, at least in part, due to the degree to which the individual is enmeshed in his or her group. One just cannot afford to deviate in goals and views, and one partakes, willingly or unwillingly, in the fate of the group. No Bosnian can escape the restraints and hardships of the war events and being a target of Serbian shellings. If one were thus inclined to deviate, the social environment tends to take immediate reprisal. In Croatia it has been extremely difficult to become a peace activist, because one would be accused of disloyalty; the same was true in the United States during the Vietnam war, and in England during the Falkland Islands conflict.

APPRAISAL

Of course, the relevance of an event to one's concerns is a matter of appraisal; that is, cognitive processes mediate between the event, the

---

[2] I am grateful to Welmoet Gerritsen for bringing the issue of the group origin of concerns to my attention. It is, of course, an issue for extensive exploration and evaluation.

concerns, and the emotion, at least in all but the most elementary physical and social cases. Appraisal thus affects emotional intensity by providing the event with relevance, but it does so in other ways as well, by what is called *secondary appraisal* (Lazarus, 1966), or *context appraisal* (Frijda, 1986). Context not only determines which particular emotion is aroused, but may also affect intensity. An event's unexpectedness influences degree of arousal and peak intensity, for instance. Other secondary or context aspects can be expected to influence overall intensity and, in particular, power.

One of these aspects is the degree of difficulty in resolving the event or in obtaining one's satisfactions. It is a condition for emotion arousal in general. As has frequently been remarked, the fact that an event is relevant to the satisfaction of some concern is not, by itself, sufficient to arouse an emotion. Danger elicits fear only when there is doubt about one's potential to meet it. Emotion emerges only when one cannot deal with the event in a straightforward instrumental fashion, or is uncertain about it. A mountain path that offers no challenge to the climber is neither frightening nor fun; the same is true for being tossed in the air as a baby (Sroufe & Waters, 1976). To elicit an emotion, the event must not merely be relevant, but also present a measure of difficulty in coping with it. Negative emotions arise when facing such difficulty; positive emotions when difficulty has been resolved or resolution appears possible. The use of the term *difficulty* in this connection is borrowed from Sartre (1948): Emotions arise when direct roads to satisfaction or safety appear to be blocked.

Other authors have used other notions. Carver and Scheier (1990) describe this aspect as a difference between expected and actual progress toward the goal; some aspects are covered by the notion of "uncontrollability" (e.g., Glass & Singer, 1972); Lazarus (1991) stresses that emotions always result from the interaction between relevance for well-being and appraised coping potential.

Difficulty admits of degrees. Violent emotion appears to be aroused by negative events when their impact is high but no escape from them is apparent. The condition for panic has been described as the state of being in imminent danger while seeing the ways of escape gradually closing (Janis, 1971). The condition for the escalation of marital quarrels has been described as the feeling of total powerlessness in diminishing discord or obtaining understanding. Violence is a last way out in many conditions of conflict, as it is for a cornered animal. Certainly, the absence of any other means but violence to ward off threat plays a cardinal role in political rhetoric and decision making regarding violent solutions to conflicts, but it has its emotional counterpart, at the individual as well as at the political level. Toch (1969) has explained the fierce aggressiveness of some adolescents due to their lack of social skill for responding to slights. Likewise, persecution of Jews during the medieval great plague has been explained as a reaction to an inexplicable and uncontrollable situation (Girard, 1982).

Controllability, appraisal of one's sense of being in control, is in many ways the opposite of difficulty. In the emotion literature it has been discussed primarily as that which attenuates fear in response to danger (Glass & Singer, 1972), or that which lets it change into a sense of challenge (Lazarus, 1966); but it would also appear to be an intensifier of anger and desire. Appraisal of controllability, it would seem, is what makes an object of lust appear accessible and an object of anger incapable of effective reprisal. Sense of controllability helps to ignore considerations that otherwise might have moderated the strength of the emotional impulse. It therefore supports giving free rein to desires—those of lust as well as destructiveness. Generally speaking, the feeling that one has the means to achieve one's emotional goals would appear to facilitate arousal of the corresponding emotions and their more or less uncontrolled manifestation. Ease of anger arousal may be expected to go along with one's power to effect intimidation, and difficulty in finding a nonviolent solution to a problem situation is often the excuse for showing one's powers to be violent. All this is to be understood materially as well as psychologically. Confidence in one's weapons leads to the luxury of getting angry at trifles, as much as to the last resort of opposition in despair; and to the feeling that one is entitled to one's emotions of desire.

Controllability appraisals contribute to emotional intensity in still another fashion. Emotional intensity, it would seem, strongly depends on one's sense that a situation of deprivation, frustration, or loss, or even of moderate satisfaction, could have been otherwise. Emotional intensity quite often does not depend on the deprivation or hardship as such, but on the additional awareness that others in comparable circumstances do not so suffer, or gain more (Runciman, 1966). One may likewise feel to be entitled to more satisfaction than one gets; I have described this as the *Law of Comparative Feeling* (Frijda, 1988). All of this can be understood as being instances of the appraisal that the emotional situation contains other options than the prevailing ones and, thus, was—in principle—controllable (Fine, 1983; Tedeschi & Nesler, 1993). In fact, the importance of perceived norm violation in the conditions for the intensity of anger may be seen as an aspect of controllability appraisal, rather than of the involvement of additional concerns.

A further, quite general example of the effect of such controllability in principle is provided by the emotional impact of attributions of blame or responsibility. Such attributions, in the case of aversive events, contribute to the emotion of anger, or may even be an essential ingredient for its arousal (Averill, 1982; Frijda, 1986; Tedeschi & Nesler, 1993); but they would also seem to contribute to the emotion's intensity, at least in regard to the impulse for undertaking restorative action—if nobody can be blamed, that is how life goes (Spinoza, 1677/1989). Again, these attributions seem to influence emotional intensity, because when someone else was to blame, it implied that he or she was free to have acted otherwise; the situation contains controllable options (Heider, 1958).

A further general condition that facilitates emotion arousal, next to difficulty and controllability, is what I will call *indubitability*. The term is inspired by Spinoza's (1677/1989) analysis of emotional intensity, which is not only the sole detailed and systematic analysis of what determines the power of emotions, but a beautiful one. In his view, any information suggesting concern relevance is by itself equivalent in its emotion-arousing power, whether it comes from something occurring in the present, from something that occurred in the past, or from something that may occur in the future; emotion-arousing power is equal for both true and imaginary events.

However, the power of emotions depends on the number of items of information that suggest concern relevance, such as threat, in proportion to the number of items that contradict such relevance. This is why an event's proximity in space and time are emotionally potent: The nearer in space and time the event, the stronger usually the fear. Anticipation of the future tends to have weaker effects than events actually there, and events heard about have weaker effects than events perceived, because more alternative courses of events remain possible. People started to fear nuclear power plants only when, after the Chernobyl disaster, their milk and spinach activated their Geiger counters. I have referred to this as *The Law of Apparent Reality* ("Emotions are elicited by events appraised as real, and their intensity corresponds to the degree to which this is the case"—Frijda, 1988, p. 352), but Spinoza's (1677/1989) conceptualization is a better one.

Examples suggesting that these factors do indeed influence emotion arousal are easy to find. When you see people dying around you, there is little room for doubt; when you have suffered personal losses, still less. This may be the principal element in explaining the switch from emotional equanimity to hatred that Glenny (1992) saw in many Krajina villagers. When he visited them in 1991, they could not imagine that the Serbo–Croatian political conflict would affect their dealings with their village neighbors. When barely a year later shooting had come to the village through the militia, the bitter hatred for the other group gave the impression of age-old hostility. The shootings had involved some of their young men, who had been forced into the militia rather than having voluntarily enlisted; whatever the causes of their engagement, however, they had been killed by Croatians.

Indubitability appears to be involved in a different way when events evoke strong associations with previous pain, anxiety, and humiliation

(Horowitz, 1976). This occurs when one is confronted with stimuli reminiscent of earlier trauma: signs linked to experienced humiliation or torture, such as behaviors that were once seen when subjected to incest (Albach, 1993; Ensink, 1992), the paraphernalia and slogans of the Chetniks from 1944 for the Croatians when displayed again in 1991, and the same for those of the Ustashas for the Serbians; or the signs of skinhead Nazi violence for many other Europeans. For many Serbians, a real conviction that a Croatian fascist revival was in the making did emerge when discrimination against Serbians in Croatia started, when people appeared carrying Ustasha symbols, when Serbian television shouted daily about what such actions meant, and when the violent emotions of those who had experienced the horrors of 45 years ago were aroused and made more vivid and psychologically near. This may well extend beyond those who had first-hand experience with such horrors through vicarious traumatization of their children or others.

In using the word *indubitability*, I am thinking of appraisals due to more or less tangible event properties like visible presence, spatial and temporal proximity, and having actually experienced suffering. A more purely psychological form, however, seems to be so highly important for the power of emotions that it merits a separate name. It has been called the *obviousness* of the event's emotional significance by Mesquita (1993). Such obviousness is, I think, responsible for much emotion power.

The emotional significance of a given event may or may not appear as something obvious to the individual. Sometimes the emotional significance of an event may be appraised as one's subjective response—a feeling that depends on one's sensitivities and concerns—and as one possible appraisal among others. But sometimes it may be appraised as obvious, as an unquestionable, obvious truth, as involving a view of things that all thinking persons would share. The opposition is a basic one. One may experience one's emotion as being something subjective, and even doubt whether one is correct in seeing things the way one does, or, on the contrary, one may feel convinced of the truth of one's appraisal and feel fully justified in it, the emotion being felt as an unavoidable outcome. Obviousness appraisal may occur with respect to the general impact of an event, but also with respect to a particular appraised feature such as the attribution of intent or offensiveness to a norm, as the event being controllable or difficult to control. It was probably clear to most or all Bosnian Serbians that their miseries were fully due to the Muslims, as presumably the Algerian fundamentalist Muslims now are convinced of the evil, harmful nature of Algerian intellectuals.

Individuals and social groups may differ in how obvious their appraisals appear to them. Mesquita (1993), in her cross-cultural study of recalled emotion incidents, asked questions like, "Do you think that another person would feel or think like you did?" and "Do you think that another person would react like you did?" Turkish respondents gave affirmative responses significantly more frequently than did Dutch respondents, and Dutch respondents answered significantly more frequently than did Turkish and Surinamese subjects that they did not know how another person would feel.

Obviousness of the appraisal is important in that it is linked to change in beliefs that emotions induce; that is, to the stable dispositional attributions regarding other people and the causes of their actions. It is linked to how justified one feels to be in feeling and doing what one feels and does; at high strength, it is a major ingredient of fanaticism. It would appear to also be linked to how drastic the emotional actions are that one feels impelled toward. There is some evidence that this is indeed the case. In Mesquita's (1993) study, Turkish subjects more frequently tended to sever contact with the offender in anger situations than did Dutch subjects, and they felt more inclined to take revenge. I return to this point because the obviousness of appraisal is one of the places where social representations and individual emotions meet. It is evident that obviousness, as well as other aspects of indubitability, is highly dependent on the judgments that are prevalent in the social environment.

RESPONSE AVAILABILITY AND EFFECTIVENESS

Behavioral inclination and the drastic nature of the resulting behavior would seem to be strengthened by the availability of the corresponding emotional behavior and by expectations of its effectiveness. I have already discussed this in connection with controllability appraisal. It appears likely that readiness for anger, as well as the power of one's anger, depend on one's capacity for angry behavior, on the endurance one can bring to raving and shouting, and on one's material and emotional capacities for outright violence. Availability, I think, facilitates not merely aggressive behavior but also the emotion of anger itself. Anger, as feeling and mode of appraisal and as impulse and mode of behavior, I propose, rises more readily when overt anger is more readily thought of, when it belongs to the things with appreciable availability or habit strength. I also suggested that lust may rise more readily, and with more power, when its target object is expected to be easily accessible.

There are no experimental data to support this proposition; it is a hypothesis. But it is, of course, in line with the massive evidence that social acceptance of violence as a means of settling disputes or enhancing personal prestige increases the likelihood of violence. Also, the likelihood of aggression increases with the availability of effective aggressive tools, such as firearms. Both apply to the Yugoslavian situation. The Balkans (at least, Bulgaria) had the highest rate of violent crime per 1,000 inhabitants in Europe in 1930, and the second highest in 1976 (Chesnais, 1981). Being proficient with a gun is a property of a true man, in those parts; he who does not know how to handle a gun is a laughingstock (at least in Serbia; Glenny, 1992).

Violence in the streets was likewise extremely common in France and England prior to the middle of the 19th century, far more common than it was there thereafter, and at least in part because it was an accepted thing to do, and because everyone carried a knife. All of this is known, but all of that violence, I dare to affirm, was not emotionally neutral, and did not simply consist of more violent manifestations of equally intense (or weak) irritations or touchiness as have Americans and Western Europeans from well-socialized social environments today. It seems likely that the emotion of anger as such was more readily aroused, was more violent, and carried more power. This means that, presumably, attributions of evil intent and appraisals of being able to exert control were more prominent or more intense, as were the control precedence of the angry impulse and how drastic the acts. That availability of aggression and readiness for blame appraisals stand in a mutual relationship is quite likely, considering the cross-cultural evidence for variations in both regards (Mesquita & Frijda, 1992), and the finding that people from more violent regions also respond with more apparent anger to insults (Nisbett, 1993).

Much of this is explained by the different norms concerning aggression, and thus by weaker inhibitory control of anger. I think, however, that this is only part of the story. It would seem that aggression as a means to resolve a conflict was more available and came more readily to mind.

MOOD AND PRIOR RESPONSE ACTIVATION

The power of emotions cannot, I think, be understood without taking into account several other, more peripheral factors. Emotional intensity depends on the individual's mood state, his or her state of health, or the state of activation of a particular emotion system at the time of the emotional event or its aftermath. High arousal renders innocent events emotionally effective, as does a state of exhaustion or irritation. Anger arousal increases sexual arousability, and vice versa (Zillmann, 1983). Several mechanisms have been proposed to account for these facilitations. Excitation transfer, Zillmann's (1979, 1983) hypothesis, is one of these: The individual attributes his or her excitation, caused earlier by something else, to the new event. Or one's prevailing state of excitation increases sensitivity to new excitatory stimuli. Excitement as well as exhaustion may also be thought to influence one's current state of disinhibition; the effects of disinhibition will be discussed shortly.

In addition, and more importantly, it seems likely that executing aggressive behavior, and perhaps other behavior that disregards what the target of that behavior may feel about it, reinforces emotions of anger and lust and may even create them. To the extent that this is true, it creates a circle of mutual enhancements, from response availability over appraisal induced by this availability to executing violent behavior, and on to emotion arousal. Emotional behavior and emotional impulses appear to stand in a circular, self-reinforcing relationship, and not merely in a linear causal one. Violent behavior, whether or not it originated in anger, is likely to strengthen anger or to make it emerge. It seems to form a basis for anger arousal when the target offers resistance, and it may generate enthusiastic reactance when aggression proves to be effective in subduing the target. There is ground for these suppositions in the cruelty of individuals who have the power to be aggressive, for example, soldiers and policemen who plunder, rape, and destroy in the course of their regular exploits. Evidence of such cruelty comes from observations of films of police violence during rioting, where their task is restricted to sedately restoring order, or of similar events. The Los Angeles police officers involved in the attack on Rodney King showed emotional vigor in excess of what presumed duty demanded, on the videotape that recorded their actions. Likewise, the Israeli soldiers beating up Palestinians in a notorious newsreel showed signs of both anger and the joys of the exertion of violence, as shown in superfluous kicks, arm breaking, as well as in facial expressions. In both cases the violence would seem to have been evoked by the helplessness of the victims and the riskless effectiveness of the aggression. Emotional behavior and emotional impulses thus appear to stand in a circular, self-reinforcing relationship, and not merely in a linear causal one.

How can such self-reinforcement be explained? The facts of retroaction are usually discussed and examined in the context of facial-feedback theory. That theory, however, does not advance a plausible mechanism, because the supposed mechanism, the generation of kinaesthetic feedback, appears to be too peripheral, bleak, or weak. Other, more essential, mechanisms can be thought of. Excitation transfer (Zillmann, 1979) has already been mentioned. Another mechanism is contained in the network activation hypothesis from Peter Lang's (1977) bio-informational theory: Emotional impulse, behavior modes, and emotional appraisal form a network, and activation of one part of the network recruits the other components. Seeking cognitive support for goals in execution provides a third. Whatever the mechanism may be, the tolerance for impulse or behavior, the sense of competence coming from the response availability or effectiveness, and the reinforcement coming from that effectiveness all appear to provide powerful contributions to the power of the emotions.

REGULATION

The last intensity determinant to discuss is regulation. Regulation includes inhibition, and I will briefly discuss the powerful role of loss of inhibition in adding to emotional intensity. Inhibitions are lost in various ways. An important means is alcohol intoxication, one of the notable facilitating conditions for destructive violence and rape in private as well as political contexts. Drunkenness is a frequent accompaniment to the raids of political gangs, as it has been in American lynch mobs and the German skinheads, Serbian Chetniks terrorizing Croatian or Bosnian settlements, and the Bosnian group rapes. Other factors are the effects of deindividuation (loss of sense of individual responsibility in crowd behavior; Zimbardo, 1970) and dehumanization (viewing the aggression target as an object rather than a human). More central to the emotion process, perhaps, is the effect of emotions that are so strong as to break down one's control; once control has collapsed, it is difficult to recuperate, as in panic, escalating quarrels, and desire after one has stopped resisting. But the most important factor would seem to be the lifting of control through direct social influence. The social environment has many such influences at its disposal: permissiveness, positive encouragement, added rewards of prestige, providing a sense of belongingness in common anger, risk taking or norm transgression, and praise for remarkable feats of nationalist fervor, articulation of hatred, risky assault, or awe-inspiring, monumental destructiveness. National governments and political movements are expert in staging such rewards. The influences of lifting restraints may come from the social environment at large, through its norms and the media, as well as from the immediate social surroundings, and operate through deindividuation (Zimbardo, 1970), emergent norms (Turner & Kilian, 1972), or group enhancement mechanisms (Rabbie & Lodwijkx, 1987).

It is clear from the earlier discussion that the social environment not only lifts inhibitions, but also can enhance felt emotion, and shape emotional expression. The notion of *display rules* falls far short of doing justice to the cultural influences on manifestations of emotion. Society does not merely tolerate; it prescribes, it encourages, and it provides models and patterns. Public indignation, enthusiastic, joyful embraces such as those of successful football players on the field, outbursts of grief, wailing and the tearing of one's clothes, and shows of religious and political awe and veneration are all examples. The norms and forms may pervade a culture. There are cultures where passions of love, jealousy, and hatred are more common than in others, and passionate expressions of emotion result from molding and shaping emotional impulses that were there prior to the expressions. This, of course, extends into emotionally sustained instrumental behavior. As I have mentioned, gun toting is common and applauded in most rural areas of Yugoslavia, just as it was or still is in some American rural areas and in subcultures of violence (Wolfgang & Ferracuti, 1967).

We must not underestimate the effects of appraisal norms and feeling norms (Hochschild, 1983). One feels emotions when one is obliged to do so; one appraises events in ways one is told to. At least this can happen and probably does not happen infrequently. Emotions quite often spring out of compulsion. When the militia goes from house to house, ordering the boys to join in the fight and combat these dastardly Ustashas, or Chetniks, or whatever, who are you not to comply with the order both to fight and to perceive Ustasha threat in everyone speaking Croatian? The power of emotion can be augmented, not merely by lifting inhibitions, not only by the examples and models of powerful emotional display, but by conforming to the emotion that others have or tell you that you should have. I have discussed this already in connection with the concerns behind aggression-inducing emotions, and have repeated it earlier in connection with appraisals, and here in connection with disinhibition and enhancements.

EMOTIONS AND BELIEFS

One further aspect remains to be discussed more fully, because it is an aspect of emotional response itself as well as of its antecedents, and one that it is essential for emotional power and the emergence of passions: the role of beliefs. Emotions in part result from beliefs, and obtain strength from their strength. The belief that others are evil and have evil intentions contributes to responding with anger to their actions.

In addition, emotions consist of beliefs, and engender additional beliefs. Belief changes form one of the aspects of emotional response. One tends to love the person who gives joy and hate the person who has made one angry, because joy leads to making dispositional attributions of loveable characteristics, and anger to the attribution of not merely acting badly, but of being bad, of always having been bad, and of remaining so forever (Frijda, 1993).

Most of the beliefs generated by emotions fade away when the emotion is over; thus, the bad beliefs that rise in one's thoughts during a quarrel dissolve after the quarrel is past. However, under certain circumstances the beliefs may remain. They become true beliefs, crystallize, and obtain truth value and stability over time. They turn into an emotional attitude or a sentiment (Frijda, Mesquita, Sonnemans, & Van Goozen, 1991). *Sentiment* is the name for an emotionally valenced belief structure, an affective schema, that defines desirable or undesirable properties of the target object. It thereby controls future appraisals and forms the basis for persistent arousal of emotions, whenever one meets the object or hears about it (Fiske, 1982). Sentiments thus contribute to the duration of the consequences of the original emotions, as well as to the time span over which new emotions emerge in further confrontations with the object.

In most instances, emotions do not so much create beliefs as strengthen and solidify beliefs that one already entertains or make one receptive to beliefs advanced by others. Emotions tend to make one accept beliefs presented by the environment or by historical tales and make them convincing and prominent. The history of Croatian Ustashas was available for providing substance to the belief that Croatians are indeed fascists inclined to cruelty when fear and anger were evoked by the first Serbo-Croatian clashes. I admit that I know of no research investigating whether the strength of beliefs resulting from emotions vary with the nature (salience, consistency, etc.) of the information contained in the belief, and whether this strength varies with the intensity of the emotion that gave rise to its emergence or acceptance. I suspect that the relationships are strong and positive.

Similarly, I do not know the conditions under which an emotion crystallizes into a sentiment, and an emotional appraisal freezes into a belief—what makes that anger turn into hatred or joy into love. Nor do I know what accounts for the stability of a belief and its affective content. One can make a fair guess, however. Analysis of self-reports of emotion incidents has suggested that emotions turn into sentiments when the emotional issue is protracted and cannot be resolved by or after the emotion (Frijda et al., 1991). A threat persists or repeats itself, an attractive object remains available either actually or in the mind, through convincing and persisting propaganda. Both the Croatian and the Serbian television stations, the HTV and RTV Belgrade, "have been singled out as two of the most culpable war criminals of the Yugoslav tragedy" (Glenny, 1992, p. 66). In other situations, an offense is of such a nature that the end of the event does not bring the end of the harm: Irrevocable loss has been inflicted, basic self-trust and self-identity feelings have been damaged (Frijda et al., 1991). Generalizations of this sort may represent a plausible account of the power and persistence of desire for revenge (Frijda, 1994). The same generalizations may also explain how deep hatreds can melt away when strife has ended, disappearing without a manifest trace within a few years. Such was the case with the hatreds of most Dutch toward the Germans, Indonesians toward the Dutch, Americans toward Japanese, and vice versa, perhaps even Serbians toward Croatians—until or unless novel threats find the obsolete, hate beliefs in the closet and dust them off.

There are several reasons for paying attention to beliefs as determinants of emotional power, in addition to what was said earlier about "obviousness," and just now about the rise of sentiments. First, as I have just stated, I think that emotions render beliefs resistant to change and correction by evidence. Facts can only strengthen, but hardly weaken, beliefs that have engendered emotions or are engendered by them. Second, beliefs dictate other behavior than mere emotions would, because the dispositional attributions dictate other appraisals. "Love" asserts a positive nature of the object, and it has, in fact, been defined as the tendency to enhance the object's "existence"; "hate" asserts the object's intrinsic badness, and has correspondingly been defined by a striving to diminish that existence (Scheler, 1923). Action matches these tendencies. Hate aims not at victory but at annihilation of the enemy. It often actually does so: It levels cities and monuments, mutilates victims, takes away their visible identities, and demolishes even their sexual identities. It may remove all traces of their ever having existed, erasing their villages, blowing their dust to the wind, and scratching their names from plaques that commemorated them (as happened to the Roman emperor Domitianus).

Finally, then, beliefs not only lead to actions (in as far as they do that). Emotionally supported beliefs also, and more commonly, I think, lead to accepting the truth of new information that matches the beliefs. They also lead to accepting, morally or emotionally, the actions performed by others that are meant to deal with those truths. They lead to accepting to participate in those actions, even if the actions are not truly approved of (one may have reservations about the desirability of sending troops, of fighting the Croats, etc.), and even if the participation is not sustained by one's emotions. The actions are accepted and followed and supported. Thus, the consequences of emotions for socially behavior may be enormous, even when that behavior is not caused by those emotions, and is not performed by those experiencing the emotions.

What I have in mind, of course, is the public support of policies, leaders, and governments that engage in socially relevant action, the approval of measures taken by the military or the police, and so forth. Nationalist frenzies in Serbia supported the measures in Albanian-inhabited Kosovo in 1989; nationalist pathos in Croatia allowed suppression of Krajina Serbian rights and the measures taken to silence their opposition. The emotions of Bosnian–Serbian women and children did not, perhaps, lead to any of them committing one cruel, ruthless act, but they did prevent the United Nations relief stock from entering Sarajevo. Their emotions helped the Bosnian–Serbian troops of Mládic to continue their violent actions.

CONCLUSION

What, then, have I said? I have asked two questions: When do emotions lead to socially relevant behavior? and What role does emotion play in such behavior? I have come to some tentative conclusions by using the analysis of emotional intensity as my guideline.

I have argued that the germ for socially consequential behavior is present in every emotion—both in its aspect of change in action readiness and in the control precedence of that readiness. The more specific question asked what determines the power of that readiness; that is, the strength of control precedence, how drastic the actions are that are prepared by the state of readiness, the extent of belief changes flowing from that readiness and giving it substance, and the duration over which control precedence and action readiness remain alive or can be evoked with ease.

What seems fundamental to any powerful emotion is a multitude of concerns or deeply rooted, central concerns. Added power then comes from a difficulty to cope with events or, on the contrary, controllability—the ease with which violence and desire can be effected. Further, power comes from how indubitable the events are, how pressing and immediate the calls for action, and, more particularly, how obvious the event's significance to the individual. Obviousness of an event's meaning—the strength of one's beliefs—would seem to be highly dependent on the beliefs shared in the social environment. A key element in why emotions may lead to behavior with social consequences are the social roots for the beliefs that motivate or sustain the behavior. Of similar importance is the availability of the behaviors that might implement the emotional goals, and how socially acceptable they are.

However, much socially relevant behavior is not performed for emotional reasons, or at least not for the reasons that might correspond with stated aims. Politics and intergroup conflict cannot be reduced to emotions; overwhelmingly, however, emotions are of importance for the support for political aims, in politicians as well as combatants, for the acceptance of the behaviors and of the means employed and for the costs involved both on one's own side and that of the antagonists. Such acceptance is a close consequence of emotions; we may assume that emotions are not merely instigated by beliefs, but that they also generate beliefs and strongly influence the acceptance and adoption of beliefs and their ensuing obviousness.

Throughout this chapter, I have mentioned the relations between emotions and beliefs and the multiple causal directions between them. I did profess my ignorance about those relationships, but I feel I share that ignorance with others, and that it is about time this should change.

Thus, most of what I have said is mere conjecture—we have little to stand on from the research on emotion. Perhaps there are some insights to be gained from the social psychology of attitude formation and opinion change, and I am insufficiently familiar with that as well. Maybe, with these insights and further work in emotion, we can understand when and why emotions lead to, or contribute to, passionate and socially consequential behavior.

What difference, then, does it make whether we do understand? Not much, I think. The stakes are higher than psychology can reach, the capital more massive than psychology can detract from. About the use of psychological insights in those matters one need not have any illusions—but that is no reason to forgo the obligation to try to obtain them.

REFERENCES

Albach, F. (1993). *Freud's verleidingstheorie: Incest, trauma, hysterie* [Freud's seduction theory: Incest, trauma, hysteria]. Unpublished doctoral thesis, University of Amsterdam.

Aristotle. (1941). *Rhetorics* (Complete works, Book 2, Chaps. 2–12). New York: Random House.

Arnold, M. B. (1960). *Emotion and personality* (Vols. I and II). New York: Columbia University Press.

Averill, J. R. (1982). *Anger and aggression: An essay on emotion.* New York: Springer.

Bain, A. (1876). The gratification derived from the infliction of pain. *Mind, 1,* 429–431.

Baumeister, R. F., & Leary, R. M. (1995). The need to belong: Desire for interpersonal attachment as a fundamental human motivation. *Psychological Bulletin, 118,* 497–529.

Brehm, J. W. (1972). *Responses to loss of freedom: A theory of psychological reactance.* Morristown, NJ: General Learning Press.

Brownmiller, S. (1976). *Against our will: Men, women and rape.* New York: Bantam.

Buunk, B., & Bringle, R. G. (1987). Jealousy in love relationships. In D. Perlman & S. Duck (Eds.), *Intimate relationships* (pp. 123–147). Beverly Hills, CA: Sage.

Carver, C. S., & Scheier, M. F. (1990). Origins and functions of positive and negative affect: A control-process view. *Psychological Bulletin, 97,* 19–35.

Chesnais, J.-C. (1981). *Histoire de la violence* [History of violence]. Paris: Robert Laffont.

Clausewitz, C. von (1987). *On war.* Harmondsworth: Penguin Classics. (Original work published 1832)

Elias, N. (1969). *The civilizing process.* New York: Urizen.

Ensink, B. (1992). *Confusing realities: A study on child sexual abuse and psychiatric symptoms.* Amsterdam: VU University Press.

Fine, M. (1983). The social context and a sense of injustice: The option to challenge. *Representative Research in Social Psychology, 13,* 15–33.

Fisk, R. (1991). *Pity the nation: Lebanon at war.* Oxford: Oxford University Press.

Fiske, S. T. (1982). Schema-triggered affect: Applications to social perception. In M. S. Clark & S. T. Fiske (Eds.), *Affect and cognition: The 17th Annual Carnegie Symposium on Cognition* (pp. 55–78). Hillsdale, NJ: Lawrence Erlbaum Associates.

Frijda, N. H. (1986). *The emotions.* Cambridge: Cambridge University Press.

Frijda, N. H. (1988). The laws of emotion. *American Psychologist, 43,* 349–358.

Frijda, N. H. (1993). The place of appraisal in emotion. *Cognition and Emotion, 7,* 357–388.

Frijda, N. H. (1994). The Lex Talionis: On vengeance. In S. H. M. Van Goozen, N. E. Van de Poll, & J. A. Sergeant (Eds.), *Emotions: Essays on emotion theory* (pp. 263–289). Hillsdale, NJ: Lawrence Erlbaum Associates.

Frijda, N. H. (in press). Spinoza and current emotion theory. In Y. Yovel (Ed.), *Spinoza by 2000* (Vol. 3). Haarlem: Brill.

Frijda, N. H., & Mesquita, B. (1994). The social roles and functions of emotions. In S. Kitayama & H. Markus (Eds.), *Emotions and culture: Empirical studies of mutual influence* (pp. 51–87). Washington, DC: APA.

Frijda, N. H., Mesquita, B., Sonnemans, J., & Van Goozen, S. (1991). The duration of affective phenomena, or emotions, sentiments and passions. In K. Strongman (Ed.), *International review of emotion and motivation* (pp. 187–225). New York: Wiley.

Frijda, N. H., Ortony, A., Sonnemans, J., & Clore, G. (1992). The complexity of intensity. In M. Clark (Ed.), *Emotion. Review of personality and social psychology* (Vol. 13, pp. 60–89). Beverly Hills, CA: Sage.

Girard, R. (1982). *Le bouc émissaire* [The scapegoat]. Paris: Grasset.

Glass, D. C., & Singer, J. E. (1972). *Urban stress: Experiments on noise and social stressors.* New York: Academic Press.

Glenny, M. (1992). *The fall of Yugoslavia: The third Balkan war.* Harmondsworth, Middlesex: Penguin.

Gray, J. A. (1982). *The neuropsychology of anxiety: An enquiry into the functions of the septo-hippocampal system.* Oxford: Oxford University Press.

Heider, F. (1958). *The psychology of interpersonal relations.* New York: Wiley.

Hochschild, A. R. (1983). *The managed heart.* Berkeley: University of California Press.

Horowitz, M. J. (1976). *Stress response syndromes.* New York: Aronson.

Hume, D. (1969). *A treatise of human nature.* Harmondsworth: Penguin Books. (Original work published 1739/1740)

Izard, C. E. (1977). *Human emotions.* New York: Plenum.

Janis, I. L. (1971). *Stress and frustration.* New York: Harcourt Brace Jovanovitch.

Lakoff, G., & Koveckses, Z. (1983). *The cognitive model of anger inherent in American English.* (Rep. No. 10). Berkeley, CA: Berkeley Cognitive Science Program.

Lang, P. J. (1979). A bio-informational theory of emotional imagery. *Psychophysiology, 16,* 495–512.

Lazarus, R. S. (1966). *Psychological stress and the coping process.* New York: McGraw-Hill.

Lazarus, R. S. (1991). *Emotion and adaptation.* New York: Oxford University Press.

Leyton, E. (1989). *Hunting humans.* Harmondsworth, Middlesex: Penguin.

Mesquita, B. G. de (1993). *Cultural variations in emotions. A comparitive study of Dutch, Surinamese and Turkish people in the Netherlands.* Unpublished doctoral dissertation, University of Amsterdam.

Mesquita, B., & Frijda, N. H. (1992). Cultural variations in emotion: A review. *Psychological Bulletin, 112,* 179–204.

Mikula, G., Petri, B., & Tanzer, N. (1990). What people regard as unjust: Types and structures of everyday experiences of injustice. *European Journal of Social Psychology, 20,* 133–149.

Nisbett, R. E. (1993). Violence and U.S. regional culture. *American Psychologist, 48,* 441–449.

Oatley, K. (1992). *Best laid schemes: The psychology of emotions.* Cambridge: Cambridge University Press.

Ortony, A., Clore, G., & Collins, A. (1988). *The cognitive structure of emotions.* Cambridge: Cambridge University Press.

Panksepp, J. (1982). Toward a general psychobiological theory of emotions. *Behavioral and Brain Sciences, 5,* 407–467.

Panksepp, J. (1993). Neurochemical control of moods and emotions: Amino acids to neuropeptides. In M. Lewis & J. M. Haviland (Eds.), *Handbook of emotions* (pp. 87–108). New York: Guilford Press.

Pearce, J. (1990). *Columbia: Inside the labyrinth.* London: Latin American Bureau.

Rabbie, J. M., & Lodewijkx, H. (1987). Individual and group aggression. *Current Research on Peace and Violence, 10,* 91–101.

Regnault, L. (1990). *Les pères du désert en Égypte au IVe siècle* [The fathers of the desert in Egypt in the 4th century]. Paris: Hachette.

Runciman, W. G. (1966). *Relative deprivation and social justice.* London: Routledge & Kegan Paul.

Sartre, J. P. (1948). *The emotions.* New York: Philosophical Library.

Scheff, T. (1994). *Bloody revenge: Nationalism, war and emotion.* Boulder, CO: Westville Press.

Scheler, M. (1923). *Wesen und Formen der Sympathie* [Nature and forms of sympathy] (5th ed.). Frankfurt: Schulte-Buhmke.

Scherer, K. R. (1984). Emotion as a multicomponent process: A model and some cross-cultural data. In P. Shaver (Ed.), *Review of personality and social psychology* (Vol. 5, pp. 37–63). Beverly Hills, CA: Sage.

Schopenhauer, M. (1819). *Die welt als wille und vorstellung* [The world as will and mental representation]. Leipzig: Reclam.

Sonnemans, J. (1991). *Structure and determinants of emotional intensity.* Unpublished doctoral dissertation, University of Amsterdam.

Spinoza, B. (1989). *Ethics.* (G. H. R. Parkinson, Trans.). London: Everyman's Library. (Original work published 1677)

Sroufe, L. A., & Waters, E. (1976). The ontogenesis of smiling and laughter: A perspective on the organization of development in infancy. *Psychological Review, 83,* 173–189.

Tajfel, H. (1981). *Human groups and social categories.* Cambridge: Cambridge University Press.

Tedeschi, J. T., & Nesler, M. S. (1993). Grievances: Development and reactions. In R. B. Felson & J. T. Tedeschi (Eds.), *Aggression and violence: Social interactionist perspectives* (pp. 13–45). Washington, DC: American Psychological Association.

Toch, H. (1969). *Violent men.* Chicago: Aldine-Atherton.

Tomkins, S. S. (1962). *Affect. Imagery and consciousness: Vol. 1. The positive affects.* New York: Springer.

Turner, R. H., & Kilian, L. M. (1972). *Collective behavior.* Englewood Cliffs, NJ: Prentice-Hall.

White, R. W. (1959). Motivation reconsidered: The concept of competence. *Psychological Review, 66,* 297–333.

Wolfgang, M. E., & Ferracuti, F. (1967). *The subculture of violence.* New York: Barnes and Noble.

Wundt, W. (1902). *Grundzüge der pysiologischen Psychologie,* Vol. 3. Leipzig, Engelmann, 5th. Ausgabe.

Yourcenar, M. (1951). *Mémoires d'Hadrien* [Hadrian's memoirs]. Paris: Plon.

Zillmann, D. (1979). *Aggression and hostility.* Hillsdale, NJ: Lawrence Erlbaum Associates.

Zillmann, D. (1983). Transfer of excitation in emotional behavior. In J. T. Caccioppo & R. E. Petty (Eds.), *Social psychophysiology: A sourcebook* (pp. 215–240).

Zimbardo, P. G. (1970). The human choice: Individuation, reason and order versus deindividuation, impulse and chaos. In W. J. Arnold & D. Levine (Eds.), *Nebraska Symposium on Motivation 1969* (Vol. 16). Lincoln: University of Nebraska Press.

Affective Neuroscience: A Paradigm to Study the Animate Circuits for Human Emotions

Jaak Panksepp
Bowling Green State University

From the moment of birth, brain emotional systems allow humans to begin operating in the world as spontaneously active organisms with a variety of ingrained values and goals that mold and become molded by experience. These genetically provided psychobehavioral systems initially help organize innate potentialities for certain feelings and instinctual behavior patterns, but they also help construct cognitive structures by assigning priorities (values) to various external events and courses of action. Gradually, cognitive plans assert a greater and greater influence on the control of action tendencies, but even as that happens, the underlying emotional systems abide as "centers of gravity" around which many of the epigentically created psychological abilities continue to revolve. In other words, even after the development of cognitive sophistication, the basic emotional systems still gauge adaptive-fitness issues via internally experienced feeling states and the consequent ruminations they promote.

By channeling thinking, the underlying emotional systems retain a decisive control over the behavioral priorities of each individual. This control is exerted internally even if individuals chose not to communicate their feelings outwardly. Such self-protective sociopolitical skills can become exceptionally well-developed in adult humans. According to such a view of ontogenetic development, it is essential to understand the intrinsically affective nature of the brain in order to understand the developing minds of children; if that is true, we shall not be able to have a satisfactory scientific understanding of human nature until we understand the deep neural structure of emotional systems that children possess as their birthright.

From a slightly different perspective, it is self-evident that most adult feelings arise from an appraisal of events within the flow of individual lives. How can we reconcile this observation with the compelling fact that the intense emotions young humans experience must arise from the character of their brain circuits? Some find these views contradictory (for an overview of opinions, see Ekman & Davidson, 1994). Others, including myself, consider them to be exquisitely compatible with each other: The potential for certain types of feelings is innate, whereas the manifestation of these feelings in the real world depends on the specific experiences of each individual. Although the two lines of analysis—of intrinsic human subjective experiences and learned brain circuit activities—have proceeded independently for some time, we have finally reached a point where they can begin to be blended into a coherent whole without doing injustice to either. The aim of this chapter is to discuss how that difficult synthesis can be accomplished. I argue that it cannot be done without brain research in other animals, and that it cannot be done without attempting to generalize the resulting facts to the human condition—a project that is rife with well-known conceptual problems (see Panksepp, 1991).

In aspiring to such a goal, it must be recognized that the search for general scientific principles and their application to real-world events are different tasks. As in physics, knowledge of the former type does not automatically provide precise knowledge of the latter, especially in circumstances where many variables are operating concurrently. Thus, even though all mammals probably share many functionally similar emotional circuits, each is expressed in disparate ecological and cultural contexts, not to mention in obviously different bodies and via the help of highly differentiated higher brain areas (e.g., neocortices) whose interconnectivities vary substantially from one mammalian species to the next. Thus, the understanding of general neuro-emotional principles in one mammalian species will not automatically provide insight into the detailed expressions of those principles in other species, but it can reveal essential ground plans. In short, there is a high likelihood that the feeling of anger in man and mouse is elaborated by very similar brain mechanisms.

There are comparable parallels in certain cognitive systems. For instance, the mechanisms of learning in the hippocampus as they are being revealed in lower animals through studies of long-term potentiation in neuronal assemblies (Teyler & DiScenna, 1984) are surely revealing important attributes of the human brain. Of course, such work tells us little about the specific events that individual organisms experience. Obviously, a detailed understanding of each instance of experience can only be achieved through a comprehensive ecological and neural analysis of each experiencing individual, and that remains prohibitively complex. Nonetheless, a clear delineation and appropriate combination of cross-species and cross-disciplinary approaches can prevent us from neglecting a study of the neural mechanisms that underlie basic human psychological abilities, especially the intrinsic faculties of the mammalian brain that mediate the basic emotions.

In this chapter, I focus on the potential impact that the findings from animal-brain research can have on a basic understanding of human emotions as well as on our conception of psychology as a unified scientific discipline. Existing evidence overwhelmingly supports the premise that the basic emotions arise from genetically ingrained neuronal operating systems that were laid down in subcortical areas fairly early in mammalian brain evolution (MacLean, 1990; Panksepp, 1981a, 1982, 1985, 1986a, 1988, 1989a, 1990a, 1991, 1992a, 1993a). This knowledge has, I believe, profound implications for the future development of psychology as a coherent science as well as for a more general understanding of certain key aspects of "human nature."

THE DILEMMA OF A PSYCHOLOGY THAT IS NOT GROUNDED IN BRAIN SCIENCE

In its short history, academic psychology has not succeeded in building a credible, shared foundation for the whole discipline. This is because such a foundation must be based on an adequate knowledge of the intrinsic functions of the brain, and until very recently that level of knowledge did not exist. Now that such information is available, a critical but generally neglected question is how to relate brain knowledge to major psychological issues. Consider the topic at hand—how can we come to scientifically understand human emotional processes as natural entities? Although it should be obvious that this cannot be done without a great deal of brain research, what is the most relevant type of research and what are the strategic maneuvers that need to be implemented in order to decipher the general principles? I briefly highlight such paradigmatic issues in this chapter (for other recent discussions of related issues, see the debate between Lazarus, 1993, and Panksepp, 1993b, as well as the synergistic views of Bunge, 1990, and Panksepp, 1990b).

Due to historical circumstances, the discipline of psychology has reached a stage where most of its intellectual and material resources are devoted to the study of the manifestations of cognitive faculties in the world as opposed to an understanding of the brain substrates from which these faculties arise. Likewise, in the study of emotions a growing cadre of investigators are presently more involved in trying to fathom how feelings govern individual lives than in the nature of brain operating systems from which emotions emerge. It would be hard to defend such an asymmetry of effort as good science, at least from the perspective of other natural sciences, which typically aspire to build new knowledge on levels of analysis immediately below the level at which their own primary focus is directed. Psychology rarely tries to do that, and often takes pains in asserting that meaningful laws can be derived without any recourse to neuroscience. Indeed, reductionism is all too commonly considered to be in poor taste (e.g., Lazarus, 1991, 1993).

This sad state of affairs is partially a lingering legacy of radical behaviorism in American psychology, which eschewed any neurologically based discussion of internal causes in the control of behavior. It is also partially due to the fact that psychology matured as a social enterprise long before neuroscience. Because of this, the "new sciences of the mind" that "overthrew" behaviorism did not nurture the desperately needed biological foundations (see Panksepp, 1988, for overview). Although cognitivism brought the concept of mind back into psychology (often in circular ways), it failed to bring the brain along for the ride. This is being rectified somewhat via the emergence of "Cognitive Neuroscience" and "neural net" computers for the study of ideas, thoughts, and perceptions, but no comparable intellectual force has emerged in the study of emotions. The premise here is that ultimately a coherent science of psychology simply cannot be constructed without a strategy that actively promotes and incorporates a deep knowledge of the basic emotional functions of the mammalian brain, via some type of interdisciplinary "affective neuroscience." That is the general approach I advocate here—a combination and blending of animal brain research and ethological behavioral analyses, which can provide much of the necessary raw data that needs to be related to key insights concerning basic psychological faculties in humans. The alternative is to continue to ignore the growing body of brain information from "lower" animals that is relevant for understanding the neural sources of affective processes in humans, which will only delay the development of psychology as a comprehensive and coherent scientific enterprise.

The neural understanding of emotional systems in animals can provide a solid cornerstone for a scientific psychology of the future. The brain systems that elaborate emotive states do similar things in all mammals. They help organize various behaviors and the physiological and hormonal changes appropriate to them; they produce internal feeling states that are the innate value structures for new learning. Human subjective experience of the various emotional states can tell us much about the types of mechanisms we should seek within the animal brain. Accordingly, the propriety of anthropomorphism in mammalian brain research should be deemed an empirical issue (based on the degree of psychoneural homology among species), as opposed to the conceptual sin it has traditionally been considered to be (Panksepp, 1982). Introspective analysis in humans helps identify basic (i.e., genetically dictated) categories of psychic states that are candidates for intensive neuroscience analysis. The subjective internal view that humans can access and speak about also provides some low-level hypotheses about the neurodynamics of the underlying brain systems. For instance, the tendency of emotions to linger after precipitating events have passed (a phenomenon that still needs to be empirically documented at the human level) should lead us to look for relatively sustained neural changes subsequent to the triggering events—changes that can continue to modify autonomic and behavioral activities and reactivities for extended periods of time.

In sum, the approach advocated here is catholic. It accepts all available sources of information—those provided by basic neuroscience, behavioral neuroscience, cognitive, and other forms of psychology—but also makes the strident assumption that scientific progress in understanding the root causes of human emotions will be impossible without a solid analysis of the brain mechanisms. Such a level of analysis may not be as essential for cognitive processes because the critical symbolic structures are represented with fidelity in the external world (Simon, 1992), but that cannot be achieved with emotional processes because the critical structures are deep in the brain, with only shadowy reflections in the external world. Without recourse to a neural analysis, psychology can do little more than describe basic feeling states, their peripheral manifestations, and their relationships to the environment. That is quite insufficient for a scientific understanding of these important phenomena. The time is now ripe for the many essential approaches to work together to help create a lasting scientific foundation in this key area of psychological functioning that cannot be generated by traditional cognitive approaches to the mind.

Within the paradigm of "affective neuroscience" envisioned here, the primitive emotional states that all humans experience provide the raw evidence concerning part of the internal psychic landscape of the mammalian nervous system which needs to be elucidated by behavioral neuroscience. Brain research in animals can provide concrete knowledge concerning such operating systems of the brain. Behavioral neuroscience provides the most robust way to test concrete neural hypotheses concerning the affective structure of the mammalian brain. Also, because of our increasing ability to ethically manipulate the neurochemistries of the human brain pharmacologically, many hypotheses from animal research can be cast in such a way that they may eventually be tested against the validating criteria of human experience.

For instance, as will be detailed later, on the basis of existing preclinical work we can predict that opioid receptor blockades will amplify feelings of loneliness and despair in humans. Such predictions can only be generated if we are willing to concurrently use the conceptual language of emotions in both human and animal research (and that is where most behavioral neuroscientists are prone to bow out of the type of enterprise that is advocated here—some claiming that emotional experience in animals is intrinsically incapable of being addressed scientifically while others simply assert that they are only interested in the neural control of animal behavior). However, investigators may increasingly become sympathetic to an "affective neuroscience" approach if they recognize that the utilization of affective language provides one of the clearest ways to link their brain studies in animals to key psychological issues in humans, and it may yield better cross-species predictions than mere behavioral analyses.

Affective language can also be useful in identifying and discussing basic brain concepts that need to be elucidated as opposed to being used as explanations of behavior. Because of recent scientific advances, we are finally able to decode the fundamental nature of emotionality in the mammalian brain (Panksepp, 1991), but there is presently remarkably little energy being devoted to the effort. Let us probe a bit further into the historical reasons for this neglect and the consequences for the development of a scientific psychology.

WHAT ARE THE PREREQUISITES
FOR A COHERENT SCIENCE OF PSYCHOLOGY?

Although the fragmentation of psychology as a coherent academic discipline has received attention from many scholars (e.g., Bunge, 1990), the rectification process has not. Indeed, many now side with the idea that fragmentation is unavoidable in a discipline as diverse as psychology (e.g., Bower, 1993; Koch, 1993) and should be accepted as *fait accompli*. I do not concur with such a pessimistic view. Of course, without credible specific proposals on how to solve the dilemma, there are few alternatives available. However, we might recall that only a few decades ago biology was in a similar conundrum, which was resolved by the discovery of the mechanisms of inheritance and DNA that operate to generate practically everything else of interest to biologists. Now, all biologists share a foundation of knowledge which gives the discipline a coherence that was unimaginable before the discovery of DNA. Similarly, medicine was transformed earlier in this century by the acceptance of a thorough knowledge of anatomy and physiological processes as an essential foundation for the field.

The time is now ripe for such an intellectual metamorphosis to transpire in psychology. The foundations for an effective passage have been laid by our new-found knowledge about the brain, especially those subcortical areas that control basic psychobehavioral processes shared by all mammals to an unmistakable extent. Many of these mechanisms are ones that still govern the basic emotional and motivational states of the human nervous system (MacLean, 1990). Although it cannot be denied that human cortical evolution adds new dimensions and puts all other brains to "shame" by the sophistication of its massive "RAM-type" memory banks and resultant cognitive skills, it is now clear that all of this is supported from below by "ROM-like" brain operating systems that are remarkably similar in all mammals (Panksepp, 1989b, 1989c). Although the ability of different species to create new functional brain structures based on learning experiences differs vastly depending on their levels of cortical sophistication, all those higher abilities remain anchored from below by very similar neurophysiological control systems that, among other things, elaborate innate biological values. Apparently because of this shared heritage, we can resonate easily with the behavioral patterns of other mammals, and that is surely one major reason we commonly cherish them as pets (Thomas, 1993).

In this article I first briefly outline a general approach to a greater acceptance of animal brain research into such basic processes as a foundation pillar for psychology and then proceed to some specific examples of how such evidence can highlight the human condition. Due to space limitations, I must be selective, and because of the amount of detailed writing I have done on the nature of brain emotional systems during the past decade, I rely heavily on already published reviews for more detailed summaries of the evidence.

AFFECTIVE NEUROSCIENCE AND THE THREE PILLARS OF A COHERENT PSYCHOLOGY

The current and central dilemma of psychology is its sectarianism—the vast diversity of rather limited interests that share no common scientific foundation (except for computational approaches, experimental design, and the general recognition of the importance of learning). Earlier in this century, behaviorists tried to establish a common foundation by establishing a consensus that scientific psychology must restrict its discussions to the objectively quantifiable actions of organisms. This plan had many empirical successes but it failed as a comprehensive strategy, and for some time now it has been supplanted, in the minds of most psychologists, by the pluralism of cognitive psychology. Unfortunately, the powerful new sciences of the mind have yet to generate a solid and inviolate scientific foundation for psychology. If anything, the field has splintered more, and sectarianism has increased.

What needs to be added now is the full and universal recognition of the place of the brain—not just the human brain, but the mammalian brain—in any coherent synthesis. I would suggest that it is among the lower brain processes, the subcortical affective and motivational circuits, rather than the higher cognitive areas, where we must presently seek the general foundation principles that psychology so desperately needs. Indeed, a neurally defensible taxonomy of affective processes has matured more rapidly than a taxonomy of cognitive processes (Panksepp, 1982, 1989a, 1989b, 1989c, 1991). This is not to deny that cognitive processes are more evident in the moment-to-moment occurrences of human lives, but to suggest that hidden affective processes are often the final arbiters of what is important to think about and to act on. Without a scientific understanding of the underlying affective processes, many cognitive processes will remain ungrounded.

In short, the concept of an "Affective Neuroscience" is aimed at promoting the needed neurobiological foundation for primary-process psychology, via a judicious combination of brain, behavioral, and mental analysis of basic emotional processes. Through this approach, we can gradually come to terms with the deep neurobiological nature of human emotionality. To do so properly we cannot avoid the abundant evidence that the primal sources of emotionality are largely subcortical (where neural homologies abound in all mammals). We must also recognize some simple constraints on evolution, such as that it can only build on preexisting solutions. A resultant conclusion is inescapable: Brain operating systems that instigate human emotions cannot be markedly different in principle from the ones that generate emotional states in other mammals. Although details will surely vary among species, existing knowledge strongly suggests that the brain sources of basic emotions such as anger, hope, fear, and sexuality are remarkably similar in all mammals (Panksepp, 1985, 1991). If so, animal brain research can tell us more about the mechanisms that underlie human emotions than any other research strategy yet available—but this must be asserted with some qualification. Obviously, the enormous cognitive potentialities of the human brain can rapidly take primitive emotions to psychological spaces that do not exist for other animals. The music, dance, and other expressive arts that emerge from the interplay of our cortico-cultural potentials with our primitive passions surpasses anything we see in other animals.

AFFECTIVE NEUROSCIENCE: A SYNTHESIS OF
PSYCHOLOGY, BEHAVIOR, AND BRAIN RESEARCH

Any synthesis that aspires to provide a scientific foundation for the psychology of basic processes must, I would submit, be constructed on three pillars—each of them equally essential for the final structure (see Figure 2.1). We must concurrently apply (a) psychological analysis, (b)

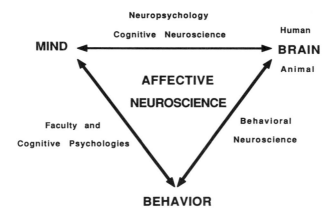

FIG. 2.1. A conceptual scheme contrasting "affective neuroscience" to other major schools of thought that are devoted to the analysis of mind–brain, brain–behavior, and mind–behavior relations.

behavioral analysis, and (c) brain analysis to those neuropsychic/neurobehavioral functions that reflect genetically ordained operating principles of the brain. Let us focus on each of these dimensions briefly.

1. As the anguish that radical behaviorism bestowed on psychology clearly demonstrated, we cannot proceed too far in understanding psychological processes and brain functions without a healthy dose of mental analysis. However, a key issue that psychology still has to resolve involves the types of psychic processes that are primitives. Which ones are given to us as genetic birthrights by the evolutionary reinforcement processes hidden in the epigenetically expressed hieroglyphics of DNA? This question should be considered in tandem with attempts to identify which processes are conserved homologously in humans and other animals. Only those processes that are, in fact, basic (i.e., genetically ingrained across mammalian species) are susceptible to a full frontal empirical attack by the application of behavioral brain research. Several emotions already fit that bill. We can presently be confident that items such as anger–rage, anxiety–fear, joy–play–happiness, sorrow–distress, and curiosity–interest–anticipatory excitement as well as various aspects of sexuality and maternal acceptance must be on any definitive list of cross-mammalian emotions (Panksepp, 1982, 1986b, 1991, 1992a, 1992b).

2. Despite all the sharp criticism that radical behaviorism has received during the cognitive revolution, we must respect and incorporate its undeniable achievements in any final synthesis. To do otherwise would be to disregard some of the most substantive empirical contributions of experimental psychology during this century. However, the one area of

behavior that still deserves greater attention than ever is the natural (ethological) behavior patterns that animals exhibit spontaneously with little prior learning (the relevant literature can be accessed through the reviews cited in the next paragraph).

It is primarily through the use of such naturalistic behavioral measures that we can develop index variables through which central state processes can be monitored most effectively (Panksepp, 1982, 1991). Thus, we should provisionally accept an animal's energetic lunging, attacking, biting, and struggling as indicators of anger–rage (Bandler, 1988; Siegel & Brutus, 1990). We should accept spontaneous freezing and fleeing as measures of fearfulness (Panksepp, 1990c; Panksepp, Sacks, Crepeau, & Abbott, 1991), the rough-and-tumble play exhibited by young animals as reflective of a state of free-flowing joyfulness (Panksepp, 1993c; Panksepp, Normansell, Cox, Crepeau, & Sacks, 1987; Panksepp, Siviy, & Normansell, 1984), and the plaintive crying of isolated young animals as reflective of their feelings of separation distress (Panksepp, 1981b; Panksepp, Herman, Vilberg, Bishop, & DeEskinazi, 1980; Panksepp, Normansell, Herman, Bishop, & Crepeau, 1988; Panksepp, Siviy, & Normansell, 1984). In addition, we should accept the spontaneous bouts of exploratory engagement and intense bodily arousal when animals are waiting for rewards to reflect the activity of anticipatory excitement/interest systems (Panksepp, 1981a, 1986a, 1992a). The discipline of psychology should spend more effort in trying to understand the brain sources of these types of intrinsic psychobehavioral tendencies.

We would also be wise to entertain the possibility that the underlying brain mechanisms in animals are homologous to those that are aroused in humans when they are overcome by similar emotional states (a premise that is increasingly supported by the evidence: Panksepp, 1985, 1989a, 1989b). In addition, it might be wise to provisionally assume that animals do experience subjective states imbued with affective meaning (Panksepp, 1990a, 1990b, 1990c, 1991, 1992a, 1993b, 1994; Thomas, 1993), and that these emotional value systems do, in fact, serve some type of control functions in generating the coherent behavior patterns that we can visually observe (see next section).

In short, I suspect we will make more progress in generating substantive understanding if we make these our starting assumptions as opposed to requiring that intrinsic central states be definitively demonstrated before they are given due consideration. To make progress, we must more fully accept and affirm the potential similarity of certain intrinsic psychobiological processes that are shared among all mammals, and formulate our theories so that animal brain research has a clear potential to shed light on the nature of human affective processes. This is not to deny species differences; they will always need to be documented. Also, this does not deny that humankind is the only species that has been substantially liberated from the mandates of natural constraints via cultural evolution, but to recognize that is more of a dilemma for a cross-species Cognitive Neuroscience than for a cross-species Affective Neuroscience.

3. Finally, and perhaps most importantly, we must cultivate a sense of the brain as the organ of mind, and we should come to regard brain science, especially the systems versions, as an essential area of knowledge for psychologists (Panksepp, 1990b, 1993b). All psychologists in training should be taught to contemplate the organ of the mind with a shared sense of comfort, wonder, and awe. To not provide such a legacy for future generations of students should be deemed an intellectual sin of present-day psychology—a sin as large as the narrow-minded one that radical behaviorism bestowed on the discipline for the better part of this century (for critique, see Panksepp, 1990b).

Although a simple-minded linear reductionism has no place in psychology, since everything an organism does emerges from the interplay of many neural systems, it is even more foolish to allow students to believe that an understanding of the animal brain has little to do with a credible scientific understanding of the human mind. We have to sustain a full regard for environmental complexities and the nature and subtlety of "information" as well as for the wonder of the many "emergent processes" that our brains can generate; nevertheless, it is remarkable that we presently do not insist that all students of psychology become conversant with the major accomplishments of the brain sciences. Students should be encouraged to think about the links that can now be empirically wrought between the basic psychological processes of humans, the corresponding behaviors of animals, and the homologous neural substrates from which they emerge in the mammalian brain. We must gradually come to terms with the types of neurodynamics that generate emotional feelings within brain, and thereby influence many cognitive processes (Panksepp, 1990a, 1990b, 1990d)—that will require animal brain research, and it will also require us to address the nature of subjectivity in other creatures.

Despite the spectacular recent advances in various forms of brain imaging, what goes on psychologically inside the brain of humans and other animals remains relatively inaccessible to direct empirical measurement. Accordingly, behavioral neuroscience, as radical behaviorism before it, continues to avoid all concepts which suggest that animals have internal experiences. Unfortunately, behavioral neuroscientists have also failed to publicly discuss what the consequences might be for the brain sciences if, in fact, other animals do have such experiences. Surely the end result of their hard-won knowledge would have to be flawed.

THE SUBJECTIVE EXPERIENCE OF EMOTIONS

We should note that other sciences have typically made major progress once they conceptualized unseen entities and developed appropriate experimental means of probing their existence and nature—means that have initially been indirect. Who, after all, has yet seen a single electron, not to mention the menagerie of quarks and other subatomic particles? Would not psychology make more progress in unraveling the neural nature of certain primitive neurodynamic processes in humans if we assumed that the ability to elaborate subjectivity is a basic function of all mammalian brains, and proceeded from that premise? Perhaps not, but the strategy remains to be adequately evaluated in the modern era of behavioral neuroscience when critical evaluation of such theoretical propositions has finally become possible. Indeed, proper evaluation of such issues can only be achieved if we first entertain and analyze such types of brain functions in animals (employing available indirect strategies), and then proceed to evaluate the resulting conclusions in humans who can provide reasonably direct feedback about their internal states.

In any event, if we provisionally accept the existence of subjectivity in other animals, we must provide some type of credible rationale for the existence of such neurodynamic inner states. Subjectivity must serve some type of adaptive function. I would suggest that hedonic feeling states provide a simple coding device for the brain, enabling it to make rapid judgments concerning the survival value of certain sensations, perceptions, and actions. Such affect-based codes may be especially effective indexing devices for the storage and retrieval of memories. Because feelings can be psychologically generalized rather than specific to each environmental situation, they may provide useful class-identifier mechanisms for new circumstances and courses of action. Because of their ability to encode memories, emotional feelings may rapidly recruit distinct classes of learned behavioral strategies in response to new challenges.

The unconditional affective experience that is intrinsic within an aroused emotional circuit (as described in the next section) may readily become conditioned to various neutral cues. Those stimuli that have been associated with unconditional feelings of dread are able to recruit avoidance strategies readily (yielding learned fears). Those stimuli that have been associated with the alleviation of homeostatic imbalances (i.e., cravings such as hunger and thirst), may develop privileged access to "expectancy or desire systems" so that flexible search and approach patterns are readily activated. Those stimuli that have been associated with feelings of irritation and frustration are more likely to recruit anger responses, and thereby help prepare the body for the challenge of dealing with thwarting situations and for competing more effectively for needed resources, and so forth and so on. Such scenarios also help explain why feelings may not always be directly evident in the behavior of organisms—their communicative function is only a secondary function of emotional process. Their deeper function is related to the generation of brain patterns that promote efficient learning and the molding of new adaptive (and sometimes maladaptive) behaviors.

In other words, if emotional systems were originally designed to provide intrinsic but flexible response strategies to life-challenging circumstances, the affective tone elaborated by these systems may provide a simple and rapid coding mechanism for the anticipation of other similar circumstances. These systems may be specific in the sense that there are several distinct natural categories of emergency responses, but they may be non-specific in their ability to promote learning that can generalize across a diversity of new emergency situations that require rapid responses.

Slow incremental learning and more deliberate cognitive appraisals may be fine for certain noncompelling circumstances, but it is hard to imagine that evolution would have failed to build in a variety of strongly ingrained action-integrating tendencies for the most important, archetypal survival issues. Once such instinctual tendencies had been constructed within the nervous system, it is hard to imagine that they would not have been used as source processes for new types of learning. Affective experience may be at the heart of these processes because of the way the brain is designed to represent the self-interests of each animal. Of course, such lines of thought must eventually force us to confront the issue of "self-identity" in animals, but that is too large and troublesome an issue to tackle in this short chapter. Just as it is a key issue in any discussion of human development (e.g., Butterworth, 1992), however, it must eventually be recognized as a key issue in animal brain research.

Just in passing, I would suggest that a "self-process" does exist in the brain as a fairly coherent neural function, and I believe it can be understood materialistically. I would suggest that the primordial self is constituted of an ancient multimodal neural net located initially at the midbrain level (in areas such as the periventricular gray and surrounding tectal and tegmental areas) that integrates primitive bodily representations from somatosensory, motor, and integrative systems such as the specific emotional ones that will be discussed in the next section. With brain evolution, this process may have ramified further in midline brain structures such as medial hypothalamus, bed nucleus of the stria terminalis, septum, hippocampus, amygdala, and frontal cortex. I assume that this primordial circuitry for "the self" can readily exploit other brain areas epigenetically and thereby comes to eventually interact intimately with many higher brain areas that integrate the details of everyday experience and waking consciousness. However, I suspect that this troublesome topic, which mainstream neuroscience still avoids like the plague, will be much easier to tackle once we have a clearer understanding of emotional circuits and the affective properties they elaborate.

EMOTIONAL CIRCUITS AND DEFINITIONS

The fundamental evidence for the existence of specific emotional circuits in the brain originally came from studies that were able to evoke clear emotive behavior patterns through discrete localized electrical stimulation of subcortical limbic areas of the brain (for summaries, see Panksepp, 1981a, 1982, 1991). This has been supplemented by the ability of specific neuro-chemical manipulations to activate and inhibit specific behavior patterns indicative of emotional states (Panksepp, 1986c, 1993a). These manipulations clearly have affective impact on animals, because they readily learn to approach or avoid such types of brain stimulation if given the chance.

More recently, a variety of longitudinally coursing neural circuits have been identified that project through limbic brain areas, and some of them, especially certain neuropeptide pathways, have the requisite charac-teristics to mediate specific emotions while others, such as the biogenic amine pathways (e.g., norepinephrine and serotonin) participate in most brain functions, including emotions, in comparatively nonspecific ways (Panksepp, 1986c, 1993a). Homologous systems also exist in the human brain, and it is unlikely that their functions are much different than those that have been revealed in animals (even though their species-typical expressions will surely vary).

In short, there exist executive systems in subcortical areas of the mam-malian brain that elaborate emotionality, but the details are just beginning to be worked out. The emerging results continue to support the type of open-ended conception I advocated some years ago (Panksepp, 1982), but there are now several additional systems and more empirical flesh on the skeleton of the original ideas (see the cited reviews from this lab 1984–1994). The thesis that the mammalian brain contains a variety of emotional command systems continues to be a useful heuristic for guiding animal research that can interface with key issues emerging from human emotion research.

The newly characterized anatomies of subcortical emotive circuits (Panksepp, 1986a, 1993a, 1994) suggest that the individual emotional systems ramify widely in the brain, resembling, if you will, a tree. The neuronal branches reach into a diversity of higher areas of the brain, and the roots distribute information via the brain stem into a variety of bodily systems. The actual trunk lines of these systems are often remarkably coalesced as they course through the diencephalon, interlinking and coordinating higher and lower brain functions. It is most reasonable presently to surmise that the feeling state of emotions emerges largely from the trunk lines of the emotional systems and from their interactions with primordial "self-representation" mechanisms of the midbrain (as alluded to before). In other words, these trunk lines appear to be the unconditional "command" or coordinating components of the basic emotional systems. In addition, certain emotional systems may also operate, in part, via paracrine processes in the brain, where the actual receptive fields for the pertinent mood-altering molecules are located at a distance from the neurons that manufacture and release the various psychoactive neuromodulators (which makes emotional systems more than mere circuits).

The many possible levels of analysis within these "tree-like" systems for the emotions suggests why there is still so much controversy in discussing emotional issues, and it also provides a possible resolution. Each level of processing within an emotional system may add new dimensions to an emotional process. For instance, let us consider some of the complexities that may emerge among the higher branches of the emotional "tree" where strategic cognitive attributions and ruminations are presumably constructed. Maybe this is where anger processes help elaborate hate, and fear processes elaborate specific anxieties and neuroses, and panic processes elaborate the thoughts of grief and the details of loneliness, and expectancy processes elaborate specific hopes and frustrations. When basic emotional systems come in contact with real world events, the higher reaches of the systems spontaneously elaborate learning and the consequent attributions about the potential causes of the emotional states. Even though primitive feelings (as evolutionary processes of the brain) do not need an external referent (only a certain type of subcortical neural arousal), they are obviously only useful for helping animals survive if each form of emotional arousal can be readily associated with real-world events.

In sum, many of the neuropeptide and amino-acid circuits that can be visualized readily with immunocytochemistry appear to be the unconditional substrates for the various basic emotions (for overview, see Panksepp, 1993a, in press). For instance, the long pathways from central amygdala to brain stem areas that Davis (this volume) describes in the context of potentiated startle appear to be the unconditional substrates for fear in the brain (Panksepp, 1982, 1990c; Panksepp, Sacks, Crepeau, & Abbott, 1991). However, this system is not just a passive information conduit, but, in some presently unfathomed way, it appears to be a key player in the generation of anxious affective experiences.

To highlight the fact that there is an unconditional "fear circuit" in the brain, and to avoid confusing that with the many vernacular meanings of such emotional terms, I will henceforth use a capitalized designation (e.g., the FEAR system) when discussing the trunk lines of specific emotional circuits (Panksepp, in press). In a sense, then, these emotive circuits resemble "hypothetical constructs" of traditional psychological theorizing, but in the context of recent advances in neuroscience, they are much more than that. They are reasonably well-characterized neural realities that are beckoning to be understood neurodynamically (i.e., psychologically).

Due to the widespread distributed influence of such systems through the neuroaxis, it is understandable why emotions have so many bodily and psychological consequences. It also helps highlight why the controversies between various theoretical perspectives to the study of emotions (such as the categorical, componential, and social constructivist views) can be so sterile (Panksepp, 1992a). Each of these levels of analysis is focusing on different aspects of each system—some focus on the overlapping "branches" interacting with cortico-cognitive processes, some on the brain stem "roots" that cause a great diversity of bodily "disturbances," and others, like myself, on the "trunk line issues," which elaborate the integrative and affective attributes of the basic emotions. In any event, I would suggest that each perspective has to come to terms with the neuroscience evidence. Without doing that, conceptual chaos is bound to prevail (for an example, see Ortony & Turner, 1990 and three subsequent commentaries with a response in Turner & Ortony, 1992). The acceptance of neurobiological foundations can help bring coherence and the possibility of rapid scientific advance to this troubled field. For instance, even the study of personality structures is being benefited by a proper conceptualization of the underlying systems (see Depue & Iacono, 1989, and Malatesta, this volume). However, before proceeding to selected empirical issues, let me share some thoughts on one traditional and troublesome issue—the problem of definitions.

THE ROLE OF DEFINITIONS
IN BASIC EMOTION RESEARCH

As may be evident from our previous discussion, I see no urgent need to have conceptual definitions for the basic emotions at the beginning of an "affective-neuroscience" research program. There are already adequate emotional labels from folk psychology that identify the putative existence of certain key types of brain systems. It is from the concurrent harvesting of behavioral, psychological, and neural knowledge about these systems that a definition of each must eventually emerge. To proceed empirically, all we need are reasonable assurances that certain types of systems exist (which comes from animal brain/behavioral and human subjective evidence) and operational definitions for the specific behavioral processes that can be used to index the presence and operations of the various brain system. Obviously, dependent measures will have to be spelled out in detail, but all measures must be deemed provisional and subject to change as more and more pertinent information is gathered (Panksepp, 1991).

What would be desirable, however, is a general conceptual definition of what type of psychoneural systems can be considered to constitute basic emotional systems. For this purpose, a conjoint application of neural circuit criteria, along with attributes derived from reliable psychological and behavioral analyses, need to be implemented. To this end, I originally suggested six types of criteria that might be useful in identifying bona fide emotional systems (Panksepp, 1982, 1986a). In addition to the self-evident psychological criterion that these systems should be capable of modifying affective feeling states, the suggested neural criteria were as follows:

1. The underlying circuits are genetically prewired and designed to respond unconditionally to stimuli arising from major life-challenging circumstances.
2. The circuits organize diverse behaviors by activating or inhibiting motor subroutines (and concurrent autonomic–hormonal changes) that have proved adaptive in the fact of such life-challenging circumstances during the evolutionary history of the species.
3. Emotive circuits change the sensitivities of sensory systems relevant for the behavior sequences that have been aroused.
4. Neural activity of emotive systems outlasts the precipitating circumstances.
5. Emotive circuits can come under the conditional control of emotionally neutral environmental stimuli.
6. Emotive circuits have reciprocal interactions with brain mechanisms that elaborate higher decision-making processes and consciousness.

The last criterion also implicitly includes the most empirically troublesome attribute of emotions, which is the subjective feeling tone. This attribute, the felt affect that accompanies emotional states, is the one that has caused the most problems for behavioral neuroscientists, not to mention psychologists in general. There simply is no easy way to deal with it; such internal states cannot be directly monitored. However, recently developed techniques such as conditioned place-preference and place-aversion tasks do begin to provide the necessary empirical handle on such issues (Carr, Fibiger, & Phillips, 1989).

Brain-imaging techniques, such as computational EEG procedures, may eventually be able to monitor these states directly. However, at the most simple behavioral level, it is generally recognized that affective valence consists of only two general dimensions—approach and avoidance. This has constrained "behavioral neuroscience" thinking about discrete emotions enormously; it is becoming evident, however, that with further work we should be able to discriminate between different types of positive and negative feeling states, but there is not enough space here to go into such difficult issues. Let me simply suggest that this can be done using various behavioral discrimination procedures (using brain stimulation as conditional stimuli) as well as related neurochemical and pharmacological ones, such as state-dependent learning paradigms. In short, we should eventually be able to create reasonably rigorous procedures and criteria for resolving some of the types of internal states an animal can have above and beyond simple approach and aversion dimensions.

At the present time the neuroscience evidence provides compelling reasons to believe that there are more than half a dozen distinct emotional command systems in the brain, including ones that mediate FEAR, RAGE, EXPECTANCY, PANIC, PLAY, MATERNAL NURTURANCE, and various male and female aspects of sexual LUST (Panksepp, 1991). Much of this work has been summarized in the other reviews already mentioned in this chapter, but for didactic purposes (to help highlight the possibilities of an "affective neuroscience") I will now focus on one of these systems, the so-called PANIC system that mediates separation distress.

THE PANIC/SEPARATION–DISTRESS SYSTEM
OF THE BRAIN

Mammalian and avian brains were designed to establish social bonds with caretakers as well as, at times, sexual partners, and clearly there are emotional circuits in the brain that were designed to respond to social separation (especially between caretaker and offspring) with internally experienced distress responses. The best objective measure of this emotional system in action is the crying or distress vocalizations (DVs) that can be evoked in young animals merely by the act of enforced social isolation. We are beginning to understand the neurobiological nature of this system (Panksepp, 1981; Panksepp, Siviy, & Normansell, 1985; Panksepp et al., 1980, 1984, 1985, 1988) and key attributes of this brain function have recently been discussed (Panksepp, Newman, & Insel, 1992). An understanding of this system will highlight the affective (albeit, not the environmental) sources of human grief and loneliness and this type of insight will have strong implications for our understanding of the sources of various social-bonding problems ranging from loss-related depression (see Panksepp, Yates, Ikemoto, & Nelson, 1991) to early childhood autism (Panksepp & Sahley, 1987). When this system is active, animals actively seek out and solicit social companionship. When it is underactive, organisms will be aloof and insensitive to the social needs of others.

Accordingly, the neurochemistries (and cognitive activities) that can dynamically inhibit this system help elaborate social reward, while the neurochemistries (and cognitive activities) that can activate this system evoke feelings of separation distress. In highly precipitous forms this distress may intensify into "panic attacks," which explains my selection of the controversial term PANIC for the circuit. We presently know much about the general anatomy and neurochemistry of this system because discrete brain stimulation can evoke DVs in various animal models (see MacLean, 1990; Newman, 1988; Panksepp et al., 1988), and we have a large number of neurochemical manipulations that can excite and inhibit this emotional response (Panksepp, 1991). The admittedly limited data from humans that is available on the topic does suggest that the key manipulations highlighted by animal studies also modulate human feelings of separation distress.

Very briefly, the trajectory of the system seems to emerge at the mesencephalic level from more ancient brain systems that mediate pain (which suggests why social loss is deemed to be painful, and why the neurochemistries that are very effective in controlling pain are also effective in controlling separation distress). The circuitry is evident at several mesencephalic locations, especially within the vicinity of the periventricular gray matter. There are strong ascending components to the system that go via the dorsomedial thalamic area to forebrain areas, with apparently the highest representations projecting to the anterior cingulate cortex (MacLean, 1990; Panksepp et al., 1988). There are also very dense representations of the system in other subcortical areas that are known to mediate sexual and maternal behaviors, such as the basal-forebrain/preoptic area, the bed-nucleus of the stria terminalis, and ventral septal area. Although there are sparse and scattered representations of this system in the amygdala and hypothalamus, the separation distress/PANIC circuit is largely a trans-thalamic emotional system, whereas others such as FEAR and RAGE are largely trans-hypothalamic (Panksepp, 1990c; Siegel & Brutus, 1990).

Our initial analysis of this system was premised on the idea that there may be fundamental neurophysiological relationships between opiate dependence and social dependence, and it was found (Panksepp, Herman, Conner, Bishop, & Scott, 1978), and soon confirmed (Kalin & Shelton, 1989; Kehoe, 1988; Wiener, Coe, & Levine, 1988), that very low doses of opiates can selectively and potently inhibit separation distress, whereas opiate antagonists can increase distress calls. It is humbling to note that this "discovery" replicated one of the first psychopharmacological findings ever recorded in history.

In Homer's Odyssey, when Helen had organized a party for the warriors who had retrieved her during the Trojan Wars, the celebrants became deeply saddened by the fact that their friend Odysseus had failed to return. According to the Fitzgerald (1963) translation, "A twinging ache of grief rose up in everyone, and Helen of Argos wept. . . . But now it entered Helen's mind to drop into the wine that they were drinking an anodyne, mild magic of forgetfulness. Whoever drank this mixture in the wine bowl would be incapable of tears that day—though he should lose mother and father both, or see, with his own eyes, a son or brother mauled by weapons of bronze at his own gate" (Book 4, lines 173–226). There is little doubt that the potion that Helen used to sustain the spirits of the celebrants was tincture of opium. Also, through the middle of this century, a common way to soothe the crying children was to rub paregoric on their gums. The soothing ingredient in that medicine is little different from that used by Helen.

We also have many literary allusions to the power of opiates to alleviate social needs. For instance, Cocteau (1957) in his diary states how opium liberated him from the need for "visits and people sitting around in circles." Recent primate work also indicates that reducing opiate tone in the nervous system with receptor antagonists increases the need for social contact (Fabre-Nys, Meller, & Keverne, 1982; Schino & Troisi, 1992). Conversely, there is direct evidence that social interactions promote opioid release in the brain (Keverne, Martensz, & Tuite, 1989; Panksepp & Bishop, 1981). From this type of evidence, we proceeded to deduce that certain human psychiatric disorders, such as early childhood autism, may be partially due to excessive endogenous activity in brain opioid systems (Panksepp, 1979), an effect that has been confirmed (Panksepp, Lensing, Leboyer, & Bouvard, 1991). The possibility for these types of predictions are a key feature of "affective neuroscience" and the specific issue of opioids and autism will be discussed in the next section.

An important point to emphasize is that there are a great number of neurochemical controls within each emotional system and most details remain to be worked out. However, we do know many of the brain chemistries that activate this emotional system as well as many that can inhibit the system. Let us briefly focus on some of the major players, while recognizing that there are also many minor influences (see Table 3.1 of Panksepp, 1991).

In our experience, the three most powerful ways to activate separation calls are the administration of curare, kainic acid, and corticotrophin-releasing hormone (CRF) into the avian brain. Indeed, this last peptide system tends to be concentrated in brain areas that contain DV circuitry. The kainic acid has been found to reflect activation of brain NMDA receptor glutamate systems (Panksepp et al., 1988) and we now also suspect that curare acts via that system because the glutamate receptor antagonist APV, which can reduce both kainic acid and NMDA-induced DVs (Normansell, 1988), can also attenuate curare-induced distress (Panksepp, 1992c, unpublished raw data). Indeed, it presently seems that glutamate is at the very heart of the trunk-line circuit that elaborates separation distress, because practically the only receptor antagonist with which we can totally eliminate DVs in animals, without producing any sedation or motor disruption, is via the blockade of glutamate receptors with APV and other NMDA receptor antagonists (see Figure 2.2).

There are also a large number of other psychopharmaceuticals that can reduce DVs modestly, but only a few have powerful and specific effects. Among the four most effective items we have discovered, three are neuropeptides (opioids, oxytocin, and prolactin), all of which have many other important effects on social behavior. The remaining one is clonidine, which stimulates alpha-2 norepinephrine (NE) receptors. Many of those clonidine-sensitive receptors are situated on NE cell bodies where they reduce neuronal firing. However, that is not the cause of the clonidine effect on DVs since total destruction of the brain NE systems does not modify the sensitivity of animals to clonidine. Clonidine reduces separation anxiety because of postsynaptic rather than presynaptic effects in the NE system (Rossi, Sahley, & Panksepp, 1983).

The ability of oxytocin and prolactin to reduce DVs (Panksepp, 1992b) is especially attractive because these peptides have been strongly implicated in maternal nurturance (Pedersen, Caldwell, Jirikowski, & Insel, 1992).

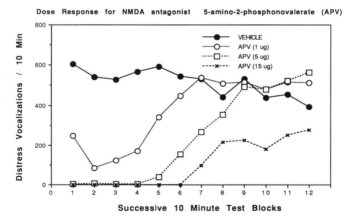

FIG. 2.2. 5-amino-2-phosphonovalerate (APV) is a glutamate receptor antagonist that specifically blocks the NMDA receptor, which is presently thought to be a key transmitter in the generation of separation distress vocalizations (DVs) within the brain. Animals (12-day-old domestic chickens) were injected into the 4th ventricle region immediately before being separated from a flock of 20 birds. Vocalizations were automatically harvested for a 2-hr period in 10-min blocks. The low dose of APV inhibited DVs reliably for 50 min, the medium dose for 70 min, and the high dose for 110 min.

Both oxytocin and prolactin can promote maternal behaviors in animals, and it is attractive to suppose that these systems may help induce the comfortable and serene mood states when mother and infant are nursing. The neuropeptide effects are quite long-lasting (Figure 2.3), which might help explain why social moods tend to linger within the brain.

For anyone to believe that humans are liberated from these types of brain emotional controls is probably foolish (even though humans can heroically overcome their dictates). Indeed, future progress in our understanding and medication of psychiatric disorders will come from the full implementation of such knowledge. I find it disquieting how little work is being conducted on these systems considering that they may be the sources of human sadness and related insecurities. As an example of how the hybridization of human and animal research via "affective neuroscience" can promote useful new insights, let me briefly summarize our ongoing work on the nature of autistic disorders.

THE BRAIN MECHANISMS OF AUTISM

As Kanner asserted in 1943, "Autistic children have come into the world with an innate inability to form the usual biologically provided affective contact with people" (p. 119). It is now generally recognized that autism

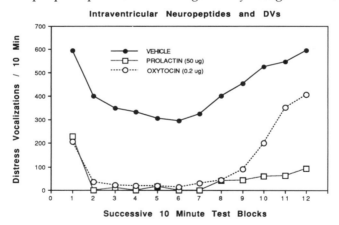

FIG. 2.3. Two neuropeptides, oxytocin and prolactin, that mediate maternal behavior also have strong inhibitory effects on separation DVs. Animals (7-day-old domestic chicks) were injected into the 4th ventricle region immediately before separation from a flock of 20–25 birds. The 50 μg dose of prolactin was approximately equipotent to the 0.2 μg of oxytocin, but the prolactin had a more prolonged action. DVs were back to normal at the 3 hr time point following oxytocin and at the 4 hr time point following prolactin. Each of these peptides produces effects that are proportionate in intensity and duration to the amount of peptide injected, suggesting how mood states may be induced in the brain.

is a brain disorder which probably arises from several etiological vectors that produce pervasive delays in neuronal development. Bauman (1987) has documented that autistic children have too many small neurons in parts of their limbic system (suggesting that selective cell death, or apoptosis, did not proceed normally), while other areas, such as the cerebellum, have too few Purkinje cells. For those who see autism to be largely a cognitive rather than an affective disorder, it may come as a surprise that the thalamic–neocortical axis, which is especially influential for the flow of thought, appears histologically normal. Although such structural changes in the brain cannot be reversed (except perhaps by very early interventions), the disorder may also be accompanied by dynamic neurochemical imbalances that may be correctable.

We suggested, on the basis of preclinical work, that one such imbalance may be excessive brain opioid activity, and proposed that opiate antagonists such as naltrexone should be capable of reducing the social aloofness of autism (Panksepp, 1979, 1981b). Because naltrexone has few known side effects, and because it can increase vocal activity and social solicitation in animals, we felt relatively confident that it should have some positive effects in some autistic children. That expectation has now been confirmed.

Work during the past few years has demonstrated that naltrexone can benefit many autistic children (Campbell et al., 1990; Herman, 1991; Leboyer et al., 1990, 1992; Panksepp & Lensing, 1991). Benefits included decreases in excessive motor activity, stereotypy, and self-injurious behavior; the medication can also evoke various positive social changes including increased desire to communicate and interact, with higher quality eye contact and interaction with the world (for summary see Panksepp, Lensing, et al., 1991). Although an endogenous opioid imbalance is surely only one facet of autism, it demonstrates that a fruitful interchange can be constructed between theoretically guided research into the brain mechanisms of emotions in animals and the sources of human emotionality. We presently remain on the near shore of this type of knowledge, but an especially appropriate place for this type of work to be pursued is in the psychology departments of our universities. From this vantage, it is disturbing to note that the amount of brain research has been diminishing alarmingly in psychology departments across the nation during the past few decades (Davis, Rosenzweig, Becker, & Sather, 1988). I personally see this trend to be undercutting the scientific future of our discipline (Panksepp, 1990d).

ON THE BLENDING OF HUMAN
AND ANIMAL BRAIN RESEARCH

Some of the most powerful knowledge in understanding emotions will come when we learn to blend the best aspects of human and animal brain research. Obviously, the most compelling translations will come when we begin to use similar techniques to analyze human and animal brain changes during emotional episodes. The number of options that we have in this arena are limited, and for the typical psychology lab they boil down to electrophysiological measures and perhaps the monitoring of neurochemical markers in urine, saliva, and, occasionally, blood. Among the available options, the most powerful analysis will probably arise from electroencephalographic (EEG) work, especially now that new and powerful computational procedures are available for analyzing the dendritic potentials that can be harvested from the surface of the human skull. Recent work has indicated that emotional changes in humans can be detected in EEG measurements (Davidson, 1993).

One distinct advantage of an EEG approach is that it is one of the few technologies whereby human and animal investigations can be pursued using an essentially identical approach. The EEG technology that may be one of the best general purpose tools for analyzing time-locked brain changes to various emotion-provoking stimuli may be the event-related desynchronization (ERD) and event-related synchronization (ERS) technology that Pfurtscheller (1991, 1992) developed at the University of Graz in Austria. Their algorithm is a way to computationally analyze for regional changes in EEG power, such as small changes in alpha blocking, as a function of timed external events. The technique has the potential to follow cognitive processes on the cortical surface in real time (Klimesch, Pfurtscheller, Mohl, & Schimke, 1990). Essentially, the technology takes frames of EEG up to several seconds in length and averages the time-related power changes as a function of baseline power during reference intervals just prior to the stimulus events of interest.

To evaluate whether this technology had the power to detect different emotional patterns on the human cortex, several years ago in Klimesch's lab I had my ERD responses analyzed as a function of doing systematic emotional exercise developed by Clynes (1978) called sentic cycles. In this exercise one expresses distinct emotions in response to periodic tone cues, and with some experience with the technique, I felt that I could in fact voluntarily control my emotional states. To see if that potentially delusional feeling corresponded to any objective change in the brain, I repeatedly expressed a series of emotions for a sufficient number of EEG recording trials (approximately 30 times for each emotion) to provide an adequate sample of each systematically experienced feeling: The successive feeling states started with "no emotion," followed successively by anger, grief, love, joy, and reverence.

As summarized in Figure 2.4, each emotion produced distinct and powerful brain changes during the four seconds following the onset of the emotional expressions (which were done minimally and bilaterally to minimize motor artifacts and artificial laterality effects). To what extent

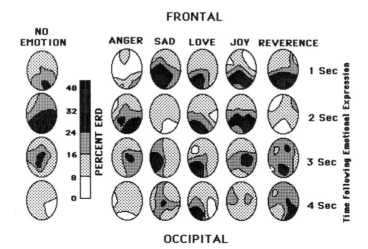

FIG. 2.4. Analysis of event-related desynchronizations (ERDs) in the author's brain during a 4 s period following the induction of emotional states using the Clynes' (1978) procedure. The expression of "no emotion" produced ERDs symmetrically in the occipital region at the 2 s time. Anger induced ERDs in the right parieto-occipital area. Sadness induced larger ERDs in the parietal regions of the left hemisphere. Love induced more posterior arousal in the left hemisphere. Joy induced right parietal arousal sweeping to the left partietal area, and reverence induced right occipito-parietal arousal. The ERD summary is based on recordings from 29 electrodes referenced to a linked-ear ground.

these changes are repeatable from session to session and subject to subject will be an interesting area of future research, but the important point is that very dramatic brain changes were evident in response to self-evoked emotional states. These changes may highlight the powerful influence that subcortical emotional systems exert on higher cortical processing. As already mentioned, what makes this especially exciting is that this is one of the few reasonably inexpensive technologies that can be applied in related animal work. This may allow us to evaluate mechanistic hypotheses in animals concerning the types of changes that are expressed on the surface of human brains.

EMOTIONAL CIRCUITS AND HIGHER PROCESSES

The analysis of human brain changes as a function of emotions remains in its infancy. The "sentic cycle" of Clynes (1978) is an excellent procedure to voluntarily evoke emotions in the laboratory, but in our experience only a minority of young undergraduates feel that they are able to do these exercises properly. Many feel self-conscious when they do them in the laboratory, and commonly report that they feel a bit silly. Others take to it quite well, and find the exercises fascinating and effective (i.e., emotionally compelling). Accordingly, that approach may only be effectively pursued in selected individuals.

A more universal approach to the question might be the use of music to modify mood states (Pignatiello, Camp, & Rasar, 1986; Terwogt & Van Grinsven, 1991). Indeed, in preliminary work we have found clear EEG–ERD changes as a function of emotional pieces of music (Panksepp, Lensing, Klimesch, Schimke, & Vaningan, 1993). One of the clearest effects was left frontal arousal to the repetition of the same emotional phrase (in this case, the first few bars of Beethoven's "Für Elise"). We are presently hoping to evaluate the brain status of autistic children using this procedure, and hopefully identify pieces of music that are able to selectively facilitate left-hemisphere speech areas in the hope of provoking these brain areas to function more effectively during language processing.

It is generally believed that emotional arousal can facilitate certain types of cognitive processing. We have conducted some preliminary research to evaluate this proposition using music. In the following experiment we determined whether the learning of neuroanatomy could be facilitated by musical feedback of the anatomical terms. Two groups of subjects ($n = 12$ per group) were asked to learn 15 anatomical areas and their respective labels using either spoken or musically sung presentations of the verbal labels. A 15-section anatomical summary of opiate receptor dispersion in the rat brain was used as the stimulus materials (see Figure 1 in Panksepp, 1986c), with each of 15 brain sections having only a single anatomical area highlighted (they were respectively from front to back within the brain: the caudate putamen, nucleus accumbens, anterior commissure, nucleus paratentalis, preoptic area, central amygdaloid nucleus, dorsomedial thalamus, parafasicular area, periventricular gray, hippocampus, interpeduncular nucleus, superior colliculus, medial raphe, inferior colliculus, and the peribrachial area).

For the control group the labels were spoken distinctly by a female language teacher and for the experimental group they were sung by the same person in a high-quality, free-form, operatic voice with considerable affective impact (all of which was prerecorded and synchronously paced with the visual presentation of the anatomical materials). Prior to the experiment, none of the subjects were familiar with the anatomical materials. As summarized in Figure 2.5, the acquisition of the neuroanatomical terms was the same in both groups, but those that had the musical feedback exhibited better retention, especially in recall tasks given several days after acquisition. This supports the idea that information integration is facilitated by concurrent musical stimulation. Whether this is due to

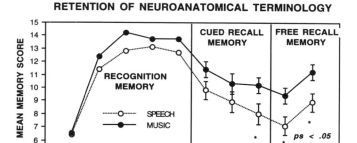

FIG. 2.5. Acquisition of anatomical terminology was not affected by musical presentation of information, but cued recall (anatomical plate provided with no verbal choices) was improved 8 days following acquisition, and free recall (no cues provided) was improved at both short and long intervals following training. Mean valves ± SEMs.

the fact that the music was able to facilitate affective arousal that promotes cognitive processing or whether via some type of direct tuning of language cortex or whether it was merely a novelty effect remains to be resolved by future work. In any event, it will be intriguing to see whether similar learning-facilitation effects can be achieved with selective arousal of specific emotional system in both animals and humans. As is well known, previous work with hypnosis has been promising but controversial (Bower, Gilligan, & Monteiro, 1981)

SUMMARY

Although one can effectively study the manifestations of emotional systems in the lives of individuals without much concern for the nature of the brain substrates, it will be impossible to understand the intrinsic behavioral, physiological, and cognitive organization these system afford an organism without such research. Likewise, the hallmark of emotionality, namely its affective nature, obviously cannot be clarified without neuroscience research. Psychology can either aspire to understand such processes neuroscientifically, or continue to treat them as unscientific concepts. We are fortunate to be working in an era during which we can finally pursue such issues in credible scientific ways. However, to do that we must forthrightly address some conceptual sticking points that have traditionally impeded our pursuit of such issues, and we will have to recognize that much of the necessary work must be conducted in other mammals (Panksepp, 1991). For addressing the nature of basic psycho-biological processes, that type of work can be more robust and important than is commonly conveyed by the term "animal model." The massive similarities in the genetic codes and brain organization of all mammals assures that. This indirect approach to understanding the human mind is quite as powerful as the computational models that have been proposed for cognitive processes (e.g., Simon, 1992), and we can surely be more certain that we are actually revealing the types of mechanisms that exist in the human brain than can the currently fashionable computational models of the mind.

From that perspective, the remarkable decline of animal research in psychology departments during the past 20 years (Davis et al., 1988) should be alarming. There are now many reasons to believe that the type of interdisciplinary work outlined in this chapter can have profound implications for understanding the fundamental substrates of human nature—perhaps more than any empirical approach that can be imple-mented in humans. The vigorous pursuit and acceptance of such knowl-edge will require psychology, as a rejuvenated scientific discipline, to rediscover and cultivate its biological roots more vigorously than it has done in the past. It will require those who pursue cognitive approaches to recognize the primitive affective underpinnings that provide the in-trinsic goals of higher mental activities. It will also require the emerging field of "behavioral neuroscience" to deal with some of the more subtle evolutionarily dictated neurodynamics of the mammalian brain. This will require a willingness to discuss the potential reality of some troublesome psychological processes that apparently emerge from the "great interme-diate net" that intervenes between the inputs and outputs within the brain. Attempting to meet that challenge is what "affective neuroscience" is about.

REFERENCES

Bandler, R. (1988). Brain mechanisms of aggression as revealed by electrical and chemical stimulation: Suggestion of a central role for the midbrain periaqueductal gray region. In A. N. Epstein & A. R. Morrison (Eds.), *Progress in psychobiology and physiological psychology* (Vol. 13, pp. 67–154) San Diego, CA: Academic Press.

Bauman, M. (1987). Limbic involvement in a second case of early infantile autism. *Neurology, 37*, 147.

Bower, G. H. (1993). The fragmentation of psychology? *American Psychologist, 48*, 905–907.

Bower, G. H., Gilligan, S. G., & Monteiro, K. P. (1981). Selective learning cause by affective states. *Journal of Experimental Psychology: General, 110*, 451–473.

Bunge, M. (1990). What kind of discipline is psychology: Autonomous or dependent, humanistic or scientific, biological or sociological? *New Ideas in Psychology, 8*, 121–137.

Butterworth, G. (1992). Origins of self-perception in infancy. *Psychological Inquiry, 3*, 103–111.

Campbell, M., Anderson, L., Small, A., Locscio, J., Lynch, N., & Choroco, M. (1990). Naltrexone in autistic children: A double-blind and placebo-controlled study. *Psychopharmacology Bulletin, 26,* 130–135.

Carr, G. D., Fibiger, H. C., & Phillips, A. G. (1989). Conditioned place preference as a measure of drug reward. In J. M. Liebman & S. J. Cooper (Eds.), *The neuropharmacological basis of reward* (pp. 264–319). Oxford, England: Clarendon.

Clynes, M. (1978). *Sentics, the touch of the emotions.* New York: Anchor.

Cocteau, J. (1957). *Opium: The diary of a cure.* New York: Grove Press.

Davidson, R. (1993). The neuropsychology of emotions and affective style. In M. Lewis & J. Haviland (Eds.), *The handbook of emotions* (pp. 143–154). New York: Guilford.

Davis, H. P., Rosenzweig, M. R., Becker, L. A., & Sather, K. J. (1988). Biological psychology's relationship to psychology and neuroscience. *American Psychologist, 43,* 359–371.

Depue, R. A., & Iacono, W. G. (1989). Neurobehavioral aspects of affective disorders. *Annual Review of Psychology, 40,* 457–492.

Ekman, P., & Davidson, R. J. (Eds.). (1994). *The nature of emotions: Fundamental questions.* New York: Oxford University Press.

Fabre-Nys, C., Meller, R. E., & Keverne, E. B. (1982). Opiate antagonists stimulate affiliative behaviour in monkeys. *Pharmacology Biochemistry & Behavior, 16,* 653–659.

Fitzgerald, R. (Trans.) (1963). *Homer's The Odyssey.* New York: Doubleday.

Herman, B. H. (1991). Effects of opioid receptor antagonists in the treatment of autism and self-injurious behavior. In J. J. Ratsey (Ed.), *Mental retardation: Developing pharmacotherapies. Progression in psychiatry* (Vol. 32, pp. 107–137). Washington, DC: American Psychiatric Press.

Kalin, N. H., & Shelton, S. E. (1989). Defensive behaviours in infant rhesus monkeys: Environmental cues and neurochemical regulation. *Science, 243,* 1718–1721.

Kanner, L. (1943). Autistic disturbances of affective contact. *Nervous Child, 2,* 217–250.

Kehoe, P. (1988). Ontongeny of adrenergic and opioid effects on separation vocalization in rats. In J. D. Newman (Ed.), *The physiological control of mammalian vocalizations* (pp. 301–320). New York: Plenum.

Keverne, E. B., Martensz, N. D., & Tuite, B. (1989). Beta-endorphin concentrations in cerebrospinal fluid of monkeys are influenced by grooming relationships. *Psychoneuroendocrinology, 14,* 155–161.

Klimesch, W., Pfurtscheller, G., Mohl, W., & Schimke, H. (1990). Event-related desynchronization, ERD-mapping and hemispheric differences for words and numbers. *International Journal of Psychophysiology, 8,* 297–308.

Koch, S. (1993). "Psychology" on "The Psychological Studies"? *American Psychologist, 48,* 902–904.

Lazarus, R. S. (1991). *Emotion & adaptation.* New York: Oxford University Press.

Lazarus, R. (1993). Lazarus rise. *Psychological Inquiry, 4,* 343–357.

Leboyer, M., Bouvard, M. P., Lensing, P., Launay, J. M., Tabuteau, F., Arnaud, P., Waller, D., Plumet, M.-H., Recasens, C., Kerdelhue, B., Dugas, M., & Panksepp, J. (1990). Opioid excess hypothesis of autism. *Brain Dysfunction, 3,* 285–298.

Leboyer, M., Bouvard, M. P., Launay, J.-M., Tabuteau, F., Waller, D., Dugas, M., Kerdelhue, B., Lensing, P., & Panksepp, J. (1992). A double-blind study of naltrexone in infantile autism. *Journal of Autism and Developmental Disorders, 22,* 311–321.

MacLean, P. D. (1990). *The triune brain in evolution.* New York: Plenum.

Newman, J. (Ed.). (1988). *The physiological control of mammalian vocalization.* New York: Plenum.

Normansell, L. (1988). *Effects of excitatory amino acids on emotional and sensorimotor behavior in the domestic chick.* Unpublished doctoral dissertation, Bowling Green State University, Bowling Green, OH.

Ortony, A., & Turner, T. J. (1990). What's basic about basic emotions? *Psychological Review,* *97*, 315–331.

Panksepp, J. (1979). A neurochemical theory of autism. *Trends in Neuroscience, 2*, 174–177.

Panksepp, J. (1981a). Hypothalamic integration of behavior: Rewards, punishments, and related psycho-biological process. In P. J. Morgane & J. Panksepp (Eds.), *Handbook of the hypothalamus, Vol. 3, Part A: Behavioral studies of the hypothalamus* (pp. 289–487). New York: Marcel Dekker.

Panksepp, J. (1981b). Brain opioids: A neurochemical substrate for narcotic and social dependence. In S. Cooper (Ed.), *Progress in theory in psychopharmacology* (pp. 149–175). London: Academic Press.

Panksepp, J. (1982). Toward a general psychobiological theory of emotions. *The Behavioral and Brain Sciences, 5*, 407–467.

Panksepp, J. (1985). Mood changes. In P. J. Vinken, G. W. Bruyn, & H. L. Klawans (Eds.), *Handbook of Clinical Neurology. Vol. 1, (45): Clinical neuropsychology* (pp. 271–285). Amsterdam: Elsevier.

Panksepp, J. (1986a). The anatomy of emotions. In R. Plutchik (Ed.), *Emotion: Theory, research and experience: Vol. 3. Biological foundations of emotions* (pp. 91–124). New York: Academic Press.

Panksepp, J. (1986b). The psychobiology of prosocial behaviors: Separation distress, play, and altruism. In C. Zahn-Waxler, E. M. Cummings, & R. Iannotti (Eds.), *Altruism and aggression, biological and social origins* (pp. 19–57). Cambridge, England: Cambridge University Press.

Panksepp, J. (1986c). The neurochemistry of behavior. *Annual Review of Psychology, 37*, 77–107.

Panksepp, J. (1988). Brain emotional circuits and psychopathologies. In M. Clynes & J. Panksepp (Eds.), *Emotions and psychopathology* (pp. 37–76). New York: Plenum Press.

Panksepp, J. (1989a). Les circuits des emotions. *Science & Vie, 168*, 58–67.

Panksepp, J. (1989b). The neurobiology of emotions: Of animal brains and human feelings. In T. Manstead & H. Wagner (Eds.), *Handbook of psychophysiology* (pp. 5–26). New York: Wiley.

Panksepp, J. (1989c). The psychobiology of emotions: The animal side of human feelings. In G. Gainotti & C. Caltagirone (Eds.), *Emotions and the dual brain. Experimental brain research series 18* (pp. 31–55). Berlin: Springer-Verlag.

Panksepp, J. (1990a). A role for "affective neuroscience" in understanding stress: The case of separation distress circuitry. In A. Oliverio (Ed.), *Psychobiology of stress* (pp. 41–58). Dordrecht: Kluwer.

Panksepp, J. (1990b). Psychology's search for identity: Can "mind" and behavior be understood without understanding the brain? *New Ideas in Psychology, 8*, 139–149.

Panksepp, J. (1990c). The psychoneurology of fear: Evolutionary perspectives and the role of animal models in understanding human anxiety. In R. Burrows (Ed.), *Handbook of anxiety* (pp. 3–58). Amsterdam: Elsevier.

Panksepp, J. (1990d). Gray zones at the emotion/cognition interface: A commentary. *Cognition and Emotion, 4*, 289–302.

Panksepp, J. (1991). Affective neuroscience: A conceptual framework for the neurobiological study of emotions. In K. Strongman (Ed.), *International reviews of emotion research* (Vol. 1, pp. 59–99). Chichester: Wiley.

Panksepp, J. (1992a). A critical role for "affective neuroscience" in resolving what is basic about basic emotions. *Psychological Review, 99*, 554–560.

Panksepp, J. (1992b). Oxytocin effects on emotional processes: Separation distress, social bonding, and relations to psychiatric disorders. *Annals of the New York Academy of Sciences, 652*, 243–252.

Panksepp, J. (1992c). [Blockade of curare induced distress vocalizations in chicks by glutamate receptor antagonists]. Unpublished raw data.

Panksepp, J. (1993a). Neurochemical control of moods and emotions: Amino acids to neuropeptides. In M. Lewis & J. Haviland (Eds.), *The handbook of emotions* (pp. 87–107). New York: Guilford.

Panksepp, J. (1993b). Where, when, and how does an appraisal become an emotion? "The times they are a changing." *Psychological Inquiry, 4,* 334–342.

Panksepp, J. (1993c). Rough-and-tumble play: A fundamental brain process. In I. MacDonald (Ed.), *Parent–child play, Descriptions and implications* (pp. 147–184). Albany, NY: SUNY Press.

Panksepp, J. (in press). Emotional circuits of the mammalian brain: Implications for biological psychiatry. In E. E. Bittar (Ed.), *Principles of medical biology.* Greenwich, CT: JAI.

Panksepp, J., & Bishop, P. (1981) An autoradiographic map of (3H) diprenorphine binding in rat brain: Effects of social interaction. *Brain Research Bulletin, 7,* 408–410.

Panksepp, J., Herman, B., Conner, R., Bishop, P., & Scott, J. P. (1978). The biology of social attachments: Opiates alleviate separation distress. *Biological Psychiatry, 9,* 213–220.

Panksepp, J., Herman, B. H., Vilberg, T., Bishop, P., & DeEskinazi, F. G. (1980). Endogenous opioids and social behavior. *Neuroscience and Biobehavioral Reviews, 4,* 473–487.

Panksepp, J., & Lensing, P. (1991). A synopsis of an open-trial of naltrexone treatment of autism with four children. *Journal of Autism and Developmental Disorders, 21,* 243–249.

Panksepp, J., Lensing, P., Klimesch, W., Schimke, H., & Vaningan, M. (1993). Event-related desynchronization (ERD) analysis of rhythmic brain functions in normal and autistic people. *Neuroscience Abstracts, 19,* 1885.

Panksepp, J., Lensing, P., Leboyer, M., & Bouvard, M. P. (1991). Naltrexone and other potential new pharmacological treatments of autism. *Brain Dysfunction, 4,* 281–300.

Panksepp, J. D., Newman, J., & Insel, T. R. (1992). Critical conceptual issues in the analysis of separation-distress systems of the brain. In K. Strongman (Ed.), *International reviews of emotion research* (Vol. 2, pp. 51–72). Chichester: Wiley.

Panksepp, J., Normansell, L., Cox, J., Crepeau, L., & Sacks, D. S. (1987). Psychopharmacology of social play. In B. Olivier, J. Mos, & P. F. Brain (Eds.), *Ethnopharmacology of agonistic behaviour in animals and humans* (pp. 132–144). Dordrecht: Martinus Nijhoff.

Panksepp, J., Normansell, L., Herman, B., Bishop, P., & Crepeau, L. (1988). Neural and neurochemical control of the separation distress call. In J. D. Newman (Ed.), *The physiological control of mammalian vocalizations* (pp. 263–300). New York: Plenum.

Panksepp, J., Sacks, D. S., Crepeau, L. J., & Abbott, B. B. (1991). The psycho- and neuro-biology of fear systems in the brain. In M. R. Denny (Ed.), *Aversive events and behavior* (pp. 7–59). Hillsdale, NJ: Lawrence Erlbaum Associates.

Panksepp, J., & Sahley, T. (1987). Possible brain opioid involvement in disrupted social intent and language development of autism. In E. Schopler & G. Mesibov (Eds.), *Neurobiological issues in autism* (pp. 357–382). New York: Plenum.

Panksepp, J., Siviy, S., & Normansell, L. (1984). The psychobiology of play: Theoretical and methodological perspectives. *Neuroscience and Biobehavioral Reviews, 8,* 465–492.

Panksepp, J., Siviy, S. M., & Normansell, L. A. (1985). Brain opioids and social emotions. In M. Reite & T. Fields (Eds.), *The psychobiology of attachment and separation* (pp. 3–49). New York: Academic Press.

Panksepp, J., Yates, G., Ikemoto, S., & Nelson, E. (1991). Simple ethological models of depression: Social-isolation induced "despair" in chicks and mice. In B. Olivier, J. Mos, & J. L. Slangen (Eds.), *Animal models in psychopharmacology* (pp. 161–181). Birkhauser: Basel.

Pedersen, C. A., Caldwell, J. D., Jirikowski, G. F., & Insel, T. R. (Eds.). (1992). Oxytocin in maternal, sexual, and social behavior. *Annals of the New York Academy of Sciences, 652.*

Pfurtscheller, G. (1991). EEG rhythm—Event-related desynchronization and synchronization. In H. Haken & H. P. Koepchen (Eds.), *Rhythms in physiological systems* (pp. 289–296). Berlin: Springer.

Pfurtscheller, G. (1992). Event-related synchronization (ERS): An electrophysiological correlate of cortical areas at rest. *Electroencephalography and Clinical Neurophysiology, 83*, 62–69.

Pignatiello, M. F., Camp, C., & Rasar, L. A. (1986). Musical mood induction: An alternative to the Velten technique. *Journal of Abnormal Psychology, 95*, 295–297.

Rossi, J., III, Sahley, T. L., & Panksepp, J. (1983). The role of brain norepinephrine in clonidine suppression of isolation-induced distress in the domestic chick. *Psychopharmacology, 79*, 338–342.

Schino, G., & Troisi, A. (1992). Opiate receptor blockade in juvenile macaques: Effect on affiliative interactions with their mothers and group companions. *Brain Research, 576*, 125–130.

Siegel, A., & Brutus, M. (1990). Neural substrates of aggression and rage in the cat. In A. N. Epstein & A. R. Morrison (Eds.), *Progress in psychobiology and physiological psychology* (Vol. 14, pp. 135–234). San Diego, CA: Academic Press.

Simon, H. E. (1992). What is an "explanation" of behavior? *American Psychologist, 3*, 150–161.

Terwogt, M. M., & Van Grinsven, F. (1991). Musical expressions of moodstates. *Psychology of Music, 19*, 99–109.

Teyler, T. J., & DiScenna, P. (1984) Long-term potentiation as a candidate mnemonic device. *Brain Research Reviews, 7*, 15–28.

Thomas, E. M. (1993). *The hidden life of dogs.* Boston: Houghton Mifflin.

Turner, T. J., & Ortony, A. (1992). Basic emotions: Can conflicting criteria converge? *Psychological Review, 99*, 566–571.

Wiener, S. G., Coe, C. L., & Levine, S. (1988). Endocrine and neurochemical sequelae of primate vocalizations. In J. D. Newman (Ed.), *The physiological control of mammalian vocalizations* (pp. 367–394). New York: Plenum.

Fear-Potentiated Startle in the Study of Animal and Human Emotion

Michael Davis
Yale University School of Medicine

THE FEAR-POTENTIATED STARTLE PARADIGM IN RATS

In studying an area as important and complex as emotion, it is important to develop experimental paradigms that allow objective measurement of emotion in animals and humans. Over the last several years, our laboratory has measured how a simple reflex is modulated by the emotion of fear.

A Central State of Fear Inferred From Increased Startle in the Presence of a Cue Previously Paired With Shock

Brown, Kalish, and Farber (1951) demonstrated that the amplitude of the acoustic startle reflex in the rat can be augmented by presenting the eliciting auditory startle stimulus in the presence of a cue (e.g., a light) that has previously been paired with a shock. This phenomenon has been termed the "fear-potentiated startle effect" and has been replicated using either an auditory or visual conditioned stimulus, whereby startle is elicited by either a loud sound or an airpuff (cf. Davis, 1986).

In this paradigm a central state of fear is considered to be the conditioned response (cf. McAllister & McAllister, 1971). Conditioned fear is operationally defined by elevated startle amplitude in the presence of a cue previously paired with a shock (see Figure 3.1). Thus, the conditioned

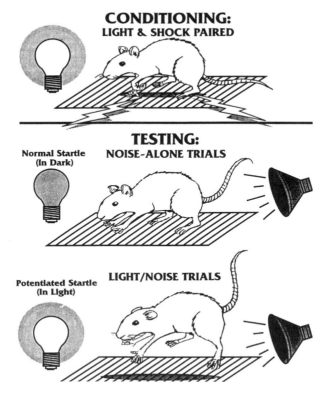

FIG. 3.1. Cartoon depicting the fear-potentiated startle paradigm. During training a neutral stimulus (conditioned stimulus) such as a light is consistently paired with a footshock. In training, a 3,700 msec light is typically paired with a 500 msec, 0.6 mA shock presented 3,200 msec after the light onset. During testing, startle is elicited by an auditory stimulus (e.g., a 100-dB burst of white noise) in the presence (Light–Noise trial type) or absence (Noise-Alone trial type) of the conditioned stimulus. In testing, the noise burst is typically presented 3,200 msec after light onset (i.e., at the same time as the shock was presented in training). It is important to note that the rat does not startle to light onset, but only to the noise burst presented alone or 3,200 msec after light onset. This is simply a cartoon; thus, the positions and postures that are pictured may not mimic the actual behavior of the animals.

stimulus does not elicit startle. Furthermore, the startle-eliciting stimulus is never paired with a shock; instead, the conditioned stimulus is paired with a shock and startle is elicited by another stimulus, either in the presence or absence of the conditioned stimulus. Fear-potentiated startle is said to occur if startle is greater when elicited in the presence of the conditioned stimulus. Potentiated startle only occurs following paired versus unpaired or "random" presentations of the conditioned stimulus and the shock, which indicates that it is a valid measure of classical conditioning (Davis & Astrachan, 1978). Discriminations between visual and auditory conditioned stimuli (Davis, Hitchcock, & Rosen, 1987) or between auditory cues or visual cues that differ in duration (Davis, Schlesinger, & Sorenson, 1989; Siegel, 1967) have also been demonstrated with potentiated startle. Increased startle in the presence of the conditioned stimulus still occurs very reliably at least one month after original training, making it appropriate for the study of long-term memory as well (Campeau, Liang, & Davis, 1990; Cassella & Davis, 1985).

It has been suggested, however, that potentiated startle may not reflect increased fear in the presence of a conditioned stimulus, but, instead, results from the animal making a postural adjustment (e.g., crouching) in anticipation of the impending footshock that is especially conducive to startle (Kurtz & Siegel, 1966). We have found, however, that in spinally transected rats rigidly held in a modified stereotaxic instrument, which prevented obvious postural adjustments, that the pinna component of startle was enhanced in the presence of a cue previously paired with a footshock (Cassella & Davis, 1986). Potentiation of startle measured electromyographically in neck muscles also occurs in the absence of any obvious postural adjustment (Cassella, Harty, & Davis, 1986). In addition, the magnitude of potentiated startle correlates highly with the degree of freezing, a very common measure of fear (Leaton & Borszcz, 1985). Taken together, therefore, the data indicate that potentiated startle is a valid measure of classical fear conditioning.

Fear-Potentiated Startle as a Model of Anticipatory Anxiety

Recently, we have found that fear-potentiated startle in rats shows considerable temporal specificity, because the magnitude of fear-potentiated startle in testing is maximal at the time after light onset in which the shock would have occurred in training (Davis et al., 1989). This suggests that fear-potentiated startle may be a sensitive measure of anticipatory anxiety. To evaluate this, three different groups of rats were used. In training, two groups received 30 light–shock pairings, using a 200-msec light–shock interval in one group and a 51,200-msec interval in the other group. The third group had lights and shocks presented in a random relationship to each other. Several days later, all groups were tested identically by presenting startle stimuli at different intervals after light onset. Figure 3.2 shows the change in startle of the two paired groups, relative to the random group, at various times after light onset. The group trained with a 200-msec light–shock interval had maximum potentiation 200 msec after light onset with no potentiation at much longer intervals.

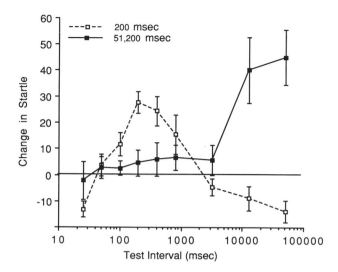

FIG. 3.2. A possible measure of anticipatory fear in rats. Mean change in startle amplitude (+ SEM) at various intervals after light onset in testing following either 200 or 51,200 msec light–shock intervals in training. Adapted from Davis, Schlesinger and Sorenson (1989), with permission from the American Psychological Association.

In contrast, the group trained with the 51,200-msec light–shock interval had maximum potentiation 51,200 msec after light onset, with little or no potentiation at much shorter intervals. These data suggest, therefore, that fear-potentiated startle was maximal at the time when the animal was anticipating receipt of shock, making it a sensitive measure of anticipatory fear or anxiety.

FEAR-POTENTIATED STARTLE IN HUMANS

Fear-Potentiated Startle in Normal Subjects

Early studies indicated that the eyeblink component of airpuff-elicited startle in humans could be potentiated when elicited at various intervals after presentation of a visual stimulus previously paired with shock (Ross, 1961; Spence & Runquist, 1958). The human eyeblink component of startle can also be elevated when subjects view unpleasant slides and reduced when they view pleasant ones (cf. Lang, Bradley, & Cuthbert, 1990).

We have been using the eyeblink component of startle in humans to measure anticipatory anxiety (Grillon, Ameli, Woods, Merikangas, & Davis, 1991). During the first session, subjects were fitted with a pair of recording electrodes over the obicularis oculi muscles in order to record the eyeblink component of the startle reflex elicited by a 106-db, 40-msec burst of white noise delivered through earphones. They then were presented with a series of startle-eliciting noise bursts, about every 30 sec, to establish a baseline level of startle and to familiarize them with the recording and acoustic stimulation procedures. During the second session, they were again hooked up with recording electrodes and also fitted with an electrode on the wrist through which they were told they might get a painful shock. They were told that during one condition (Threat) electric shocks could be delivered to their wrists. They were informed that one to three electric shocks might be given during the experiment and that the intensity of shock would increase with the passage of time. It was also stressed that the second and third shocks, if delivered, would be more intense than the preceding shock(s). In the other condition (No Threat) they were told that no shocks would occur. The acoustic startle reflex was elicited four times, about every 30 sec, during each of 13 blocks of either Threat or No Threat conditions counterbalanced across the session and across subjects. The subjects actually received only one shock, which came toward the end of the session 10 sec before the first startle stimulus in the block associated with the fourth threat condition (i.e., Block 8 or 9).

Figure 3.3 shows that the eyeblink component of the startle reflex was larger during periods in which subjects anticipated shock than in periods

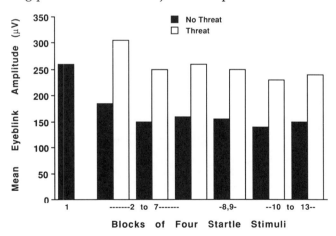

FIG. 3.3. Anticipatory anxiety in humans produces potentiation of the eyeblink. Mean eyeblink amplitude during periods in which subjects were told either they would not get a shock (No Threat condition—black bar) or that they might get a shock (Threat condition—white bar). Blocks 2–7 were presented before the occurrence of shock and Blocks 10–13 after its occurrence. Adapted from Grillon, Ameli, Woods, Merikangas, and Davis (1991), with permission from the Society for Psychophysiological Research.

when they did not. Importantly, this effect occurred in each of the blocks when they were anticipating shock before the actual shock was given. This has turned out to be an extremely reliable effect, which has been shown by over 90% of the subjects tested thus far. Moreover, the magnitude of this effect did not substantially change during Threat and No Threat conditions following presentation of the shock. In fact, for some subjects, the level of startle potentiation was actually smaller once they received the shock, which they rated as only mildly unpleasant. Hence, anticipation of shock, rather than actual presentation of shock, was the important factor in potentiating the startle reflex.

In another experiment (Grillon, Ameli, Merikangas, Woods, & Davis, 1993), subjects were given a series of startle stimuli in an initial phase of the experiment to assess their baseline level of startle. They were then told that different colored lights would be presented and that shocks might be administered during the last 10 sec after a 45-sec red light came on but definitely would not be given when a green light came on immediately thereafter. For other subjects, the green light signalled shock and the red light signalled no shock. The acoustic startle reflex was then elicited at various times after onset of either the red or green light. Figure 3.4 shows that the overall level of startle was generally higher when the

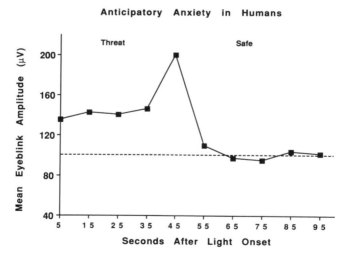

FIG. 3.4.   Temporal specificity of anticipatory anxiety in humans measured by potentiation of the eyeblink. Mean eyeblink amplitude elicited at various times after onset of a light that either signals that a shock might occur during the last 10 sec of illumination (Threat condition) vs. a differently colored light that signals a shock will not occur (No Threat condition). Adapted from Grillon, Ameli, Merikangas, Woods, and Davis (1993), with permission from the Society for Psychophysiological Research.

light that signalled shock came on (Threat) than when the other light was on (No Threat), consistent with our earlier study. Most importantly, however, the magnitude of this difference was greatest 45 sec after the onset of the light that signalled shock, exactly at the time when the subjects were anticipating the shock. When the other light then came on, startle levels rapidly declined back to a stable baseline.

These data indicate, therefore, that anticipation of a shock is sufficient to elevate the eyeblink component of startle in humans, making it a sensitive measure of anticipatory anxiety. Moreover, normal subjects show a rapid decline in anxiety, measured with fear-potentiated startle, when a signal comes on telling them that there is no longer a threat of shock. Currently, we are using this paradigm to measure the onset and offset of anxiety in different groups of people, including psychiatric patients with different types of anxiety disorders, in an effort to evaluate the temporal aspects of individual differences in anticipatory anxiety and responsivity to safety signals.

Relationship Between State and Trait Anxiety and Fear-Potentiated Startle

When this same paradigm was tested in college students who differed in their levels of state and trait anxiety, several differences emerged (Grillon, Ameli, Foot, & Davis, 1993). Individuals who rated high on state anxiety using the Spielberger State–Trait Anxiety Inventory had higher levels of fear-potentiated startle at the 45-sec test point. Moreover, when the safe, green light came on, fear-potentiated startle did not immediately return to baseline, but remained high for an unusually long period of time. However, these differences seemed wholly dependent on the state of fear during the part of the experiment when shocks might be delivered because the groups did not differ on baseline levels of startle during the initial phase of the experiment and trait anxiety measured by the same scale did not correlate with any of the startle measures.

Fear-Potentiated Startle in Panic Patients

When this same startle test was administered to patients diagnosed with panic disorder (Grillon, Ameli, Goddard, Woods, & Davis, 1994), the results were considerably more complicated (see Figure 3.5). Overall, there were no significant differences between panic patients and age-matched controls. However, when the data were analyzed separately for young (age < 40 years old) versus old (age > 40 years old) patients several differences emerged. Overall, startle levels were generally lower for older versus younger people, a common finding within the literature on human startle. Young panic patients, compared to age-matched controls, had

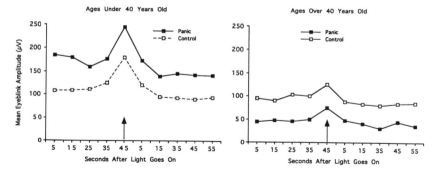

FIG. 3.5. Mean eyeblink amplitude elicited at various times after onset of a light that either signals that a shock might occur during the last 10 sec of illumination (Threat condition) vs. a differently colored light that signals a shock will not occur (No Threat condition). Data are shown separately for panic patients below 39 years of age vs. age-matched controls and for panic patients greater than 40 years old vs. age-matched controls. Adapted from Grillon, Ameli, Goddard, Woods, and Davis (1994), with permission from the Society for Research in Biological Psychiatry.

generally higher levels of startle throughout testing, which became significant during the period when shocks were anticipated.

In contrast, older panic patients had generally lower overall levels of startle compared to age-matched controls, although this difference was not statistically significant. When these differences in startle level were normalized for each group, they all showed comparable magnitudes of fear-potentiated startle that peaked at the time shock was anticipated. The fact that startle levels of the young panic patients did not differ significantly from their age-matched controls in baseline startle suggests that the abnormally high levels of startle in the young panic patients did not reflect chronic exaggerated startle, but a high level of generalized anxiety elicited by the threat of shock. The fact that their levels of startle did not normalize completely when the green, safe light came on suggests that these young panic patients were not responding appropriately to safety signals. The generally lower levels of startle in the older panic patients was not expected. Although it might reflect some sort of protective mechanism that has developed over time, this effect clearly needs more study.

NEURAL SYSTEMS INVOLVED IN FEAR-POTENTIATED STARTLE

A major advantage of the potentiated startle paradigm is that fear is measured by a change in a simple reflex. Hence, with potentiated startle, fear is expressed through some neural circuit that is activated by the fear-eliciting stimulus and ultimately impinges on the startle circuit. Fig-

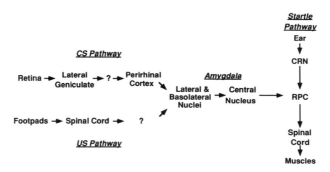

FIG. 3.6. Proposed neural pathways involved in fear-potentiated startle using a visual conditioned stimulus. Inputs from both the retina, via a projection involving the ventral lateral geniculate nucleus and the perirhinal cortex, and pain afferents in the spinal cord may converge at the lateral and basal nuclei of the amygdala. After being paired with a shock, the light may activate the lateral and basal amygdaloid nuclei, which in turn project to the central amygdaloid nucleus. Activation of the central nucleus of the amygdala may be both necessary and sufficient to facilitate startle through a direct connection to the nucleus reticularis pontis caudalis, an obligatory part of the acoustic startle pathway.

ure 3.6 shows a schematic summary diagram of the neural pathways that we believe are required for fear-potentiated startle in rats using a visual conditioned stimulus. These pathways involve convergence of the conditioned stimulus and the unconditioned shock stimulus at the lateral and basolateral amygdala nuclei, which project to the central nucleus of the amygdala, which then projects directly to a particular nucleus in the acoustic startle pathway.

The Acoustic Startle Pathway

In the rat, the latency of acoustic startle is 6 msec recorded electromyographically in the foreleg and 8 msec in the hindleg (Ison, McAdam, & Hammond, 1973). This very short latency indicates that only a few synapses could be involved in mediating acoustic startle. Using a variety of techniques (Davis, Gendelman, Tischler, & Gendelman, 1982), we have proposed that the acoustic startle reflex is mediated by the ventral cochlear nucleus, an area just medial to the ventral nucleus of the lateral lemniscus (the paralemniscal zone or the central nucleus of the acoustic tract), an area just dorsal to the superior olives in the nucleus reticularis pontis caudalis, and motor neurons in the spinal cord. Bilateral electrolytic lesions in each of these nuclei eliminate startle, whereas lesions in a variety of other auditory or motor areas do not. Startle-like responses can be elicited electrically from each of these nuclei, with progressively shorter latencies as the electrode is moved down the pathway.

More recently, using very discrete electrolytic or NMDA lesions, we have found that startle seems to involve a continuum of cells in the nucleus reticularis pontis caudalis, lying just medial and ventral to the motor nucleus of the fifth, extending from the most anterior to the most posterior part of the motor nucleus of the fifth (Lee, Lopez, Meloni, & Davis, 1994). NMDA-induced lesions of this area eliminate acoustic startle, whereas discrete lesions of the paralemniscal zone or the ventral nucleus of the lateral lemniscus do not. This is consistent with a recent report showing that quinolinic acid-induced lesions of this area also depress acoustic startle and that the magnitude of depression correlated with the number of giant reticulospinal neurons destroyed by the lesion (Koch, Lingenhohl, & Pilz, 1992). These data lend strong support to the hypothesis that cells in the nucleus reticularis pontis caudalis mediate acoustic startle. In fact, it is possible that direct inputs from the cochlear nucleus to this part of the nucleus reticularis pontis caudalis (e.g., Lingenhohl & Friauf, 1992) or from cochlear root neurons embedded in the auditory nerve (Lee et al., 1994) are sufficient to mediate acoustic startle without an intermediate synapse. If so, this would make the acoustic startle pathway even simpler than we originally thought. In fact, we have recently found that very discrete lesions of the cochlear root neurons essentially eliminate the acoustic startle reflex (Lee et al., 1994).

Determining the Point in the Startle Pathway Where Conditioned Fear Modulates Neural Transmission

We have attempted to determine the point within the startle circuit where the visual conditioned stimulus ultimately modulates transmission following conditioning. To do this, startle-like responses were elicited electrically from various points along the startle pathway before and after presentation of a light that was either paired or not paired with a shock in different groups of rats (Berg & Davis, 1985). These experiments showed that startle elicited electrically from either the ventral cochlear nucleus or from the paralemniscal zone was potentiated by a conditioned fear stimulus, whereas elicitation of startle in the nucleus reticularis pontis caudalis or beyond was not. Potentiation of electrically elicited startle could be blocked by diazepam at doses that had no effect whatsoever on baseline levels of electrically elicited startle (Berg & Davis, 1984). Based on these and other data (see next section), we have concluded that fear ultimately alters transmission at the nucleus reticularis pontis caudalis.

Effects of Amygdala Lesions on Fear-Potentiated Startle

Converging evidence now indicates that the amygdala, and its many efferent projections, may represent a central fear system involved in both the expression and acquisition of conditioned fear (cf. Davis, 1992). The amygdala receives highly processed sensory information from all modalities through its lateral and basolateral nuclei. In turn, these nuclei project to the central amygdaloid nucleus, which then projects to a variety of hypothalamic and brainstem target areas that are involved in the specific signs of fear and anxiety. Electrical stimulation of the amygdala elicits many of the behaviors used to define a state of fear, whereas stimulation of selected targets areas of the amygdala produces more selective effects. Conditioned fear may result when a formerly neutral stimulus now comes to activate the amygdala by virtue of pairing the neutral stimulus with aversive stimulation. In fact, the amygdala has long been implicated in the evaluation and memory of emotionally significant stimuli. In view of these data, we wondered whether lesions of the amygdala would block the expression of fear-potentiated startle.

Effects of Lesions of the Central Nucleus of the Amygdala on Fear-Potentiated Startle. Rats were given 10 light–shock pairings on two successive days (Hitchcock & Davis, 1986). At 24–48 hr following training, groups of rats received either bilateral transection of the cerebellar peduncles, bilateral lesions of the red nucleus (which receives most of the cerebellar efferents), or bilateral lesions of the central nucleus of the amygdala. Control animals were sham operated. Three to four days after surgery, the rats were tested for potentiated startle. Fear-potentiated startle was completely blocked by lesions of the central nucleus of the amygdala. In this same experiment, transection of the cerebellar peduncles or lesions of the red nucleus did not block potentiated startle. A visual prepulse test indicated that the blockade of potentiated startle observed in animals with lesions of the amygdala could not be attributed to visual impairment. In fact, blockade of fear-potentiated startle by amygdala lesions is not specific to the visual modality, because lesions of the central nucleus of the amygdala also blocked fear-potentiated startle when an auditory rather than a visual conditioned stimulus was used (Hitchcock & Davis, 1987).

The absence of potentiation in the animals with amygdala lesions did not simply result from a lowered startle level ceiling, because the amygdala-lesioned animals could show increased startle with increased stimulus intensity or following administration of strychnine (Hitchcock & Davis, 1986), a drug that reliably increases startle at subconvulsant doses (Kehne, Gallager, & Davis, 1981). Taken together, the results of these experiments support the hypothesis that the amygdala is involved in the expression of conditioned fear. Moreover, the cerebellum does not seem to play a role in fear-potentiated startle, even though more recent data now indicate that the cerebellar vermis is apparently very important in the modulation of other measures of fear (cf. Supple & Leaton, 1990).

The Role of Various Amygdala Projection Areas in Fear-Potentiated Startle. The central nucleus of the amygdala projects to a variety of brain regions via two major efferent pathways, the stria terminalis and the ventral amygdalofugal pathway. The caudal part of the ventral amygdalofugal pathway is known to project directly to many parts of the pons, medulla, and spinal cord. Inagaki, Kawai, Matsuzaki, Shiosaka, and Tohyama (1983) reported direct connections between the central nucleus of the amygdala and the exact part of the nucleus reticularis pontis caudalis that is critical for startle (an area just dorsal to the superior olives). We have confirmed this direct connection using anterograde (*Phaseolus vulgaris*-leucoagglutinin [PHA-L]) and retrograde (Fluoro-Gold) tracing techniques (Rosen, Hitchcock, & Davis, 1991) and have been systematically lesioning various points along the output pathways of the amygdala to evaluate the role of these projections in fear-potentiated startle (Hitchcock & Davis, 1991).

A diagram of the output pathways of the central nucleus of the amygdala and the effects of lesions at various points along this pathway are summarized in Figure 3.7. Lesions of the stria terminalis itself, or the bed nucleus of the stria terminalis, a major projection area of this pathway, do not block potentiated startle. Knife cuts of the rostral part of the ventral amygdalofugal pathway, which would interrupt its projections to the rostral lateral hypothalamus and substantia innominata, also fail to block potentiated startle. On the other hand, lesions of the caudal part of the ventral amygdalo- fugal pathway, at the point where it passes through the subthalamic area and cerebral peduncles, completely block potentiated startle. Lesions of the substantia nigra, which receives central amygdaloid nucleus projections as well as fibers of passage from the central nucleus of the amygdala to more caudal brainstem regions, also block potentiated startle. This blockade does not seem to involve dopamine cells in the zona compacta because infusion of the dopamine neurotoxin 6-OHDA into the substantia nigra did not block potentiated startle despite an over 90% depletion of dopamine in the caudate nucleus. Finally, lesions of the lateral tegmental field, caudal to the substantia nigra, also block fear-potentiated startle.

Effects of Lesions of the Lateral and Basolateral Nuclei of the Amygdala. Most sensory information enters the amygdala through its lateral and basolateral nuclei that then project to the central nucleus which, as discussed above, projects directly to the acoustic startle pathway. The lateral nucleus of the amygdala provides a critical link for relaying auditory information to the central nucleus of the amygdala during fear conditioning (LeDoux, Cicchetti, Xagoraris, & Romanski, 1990). We have found that NMDA-induced lesions of the lateral and basolateral nuclei cause a com-

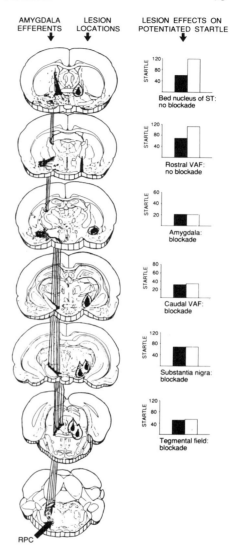

AMYGDALA   LESION   LESION EFFECTS ON
EFFERENTS   LOCATIONS   POTENTIATED STARTLE

FIG. 3.7. Lesions interrupting the pathway from the central nucleus of the amygdala to the RPC, but not lesions interrupting other central nucleus efferent pathways, block fear-potentiated startle. Left panel: A series of coronal rat brain sections, with the top section being the most rostral. The left sides of the sections show a schematic representation, based on PHA-L tracing studies, of the efferent pathways of the central nucleus of the amygdala. The right sides of the sections show representative lesions that interrupted the central nucleus efferent pathways at various levels. The black areas represent the cavities produced by the lesions and the stippled areas represent the surrounding gliosis. Right panel: Graphs showing the effects of bilateral lesions in each area on fear-potentiated startle. The graphs show the mean amplitude startle response on Noise-Alone trials (black bars) and Light–Noise trials (white bars) in rats given bilateral lesions in the locations shown in the corresponding brain section to the left of the graph. Adapted from Hitchcock and Davis (1991) with permission from the American Psychological Association.

plete blockade of fear-potentiated startle when the lesions were made before or after training, but before testing (Sananes & Davis, 1992). NMDA lesions also blocked shock sensitization, provided that they completely destroyed the most anterior and ventral part of the basolateral nucleus.

Effects of Electrical Stimulation of the Amygdala on Startle. Electrical stimulation of the amygdala has been reported to produce fear-like behaviors in many animals, including humans (cf. Davis, 1992). We have found that startle is an extremely sensitive index of amygdala stimulation because low-level electrical stimulation of the amygdala (e.g., 40–400 μA, 25 ms trains of 0.1 ms square wave cathodal pulses) markedly increases acoustic startle amplitude (Rosen & Davis, 1988a) with no obvious signs of behavioral activation during stimulation at the stimulation currents and durations used.

With electrical stimulation of the amygdala, the excitatory effect on startle appears to develop very rapidly. By eliciting startle at various times before and after electrical stimulation of the amygdala, we estimate a transit time of about 5 msec from the amygdala to the startle pathway (Rosen & Davis, 1988b). The rapidity of action means that the increase in startle is not secondary to autonomic or hormonal changes that might be produced by amygdala stimulation, because these would have a much longer latency.

In addition, electrical stimulation of the amygdala alone does not elicit startle at these currents and electrical stimulation of several other nearby brain areas such as the endopiriform nucleus, fundus striati, internal capsule, or some sites in the basolateral nucleus of the amygdala does not increase startle. Finally, using electrically elicited startle, electrical stimulation of the amygdala appears to modulate startle at the level of the nucleus reticularis pontis caudalis (Rosen & Davis, 1990), like conditioned fear and shock sensitization. In fact, Koch and Ebert (1993) have now found that electrical stimulation of the central nucleus of the amygdala increases the firing rate of cells in nucleus reticularis pontis caudalis driven by auditory stimuli. They also report that excitation of cells in the central nucleus of the amygdala via local administration of NMDA increases the amplitude of the acoustic startle reflex.

The Role of Non-NMDA Ionotropic Receptors in the Amygdala in the Expression of Fear-Potentiated Startle. Other studies in our laboratory using induction of the immediate early gene, *c-fos*, as a marker of neuronal activation supports the hypothesis that a conditioned fear stimulus activates the amygdala (Campeau et al., 1991), consistent with electrophysiological evidence (e.g., Pascoe & Kapp, 1985). However, it does not identify the neurotransmitter systems that might be involved in such an activation. Electrophysiological studies indicate that amygdaloid neurons can be activated by glutamate acting on both NMDA and non-NMDA receptors (Nose, Higashi, Inokuchi, & Nishi, 1991; Rainnie, Asprodini, & Schinnick-Gallagher, 1991). To test the role of non-NMDA receptors, rats were implanted with bilateral cannulae aimed at the basolateral nuclei of the amygdala. After recovery from surgery, they received 10 pairings of a visual or auditory conditioned stimulus (CS) with footshock on each of two days. On the next day, they received a short fear-potentiated startle test and were assigned to equivalent groups based on their performance in this test. One or two days later, they were infused with either 0.025, 0.25, or 2.5 µg of 6-cyano-7-nitroquinoxaline-2,3-dione (CNQX), a non-NMDA ionotropic antagonist, or its vehicle into each side of the amygdala and tested 5 min later for fear-potentiated startle.

Figure 3.8 shows that CNQX dose-dependently blocked the expression of fear-potentiated startle to both visual and auditory conditioned stimuli. Provided that CNQX remained localized to the amygdala, these data indicate that activation of non-NMDA receptors in the amygdala is necessary for the expression of fear-potentiated startle. In contrast, other studies showed that local infusion of NMDA antagonists into the amygdala did not block the expression of fear-potentiated startle (Campeau, Miserendino, & Davis, 1992; Miserendino, Sananes, Melia, & Davis, 1990).

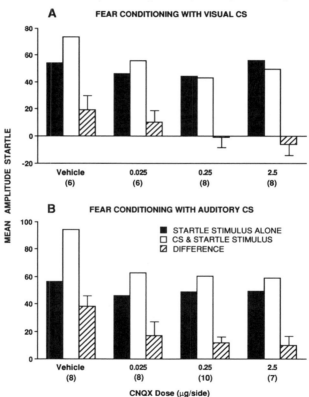

FIG. 3.8. Mean startle amplitudes in the presence and absence of the visual (A) or auditory (B) CS, and the difference scores (+ SEM), after pretest intra-amygdala infusion of various doses of CNQX or its vehicle, NaOH. The number of animals in each group is indicated in the parentheses. From Davis, Falls, Campeau, and Kim (1993) with permission from Elsevier Science Publishers.

The Role of the Perirhinal Cortex in Fear-Potentiated Startle. The aforementioned data suggest, therefore, that visual input critical for the expression of fear-potentiated startle using a visual conditioned stimulus may enter the amygdala through the lateral and/or basolateral nuclei. At the present time, however, the visual pathway(s) critical for fear-potentiated startle using a visual conditioned stimulus linking the retina to these basolateral nuclei are still unclear. Recently, we have found that complete removal of all primary and secondary visual corties does not block the expression of fear-potentiated startle using a visual conditioned stimulus (Rosen, Hitchcock, Sananes, Miserendino, & Davis, 1992).

In contrast, relatively small electrolytic lesions of the perirhinal cortex completely block fear-potentiated startle, provided the lesion included an area of perirhinal cortex just dorsal and ventral to the rhinal sulcus (see Figure 3.9; Rosen et al., 1992). Animals with dorsal but not ventral damage did not have a blockade of potentiated startle. This is especially interesting because McDonald and Jackson (1987) found heavy retrograde and

No Blockade

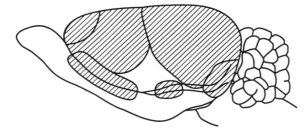

Blockade

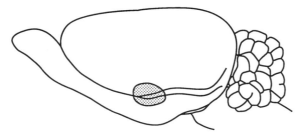

FIG. 3.9. Top panel shows a schematic saggital perspective summarizing cortical lesions that did not completely block fear-potentiated startle using a visual conditioned stimulus. Bottom panel shows a schematic representation of the lesion that did block fear-potentiated startle. From Rosen et al. (1992) with permission from the Society for Neuroscience.

anterograde labeling in the basolateral and especially the lateral nucleus of the amygdala after HRP–WGA deposits in the perirhinal cortex. Most of the connections between the lateral nucleus and the perirhinal cortex involve the area of the perirhinal cortex dorsal to the rhinal sulcus, whereas the connections between the basolateral and accessory basolateral nucleus involve the area below the rhinal sulcus. It is thus possible that visual information is relayed from the area of the perirhinal cortex just below the rhinal sulcus to the basolateral nucleus. We currently are using retrograde tracing techniques to evaluate how subcortical visual information might get to this area of the perirhinal cortex.

How Might the Amygdala Modulate Transmission at the Nucleus Reticularis Pontis Caudalis so as to Increase Acoustic Startle Amplitude?

At the present time, we do not know how the amygdala might modulate transmission at the nucleus reticularis pontis caudalis so as to increase acoustic startle amplitude. One possibility would be that the amygdala projects directly to reticulospinal neurons and changes their excitability. Activation of the amygdala by a conditioned fear stimulus would thus increase the excitability of RPC neurons, allowing more neurons to be activated by the startle stimulus, leading to a larger startle response. In fact, electrical stimulation of the central nucleus of the amygdala has been shown to increase the responsiveness of cells in the RPC to a startle eliciting stimulus in anesthetized rats (Koch & Ebert, 1993). In many cells electrical stimulation of the amygdala by itself induced spikes in these same cells, which is perhaps consistent with recent data showing that high levels of electrical stimulation of the amygdala can elicit startle-like responses in unanesthetized rats (Yeomans & Pollard, 1993).

Another possibility is that the amygdala projects to terminals in the RPC originating from neurons in earlier parts of the startle pathway. Activation of this axonal–axonal connection could result in greater transmitter release from the terminals within the startle circuit, leading to a larger startle response. This "presynaptic" mechanism is attractive because electrical stimulation of the amygdala at low currents and short durations does not produce any observable behavioral changes yet markedly increases the amplitude of the acoustic startle reflex (Rosen & Davis, 1988a). Moreover, a conditioned fear stimulus has never been shown to actually elicit a startle response by itself, but instead only modulates startle amplitude elicited by a second stimulus.

Although we do not have any direct data bearing on this question, we are currently testing how local infusion of drugs into the RPC affects startle in an effort to (a) determine the identity of the transmitter that actually mediates startle at this level of the pathway and (b) identify mechanisms that might be expected to increase or decrease release of this transmitter.

   Because the startle reflex is so rapid, we hypothesized that excitatory amino acids released from terminals of cells originating in earlier parts of the startle pathway acting through receptors on RPC neurons might mediate acoustic startle at this level of the circuit, similar to that suggested at the level of the spinal cord (Boulis, Kehne, Miserendino, & Davis, 1990). To test this, the startle response was tested in rats chronically implanted with bilateral cannulae aimed at the nucleus reticularis pontis caudalis, before and after infusion of the excitatory amino acid antagonists g-D-glutamylglycine (DGG), DL-2-amino-5-phosphonopentanoic acid (AP5), and 6-cyano-7-nitroquinoxaline-2,3-dione (CNQX). Local infusion of each of these compounds significantly reduced startle amplitude by as much as 70–80%. Figure 3.10 shows that AP5 and CNQX attenuated startle over a similar dose range. Moreover, compared to earlier studies (Spiera & Davis, 1988) very low does of these compounds substantially reduced startle amplitude, indicating that the nucleus reticularis pontis caudalis may be much more sensitive to these compounds than other nuclei along the primary startle pathway. These results suggest that at this level of the startle pathway an excitatory amino acid neurotransmitter may mediate acoustic startle, and that both NMDA and non-NMDA receptor subtypes may be important for the expression of the acoustic startle response. Very similar results have also been reported by Krase, Koch, and Schnitzler (1993).

   In many parts of the brain, the release of glutamate can be increased by activation of cAMP. Hence, if the amygdala released a neurotransmitter positively coupled to cAMP onto presynaptic terminals in the RPC it could increase transmitter release and increase startle amplitude. To address this, we have been testing startle before and after infusion of the cAMP analogue, 8-bromo-cAMP into the RPC (de Lima & Davis, 1994). Figure 3.11 shows that 8-bromo cAMP (2.5 μg/0.5 0 μl) causes a dramatic increase in startle amplitude following direct infusion into the RPC. Most impressive is the fact that this dose of 8-bromo-cAMP does not, by itself, produce any observable change in behavior. Its presence is only obvious when the startle stimulus is given. This effect only occurs when cannulas are in the part of the RPC that we know is critical for startle based on chemical lesioning studies, indicating that 8-bromo-cAMP does not spread very far after these infusion volumes. Currently, we are evaluating whether local infusion of cAMP-dependent protein kinase inhibitors will block this excitatory effect of 8-bromo-cAMP. If so, then the critical experiment will be to test whether local infusion of cAMP-dependant protein kinase inhibitors into the RPC will block conditioned fear at doses that have little or no effect on baseline levels of startle. Other studies using microdialysis with probes located in the RPC will test whether a startle stimulus results in a release of glutamate in the RPC and whether this effect is increased by local infusion of

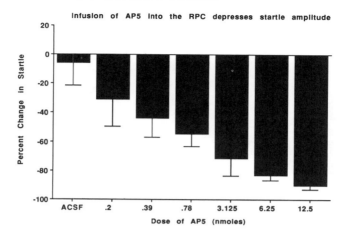

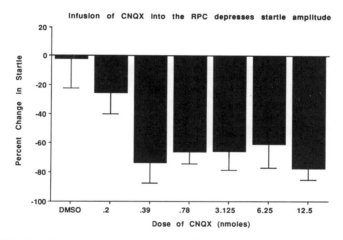

FIG. 3.10. Percent change in startle amplitude after local infusion into the nucleus reticularis pontis caudalis of various doses of the NMDA receptor antagonist AP5 (top panel) or the non-NMDA antagonist CNQX (bottom panel). Percent change was computed using the mean startle amplitude over the 10 startle stimuli presented at a 30 sec interval immediately before and after drug infusion. Adapted from Miserendino and Davis (1993) with permission from Elsevier Science Publishers.

8-bromo-cAMP. If so, then comparable experiments will test whether a startle-induced release of glutamate will be increased by either electrical stimulation of the central nucleus of the amygdala or, most importantly, presentation of a conditioned fear stimulus. If so, local infusion into the RPC of a cAMP-dependent protein kinase inhibitor should block the expression of conditioned fear.

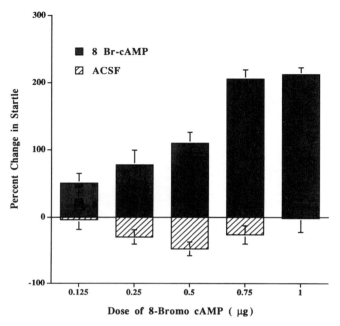

FIG. 3.11. Percent change in startle, relative to an initial infusion of ACSF, after infusion of various doses of 8-bromo-cAMP in 10 rats or repeated infusions of ACSF in another 10 rats. The mean startle amplitude over a 20-min period after an initial infusion of ACSF was first subtracted from the mean startle amplitude over the 10 min prior to infusion. This difference was then subtracted from the mean startle amplitude over a 20-min period after each of the following infusions and converted into a percent change relative to the initial ACSF difference.

INHIBITION OF FEAR

A great deal of progress has thus been made in determining the neural systems involved in the acquisition and expression of fear and anxiety. Although it is important to understand how fear and anxiety are acquired, it is equally important to understand how, once acquired, fear and anxiety are reduced. Clinically, the inability to eliminate fear and anxiety ranks as one of the major problems in psychiatry. Moreover, we are beginning to find that certain individuals do not respond appropriately to safety signals (e.g., the green light which should tell them that no shocks will occur). Curiously, however, practically nothing is known about the neural systems that may be involved in the reduction or elimination of conditioned fear. We have recently begun to investigate learning paradigms that measure the reduction of conditioned fear. Our hope is that these procedures will allow us to identify the neural systems responsible for reducing or eliminating fear and anxiety.

External Inhibition

Anecdotal reports suggest that one method for reducing fear or anxiety in any situation is to shift attention away from the fear- or anxiety-provoking stimulus. Interestingly, although the provoking stimulus may still be present in these situations, attending to some other stimulus serves to reduce fear and anxiety. Such "distracter" effects have been documented in the animal learning literature (Brimer, 1970; Pavlov, 1927; Pennypacker, 1967). In general, when a novel stimulus is presented slightly before or at the same time as a well-trained conditioned stimulus, the conditioned response will be disrupted. This nonassociative disruption of conditioned responding has been described in many ways (e.g., generalization decrement, distraction, external inhibition) but it is not understood at the neural level. The question of interest is whether such novel stimuli engage neural systems that naturally participate in reducing fear and anxiety.

To begin to investigate the distracter effect using fear-potentiated startle, rats were given 10 noise CS–footshock pairings on each of two days and subsequently tested for fear-potentiated startle. The amplitude of acoustically elicited startle was measured in the presence or absence of the noise CS (standard fear-potentiated startle) as well as in the presence of the noise CS in compound with a novel light (i.e., a distracter trial). Figure 3.12 shows that there was substantial fear to the noise CS as

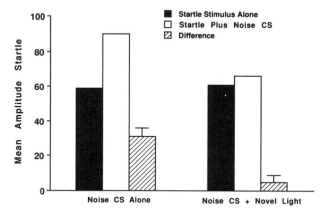

FIG. 3.12. Panel A: Mean amplitude startle response in the absence (black bar) or presence (gray bar) of a noise CS plus the difference between these two trial types (+ S.E.M.) in the standard fear-potentiated startle paradigm. Panel B: Mean amplitude startle response in the absence (black bar) or presence (hatched bar) of a noise CS accompanied by presentation of a novel visual stimulus plus the difference between these two trial types (+ S.E.M.) From Davis, Falls, Campeau, and Kim (1993) with permission from Elsevier Science Publishers.

evidenced by greater startle amplitude in the presence of the noise than in its absence. However, there was substantially less fear-potentiated startle to the noise when it was accompanied by the novel light. This suggests that the novel light had the ability to interfere with or inhibit the fear otherwise produced by the noise CS. However, when the amplitude of startle was pharmacologically increased to levels comparable to those produced by the fear-producing noise CS, startle was not inhibited by the light. This suggests that the light does not simply act by inhibiting the startle reflex, but instead exerts an inhibitory influence on the fear produced by the noise CS, perhaps via an inhibitory action exerted at or afferent to the amygdala. We hope to test this by measuring whether a novel light will diminish startle that is elevated directly by chemical stimulation of the amygdala (e.g., via NMDA; Koch & Ebert, 1993).

Conditioned Inhibition

Another procedure that can modulate the responding to otherwise fear-producing CSs is conditioned inhibition. In the typical conditioned-inhibition procedure, conditions are arranged such that one stimulus, denoted as A, predicts shock while another stimulus X, predicts the absence of shock. The result of this procedure is that A comes to elicit a fear reaction when presented alone but not when it is accompanied by X, the conditioned inhibitor.

Interestingly, extinction, which is another way to measure a reduction of fear, has been considered a special case of conditioned inhibition (e.g., Bouton, 1991) in that the experimental context predicts that the CS will not be followed by shock (cf. Bouton & Bolles, 1985; Bouton & King, 1983, 1986). The conditioned inhibition procedure, however, offers advantages over the extinction procedure. In the conditioned inhibition procedure, the reduction of fear is under the control of an explicit CS, rather than under the control of contextual cues. Moreover, fear reduction is assessed at the same time as fear production, allowing one to disentangle the inhibition of fear from a more global disruption in fear performance or stimulus processing.

Because of the possible advantages of the conditioned inhibition procedure, we have devised a procedure for obtaining conditioned inhibition of fear-potentiated startle. Rats underwent 2 days of training in which one stimulus, denoted as A+ (either light or noise CS), was repeatedly paired with footshock. Following this, the rats underwent 5 additional days of training in which a serial compound, denoted as X*A−, was not paired with shock (X was the alternative light or noise CS). A+ training was continued during this second phase. Conditioned inhibition was assessed by measuring the amplitude of the startle reflex in the presence or absence of A when it was or was not preceded by X (i.e., A or X*A).

Figure 3.13 shows substantial fear to A as evidenced by greater startle amplitude in the presence of A than in its absence. However, the rats did not show fear-potentiated startle to A when it was preceded by X. This suggests that X had acquired the ability to inhibit the fear produced by A. In contrast to the nonassociative inhibition of conditioned fear that is produced by the simultaneous presentation of a novel stimulus with a fear-producing CS (see previous discussion), the inhibitory effect of X was dependent on the rats having been given explicit, nonreinforced presentations of the serial X*A compound. In control experiments, rats that had never received X prior to testing or rats given X and A in an explicitly unpaired fashion did not show inhibition of fear-potentiated startle to A when preceded by X. Therefore, the inhibitory effect of X on A is dependent on nonreinforced, serial X*A presentations in training.

In order to demonstrate that X in the conditioned inhibition paradigm functions as an inhibitor of fear, it is necessary to demonstrate that X is capable of inhibiting fear produced by another CS. To examine transfer of inhibition, rats were given A + footshock pairings (A was either a light,

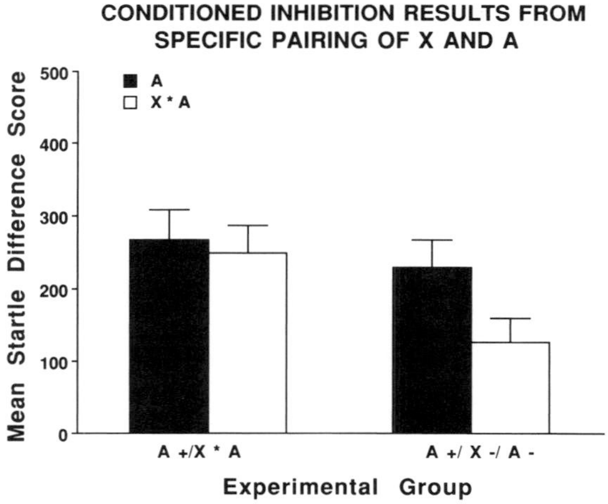

FIG. 3.13. Left bars: Mean change in startle amplitude (i.e., difference in mean startle amplitude in the presence vs. the absence of the conditioned stimulus [A] or a compound stimulus [X*A]) in rats where cue A signaled shock during training and compound X*A signaled the absence of shock. Right bars: Comparable data in animals where A and X were not presented in compound to signal the absence of shock. The results show that compound X*A only inhibited fear-potentiated startle when X*A had previously predicted the absence of shock. From Davis, Falls, Campeau, and Kim (1993) with permission from Elsevier Science Publishers.

noise, or fan CS). In a second phase, rats were given 5 additional days of training in which the serial compound X*A– was not paired with shock (all CSs were counterbalanced). In the final 2 days of the second phase C + footshock training was introduced. A + training was continued during the entire second phase. Conditioned inhibition and the transfer of inhibition was assessed by measuring the amplitude of noise-elicited startle in the presence or absence of A and C when they were or were not preceded by X (i.e., A, C, X*A, or X*C). The results showed that the fear to A was reduced when A was preceded by X, replicating our previous findings. More importantly, however, fear to C was also inhibited by X, indicating that X is able to inhibit fear produced by a CS other than the one with which it was trained. Therefore, the inhibition of fear-potentiated startle by X cannot readily be attributed to a configural discrimination. Taken together, these results suggest that X acquires the ability to inhibit fear-potentiated startle.

Because so much is known about the neural systems mediating the acquisition and performance of fear-potentiated startle, we are now in a position to begin to ask which structures may be responsible for the reduction of conditioned fear.

Measuring Inhibition of Fear in Humans

Recently, we have begun to develop experimental procedures that we hope will provide direct measurements of fear inhibition in humans. In our first effort in this regard (Grillon, Falls, Ameli, & Davis, 1994) the startle reflex was measured during anticipation of shock in Threat or No Threat (safe) conditions, signaled by three different colored lights. Two lights signaled safe conditions and the other light signaled the threat condition. In Phase I, the lights alternated, each presentation consisting of one colored light. In Phase II, the lights were presented alone or in the two combinations of safe 1 (or safe 2) + threat and safe 1 + safe 2. In both phases the contingency between the lights was carefully explained to the subjects. It was emphasized that no shock could be administered when the safe and threat lights were on together. On later testing, all subjects said they understood and believed the instructions.

The results showed that in Phase I, startle was increased in the threat-alone compared to the safe-alone condition, consistent with our previous work. In Phase II, even though startle in the safe + threat condition was smaller than in the threat-alone condition, it was larger than in the safe 1 + safe 2 condition. Hence, startle amplitude reflected active inhibition of fear by the safe light along with a non-zero level of residual fear, despite the fact that subjects understood and believed that no shock could occur when a safe light was on.

Future Directions

One of the problems with these experiments is that it is never quite clear whether the subjects truly understand all of the instructions. Moreover, when testing different groups of patients, it is not clear when differences emerge whether it is because of fundamental differences in processing emotional stimuli or simply because of confusion over specific instructions in the experiment. Because of this, we are now using purely conditioning procedures in humans, using experimental procedures essentially identical to those described here earlier in rats. Thus far we are obtaining very reliable conditioned fear-potentiated startle in humans that looks strikingly similar to the data we normally obtain in rats. In the near future, we plan to measure conditioned inhibition in humans and then evaluate whether psychiatric patients with different types of anxiety disorders fail to develop conditioned inhibition or develop abnormal conditioned inhibition. In parallel, we hope to determine what brain areas in rats may be activated by a conditioned inhibitor and whether these project to and inhibit the amygdala, or instead project to points along the neural circuitry afferent or efferent to the amygdala. Once this is accomplished, we hope to determine what neurotransmitters are involved. By analyzing how the brain has evolved to inhibit fear naturally (i.e., in the presence of safety signals) we hope to develop drugs that may facilitate this process. If specific types of anxiety disorders are associated with abnormal conditioned inhibition, such drugs might prove to be especially efficacious in treating such disorders.

SUMMARY

The fear-potentiated startle paradigm has proven to be a sensitive test to measure fear in both rats and humans. In rats, this test measures conditioned fear by an increase in the amplitude of a simple reflex (the acoustic startle reflex) in the presence of a cue previously paired with a shock. Electrical stimulation techniques suggest that a visual conditioned stimulus ultimately alters acoustic startle at a specific point along the acoustic startle pathway. The lateral, basolateral, and central amygdaloid nuclei and the caudal branch of the ventral amygdalofugal pathway projecting to the brainstem are necessary for potentiated startle to occur. The central nucleus of the amygdala projects directly to one of the brainstem nuclei critical for startle and electrical stimulation of this amygdaloid nucleus increases startle amplitude. Chemical or electrolytic lesions of either the central nucleus or the lateral and basolateral nuclei of the amygdala block the expression of fear-potentiated startle. The perirhinal cortex, which projects directly to the lateral and basolateral amygdaloid nuclei, plays a critical role in the expression of fear-potentiated startle using either visual or auditory conditioned stimuli. The expression of fear-potentiated startle is blocked by local infusion into the amygdala of the non-NMDA ionotropic glutamate antagonist CNQX, suggesting the conditioned fear results from a release of glutamate in the amygdala. Glutamate may also mediate startle at the level of the nucleus reticularis pontis caudalis.

In humans, the eyeblink component of the startle reflex can be increased by anticipation of shock, with the largest increase at the time the shock is expected. The magnitude of this effect correlates with the level of state anxiety during testing and is larger in young panic patients compared to age-matched controls. In some instances, abnormal levels of startle seem to be attributable to a failure to respond appropriately to safety signals. Hence, we have begun to investigate brain systems that might be involved in the inhibition of fear. We have established a reliable procedure for producing both external and conditioned inhibition of fear-potentiated startle in rats and hope to develop similar experimental paradigms in humans to assess whether patients with different types of anxiety disorders fail to respond appropriately to conditioned inhibitors. If they do, then a better understanding of brain systems and neurotransmitters involved in the inhibition of fear may ultimately lead to better treatments for these disorders.

ACKNOWLEDGMENTS

This research was supported by National Institute of Mental Health Grants MH–25642 and MH–47840, Research Scientist Development Award MH–00004, a grant from the Air Force Office of Scientific Research, and the State of Connecticut. I thank Leslie Fields for help in typing.

REFERENCES

Berg, W. K., & Davis, M. (1984). Diazepam blocks fear-enhanced startle elicited electrically from the brainstem. *Physiology and Behavior, 32,* 333–336.

Berg, W. K., & Davis, M. (1985). Associative learning modifies startle reflexes at the lateral lemniscus. *Behavioral Neuroscience, 99,* 191–199.

Boulis, N., Kehne, J. H., Miserendino, M. J. D., & Davis, M. (1990). Differential blockade of early and late components of acoustic startle following intrathecal infusion of 6-cyano-7-nitroquinoxaline-2,3-dione (CNQX) or D,L-2-amino-5-phosphonovaleric acid (AP-5). *Brain Research, 520,* 240–246.

Bouton, M. E. (1991). A contextual analysis of fear extinction. In P. R. Martin (Ed.), *Handbook of behavior therapy and psychological science: An integrative approach* (pp. 435–453). New York: Pergamon Press.

Bouton, M. E., & Bolles, R. C. (1985). *Context, event-memories, and extinction.* Hillsdale, NJ: Lawrence Erlbaum Associates.

Bouton, M. E., & King, D. A. (1983). Contextual control of conditioned fear: Tests for the associative value of the context. *Journal of Experimental Psychology: Animal Behavior Processes, 9,* 248–256.

Bouton, M. E., & King, D. A. (1986). Effect of context with mixed histories of reinforcement and nonreinforcement. *Journal of Experimental Psychology: Animal Behavior Processes, 12,* 4–15.

Brimer, C. J. (1970). Disinhibition of an operant response. *Learning and Motivation, 1,* 346–371.

Brown, J. S., Kalish, H. I., & Farber, I. E. (1951). Conditional fear as revealed by magnitude of startle response to an auditory stimulus. *Journal of Experimental Psychology, 41,* 317–328.

Campeau, S., Hayward, M. D., Hope, B. T., Rosen, J. B., Nestler, E. J., & Davis, M. (1991). Induction of the c-fos proto-oncogene in rat amygdala during unconditioned and conditioned fear. *Brain Research, 565,* 349–352.

Campeau, S., Liang, K. C., & Davis, M. (1990). Long-term retention of fear-potentiated startle following a short training session. *Animal Learning & Behavior, 18,* 462–468.

Campeau, S., Miserendino, M. J. D., & Davis, M. (1992). Intra-amygdala infusion of the N-methyl-D-Aspartate receptor antagonist AP5 blocks acquisition but not expression of fear-potentiated startle to an auditory conditioned stimulus. *Behavioral Neuroscience, 106,* 569–574.

Cassella, J. V., & Davis, M. (1985). Fear-enhanced acoustic startle is not attenuated by acute or chronic imipramine treatment in rats. *Psychopharmacology, 87,* 278–282.

Cassella, J. V., & Davis, M. (1986). Habituation, prepulse inhibition, fear conditioning, and drug modulation of the acoustically elicited pinna reflex in rats. *Behavioral Neuroscience, 100,* 39–44.

Cassella, J. V., Harty, P. T., & Davis, M. (1986). Fear conditioning, pre-pulse inhibition, and drug modulation of a short latency startle response measure electromyographically from neck muscles in the rat. *Physiology & Behavior, 36,* 1187–1191.

Davis, M. (1986). Pharmacological and anatomical analysis of fear conditioning using the fear-potentiated startle paradigm. *Behavioral Neuroscience, 100,* 814–824.

Davis, M. (1992). The role of the amygdala in fear and anxiety. *Annual Review Neuroscience, 15,* 353–375.

Davis, M., & Astrachan, D. I. (1978). Conditioned fear and startle magnitude: Effects of different footshock or backshock intensities used in training. *Journal of Experimental Psychology: Animal Behavior Processes, 4,* 95–103.

Davis, M., Falls, W. A., Campeau, S., & Kim, M. (1993). Fear-potentiated startle: A neural and pharmacological analysis. *Behavioural Brain Research, 58,* 175–198.

Davis, M., Gendelman, D. S., Tischler, M. D., & Gendelman, P. M. (1982). A primary acoustic startle circuit: Lesion and stimulation studies. *Journal of Neuroscience, 6,* 791–805.

Davis, M., Hitchcock, J. M., & Rosen, J. B. (1987). Anxiety and the amygdala: Pharmacological and anatomical analysis of the fear-potentiated startle paradigm. In G. H. Bower (Ed.), *The psychology of learning and motivation* (pp. 263–305). New York: Academic Press.

Davis, M., Schlesinger, L. S., & Sorenson, C. A. (1989). Temporal specificity of fear conditioning: Effects of different conditioned stimulus–unconditioned stimulus intervals on the fear-potentiated startle effect. *Journal of Experimental Psychology: Animal Behavior Processes, 15,* 295–310.

deLima, T. C. M., & Davis, M. (1994). Involvement of cAMP in the acoustic startle response at the level of the nucleus reticularis pontis caudalis. *Society of Neuroscience Abstracts, 20,* 1763.

Grillon, C., Ameli, R., Foot, M., & Davis, M. (1993). Fear-potentiated startle: Relationship to the level of state/trait anxiety in healthy subjects. *Biological Psychiatry, 33,* 566–574.

Grillon, C., Ameli, R., Goddard, A., Woods, S. W., & Davis, M. (1994). Baseline startle and fear-potentiated startle in panic disorder patients. *Biological Psychiatry, 35*, 431–439.

Grillon, C., Ameli, R., Merikangas, K., Woods, S. W., & Davis, M. (1993). Measuring the time course of anticipatory anxiety using the fear-potentiated startle reflex. *Psychophysiology, 30*, 340–346.

Grillon, C., Ameli, R., Woods, S. W., Merikangas, K., & Davis, M. (1991). Fear-potentiated startle in humans: Effects of anticipatory anxiety on the acoustic blink reflex. *Psychophysiology, 28*, 588–595.

Grillon, C., Falls, W. A., Ameli, R., & Davis, M. (1994). Safety signals and human anxiety: A fear-potentiated startle study. *Anxiety, 1*, 13–21.

Hitchcock, J. M., & Davis, M. (1986). Lesions of the amygdala, but not of the cerebellum or red nucleus, block conditioned fear as measured with the potentiated startle paradigm. *Behavioral Neuroscience, 100*, 11–22.

Hitchcock, J., & Davis, M. (1987). Fear-potentiated startle using a tone conditioned stimulus: Effect of amygdala lesions. *Physiology and Behavior, 39*, 403–408.

Hitchcock, J. M., & Davis, M. (1991). The efferent pathway of the amygdala involved in conditioned fear as measured with the fear-potentiated startle paradigm. *Behavioral Neuroscience, 105*, 826–842.

Inagaki, S., Kawai, Y., Matsuzaki, T., Shiosaka, S., & Tohyama, M. (1983). Precise terminal fields of the descending somatostatinergic neuron system from the amygdala complex of the rat. *Journal Hirnfursch, 24*, 345–365.

Ison, J. R., McAdam, D. W., & Hammond, G. R. (1973). Latency and amplitude changes in the acoustic startle reflex of the rat produced by variation in auditory prestimulation. *Physiology & Behavior, 10*, 1035–1039.

Kehne, J. H., Gallager, D. W., & Davis, M. (1981). Strychnine: Brainstem and spinal mediation of excitatory effects on acoustic startle. *European Journal of Pharmacology, 76*, 177–186.

Koch, M., & Ebert, U. (1993). Enhancement of the acoustic startle response by stimulation of an excitatory pathway from the central amygdala/basal nucleus of Meynert to the pontine reticular formation. *Experimental Brain Research, 93*, 231–241.

Koch, M., Lingenhohl, K., & Pilz, P. K. D. (1992). Loss of the acoustic startle response following neurotoxic lesions of the caudal pontine reticular formation: Possible role of giant neurons. *Neuroscience, 49*, 617–625.

Krase, W., Koch, M., & Schnitzler, H. U. (1993). Glutamate antagonists in the reticular formation reduce the acoustic startle reflex. *NeuroReport, 4*, 13–16.

Kurtz, K. H., & Siegel, A. (1966). Conditioned fear and magnitude of startle response: A replication and extension. *Journal of Comparative Physiology and Psychology, 62*, 8–14.

Lang, P. J., Bradley, M. M., & Cuthbert, B. N. (1990). Emotion, attention, and the startle reflex. *Psychology Reviews, 97*, 377–395.

Leaton, R. N., & Borszcz, G. S. (1985). Potentiated startle: Its relation to freezing and shock intensity in rats. *Journal of Experimental Psychology: Animal Behavior Processes, 11*, 421–428.

LeDoux, J. E., Cicchetti, P., Xagoraris, A., & Romanski, L. M. (1990). The lateral amygdaloid nucleus, sensory interface of the amygdala in fear conditioning. *Journal of Neuroscience, 10*, 1062–1069.

Lee, Y., Lopez, D., Meloni, E., & Davis, M. (1994). A primary acoustic startle circuit: Role of auditory root neurons and nucleus reticularis pontis caudalis. *Society for Neuroscience Abstracts, 10*, 1009.

Lingenhohl, K., & Friauf, E. (1992). Giant neurons in the caudal pontine reticular formation receive short latency acoustic input: An intracellular recording and HRP study in the rat. *Journal of Comparative Neurology, 325*, 473–492.

McAllister, W. R., & McAllister, D. E. (1971). Behavioral measurement of conditioned fear. In F. R. Brush (Ed.), *Aversive conditioning and learning* (pp. 105–179). New York: Academic Press.

McDonald, A. J., & Jackson, T. R. (1987). Amygdaloid connections with posterior insular and temporal cortical areas in the rat. *Journal of Comparative Neurology, 262,* 59–77.

Miserendino, M. J. D., & Davis, M. (1993). NMDA and non-NMDA antagonists infused into the nucleus reticularis pontis caudalis depress the acoustic startle reflex. *Brain Research, 623,* 215–222.

Miserendino, M. J. D., Sananes, C. B., Melia, K. R., & Davis, M. (1990). Blocking of acquisition but not expression of conditioned fear-potentiated startle by NMDA antagonists in the amygdala. *Nature, 345,* 716–718.

Nose, I., Higashi, H., Inokuchi, H., & Nishi, S. (1991). Synaptic responses of guinea pig and rat central amygdala neurons in vitro. *Journal of Neurophysiology, 65,* 1227–1241.

Pascoe, J. P., & Kapp, B. S. (1985). Electrophysiological characteristics of amygdaloid central nucleus neurons in the awake rabbit. *Brain Research Bulletin, 14,* 331–338.

Pavlov, I. P. (1927). *Conditioned reflexes.* Oxford, UK: Oxford University Press.

Pennypacker, H. S. (1967). External inhibition of the conditioned eyelid reflex. In G. A. Kimble (Ed.), *Foundations of conditioning and learning* (pp. 528–544). New York: Appleton-Century-Crofts.

Rainnie, D. G., Asprodini, E. K., & Shinnick-Gallagher, P. (1991). Excitatory transmission in the basolateral amygdala. *Journal of Neurophysiology, 66,* 986–998.

Rosen, J. B., & Davis, M. (1988a). Enhancement of acoustic startle by electrical stimulation of the amygdala. *Behavioral Neuroscience, 102,* 195–202.

Rosen, J. B., & Davis, M. (1988b). Temporal characterizations of enhancement of startle by stimulation of the amygdala. *Physiology and Behavior, 44,* 117–123.

Rosen, J. B., & Davis, M. (1990). Enhancement of electrically elicited startle by amygdaloid stimulation. *Physiology and Behavior, 48,* 343–349.

Rosen, J. B., Hitchcock, J. M., Miserendino, M. J. D., Falls, W. A., Campeau, S., & Davis, M. (1992). Lesions of the perirhinal cortex but not of the frontal, medial prefrontal, visual, or insular cortex block fear-potentiated startle using a visual conditioned stimulus. *Journal of Neuroscience, 12,* 4624–4633.

Rosen, J. B., Hitchcock, J. M., Sananes, C. B., Miserendino, M. J. D., & Davis, M. (1991). A direct projection from the central nucleus of the amygdala to the acoustic startle pathway: Anterograde and retrograde tracing studies. *Behavioral Neuroscience, 105,* 817–825.

Ross, L. E. (1961). Conditioned fear as a function of CS–UCS and probe stimulus intervals. *Journal of Experimental Psychology, 61,* 265–273.

Sananes, C. B., & Davis, M. (1992). N-Methyl-D-Aspartate lesions of the lateral and basolateral nuclei of the amygdala block fear-potentiated startle and shock sensitization of startle. *Behavioral Neuroscience, 106,* 72–80.

Spence, K. W., & Runquist, W. N. (1958). Temporal effects of conditioned fear on the eyelid reflex. *Journal of Experimental Psychology, 55,* 613–616.

Spiera, R. F., & Davis, M. (1988). Excitatory amino acid antagonists depress acoustic startle after infusion into the ventral nucleus of the lateral lemniscus or paralemniscal zone. *Brain Research, 445,* 130–136.

Supple, W. F., Jr., & Leaton, R. N. (1990). Lesions of the cerebellar vermis and cerebellar hemispheres: Effects on heart rate conditioning in rats. *Behavioral Neuroscience, 104,* 934–947.

Yeomans, J. S., & Pollard, B. A. (1993). Amygdala efferents mediating electrically evoked startle-like responses and fear potentiation of acoustic startle. *Behavioral Neuroscience, 107,* 596–610.

4

A Goal-Based Approach to Memory
for Emotional Events: Implications
for Theories of Understanding
and Socialization

Nancy L. Stein
Maria D. Liwag
Elizabeth Wade
University of Chicago

This chapter presents an analysis of children's memories for real-life emotional events. The events in question are those that have evoked emotional reactions in 3- to 6-year-old children, by their own admission and by reports from their parents. In discussing these studies, we describe a theory of emotional understanding that accounts for the nature, content, and organization of emotional memories. We then illustrate how memory for emotional events reflects the ways in which people think about emotional experience and how they organize their knowledge about emotion.

Throughout this chapter, we stress the need for an elaborated model of emotional understanding and goal-directed thinking that addresses the core issues related to the organization of emotional experience. Specifically, the thinking and memory processes that are carried out during the understanding of emotional experience need more definition and elaboration, not only in terms of the functional significance of emotion (Campos, 1994), but in terms of the content of the thinking and appraisal processes that regulate and underlie memory for emotional events.

Many investigators have undertaken the creation of theories of emotional appraisal (e.g., see the edited volumes of Frijda & Oatley, 1994, and Stein & Oatley, 1992), and several of these attempts have described appraisal dimensions that are related to the experience of specific emotions (Frijda, 1987, 1994; Higgins, 1991, this volume; Lewis, 1992; Oatley & Johnson-Laird, 1987; Roseman, 1991; Smith & Lazarus, 1993; Stein & Jewett, 1986; Stein & Levine, 1987, 1989; Stein, Trabasso, & Liwag, 1993).

In this chapter, we model the emotional understanding process by show-ing how appraisals are carried out over the course of an emotional experience. We then use data from our studies of children's and parents' memory for real-life emotional events to test some implications and hypotheses derived from this model.

A central issue in any theory of emotional understanding concerns the nature and structure of emotion categories. In particular, some researchers question whether the concept of a basic emotion is useful in describing the organization of emotional experience (see Ortony, Clore, & Foss, 1987; Ortony & Turner, 1990; Stein & Oatley, 1992). The reason for this query, in part, is the difficulty in defining what a basic emotion is, which emotions are basic, and what dimensions are unique to each basic emo-tion. Indeed, the debate over the idea of a basic emotion has focused on the very definitions of emotion and emotional experience. How do we know when we or others have experienced an emotional reaction? What dimensions define an emotional reaction? If we succeed in specifying the conditions under which emotional reactions occur, what dimensions are critical to distinguishing among the specific emotions?

In order to explore more fully the appraisals and evaluations that link events and emotions, and to determine the nature and boundaries of emotional categories (e.g., Is each emotion category "discrete" such that a set of unique dimensions characterize each emotion? Do all experiences of fear have at least one common defining characteristic, despite the differences in events and physiological reactions that might accompany fear?), we present data from two studies where preschool children have either generated or identified real-life events that evoked different emo-tional reactions.

Our conclusion, on examining the evidence from our own and other studies of real-life emotion, is that for happiness, anger, sadness, and fear, each emotion maps onto a characteristic pattern of goal–outcome rela-tionships. The critical goal–outcome relationships that differentiate among the four emotions are whether one desires or does not desire to maintain a particular goal, in conjunction with whether or not goal failure or success occurs. Specific beliefs about the probability of reinstating or maintaining a goal, in conjunction with specific goal–outcome relation-ships, further differentiate among the four emotions. Thus, happiness, sadness, anger, and fear each have unique patterns of goal–outcome relationships and goal reinstatement beliefs associated with them.

We also show that the events associated with the emotion of happiness are distinctly separate from those events that elicit the negative emotions. Therefore, if we had examined only the positive emotion of happiness, we would have concluded, indeed, that happiness maps onto a set of events unique only to happiness. We show, however, that fear, anger, and sadness do not always map onto different events. Specifically, those events that elicit anger are just as likely to elicit sadness. Moreover, even though fear is elicited by a set of events that is often distinct from those that elicit anger and sadness, some overlap can still be observed (Stein, Trabasso, & Liwag, in press). Thus, the correspondence between an event and an emotion is always a function of evaluating goal–outcome relationships in connection with the event. The critical component is whether or not events are thought to have caused the success or failure of important goals. Beliefs about the ability to reinstate a failed or attained goal or to prevent specific goal states from occurring are also germane to eliciting and differentiating among the emotions.

We show that happiness, sadness, anger, and fear are each associated with a particular type of subsequent goal and plan of action. For example, the desire to prevent certain states from occurring is almost always associated with fear, whereas the desire to seek revenge is frequently associated with anger. Similarly, the desire to continue a current goal state is associated with happiness more than with any other emotion. A small set of goals and plans, especially those associated with reinstating a goal, are elicited in response to both anger and sadness, and we provide an explanation for this overlap. Rather than conclude that the four emotion categories of happiness, sadness, anger, and fear do not have discrete defining features and boundaries, we argue that particular plans and actions are often linked to more than one emotion because children gravitate toward plans that lead to positive goal attainment, even if these plans are not feasible at the moment. Although children may not achieve what they want in the real world, they always have the option of attaining success in pretense, fantasies, and hypothetical thinking.

Because of children's rapidly developing skill for blaming, fantasy, and hypothetical thinking, the sequential reasoning and decision making carried out during an emotional episode are as important as the initial emotional response to a precipitating event. Children as young as 3 clearly make distinctions between what they want and what they can have, they have a good memory for situations that run counter to their desires, and they are quite skilled at inventing scenarios that result in goal success rather than failure. In fact, hypothetical and wishful thinking may function to direct future problem-solving attempts, and these wishes and plans may result in a restructuring or reevaluation of memory for an event.

Understanding the dynamics of thinking during emotional events provides additional insights into the knowledge children have acquired about personal and social problem solving. What may look like disconnected, irrational, mindless behavior on the part of a child who experiences an emotion rarely is. Emotional behavior always results from value judgments about the desirability of specific goal states, events, and people, and it always involves accessing beliefs about whether or not desired goal states are attainable. To the extent that desirability and certainty evaluations are made about a goal, both children and adults engage in planning to achieve or maintain their desired states, and they also make plans to change, avoid, or get rid of undesired states.

Examining young children's memories for emotional events allows us to determine whether their knowledge and thinking about emotional experience is similar to those of adults. Our data indicate that children and their parents have strikingly similar schemes for encoding and remembering emotional events. Thus, when children talk about a time when they were angry, they use the same pattern of appraisals and evaluations as their parents do. This similarity, however, does not mean that for a given event children report experiencing the same emotion as their parents say they have. Children's memories often differ from their parents because children and parents focus their attention on different components of the event at the time of encoding. Each brings different memories and knowledge to the interpretation of the event, along with different goals. Moreover, children who experience an emotional reaction to an event sometimes ruminate about the event long after its occurrence (Stein, Trabasso, & Liwag, in press). In the process of rumination, postevent information may be added to the representation of the original emotional experience. Thus, children's memory for an emotional event often spans a greater time period than their parents' memories and may contain information that occurred after the initial event took place.

Describing the structure and organization of emotional memories illustrates the ways in which information from different time periods is integrated into a single representation. If we can generate an explanation for this integration, we can better describe the mental schemes used to construct and regulate the memory representation at the time of encoding. Although a good number of models of the appraisal process have been developed (Frijda, 1987; Lazarus, 1991; Oatley & Johnson-Laird, 1987; Stein & Levine, 1990; Stein & Trabasso, 1992; Stein, Trabasso, & Liwag, 1993, in press), few describe the sequence of processes that take place over the course of situated emotional understanding. Rather, most models focus only on listing the events, goal–outcome combinations, and certainty appraisals that lead people to experience different types of emotions.

Identifying the correspondence between goal–outcome states and specific emotions is critical to the development of a model of emotional understanding. However, more than outcome evaluations are made during the experience and understanding of an emotional event. People make judgments about the *consequences* of acting on their desires, and often revise their plans of actions in response to these evaluations, especially if they realize that their plans will result in negative outcomes (Folkman

& Stein, in press; Stein & Levine, 1989; Stein & Trabasso, 1989). Moreover, extensive analyses of the causes of a precipitating event are often carried out so that similar situations can be avoided in the future. People also engage in what we (Folkman & Stein, in press) call the *regret syndrome*, where they chastise themselves for undertaking a series of actions that have resulted in disastrous outcomes, and subsequently engage in real and hypothetical attempts to "undo" the harm, even though the harm cannot be undone. Finally, emotional understanding forces the revision of deeply held beliefs so that new plans of action can be formulated to ensure well-being.

It becomes necessary to revise currently held beliefs in almost every emotional situation, especially those that result in irrevocable loss (Folkman & Stein, in press; Wortman & Silver, 1990), where no possibility of goal reinstatement exists. In cases of irrevocable loss, new goals must be formulated, and connections must be made between the positive values that people hold so deeply and newly formulated plans that might succeed in keeping these values intact. Only by studying the dynamics of the understanding process will we be able to describe more fully the nature of the changes in beliefs, knowledge, and goals that occur during emotional experience.

A MODEL OF EMOTIONAL UNDERSTANDING AND MEMORY

The process of remembering an emotional event is a function of the way in which the event was understood. Understanding involves perceptual analysis, evaluation, and inference making. Therefore, a memory is never an exact replica of the original emotional experience, even if the memory is activated and retrieved immediately after an emotional event is experienced. Remembering is always constrained and influenced by personal knowledge (e.g., current affective, goal, and knowledge states) and by the inference processes that take place during the encoding of an event. Although emotional memories can be quite accurate, they are never all-encompassing (Ornstein, Shapiro, Clubb, & Follmer, in press; Ross, in press; Stein, Trabasso, & Liwag, 1993, in press; Stein, Wade, & Liwag, in press).

To respond emotionally means to activate specific goals and content knowledge in relationship to an event that has occurred either in the external environment or internally, upon reflection on past or anticipated events. When specific goals and knowledge are activated, attention is directed to those parts of an emotion episode that directly relate to these current goal and knowledge states. Thus, attention is diverted away from other parts of the episode. As we illustrate in our description of on-line inference processes during emotional understanding, activating specific goals narrows and focuses attention because each activated goal carries with it a set of knowledge, plans, and appraisals that need evaluation if people are to respond to an ongoing event.

When people evaluate how an event has affected their goals and plans, the products of these evaluations become part of the memory representation for the event. For example, if people decide that a particular plan may be thwarted by another person, their subsequent memory of the event will include their thoughts and emotional evaluations related to the thwarted plan. Some people may even transform the threat of plan blockage into one of actually having a plan blocked (Nezworski, Stein, & Trabasso, 1981); thus, memory for emotional events includes the thoughts and inferences made about a specific event as well as the information that can be encoded from the actions surrounding an event.

The assertion that memory for events is constrained by personal preferences, desires, and values is not new. Bartlett (1932), in his seminal work on everyday memory, made the same claim. He believed that current attitudes, desires, and prior knowledge guided and organized all memory. The problem for Bartlett, as for all of us who study memory in everyday contexts, was how to characterize and describe the representation of an event that results from the interaction of prior knowledge with information encoded from the external unfolding of the event. The task is difficult and entails tolerating complex network representations (Stein & Trabasso, 1982). At the same time, the nature of goal-directed thought and action is heavily constrained by the types of prior knowledge acquired about emotional experience. In a series of recent papers (Folkman & Stein, in press; Liwag & Stein, in press; Stein & Levine, 1987, 1989, 1990; Stein & Trabasso, 1992; Stein, Trabasso, & Liwag, 1993), we have described many of the constraints that are placed on emotional understanding, and have illustrated how these constraints regulate the inferences and evaluations made during the experience of an emotional event.

According to our theory (Folkman & Stein, in press; Stein & Levine, 1987, 1989, 1990; Stein, Trabasso, & Liwag, 1993, in press), people prefer to be in states of goal satisfaction and maintenance rather than in states of goal failure or goal abandonment. They continually monitor the status of their goals, especially those that are directly related to maintaining states of well-being. Thus, positive outcomes are preferred over negative outcomes of loss, abandonment, or pain. This assumption is similar to the pleasure–pain principle in Freud's motivational theory, and it underlies almost all current approaches to the study of emotional experience, especially those that deal with pain and loss (see Kahneman, Frederickson, Schreiber, & Redelmeier, 1993; Salovey & Smith, in press, for the latest adaptation of the pleasure–pain principle to memories for painful events).

Only six different combinations of goal–outcome states can occur. Given a goal that is valued and considered desirable, a person may want something and attain it; they may want it, but not attain it; or they may want it, but be uncertain of its attainment. Similarly, given a goal that is considered undesirable, a person may not want to attain the goal, but attain it; they may not want it, and not attain it; or they may not want it, but be uncertain of its attainment.

As we have noted in past studies (Stein & Levine, 1987, 1990; Stein & Trabasso, 1989, 1992; Stein, Trabasso, & Liwag, 1993, in press), each of these combinations of goal–outcome states is associated with particular emotions. Happiness is associated with two goal–outcome states: wanting something and attaining it and not wanting something and not attaining it (i.e., avoiding it). Fear is associated with two outcomes states: not wanting something but being uncertain as to whether the state can be avoided and wanting something but not being certain that the goal can be attained. Anger and sadness are both associated with states of wanting something but not attaining it or not wanting something, but having the state occur. Thus, four of the five basic emotions identified by Ekman (1977) can be described in part by specific combinations of goal–outcome states that result during the monitoring of changes in the status of specific goals.

For an event to be defined as one that elicits an emotion, however, more than the changes in the status of goal–outcome states must be appraised. Beliefs about whether or not valued goals can be attained, maintained, reinstated, or avoided must be activated. Beliefs are states of knowledge about the world that refer to the way in which the world has functioned in the past, is functioning in the present, and will function in the future. Thus, beliefs carry a truth value about the way the world was or is or will be, and they carry expectations about the present or future, as well as feelings of certainty regarding the occurrence of events in the past.

The activation of beliefs about the probability of reinstating a goal in conjunction with appraisals about the certainty of goal–outcome states occurring allows a differentiation between the emotions of happiness, sadness, anger, and fear. In particular, beliefs about the probability of reinstating or avoiding a goal are used in differentiating between anger and sadness. Anger is evoked when people want something, have failed to attain it, and believe that their goal can be reinstated. Sadness is evoked when people want something, have failed to attain it, and believe that the goal cannot be reinstated. Similarly, both emotions can be evoked when people want to *avoid* a particular state, usually an aversive or painful state, and fail in their attempts to do so. If people believe they can eventually get out of that aversive state, they get angry—if they believe that they can do nothing about the current aversive state, they feel sad (Levine, in press).

Roseman (1991) and Smith and Lazarus (1993) have all argued that anger is an emotion directed toward an agent or event that caused the failure of a goal, whereas sadness is not. We (Stein & Levine, 1987, 1989, 1990) have argued and have illustrated that inferences about the agentive nature of goal failure are not necessary for anger to occur. Both children and adults get quite angry when they are put in an aversive state, independent of whether an animate being has caused their anger. The emotion of anger can be evoked as soon as a painful end state is experienced and beliefs about reinstating a goal are accessed. Inferences about the causal or consequential nature of the agent are often made *after* the emotion of anger has been experienced, not before its evocation. The same is true with regard to sadness. During sad experiences, attention is often focused on the consequences of sadness, but sadness can occur without consequential rumination. The essential feature of sadness, in conjunction with a goal–outcome appraisal, is the activation of the belief that a failed goal *cannot* be reinstated. Thus, the components necessary to evoke anger and sadness are simpler than Roseman (1991) or Smith and Lazarus (1993) proposed.

Anger, however, is not evoked solely by the accessing of beliefs about goal reinstatement (Oatley & Johnson-Laird, 1987), nor is anger evoked solely by the presence of certain goal–outcome states (Ortony & Turner, 1990). Both goal–outcome states and beliefs about reinstatement must be considered in order to distinguish between the emotions of anger and sadness (Stein & Trabasso, 1992). Furthermore, the evocation of the four emotions of happiness, anger, sadness, and fear are not dependent on the activation of "action tendencies," as Frijda (1987) proposed.

According to Frijda, emotional evocation is intimately connected to the *tendency* of the organism to carry out specific types of actions. Tendency is a difficult concept because it encodes multiple meanings. However, Frijda uses tendency to signify a readiness to execute action and a readiness to achieve or maintain a particular state. According to Frijda, however, emotional action is not intentional action: Emotional actions result from "impulses" or "urges." However, his definition of an action tendency rests on the activation of a plan of readiness, and plan activation, in most cases, is intentionally based.

Frijda's use of action tendency to define and differentiate among the emotions has two inherent difficulties. By using the concept of tendency, he clusters appraisals and evaluations that are separable and occur in a particular causal or temporal sequence. Therefore, Frijda cannot specify the exact nature of the appraisal and inference sequence that occurs in conjunction with emotional "impulses" or "urges." Second, Frijda assumes that the goal plan regulating an urge or an impulse is not conscious and not subject to volitional thought. That is, emotions are somehow regulated by plans, but these plans are not available to conscious thought; rather, they are run off automatically such that an emotional response simulates a rapid behavioral reflex. However, evaluations do get carried out because different action tendencies are activated in terms of the experience of different emotions.

Our theory of emotional understanding is similar to Frijda's in that it is based on intentional action and the construction of plans in response to the monitoring of changes in valued goal states. We (Stein & Jewett, 1986; Stein & Levine, 1987; Stein & Trabasso, 1992; Stein, Trabasso, & Liwag, 1993, in press) differ from Frijda, however, in that we postulate conscious awareness of the goals that change in status. Moreover, the plans formulated in response to the activation of desires are also available to consciousness. Young children and adults alike can verbalize what they want and what they need to do in order to get something, and these verbalizations are frequent in spontaneous talk about emotional experience (Stein, Trabasso, & Liwag, in press).

The reason that investigators may conclude that emotional responses are unconscious, unintentional, and not privy to reflection is that emotion is studied most often in a retrospective fashion with no examination of the on-line sequential processes that occur during the emotional experience. Even if on-line experience is observed, some investigators still assume that the speed of emotional arousal negates any type of reflective processing (Zajonc, 1980).

In our theory of emotional understanding, we consider the thinking, encoding, and retrieval of information both during and after an emotional experience. Although thinking aloud about on-going experience can never simulate all thought processes that get activated, observing the stream and direction of talk during an emotional experience allows us to describe the content of the mental schemes and processes that are used to understand dynamic emotional situations. The fact that different types of thinking and memory processes get carried out during emotional experience then becomes more apparent. The appraisal processes that lead to the evocation of one emotion and not another also become better understood.

The memory and appraisal processes carried out during emotional experiences can be modeled by using as a guide the sequential thoughts generated by subjects as they proceed through an emotion episode. Table 4.1 contains four categories of appraisals that are almost always carried out during emotional experience. Answers to these questions indicate both the common and unique appraisals made across all emotional experiences. Understanding is always situated and dependent on the specific precipitating event and the conditions surrounding the event. At the same time, the mental schemes activated during emotional experience are similar across situations. Even though each emotional experience is

TABLE 4.1
The Content of Appraisals Made During
the Experience of an Emotional Event

What Happened?

---

1. What type of event occurred?
2. Have my goals been affected?
3. Which goals have changed in status?
4. How have the goals changed (have they failed or succeeded)?
5. Who or what caused the change in the status of the goal?
6. Did an agent mean to intentionally affect the success or failure of my goals?
6. What are the consequences of the change in the goal's status?
7. What beliefs have been violated and updated due to the change?
8. Do I think the goal can be reinstated, maintained, or avoided?

What Can I Do About It?

---

1. What do I want to do about it?
2. Is an action plan available that would reinstate or modify the desired goal?
3. How do I feel about it?
4. What are the reasons for my emotional reactions?

What Did I Do?

---

1. Did I carry out actions in the service of attaining or maintaining the goal?
2. What were the actions?
3. Were the actions the same as the one I planned to enact?

What Were the Results of My Actions?

---

1. What were the outcomes?
2. Did the outcomes result in the achievement or failure of a desired goal?
3. Did any unintended outcomes result from goal achievement or failure?
4. Did the unintended outcomes cause a reevaluation of the desired goals at stake?
5. How did the outcomes affect the success or failure of other desired goals?

---

unique, situated, and constrained by specific operating conditions, the types of appraisals and the functional role these appraisals play are similar across situations. All emotional responses result from the perception of a change in the status of a valued goal with respect to the success or failure of attaining, maintaining, or avoiding a particular goal state. Emotional responses are not planned and are elicited when changes in the status of a goal are unexpected and violate expectations about what should be occurring in a given situation.

An excellent example of the uncontrollable and unexpected nature of emotional reactions comes from our analysis of bereavement narratives of male caregivers whose partners have just died from AIDS (Stein, Folkman, Christopher-Richards, & Trabasso, 1994). These caregivers knew for quite some time that their partners would not recover from the HIV virus; all knew that their partners would die. Many attempted to assist their partners in making death easier, because of the ravaging, horrendous effects of the disease. When the deaths of their partners came, two prototypic emotions were experienced across caregivers: relief and sadness. Caregivers' relief was intimately associated with not having to see their partners suffer or be in pain anymore. Sadness was associated with never being able to see their partners again. For many caregivers, sadness was overwhelmingly intense, even when they had done much to prepare themselves for their partner's death.

These caregivers were not able to predict just how dependent they would be on their partners for companionship and comfort. Never being able to see, touch, or be in close proximity to their partners was also overwhelming to many. Not having any access to what caregivers felt were the best qualities of their partners was the single most important theme expressed during bereavement ruminations. These caregivers' narratives illustrate that an event like death elicits intense sadness, despite the fact that certain parts of the death process are predictable. The death of a spouse or lover blocks not just one but many goals, such that an entire *network of goals* is affected. When caregivers report that they have dealt with the upcoming loss of their partner, in a sense they are accurate. They do know that their partner will die, and they envision how they will feel and what they will do.

When death occurs, however, much of what they envisioned does not come to pass. Although they thought they knew what it would be like, they realize that they were not able to predict everything. The caregivers became cognizant of the many other goals that were blocked. These goal blockages indicate that beliefs about the world are incorrect and in need of revision. Thus, the person experiencing the emotion is forced to reevaluate the conditions that lead to the attainment of their goals. In the process of reevaluating their beliefs, they change many of their working assumptions about the ease or difficulty of attaining certain goals as well as the value of the goal under consideration.

If we accept the fact that emotional reactions are not planned, that they are intimately related to learning, that children experience emotional reactions from infancy onward, and that emotional reactions permeate every aspect of our existence, it seems ironic that many researchers postulate a late development of emotional understanding. Some researchers conclude that children lack a basic understanding of the nature and structure of their own and other people's beliefs until the age of 3 or 4 (Astington & Gopnik, 1991; Higgins, 1991). If interviewed properly, however, even 2-year-olds evidence a good understanding of emotion, deception, belief violation, and intentionality (Chandler, Fritz, & Hala,

1989; Dunn, 1989; Wellman, 1991). The task for us, as theorists interested in on-line thinking about and memory for emotional events, is to specify the knowledge that children and adults use to understand and represent emotional events.

ON-LINE APPRAISALS DURING EMOTIONAL EXPERIENCE

Since emotional responses reflect changes in the status of valued goals, the mental schemes used to understand precipitating events necessitate the interpretation and ramifications of goal success and failure. Thus, a precipitating event will be appraised in terms of the identification of the type of event that caused the shift, a determination of its causes and consequences, construction of a plan to cope with the change in the status of goals, the undertaking of action, if the plan specifies it, and the evaluation of the consequences of the actions and outcomes associated with the coping responses. The essence of this appraisal process can be captured by four fundamental questions: (a) What happened?; (b) What can I do about it?; (c) What did I do about it?; and (d) What are the results of carrying out a plan of action?

Although many thinking and memory processes associated with emotional experience are simultaneous in nature, the four categories of appraisals are not. Since some goals must be carried out before others can be achieved, goals must be organized into a sequential hierarchy—a person cannot evaluate the outcomes of a plan or action until the plan has been formulated. Similarly, decisions about appropriate plans of actions cannot be made without a representation of what happened with respect to an event that precipitated an emotion.

Emotional reactions can be elicited in any of the subcomponents of the appraisal process. The critical dimensions that control emotional arousal are perceived changes in the attainability of valued goals and the activation of beliefs about goal reinstatement and maintenance. We illustrate how four different emotions can be elicited during the on-line appraisal processes listed in Table 4.1. We begin by discussing the appraisal processes associated with the question *What happened?*

When a precipitating event occurs, the experiencer must first recognize that valued goals have shifted in status. Determining what happened focuses on identifying incoming information and comparing the interpretation to what is already known about such an event. Even though a description of what happened can often be simply stated, many memory and appraisal processes are carried out in order to arrive at a final interpretation. Retrieving information from long-term memory, using this information to first identify the event, and then comparing incoming information to what is already known are three such memory processes, most of which are unavailable to consciousness.

Johnson and Hirst (1993) and Johnson and Malthaup (1991) have constructed a model of memory that allows multiple entry into memory, assuming that modular systems are operating during the encoding and representation of any event. The types of processes they list are similar to the ones mentioned here, in that retrieval, identification, and comparative processes are described. The hallmark of the Johnson et al. theory is that memory processes are categorized into two different types: perceptual and reflective. The perceptual system is composed of two different types of processes: P1 and P2. P1 processes are not available to conscious attention and consist of processes such as locating a stimulus or an event, resolving stimulus configurations, tracking stimuli, and extracting invariants from perceptual arrays. P2 processes are more available to consciousness and involve identification, examination, structuring, or abstracting a pattern of organization across temporally extended stimuli.

It should be noted that almost all P1 and P2 processes are used in the process of answering each of the four categories of appraisal questions listed in Table 4.1. All memory processes described by Johnson and her colleagues are controlled by a schema that allows the experiencer to focus on the *causal implications* of the precipitating event. The importance of the event for emotional responsivity will be determined by whether or not the event is perceived to stand in direct relationship to successful or failed goals that are personally relevant and of value to the experiencer.

The questions listed in the first appraisal subcomponent, *What Happened?*, promote inferences about the positive or negative *value* of an event and whether goals relevant to the event have been attained, threatened, or blocked. Table 4.2 contains 22 different events that were generated when children, 2½ to 6 years of age, were asked to nominate events that had made or would make them or another child feel happy, sad, angry, and afraid. Parents of these same children generated the same types of events when asked to describe situations where they actually observed their children become happy, sad, angry, or afraid. In fact, nearly all parental events were captured by the taxonomy in Table 4.2.

The important results from this taxonomy, with respect to categories of emotional events, is that the events that provoke happiness do not overlap with any of the events that provoke the three negative emotions. For the three negative emotions, fear events are quite discriminable when compared to the events that provoke anger and sadness. Although there is some overlap in that one or two events provoke all three negative emotions, especially for the event of being intruded on, fear is unique in that being threatened, encountering a supernatural creature, and having

TABLE 4.2
Percent of Children Nominating Events in Each Category

Event Categories	Emotion			
	Happy	Angry	Sad	Afraid
CHILD . . .				
Is reunited with significant others	3			
Plays	23			
Celebrates birthdays/holidays	3			
Gives or receives affection	10			
Gets desirable objects	25			
Engages in desirable activities	15			
Avoids a bad situation	8			
Is denied desirable objects		6	5	
Is prohibited from desirable activities		11	9	
Is denied affection/companionship			2	
Has goals in conflict with others'		2		
Is unable to get desirable objects		2	8	
Is unable to engage in desirable activities		2	3	
Is separated from significant others			3	
Has possessions taken away/destroyed		2	3	
Has expectations not met		3	2	
Is forced to do something		3		
Is punished		5	8	
Is intruded on		31	19	10
Is physically harmed		20	23	9
Has experience related to death		2	2	2
Sees others harmed or in pain			2	2
Is left alone			2	3
Has nightmares/bad dreams				3
Experiences undesirable sensory stimuli		2		15
Perceives a threat				12
Encounters supernatural creatures				30

nightmares are specific only to this emotion. Experiencing undesirable sensory stimuli also induces primarily a fear experience.

Thus, if we had access only to event information to determine whether the boundaries among the four basic emotions are discrete, we would have to say that happiness and fear do correspond to classes of events that are unique to those emotions. The cluster analysis in Figure 4.1 supports this assertion by showing that the amount of statistical distance among the four categories is the greatest when happiness is compared to the three negative emotions. Within the negative emotions, fear lies approximately halfway between the enormous distance between happiness and the negative emotions and the short distance between anger and sadness.

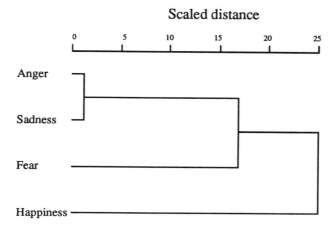

FIG. 4.1. Cluster analysis of event categories.

The problem for theories of discrete emotions is the significant overlap between anger and sadness in terms of the events that provoke each emotion. Although being intruded on (e.g., invasion of physical space or property) generates anger more often than sadness, the other events nominated for anger are just as likely to generate sadness. Similarly, sad events overlap with anger events, with the exception of three events: being left alone, being denied affection, and seeing others harmed or in pain. The first two events result in loss states, while the third event results in an aversive state.

If emotion concepts are organized according to discrete conceptual spaces, we need information about the underlying appraisal processes that accompany anger and sadness. We therefore examined four dimensions in terms of the appraisals that corresponded to each of the four emotions: (a) the goal outcome states that were reported to provoke each of the four emotions; (b) the reasons given for the evocation of each emotion; (c) the wishes generated in response to coping with goal success, goal failure, or a perceived threat to a goal; and (d) the actions actually carried out in response to the emotion.

The data presented to examine these four dimensions were generated by the same children participating in our first study of self-generated emotional events. The main difference between the two studies is that in our second study, parents generated the precipitating events to which children responded. Children were given instructions to try to remember everything about their parents' nominated event, without being given any information about what their parents reported about the event. Children were asked the following series of questions: (a) *Recognition of Precipitating Event*—Do you remember this event?; (b) *Recall of Emotion*—

How did you feel when this happened?; (c) *Recall of Emotion Episode*—Can you tell me exactly what happened? What did you think about? What did you do?

After they completed their initial narration, they were asked the following series of probe questions: (a) *Reasons*—Why did (event) make you feel (emotion)?; (b) *Wishes/Plans*—What did you wish you could do?; and (c) *Actions*—What did you do? The probe questions used to elicit the spontaneous and probed narratives correspond to the appraisal questions outlined in Table 4.1.

The results of our goal–outcome analysis illustrate the specific combinations of goals and outcomes that are associated with the experience of each of four emotions. The reporting of goal–outcome states occurred spontaneously during the recall of an emotional episode or in response to "why" probe questions focusing on reasons for experiencing each particular emotion. As the data indicate in Table 4.3, goal–outcome states reported for happiness are distinct from goal–outcome states reported for the three negative emotions. Children most often associate getting something that they want (e.g., a desired toy or favorite food, a special treat, etc.) with the experience of happiness.

Although the prevention of undesired goals (e.g., I didn't want him to hit me, and my brother stopped him) is also associated with happiness, these goal–outcome combinations were generated less frequently than the attainment of desired states. Children may link the prevention of undesired states to the experience of happiness when they consciously perceive that they have also attained desirable goals. In contrast, they may use a new word such as "relief" to signal prevention states not immediately associated with the attainment of desired goals.

Whether children conceive of *happiness* and *relief* as distinct emotion concepts needs to be investigated. Roseman (1991) has argued that the concept of happiness embeds both joy and relief such that joy is specific to the attainment of desired states and relief to the prevention of undesired states. Our data, however, suggest that children may not embed the

TABLE 4.3
Percent of Children Mentioning Goal/Outcome Appraisals

	Emotion			
Goal/Outcome Appraisals	*Happy*	*Angry*	*Sad*	*Afraid*
Want–Have	74		2	
Not want–Not have	15			
Want–Not have	7	43	62	
Not want–Have	2	57	29	29
Not want–Have (Uncertain)			2	71

meanings of both joy and relief in their concept of happiness. For young children aged 2½ to 6 years, the prototypic events causing happiness were ones that led to the attainment of desired goals (see Table 4.1). Children rarely nominated the prevention of undesired states as causes of happiness. We (Trabasso, Stein, & Johnson, 1981) reported similar results in an earlier study on children's causal understanding of emotions.

Our contention is that children are more likely to use value terms, such as *feeling not so bad* or *feeling better*, to describe the experience of having undesired states prevented. When children finally learn that the word *relief* captures the meaning associated with the prevention of undesired states, they may then begin using *relief* to signal the presence of the feelings evoked when goal failures and more disastrous consequences have been avoided.

Goal–outcome states associated with anger and sadness were limited to desired states that were not attained and undesired states that had to be tolerated. Although both goal–outcome combinations were generated for both anger and sadness, aversive (undesired) states were associated with anger more than with sadness. Conversely, children associated lack or loss of a desired state with sadness more than with anger. These results replicate and support those reported by Stein and Levine (1989), who examined children's and adults' causal understanding of anger, sadness, and happiness. They discovered that both children and adults were more likely to respond to an aversive state with anger than with sadness, whether or not an animate agent caused the aversive state.

Stein and Levine also reported that children were more likely to respond to loss states with sadness rather than with anger. Adults, however, were sensitive to who or what caused the particular loss state. If a physical event caused the loss state, almost all adults responded with sadness. If an animate agent caused the loss state, adults were more likely to respond with anger or with a combination of anger and sadness, indicating the importance of agency in the adult conception of anger, especially when an agent intentionally inflicted harm on another person. For 3-year-old children, however, the presence of agency did not guarantee that anger would be experienced. Three-year-old children often felt sad when they lost something, despite the fact that they understood that an animate agent caused their loss, sometimes intentionally. Focusing on an intentional agent as the cause of the loss was not sufficient for eliciting anger in young children. Thus, these data suggest that the theories of both Smith and Lazarus (1993) and Roseman (1991), who defined anger in terms of its relationship to agency, do not apply to the emotional understanding of preschool children.

Making agency a prerequisite for the experience of anger may unnecessarily complicate the conceptual representation of anger, for theories of both children's and adults' emotional understanding. Although prototypic reports of adult anger include events that refer to agents acting in intentionally harmful ways (Shaver, Schwartz, Kirson, & O'Connor, 1987), anger prototypes are significantly influenced by cultural norms that specify conditions under which anger can be appropriately expressed (Stein & Levine, 1989). Adults may not report angry feelings precipitated by inanimate objects or physical occurrences, because in their culture such expressions are not considered appropriate.

Nonetheless, adults have been observed to experience anger to painful or aversive events that involve no animate agent. Berkowitz (1989) has shown that aversive and painful events elicit anger without any animate agent causing the aversive event. Our data and theory support Berkowitz' contentions. If Berkowitz' and our data can be replicated over many situations, conceptualizations of anger involving other-blame such as those of Roseman (1991) and Smith and Lazarus (1993) need to be revised with respect to the minimal number of dimensions necessary to elicit anger.

Regarding fear, the most frequent goal–outcome states reported were the desire to avoid an aversive state, where the outcome was uncertain. Our theory predicts that fear involves uncertainty about the outcome state—fear is essentially an emotion that occurs in response to threat. In talking about fear, even 3-year-old children recognized this and talked about future outcome states that could occur but that were not desirable. The use of the future tense, such as *He's going to hit me*, or the use of the perfect conditional, *He was going to hit me*, were used to signal outcome states that had not yet occurred.

Our theory did not predict fear responses to aversive states (being put in an undesirable state). However, the mention of these states was quite understandable, given the context of a fear situation. Children would often mention the *event* that caused a change in the status of a goal rather than the outcome state that was now uncertain for them. Thus, many children who talked about supernatural beings like monsters and ghosts did so by saying, "Well, I was afraid because there was a monster in a my room," signaling the presence of a state that children did not desire. In such a state, however, the children might still be uncertain of future negative outcomes, such as whether or not the monster would now harm them.

Data from the Stein and Levine (1989) and Stein and Jewett (1986) studies support the claim that children first focus on the specific state changes that occur in their environment. They then focus on exactly what the event signals in terms of maintaining their well-being. In these studies, the shifting focus of attention was demonstrated by asking children two "why" questions, one in connection to their fear reaction, the next in connection with the answer they gave to the first "why" question. Thus, the procedure went as follows:

E: You said you were afraid last night. Why were you afraid?
C: There was a monster in my room.
E: What about a monster being in your room made you afraid?
C: Well, he could eat me.

Using this technique allowed us to reveal that the events that cause an initial change in the environment are first noticed because they function to set up a threat to relevant goals. An explanation for fear is then elicited, given that the conditions are now set up to provoke the emotion.

Table 4.4 contains the reasons generated for the four different emotions. Two findings are immediately evident. First, anger and sadness are distinguishable by two dimensions: reference to agency and a focus on the consequence of a loss or an aversive state. Agency is mentioned as a reason significantly more for anger than for sadness. However, children focus on the consequences when they are feeling sad, and they never focus on the consequences when providing reasons for anger. Thus, we can begin to understand how agency gradually becomes part of the anger repertoire that children are acquiring.

At the same time, approximately half of the children, when explaining their anger, did not focus on agency. Rather, they focused on the value of the blocked goal and how important it was for them to attain it. They also focused on the type of event that blocked their goal. These data indicate that anger is indeed associated with a reference to agency, but this reference is not a prerequisite for the experience of anger, at least in children's conscious reasons for their own anger.

The more interesting finding, with respect to causal thinking, is that reasons for three emotions are focused on the consequences of the threat, attainment, or loss of a goal. This focus signifies that children have made appraisals about goals and preferences that have been affected in addition to their primary goal under consideration. These data also suggest that young children use planning schemas to determine how their goals are hierarchically related to one another. For example, a child might say, "I

TABLE 4.4
Percent of Children Mentioning Reasons for Emotions

	Emotion			
Reasons	Angry	Sad	Afraid	Happy
Precipitating event	22	8	14	9
Goals/Preferences	44	39	7	40
Consequences	0	31	61	30
Violations	11	8	4	8
Agent	56	33	43	29

was sad because my toy got broken, and now I can't play with Alan." The child might also say, "I was happy because she gave me back my toy, and now I can play with Alan." Planning schemas allow people to hierarchicalize their goals and determine the causal relationships among them. Some goals function as the superordinate goal—the ultimate goal to be attained. Other goals function as subordinate goals—those that must be attained before the superordinate goal can be attained. The reasons given for each emotion suggest that children take into consideration the consequences of an event and determine how they feel about the consequences as well as the focal goal success or failure.

Table 4.5 contains the types of wishes that children generated in response to feeling one of four different emotions. Again, the wishes that accompany happiness do not overlap with the wishes for any other emotion—all wishes generated in response to feeling happy were either to maintain the present goal state or to attain new goals as a function of attaining the focal goal. Fear was quite distinct from anger and sadness, in that over 90% of all subjects wanted to prevent an undesirable state from occurring. Thus, in every dimension, *happy* and *fear* are clearly separable from one another, and they are distinct with respect to the emotions of anger and sadness.

Again, the greatest amount of overlap in wishes occurred between anger and sadness. The wishes for each emotion, however, could be characterized differently. Anger resulted in two primary wishes: desires to reinstate the original goal or to seek revenge. Sadness, on the other hand, resulted in desires to reinstate or to substitute new goals. Our theory (Stein & Levine, 1990; Stein, Trabasso, & Liwag, 1993) specifies that reinstatement will be the primary wish under conditions of goal failure, independent of both the emotion experienced and the possibility of reinstatement. Wishes function to help one cope with the devastation of loss by providing guidelines as to what is liked and preferred. They

TABLE 4.5
Percent of Children Mentioning Wishes

| Wishes | Emotion | | | |
	Angry	Sad	Afraid	Happy
Maintain original goal				37
Attain new goal				47
Reinstate original goal	40	36	8	
Substitute new goal	20	46		
Abandon original goal		2		
Revenge	40	8		
Prevent undesirable state		8	92	

also help in the generation of goals that can substitute for failed goals. By comparing what is possible to what is desired, people learn to broaden their preferences by creating new connections between old preferences and achievable goal states. Without guidelines as to which goals should be valued and achieved, people would not be able to create new, meaningful goals.

The fact that approximately half the children who experienced sadness already planned to substitute another goal implies that they were aware that they simply could never reinstate their old goal. Some children generated substitute goals when they got angry, but not to the degree that they did when sad. Rather, 40% of the angry children sought revenge, which rarely occurred in reports of sadness.

Table 4.6 contains a description of the actions children carried out as a function of feeling four different emotions. Again, happiness and fear remain distinct from each other and from anger and sadness. Furthermore, the relationship between what children wanted to do and what they did is very high. If children said they wished to maintain their achieved goal, they usually engaged in actions related to maintenance. If they said they wanted to achieve new goals, they usually attempted to do just that. Similarly, the desire to prevent aversive states from occurring most often resulted in actions that attempt to prevent those aversive states.

The discrepancies between wishes and actions occurred primarily under conditions of goal failure. Children discovered that little hope existed for reinstating their original goals, even though they initially believed that their goal could and should be reinstated. In many cases, children initially tried to carry out plans to reinstate their goal, but failed again. Upon their second failure, they either substituted a new goal or sought revenge.

The difficulty in differentiating anger from sadness is, in part, due to a failure to trace the dynamics of the emotional reaction through the

TABLE 4.6
Percent of Children Mentioning Actions

	Emotion			
Actions	Angry	Sad	Afraid	Happy
Maintain original goal				48
Attain new goal				34
Reinstate original goal	13	12	3	
Substitute new goal	38	35	16	
Abandon original goal	6	15	3	
Revenge	38	10		
Prevent undesirable state		13	71	

goal-directed episode to its resolution. When desired goals fail, children often become preoccupied with their failed goal until they determine definitely whether they can or cannot reinstate their original goal. During this period of decision making, thinking, and planning, children often experience additional emotions in their attempts at reinstating a goal. Therefore, they often report the last emotion experienced and often disagree with their parents, who have observed their children expressing anger, sadness, fear, or happiness. Disagreements among children and parents is particularly common for parent-nominated events of anger.

In our parent–child study of emotional events (Stein & Liwag, 1994; Stein, Trabasso, & Liwag, in press), children agreed with their parent's appraisal of anger only 22% of the time. Instead of responding to the parent-nominated event with anger, children most frequently responded with either sadness or happiness. Upon analysis of the time lines of both the parent and child reports, we discovered that children often reported sadness to anger-provoking events because their narratives incorporated subsequent episodes and attempts to resolve their goal failure. Similarly, when children reported that they felt happy about those events that parents nominated as causing anger, children included subsequent episodes where they did manage to succeed at attaining their goals. Thus, the ways in which children link their emotional responses to a precipitating event may be in relation to their final goal resolution rather than to their initial goal. They often delete segments of the experienced event sequence and make their report coherent in terms of their final resolution. If probed, however, for information about additional emotional responses, even our very young children can easily fill in critical information about their initial emotional responses. We found that 60% of children who initially disagreed with their parents concerning the expression of anger did admit to experiencing anger in addition to the emotion they initially reported. Moreover, they were quite capable of giving accurate reasons as to why they experienced an emotion in addition to the one they first reported.

These data are important because they illustrate the difficulty of determining exactly what inferences are being made about each segment in an emotion episode. Care must be taken to collect an on-line account of the thinking during an emotional experience so that the temporal and causal inferences can be plotted.

CONCLUSIONS

The theory and data presented in this chapter offer support for the usefulness of a theory of emotional understanding that attempts to chart the inferences and appraisals made during the experience and recall of emotional events. Collecting spontaneous narrations, either in retrospective or on-line situations, allows a more accurate description of the content of inferences made in understanding and remembering events. The data presented show unambiguously that children from the ages of 2½ to 6 years can recall emotion narratives and answer probe questions about their thinking and reasoning.

Our narrative data show that personal and social desires, the changes that occur in the ability to attain these desires, the knowledge children have about the conditions under which these desires can and cannot be achieved, and plans of action in the service of goal attainment are at the core of emotional knowledge and experience. In their narrations, 3-year-old children oriented a listener to those events that produced different emotions, signaled the importance of these emotions by connecting each emotion to its causes, and talked about emotions in terms of different types of outcomes and future consequences. Moreover, the children acknowledged, especially in anger situations, that their beliefs about other people's actions were at the core of their emotional reactions. Violations of personal or social norms were connected to reasons for anger, and children responded to these violations by changing subsequent goals and plans in order to accommodate their updated beliefs about the current situation.

When children's spontaneous narrations were compared to the information that was elicited through more detailed probe questions, we found that the two could be differentiated by future versus past orientations. Children's spontaneous narratives focused more often on the *planning process*, the actions undertaken, and interpretations that would help in future situations. Responses to probe questions contained more information about *explanations* for emotional responses, beliefs that had been violated, the unexpected nature of the emotional event, and the types and depth of feeling children had about desired goals. Thus, on-line narration may be biased toward the future because of demands to adapt to changing circumstances. This bias, however, does not mean that children are incapable of giving correct explanatory responses. Rather, our data suggest that explanatory responses are often embedded or implied in the formulation of children's plans.

The study of on-line thinking processes enriches the study of emotion in several ways. First, these studies provide detailed information about the inference processes that occur during and after emotional experience. Detailing the content of thoughts provides more direct evidence about the appraisals that are made during an emotional reaction. Describing the sequential nature of the thinking process also shows, unambiguously, the dynamic and complex nature of emotional understanding. Specifically, our data illustrate that a precipitating event may have multiple consequences and affect more than one desired goal. To the extent that children are aware of this multiplicity, they will report experiencing more than one emotion, or they will report the different goals that have been affected by the event. Thus, the notion of a one-to-one correspondence between a single event and a single emotion may need revision.

At the same time, children's narrations illustrate that children can focus on a single emotion, and in doing so can provide causal information that connects the emotion to the precipitating event, beliefs, goals, plans, actions, and outcomes. Our contention is that the process of narration itself provides an opportunity to better understand the sequence of events that precipitated the emotion. During narration, either on line or retrospectively, children have a chance to reflect on just what they do understand about the emotional situation and what they need to do to gain more information about the event.

To the extent that we detail the understanding process, we can examine the nature of memory representations and make predictions about the content and accuracy of memories. In a series of studies (Stein & Liwag, 1994; Stein, Trabasso, & Liwag, in press; Stein, Wade, & Liwag, in press; Wade & Stein, 1994), we have described the appraisals and inferences children make during retrospective narration, and have compared children's recollections to their parents' recollections for the same event. Our data from these studies suggest that point of view and the operating goals of both parents and children are critical in predicting not only the types of inferences made about an ongoing event, but the focus of attention during encoding. Specifically, when children provide reports about their emotional experiences they include information about episodes that occurred after the event under consideration. They do so because their goal in narrating is to establish how they resolved the problem or the changes created by a precipitating event.

Parents, on the other hand, do not include these subsequent episodes in their recollections of the event, primarily because parents often do not have access to the subsequent episode. Even if parents do have access to this information, they often focus their attention on whether their children's behavior is conforming to their expectations. Parents' recollection of children's emotional experience is thus often constrained more to the immediate behavior following the precipitating event and to those behaviors that are most important to their own goals. Describing the goals of parents and children, their expectations, and their plans for carrying out an interchange with each other should provide data from which a set of predictions can be made about the focus of attention and memory during the actual interchange. If understanding is goal-directed, the appraisals and inferences that each participant makes during an interaction should follow from the types of goals each has activated during the interchange. Future studies will be necessary to determine whether a goal-based approach provides the accuracy and detail of prediction that our results suggest.

Finally, the narration of emotional experiences provides a method for testing many current hypotheses regarding the concept of basic emotions. The debate rages over which emotions are basic for two primary reasons: First, investigators often have different definitions of basic emotions; second, they often confuse the language and vocabulary of emotion with the experience of emotion. Simply defining the meaning of various emotional terms may not capture the emotional experience itself—using a narrative analysis of real-life situations provides a mechanism to bridge language issues with experience issues.

ACKNOWLEDGMENTS

This research was funded in part by grants from the Smart Foundation on Early Learning to Nancy L. Stein, from the National Institute of Child Health and Human Development (Grant No. HD 25742 to Tom Trabasso and Nancy L. Stein, and Grant No. HD 17431 to Tom Trabasso), from the Spencer Foundation to Tom Trabasso, and by a Harris Fellowship from the Harris Center for Developmental Studies to Maria D. Liwag. We want to thank Tom Trabasso for his valuable conceptual suggestions throughout the project and Linda Levine for her theoretical and administrative assistance. Finally, we want to thank the teachers, children, and parents who participated in the study for sharing their time, memories, and emotions with us.

REFERENCES

Astington, J., & Gopnik, A. (1991). Developing understanding of desire and intention. In A. Whiten (Ed.), *Natural theories of mind: Evolution, development, and simulation of everyday mindreading* (pp. 39–50). Oxford, England: Blackwell.

Bartlett, F. C. (1932). *Remembering: A study in experimental and social psychology.* London: Cambridge University Press.

Berkowitz, L. (1989). Frustration–aggression hypothesis: Examination and reformulation. *Psychological Bulletin, 106,* 59–73.

Campos, J. (1994). The new functionalism in emotion. *SRCD Newsletter,* Spring Issue.

Chandler, M. J., Fritz, A. S., & Hala, S. (1989). Small scale deceit: Deception as a marker of 2, 3, & 4-year olds' early theories of mind. *Child Development, 60,* 1263–1277.

Dunn, J. (1989). *The development of social understanding.* New York: Cambridge University Press.

Ekman, P. (1977). Biological and cultural contributions to body and facial movement. In J. Blacking (Ed.), *Anthropology of the body* (pp. 34–84). London: Academic Press.

Folkman, S., & Stein, N. L. (in press). The analysis of belief and goal processes during reports of stressful events by caregivers of men with AIDS. In N. L. Stein, P. A. Ornstein, B. Tversky, & C. Brainerd (Eds.), *Memory for everyday and emotional events*. Hillsdale, NJ: Lawrence Erlbaum Associates.

Frijda, N. H. (1987). Emotion, cognitive structure, and action tendency. *Cognition and Emotion, 1*, 115–144.

Frijda, N. H. (1994). Appraisal and beyond: The issue of cognitive determinants of emotion. *Cognition and Emotion, 7*(3/4), 225–231.

Frijda, N. H., & Oatley, K. (Eds.). (1994). *Cognition and Emotion, 7*(3/4).

Higgins, E. T. (1991). Development of self regulatory and self evaluative processes: Costs, benefits, and tradeoffs. In M. R. Gunnar & A. L. Sroufe (Eds.), *Self processes and development: The Minnesota Symposium on Child Psychology* (Vol. 23, pp. 125–165). Hillsdale, NJ: Lawrence Erlbaum Associates.

Johnson, M. K., & Hirst, W. (1993). MEM: Memory subsystems as processes. In A. F. Collins, S. E. Gathercole, M. A. Conway, & P. E. Morris (Eds.), *Theories of memory* (pp. 241–286). Hillsdale, NJ: Lawrence Erlbaum Associates.

Johnson, M. K., & Malthaup, K. S. (1991). Emotion and MEM. In S. A. Christianson (Ed.), *The handbook of emotion and memory: Current research and theory* (pp. 33–66). Hillsdale, NJ: Lawrence Erlbaum Associates.

Kahneman, D., Frederickson, B. L., Schreiber, C. A., & Redelmeier, D. A. (1993). When more pain is preferred to less: Adding a better ending. *Psychological Science, 4*(6), 401–405.

Lazarus, R. S. (1991). *Emotion and adaptation*. New York: Oxford University Press.

Levine, L. (in press). Young children's understanding of the causes of anger and sadness. *Child Development*.

Lewis, M. (1992). *Shame: The exposed self*. New York: The Free Press.

Liwag, M. D., & Stein, N. L. (in press). Children's memory for emotional events: The importance of emotion-related retrieval cues [Special issue on everyday memory]. *Journal of Experimental Child Psychology*.

Nezworski, M. T., Stein, N. L., & Trabasso, T. (1981). Story structure versus content effects on children's recall of stories. *Journal of Verbal Learning and Verbal Behavior, 21*, 196–206.

Oatley, K., & Johnson-Laird, P. (1987). Toward a cognitive theory of emotions. *Cognition and Emotion, 1*, 29–50.

Ornstein, P. A., Shapiro, L. R., Clubb, P. A., & Follmer, A. (in press). The influence of prior knowledge on children's memory for salient medical experiences. In N. L. Stein, P. A. Ornstein, B. Tversky, & C. Brainerd (Eds.), *Memory for everyday and emotional events*. Hillsdale, NJ: Lawrence Erlbaum Associates.

Ortony, A., Clore, G. L., & Foss, M. A. (1987). The referential structure of the affective lexicon. *Cognitive Science, 11*, 341–364.

Ortony, A., & Turner, T. J. (1990). What's basic about basic emotions. *Psychological Review, 97*, 315–331.

Roseman, I. J. (1991). Appraisal determinants of discrete emotions. *Cognition and Emotion, 5*, 161–200.

Ross, M. (in press). Validating memories. In N. L. Stein, P. A. Ornstein, B. Tversky, & C. Brainerd (Eds.), *Memory for everyday and emotional events*. Hillsdale, NJ: Lawrence Erlbaum Associates.

Salovey, P., & Smith, A. F. (in press). Memory for painful experiences. In N. L. Stein, P. A. Ornstein, B. Tversky, & C. Brainerd (Eds.), *Memory for everyday and emotional events*. Hillsdale, NJ: Lawrence Erlbaum Associates.

Shaver, P., Schwartz, J., Kirson, D., & O'Connor, C. (1987). Emotion knowledge: Further explorations of a prototype approach. *Journal of Personality & Social Psychology, 52*(6), 1061–1086.

Smith, C. A., & Lazarus, R. S. (1993). Appraisal components: Core relational themes and the emotions. *Cognition and Emotion, 7*(3/4), 233–269.

Stein, N. L., Folkman, S., Christopher-Richards, A., & Trabasso, T. (1994, September). *A goal processes approach to predicting positive morale and depression from the analysis of bereavement narratives.* Paper presented at the Rashomon Conference, Center for AIDS Prevention Studies, San Francisco, CA.

Stein, N. L., & Jewett, J. (1986). A conceptual analysis of the meaning of basic negative emotions: Implications for a theory of development. In C. E. Izard & P. Read (Eds.), *Measurement of emotion in infants and children* (Vol. 2, pp. 238–267). New York: Cambridge University Press.

Stein, N. L., & Levine, L. (1987). Thinking about feelings: The development and use of emotional knowledge. In R. E. Snow & M. Farr (Eds.), *Aptitude, learning, and instruction: Vol. 3. Cognition, conation, and affect* (pp. 165–197). Hillsdale, NJ: Lawrence Erlbaum Associates.

Stein, N. L., & Levine, L. (1989). The causal organization of emotion knowledge: A developmental study. *Cognition and Emotion, 3*(4), 343–378.

Stein, N. L., & Levine, L. (1990). Making sense out of emotional experience: The representation and use of goal-directed knowledge. In N. L. Stein, B. Leventhal, & T. Trabasso (Eds.), *Psychological and biological approaches to emotion* (pp. 45–73). Hillsdale, NJ: Lawrence Erlbaum Associates.

Stein, N. L., & Liwag, M. D. (1994). *Parents' and children's memories for emotional events.* Unpublished manuscript, University of Chicago.

Stein, N. L., & Oatley, K. (Eds.). (1992). Basic emotions: Theory and measurement [Special Issue on Basic Emotions]. *Cognition and Emotion, 6*(3/4), 161–168.

Stein, N. L., & Trabasso, T. (1982). What's in a story: An approach to comprehension and instruction. In R. Glaser (Ed.), *Advances in instructional psychology* (Vol. 2, pp. 213–267). Hillsdale, NJ: Lawrence Erlbaum Associates.

Stein, N. L., & Trabasso, T. (1989). Children's understanding of changing emotion states. In C. Saarni & P. Harris (Eds.), *The development of emotional understanding* (pp. 50–77). New York: Cambridge University Press.

Stein, N. L., & Trabasso, T. (1992). The organization of emotional experience: Creating links among emotion, thinking, language and intentional action [Special Issue on Basic Emotions]. *Cognition and Emotion, 6*(3/4), 225–244.

Stein, N. L., Trabasso, T., & Liwag, M. D. (1993). The representation and organization of emotional experience. Unfolding the emotional episode. In M. Lewis & J. Haviland (Eds.), *Handbook of emotion* (pp. 279–300). New York: Guilford.

Stein, N. L., Trabasso, T., & Liwag, M. (in press). The Rashomon Phenomenon: Personal frames and future oriented appraisals in memory for emotional events. In M. Haith (Ed.), *Future oriented processes.* Chicago: University of Chicago Press.

Stein, N. L., Wade, E., & Liwag, M. D. (in press). A theoretical approach to understanding and remembering emotional events. In N. L. Stein, P. A. Ornstein, B. Tversky, & C. Brainerd (Eds.), *Memory for everyday and emotional events.* Hillsdale, NJ: Lawrence Erlbaum Associates.

Trabasso, T., Stein, N. L., & Johnson, L. R. (1981). Children's knowledge of events: A causal analysis of story structure. In G. Bower (Ed.), *Learning and motivation* (Vol. 15, pp. 237–282). New York: Academic Press.

Wade, E., & Stein, N. L. (1994, July). *Children's memories for real and hypothetical events.* Paper presented at the Society for Text and Discourse Meetings, Washington, DC.

Wellman, H. (1991). From desires to beliefs: Acquisition of a theory of mind. In A. Whiten (Ed.), *Natural theories of mind: Evolution, development, and simulation of everyday mindreading* (pp. 19–38). Oxford, England: Blackwell.

Wortman, C. B., & Silver, R. C. (1990). Successful mastery of bereavement and widowhood. In P. Baltes & M. M. Baltes (Ed.), *Successful aging: Perspectives from the behavioral sciences* (pp. 225–264). New York: Cambridge University Press.

Zajonc, R. (1980). Feeling and thinking. Preferences need no inferences. *American Psychologist, 39,* 117–123.

5

An Epigenetic Perspective on Emotional Development

Joseph J. Campos
Rosanne Kermoian
David Witherington
University of California at Berkeley

In recent years there have been significant contributions to the description of emotional development without comparable attention to the processes underlying such transitions. Current work has advanced our understanding of such topics as emotion regulation and the origins of "complex" emotions (e.g., empathy, shame, guilt), and has led to remarkable advances in our measurement techniques (e.g., frontal EEG and adrenocortical assessments). However, with few exceptions (e.g., Camras, 1992; Fogel et al., 1992), researchers have steered away from theory and research on how emotions emerge and develop. In this chapter, we propose an epigenetic[1] approach to emotional development and then document how the interaction between the person and environment brings about qualitative changes in the generation of emotion, as well as its consequences.

Over 30 years ago, epigenetic explanations revolutionized the field of emotional development (Hunt, 1961). One of the most influential explanations stemmed from the theorizing of Hebb (1946, 1949) and has been called "discrepancy theory." More specifically, perceptual encounters with events in the environment were said to establish a set of memory bases against which new stimuli and events are compared. The degree

---

[1]Epigenesis refers to the differentiation and the emergence of new physiological and psychological structures from simpler and more global ones. Epigenesis contrasts with older views that stress development as growth of preexisting structures. Virtually all contemporary epigenetic views assume that development occurs as a consequence of organism–environment interactions, but differ in the degree of emphasis they give to one interactant.

of discrepancy from past experience then accounts for both the intensity and the affective valence of an event, with moderate but assimilable discrepancy resulting in smiles of assimilation and unresolvable mismatch resulting in frank distress.

Another influential epigenetic explanation, taken by ethologists and psychoanalysts, emphasizes the importance of neurophysiological maturation in the development of emotion. This biobehavioral approach focuses on maturation as a central organizer for emotional development to explain qualitative changes in emotion that coincide with major changes across domains of functioning—cognition, perception, and social behavior (Bowlby, 1973; Emde, Gaensbauer, & Harmon, 1976; Spitz, 1965). In contrast to discrepancy theory, biobehavioral approaches suggest that emotional development is principally (although not exclusively) maturational and a result of the endogenous unfolding of a genetic blueprint. Although noting the importance of deprivation of social interaction and physical stimulation, biobehavioral approaches otherwise paid little attention to less extreme environmental factors outside the individual that can modify the course of emotional development.

Both epigenetic accounts offer single-process explanations of emotional development, either in very general terms (i.e., rapid brain development as a central organizer affecting many domains of functioning simultaneously) or in more specific terms (i.e., degree of discrepancy from past experience as the organizer of subsequent emotional development). The epigenetic perspective we present differs from these accounts in several ways. We agree that multiple processes, both experiential and neurophysiological, underlie emotional development, but we propose a more constructionist stance, in which developmental changes, especially in emotion, come about as a function of quite specific transactions between the organism and the environment. In addition, we stress the person's active role in the generation of very specific experiences that lead to emotional development, rather than the person's passive exposure to stimulation. Finally, we propose that issues of process cannot be studied without regard to the physical and social context in which they operate, and cannot be adequately interpreted without considering the effects on future development of the physical and social changes brought about by the process in the first place. In sum, our perspective highlights the crucial organizing role of changes in the relation of the person to the environment in the development of both structural and functional changes in emotion.

We propose two central epigenetic principles to guide our search in identifying specific experiences that organize emotional development and that, in turn, profoundly change the nature of the interaction of the organism with the social and physical world. These principles, derived from the conceptual framework of Kuo (1976), Gottlieb (1983, 1991), and Lerner (1986, 1991), are as follows:

Principle I. The appearance of a developmental change can generate experiences that set the stage for widespread changes in psychological development. These changes are then reflected in long-lasting and pervasive changes in the organism's relation to the environment.

Principle II. Changes in the person bring about bidirectional changes in person–environment relations that set the stage for further development.

The period of infancy provides particular insight into these principles of epigenetic change because of the number of transitions infants undergo, the rapidity of change, and the widespread effects of these developments on infants and their environments. Nowhere in infancy are the ways in which new abilities radically alter infants' relation to the environment more apparent than in attainment of motoric acquisitions (Bertenthal, Campos, & Barrett, 1984). As infants begin to reach, crawl, and walk, their space for exploration and action expands dramatically to encompass more of the world around them. A powerful way in which motoric acquisitions drive development comes about through events and obstacles the organism encounters daily and the subsequent adaptations to these new demands. As the infant gains new capabilities, these new abilities necessarily result in new experiences. The encounters and adaptations bring about still other important changes in the relation of the organism to the environment. In sum, motoric developments bring about new levels of intentionality, new means by which goals can be attained, new opportunities for both success and frustration in dealing with the world, new attributions from the parents, different qualities of emotional response from the caregivers, and a substantially reorganized emotional constellation in the infant.

In this chapter we present evidence on how the acquisition of one motoric skill—self-produced locomotion via prone progression—generates many new experiences, and how these experiences are orchestrated to bring about emotional development. More specifically, we instantiate Principle I by examining the epigenetic basis for the development of wariness of heights. We illustrate the degree to which self-produced locomotion establishes the experiential groundwork, through the act of coupling visual and vestibular input, for the emergence of fear of heights. We instantiate Principle II by demonstrating how locomotor experience sets the stage for socioemotional changes in the family system, including increases in anger displays and other positive and negative emotions.

LOCOMOTOR EXPERIENCE, EPIGENETIC
PROCESSES, AND THE WARINESS OF HEIGHTS

Because fear (or, in its less intense form, wariness) of heights is basic to our everyday survival, many researchers have assumed a maturational basis for its origins, suggesting that the subject is genetically predisposed to respond to heights with fear (Emde, Gaensbauer, & Harmon, 1976; Freedman, 1974; Kagan, Kearsley, & Zelazo, 1978). However, three decades of research have sharply called into question any simple maturational explanation. Far from the result of a phylogenetically entrained behavioral unfolding, wariness of heights arises in infancy as a function of experientially constructed processes, ones that are engendered by self-produced locomotion (Campos, Bertenthal, & Kermoian, 1992; Campos, Hiatt, Ramsay, Henderson, & Svejda, 1978). As such, understanding the processes by which locomotor experience facilitates the emergence of wariness of heights may afford a fundamental insight into explanations of important developmental changes in emotion in other states besides fear.

The link between locomotion and avoidance of heights indicating fear is nothing new; in fact, Walk and Gibson (1961), in their seminal monograph on visual depth perception, concluded that avoidance of depth-at-an-edge, while governed by essentially innate mechanisms, nonetheless awaited the maturation of locomotor capacities for its manifestation. Their general principle was that avoidance of heights is evident as soon as the animal can locomote. Locomotion, for Walk and Gibson and for many of the researchers who followed them, thus served not as an experiential means for engendering the emergence of avoidance of heights but as a maturational acquisition that permitted depth perception to be clearly manifested by an animal. The possibility that the fear of heights was the epigenetic outcome of processes brought about by experiences with locomotion was never seriously considered.

THE IMPORTANCE OF EXPERIENCE
ON VISUAL CLIFF BEHAVIOR

Although reports since Walk and Gibson (1961) have established in a number of species the influence of rearing environments on depth avoidance (e.g., Schiffman, 1970; Seitz, Seitz, & Kaufman, 1973), the animal work of Hein and his colleagues best exemplifies an experiential epigenetic account of the emergence of wariness of heights. Although not assessing fear per se, Held and Hein's (1963; Hein, 1972) work rendered the maturationist position less tenable by demonstrating the importance of self-produced locomotion in various aspects of visually guided behavior.

Held and Hein manipulated the manner in which dark-reared kitten littermates received exposure to patterned visual stimulation by using a "carousel." The carousel is a cylindrical device in which one kitten's active movements were mechanically yoked to a gondola within which the kitten's littermate was passively transported. Both the active and the passively moved kittens thus received equivalent amounts of visual stimulation, but only one member of the pair obtained systematically self-generated visual stimulation and sensorimotor coordination. Each kitten was then tested on the visual cliff (Gibson & Walk, 1960), a table with a glass top divided into a "deep" side, with a patterned surface four feet beneath the top and a "shallow" side, with a patterned surface directly below the glass. Those kittens who had experience moving actively responded to the visual cliff by descending to the shallow side, but not to the deep side; in sharp contrast, the passively transported kittens responded by descending to the deep side as readily as to the shallow.

When subsequently given the opportunity to locomote in an illuminated environment, the kittens who had previously been passively transported systematically avoided the deep side. However, these passively moved kittens required significantly more hours of experience with coupling visual stimulation and self-produced movement to demonstrate visual cliff behavior comparable to that of their active littermates (Hein, Held, & Gower, 1970). From these results, Hein and his collaborators concluded that the emergence of visually controlled behavior depends on experience with visual stimulation that systematically co-occurs with, and derives from, self-produced movement. Furthermore, asystematic visuomotor experience actually undermined the development of visually guided behavior, a point that underscores the importance of specific experience in the development of performance on the visual cliff.

To rule out the possibility that the passively moved kittens were somehow delayed in developing motor control relative to the actively moving ones, a study was done in which the same animal served as both the experimental (actively moving) subject and the comparison (passively moved) subject. This feat was brought about by allowing dark-reared kittens to move about actively on the kitten carousel while one eye was covered. The same kittens were also exposed to passively generated visual stimulation by exposing the previously covered eye while moved about in the gondola. When tested monocularly on the visual cliff with the eye uncovered while actively moving, the kittens consistently descended onto the shallow side of the cliff. When tested with the eye uncovered while passively moved about, however, the same kittens failed to perform differentially toward the shallow and deep sides (Hein & Diamond, 1971). Taken as a whole, these studies demonstrate the importance of specific, actively generated experience, through an animal's interactions with the environment, in understanding the emergence of visually guided behavior on the deep or the shallow side of the cliff.

Can we infer fear or wariness of heights from these assessments of visually guided behavior? Methodologically, Hein and his colleagues employed a preference procedure whereby kittens were placed on a centerboard that bisects the visual cliff into a deep and a shallow side and were allowed to descend to either side. Although systematic preference for one side entails avoidance of the other side, as such, their results actually assess a preference for one side versus the other; only by inference can we say that preference for one side of the cliff implies fearfulness of the other side.

In their reexamination of Held and Hein's (1963) kitten findings, Walk, Shepherd, and Miller (1988) argued for precisely this distinction between preference and fear. When dark-reared kittens were passively exposed to light, deprived of any visuomotor feedback from self-produced locomotion, but given an attention-stimulating environment to view, these kittens preferentially descended to the shallow side of the visual cliff just like those who actively generated correlated visuomotor feedback through self-produced locomotion. This finding shows that in the absence of locomotor experience, a kitten's passive exposure to a stimulating environment is sufficient for the development of preference for the shallow side.

Walk et al. (1988) suggested that these results, as well as those of Hein and colleagues, demonstrate that behavioral discrimination of depth does not depend on locomotor experience. However, depth perception and preference for the shallow side may be dissociable from fearfulness, and locomotor experience may influence the development of emotion more than that of depth perception. This distinction between preference and wariness is particularly noteworthy because studies with human infants have not typically employed a preference procedure.

To examine the effect of testing condition in infant behavior, Walk (1969) compared human infants in a "bisection" condition, comparable to Held and Hein's (1963) preference paradigm, with infants in the more commonly used "crossing" condition. In the crossing condition, infants are placed on the centerboard of the cliff and are then coaxed by their mothers to cross over either the deep or shallow side, whereas in the bisection condition, infants move to their mothers down a narrowing centerboard and can "choose" to move onto either the deep or the shallow side. Walk (1969) showed that infants with little locomotor experience almost exclusively moved to the shallow side in the bisection condition, but were able to be coaxed over the deep side in the crossing condition. Walk et al. (1988) concluded, therefore, that the bisection procedure demonstrated the presence of depth perception, at the same time that infants with minimal locomotor experience were showing little avoidance of crossing the deep side to reach the mother. In summary, there is convincing evidence that locomotor experience affects avoidance of heights, but not necessarily the perception of depth.

IMPORTANCE OF EXPERIENCE IN WARINESS
OF HEIGHTS IN HUMAN INFANTS

In studies of human infants conducted in our laboratory, a number of research methods have been used to study the link between locomotor experience and the emergence of wariness of heights. For instance, to compare prelocomotor and locomotor infants we developed a method of assessing wariness that does not require infants to crawl across the cliff. Infants are instead lowered over each side of the visual cliff while their heart rates are sampled. The use of heart rate to index fear is based on the assumption that cardiac decelerations accompany increases in attention and orienting, and that cardiac accelerations accompany increases in muscular tension, and respiratory depth and frequency.[2]

Comparisons between prelocomotor and locomotor infants at 7.3 months of age revealed significant differences between the groups. Locomotor infants showed significant cardiac acceleration when lowered over the deep side of the cliff but not over the shallow side (Bertenthal & Campos, 1990; Bertenthal et al., 1984). In contrast, prelocomotor infants showed no difference in cardiac acceleration from baseline on either the deep or shallow sides. The onset of locomotion thus precedes evidence of wariness of heights.[3]

To assess the role of experience on the emergence of wariness, we have employed converging research operations analogous to the "enrichment" and "deprivation" research strategies commonly used by psychobiologists. Prelocomotor infants with enriched opportunities for locomotor experience provided in the form of "walker" usage showed cardiac accelerations when lowered over the deep side of the cliff, in contrast to

---

[2]The fundamental assumption linking the direction of heart rate change to attentiveness and wariness has been confirmed by using stimuli other than heights that show a developmental shift from attentiveness to wariness, such as various studies using the infant's reaction to approaching strangers (e.g., Campos, 1976; Campos, Emde, Gaensbauer, & Henderson, 1975; Kagan, 1974; Kagan & Lewis, 1965; Sroufe & Waters, 1977).

[3]It is important to note that differences in cardiac activity in infants with different locomotor histories do not reflect the development of depth perception. Every infant lowered to the shallow side of the cliff, whether prelocomotor or locomotor, extended arms in preparation for contact with the approaching solid surface, whereas no infant showed a visual placing response on the deep side. In fact, infants as young as 2 months of age discriminate the deep from the shallow side, in the form of cardiac deceleration over the deep side (Campos, Langer, & Krowitz, 1970).

matched prelocomotor comparison infants who had no walker experience and whose heart rates were deceleratory. Similarly, we studied "deprivation" of locomotor experience in a longitudinal case study of an orthopedically handicapped infant who was delayed in locomotor onset because of the use of a heavy cast applied to correct a clubfoot condition. Only at 10 months of age, after the cast had been removed and he had begun to move independently, did this infant respond with cardiac acceleration when lowered over the deep side of the cliff. These results demonstrate that even in the absence of the development of prone progression, infants' active movement experience facilitated the emergence of wariness of heights (Campos, Bertenthal, & Kermoian, 1992).

Additional evidence for the role of experience comes from tests of infants differing in duration of locomotor experience and using the crossing procedure described earlier in which the mother calls to the infant from over the deep or the shallow side of the cliff. The longer infants had been locomoting the more likely they were to avoid the deep side of the cliff. These findings on the duration of locomotor experience held regardless of whether infants began to crawl somewhat early (at 6 months), at a normative age (about 7 months), or somewhat late (about 8 months). In sum, the use of different research methods and converging research operations reveals a highly consistent picture of the emergence of wariness of heights in the human infant: Self-produced locomotor experience facilitates the development of both cardiac and behavioral avoidance indices of wariness (Campos, Bertenthal, et al., 1992).

CRITIQUE OF HUMAN WORK

The conclusion that locomotor experience is important for the onset of wariness of heights has been challenged by several researchers. Scarr and Salapatek (1970) first reported a negative correlation between avoidance of the deep side of the cliff and locomotor experience, suggesting that more experience locomoting predicted less avoidance of the deep side of the visual cliff. Underscoring this finding, Rader and her colleagues (Rader, Bausano, & Richards, 1980; Richards & Rader, 1981, 1983) found that the age at which infants begin to locomote predicted avoidance on the cliff more readily than experience with locomotion. Moreover, duration of locomotor experience failed to predict avoidance independent of age of locomotor onset. Specifically, Rader and colleagues reported that, in general, infants who began locomoting at an early age crossed the deep side, whereas infants who began locomoting later in infancy avoided the deep side. These findings suggested to Rader and her colleagues the notion of a maturationally determined visuomotor program that enabled locomoting infants to utilize visual information that affords a traversable surface in directing their behavior. If infants begin to locomote prior to the maturation of this program, then they will rely on tactile information to guide their action on the cliff. As a result of this formulation, Rader and her colleagues questioned the mediation of avoidance of heights by locomotor experience.

Replying to this challenge, Bertenthal and Campos (1984) pointed to the presumption in Rader's work of a linear relation between locomotor experience and wariness of heights. If locomotor experience is associated with wariness of heights in a nonlinear, step-function manner, then the points of experience at which infants are sampled are crucial for an accurate assessment of the qualitative shift in functioning. In fact, Campos and his colleagues have consistently found that 1 month of crawling experience is sufficient for the emergence of wariness of heights. Rader and her colleagues, however, selected infants with either one or two months of locomotor experience. Her studies may thus have sampled the subsequent plateau in responding and missed the point of transition, generating interpretational ambiguity. This ambiguity in Rader's work, coupled with the converging research evidence from the work of both Hein and Campos and their colleagues, provides convincing evidence for locomotor experience as an antecedent of wariness of heights (Campos, Bertenthal, et al., 1992).

A PROCESS ACCOUNT OF THE EMERGENCE OF WARINESS OF HEIGHTS

What specifically about locomotor experience gives rise to wariness of heights? In previous publications, we speculated on two factors—falling experiences (Walk, 1966) and emotional communication from the mother when the child is approaching a dangerous dropoff (Campos & Stenberg, 1981). However, neither of these can account for the behavior of kittens in the carousel studies, in which not only were falls associated with heights experimentally precluded, but the mother cat was not in the cliff room to signal to her kittens.

As an alternative hypothesis, we have more recently attempted to explain the onset of wariness of heights as the result of two experientially produced perceptual constructions that are brought about by experience locomoting. The constructions are (a) the use of peripheral optic flow that creates a sense of self-motion, and (b) the coordination of the visual information that specifies self-motion with vestibular and kinesthetic stimulation that specifies the same activity. The explanation then proposes that heights generally involve conditions in which vestibular and kines-thetic input exist (e.g., because of head movements), but in which peripheral visual stimulation is absent or greatly diminished (because when one looks down from a height, the ground that creates the peripheral visual stimulation is absent). Finally, the explanation holds that visual–vestibular decoupling of the sort encountered in heights is affectively disturbing, and sufficient to mediate avoidance behavior (Bertenthal & Campos, 1990). This hypothesis clearly illustrates the principle that a developmental acquisition in one domain creates experiences that make the emergence of new psychological phenomena in rather different domains possible.

LOCOMOTOR EXPERIENCE AND SENSITIVITY TO VISUAL PROPRIOCEPTION

Our explanation of the onset of wariness of heights begins with Gibson's (1979) notion of visual proprioception. This term refers to the fact that visual information can specify self-movement independent of kinesthetic feedback from the vestibular system, or the muscles, joints, and skin. Visual proprioception operates as follows: As an observer moves through the environment, the visual system receives specific patterns of optic flow that specify the observer's direction and velocity of motion. When the observer's line of sight coincides with the direction of motion, these patterns of optic flow assume a radial (i.e., expanding) structure in the central visual field, and a lamellar (i.e., parallel) structure in the visual periphery. According to Gibson, these patterns of optic flow (radial and lamellar) are sufficient to create in the perceiver a sense of self-movement. Gibson proposed that these patterns are either innately effective, or require detection only through perceptual learning to be effective. We shall present evidence that experience with self-produced locomotion makes functional the detection of peripheral optic flow (more specifically, that only after experience with self-produced locomotion does the infant respond with self-movement to peripheral optic flow displays alone).

Evidence that observers use visual information to detect self-motion even in the absence of kinesthetic feedback comes from a series of studies of adults and children conducted in a "moving room." In this apparatus the walls and ceiling can be moved around an observer who is, in fact, stationary, but who nevertheless experiences the illusion of self-motion. Both adults and young children demonstrate postural compensation especially to peripheral optic flow patterns, as if they themselves had moved, even though—to reiterate—the subject in fact has not moved (e.g., Bertenthal & Bai, 1989; Lishman & Lee, 1973). These findings related to the moving room suggest that optic flow in the visual field specifies self-motion so powerfully that it overrides vestibular and kinesthetic stimulation providing the opposite perceptual information (viz., that there was no self-motion).

By 7 months, infants show signs of integrating visual and vestibular input by responding with postural compensation to optic flow patterns that include both radial and lamellar structure (Berthenthal & Bai, 1989). In our laboratory we have found that only following locomotor onset do infants posturally compensate to peripheral lamellar optic flow in the absence of central optic flow (Higgins, Campos, & Kermoian, 1994). Prelocomotor infants of the same age who have had experience moving in a walker show postural compensations to lamellar peripheral optic flow comparable to endogenously locomoting infants. These findings suggest that experience engendered through self-produced locomotion facilitates the progressive specification of optic flow in the perception of self-motion. Locomotor experience, in other words, enables the infant to perceive self-motion by using increasingly smaller portions of the visual field (i.e., a shift from needing both radial and lamellar optic flow to needing only lamellar flow in the visual periphery to specify self-motion). How, in turn, do infants finely tune visual–vestibular coordination so as to respond to peripheral visual optic flow by itself?

We have proposed that prelocomotor and locomotor infants have vastly different exposures to peripheral optic flow while moving forward. More specifically, locomotor infants must visually attend to their spatial layout as they direct themselves forward. In so doing, they will typically direct their line of sight in a manner that spatially coincides with the direction of their motion. Since locomotor infants direct their attention along their line of movement, they experience congruence between vestibular feedback about angular acceleration, and visual input about forward motion. (Given that the visual periphery encompasses such a large portion of the visual field, optic flow in the visual periphery—specifically, lamellar optic flow— becomes primary to the perception of self-motion.) Thus, locomoting infants will increasingly experience a strong degree of correlation between specific visual and vestibular inputs specifying self-motion.

In contrast, few experiences in the everyday lives of prelocomotor infants constrain their direction of looking during movement. When pre-locomotor infants are passively moved, nothing demands that they direct their attention toward their forward line of motion. As such, the visual input they receive while being moved forward can take any number of patterns besides the lamellar one, depending on the infant's head and body position while carried. Prelocomotor infants, therefore, will rarely experience correlated visual–vestibular input specifying self-motion.

To summarize the argument so far, we propose that as infants gain experience moving themselves voluntarily, they construct specific patterns of correspondence between the optical and vestibular input as they move. Through the experience of constructing these correlated inputs, infants increasingly expect the specific correlations they generate. This expectation creates the basis for the process that results in the emergence of fear of heights. In the context of heights, the expectation of visual and vestibular information jointly specifying the same degree and direction of self-movement is violated: When at an edge, the infant gets vestibular feedback from head movement, but very little peripheral optic flow because depth typically lacks peripheral visual texture—there is no more ground around oneself. This discrepancy may lead infants to experience a sense of vertigo, or loss of balance, either of which can lead to dysphoria, and may cause avoidance of heights or cardiac accelerations.

In conclusion, we propose that the generation of fear of heights involves the violation of a specific expectation of correlated visual and vestibular input specifying self-movement. This expectation constitutes the basis for a significant person–event transaction, such as an expectation of a possible loss of support. A central part of the affective significance in visual–vestibular mismatch derives from the hedonic quality of vestibular stimulation itself, which can be a powerful source of negative emotion.

VISUAL PROPRIOCEPTION AND WARINESS OF HEIGHTS: AN EXPERIMENTAL TEST

Recent evidence from our laboratory provides preliminary support for the hypothesis that fear of heights may be predicted by the degree of responsiveness of newly locomoting infants to peripheral optic flow specifying self-motion (Witherington, Campos, & Kermoian, 1995). In this study, we have tested 8.5-month-old locomoting infants both in the moving-room apparatus and on the visual cliff. We hypothesized that infants' postural compensation to lamellar optic flow presented to the visual periphery in the moving room would predict avoidance of the deep side of the visual cliff, and, conversely, that low levels of postural responsiveness to peripheral optic flow would be related to minimal visual cliff avoidance. Our findings have so far supported the hypothesis: Coordination of postural compensation with direction and velocity of peripheral optic flow as assessed in the moving room strongly predicts avoidance of the deep side of the visual cliff. Thus, sensitivity to peripheral optic flow derived from locomotor experience appears to facilitate the emergence of wariness of heights.

LOCOMOTOR EXPERIENCE ORGANIZES SOCIOEMOTIONAL CHANGES IN PERSON/ENVIRONMENT RELATIONS

In the studies of wariness of heights, locomotion was shown to make possible a number of new experiences, such as the coupling of visual and vestibular information that in turn facilitated the emergence of emotion in new contexts. However, locomotion may act through strikingly different processes to change the relation between infants and their social world. In our work, we have begun to delineate how locomotor experience serves as a setting event for changes in the quality and intensity of the expression of affect by both infants and their parents (Campos, Kermoian, & Zumbahlen, 1992). In addition, we hypothesized how such changes in the family system following the onset of infant creeping set the stage for future developments in the infant.

CHANGES IN ANGER IN THE FAMILY SYSTEM

We expected that the radical changes in infants and their environments following the onset of creeping would produce a major reorganization in the affective climate of the family. For example, as infants begin to move independently, we predicted that they would be more likely to engage in behavior that is unacceptable to the parents, such as manipulating dangerous objects. Such encounters would make infants likely recipients of parental anger and might also serve as a sign to the parents of their infants' autonomy and the need to expect their infants to be increasingly responsible for their own actions. These new parental attributions of responsibility would thus create expectations for infants to comply to their parents' rules of conduct; violations of those rules could then lead to parental anger.

Findings come from a study in which we interviewed parents of prelocomotor and locomotor 8-month-old infants about changes taking place in their parenting behavior and their infants' behavior in the past weeks. We found that although all of the parents clearly acknowledged that their infants had goals and intentions, only the parents whose infants were moving about voluntarily began to expect their infants to choose goals that the parents deemed appropriate. Specifically, parents of locomotor infants began to make new demands of their infants, as if to teach them right from wrong, and began to expect their infants to at least attempt to comply with their demands.

The parents of locomoting infants principally made new demands by using their voices to regulate their infants' behavior. This use of the voice may become salient because parents find it tiresome to continually remove the infant from a prohibited object. In addition, parents may not be able to move rapidly enough to remove their infants from danger. Thus, the voice can be effective across distances, and, unlike facial expressions, does not require the infants to orient toward the parents to receive the emotional communication. However, the most important characteristic of the voice is that it is peremptory; it can be graded in intensity and modulated in tonal pattern to produce the desired effect of encouraging or inhibiting infant behavior. It is thus not surprising that parents rely on vocal signaling after their infants begin to crawl, given the unique qualities of vocal communications for distal interaction.

In addition to parents' regulating their infants' behavior via vocal signals, only parents of locomoting infants reported physically punishing their infants as a means of controlling prohibited behavior. A typical context for use of punishment was one in which the parents' utterance of "no," even in a stern tone of voice, was not enough to gain the infants' compliance. The parents' use of punishment in such contexts seemed multidetermined. It represented the parents' new concerns about socializing infants to parental goals, the increased importance to parents that their infants meet their expectations, and the parents' emerging recognition that verbal signals alone, in the absence of physical action, may not always bring about compliance.

Taken together, these findings suggest that the onset of locomotion affects parents' socialization of their infants and begins the process of actively preparing infants for entry into a larger world—a world with increased social demands, physical dangers, and opportunities. Although these findings may imply that changes in the infant following locomotor onset come about primarily as a consequence of new parental attribution, our data suggest that such an interpretation is overly simplistic: Infants are also changing as a consequence of their own activity.

We hypothesized that many of the emotional changes taking place in infants following the onset of locomotion stem from the close link that exists between infants' emotions and their goals (Campos, Campos, & Barrett, 1989; Campos, Mumme, Kermoian, & Campos, 1994; Frijda, 1986; Lazarus, 1991). Positive affect in the newly locomoting infants should increase as a result of new levels of self-efficacy as goals are attained; negative affect should similarly increase as a result of the frustration experienced as infants' newly attainable goals are thwarted. With the onset of locomotion, then, infants are likely to undergo a burgeoning of both positive and negative affect because self-produced locomotion generates the possibility of new goals, new means to obtain these goals, and new opportunities for clashes between infants' goals and those of social agents.

In our interview study, the clearest change reported by parents of locomotor infants was the increase in their infants' expression of anger, including the frequency, intensity, and patterning of anger. Parents of locomotors reported that their infants were more likely to express anger, show extreme displays of anger, and have temper tantrums. These increases in anger seemed to be the result of frustrated attempts by locomoting infants to attain a goal. Parents of locomotor infants also reported that their infants were more difficult to distract and would no longer accept the parental offer of another goal or activity. In sum, our data show dramatic changes in both infants and their parents following the onset of locomotion.

CHANGES IN ATTACHMENT AND POSITIVE AFFECT

In addition to major changes in parental expression of anger following locomotor onset, we expected that parents would give new meaning to their infants' proximity. Before infants become mobile, parents can control the distance of their infants from them; afterward, infants begin to share in the control of proximity. Infants' initiative in moving away from their parents may, in turn, lead to changes in parental affection: What parents lose in time near their infants may be compensated for by increases in the intensity of affection when the dyad is close. It is also possible that after infants begin to move, their parents perceive them as more independent, more like a "real person," and more fun to interact with. As a result, parents may begin to express more "grown-up" affection, for example, by decreasing rocking. Indeed, we found that parents of locomotor infants tended to report changes in the intensity and quality of expression of positive affect toward their infants such as tighter hugs, rougher play, and vocal expressions of affection.

Just as we predicted that locomotion would change the parents' relation to their infants, we predicted that crawling should reorganize the infants' emotional life by altering their attachment system. The capacity to seek proximity may bring about the transition to use the parents as discriminated attachment figures (Ainsworth, Blehar, Waters, & Wall, 1978; Bowlby, 1969). Specifically, locomotion should markedly facilitate the use of parents as both a secure base for exploration and a haven of safety. According to ethological attachment theory, the new use of parents as differentiated attachment figures may then increase the infants' sensitivity to their departures. As a result, new and higher levels of separation distress may be evident. In sum, by reason of ecological, motivational, signaling, and instrumental behavioral factors, crawling onset may be crucial for understanding changes in infants' emotional development (Mahler, Pine, & Bergman, 1975).

Our interview study confirmed many of these predictions. Locomotor infants were reported to have heightened reactions to their parents' departures—becoming both more aware of such comings and goings, and more likely to respond to departures with pre-cry faces and mild fussing. In addition to the heightened level of response to parental departure, locomotor infants' responses appeared to be specific to the parents, and could not be accounted for as a new response to being left alone, in the company of a stranger, or even a familiar person other than the parents. Further reports of new forms of attachment included increases in positive emotionality, with locomotor infants being more likely to show new or more intense affection such as hugging, kissing, and patting of their parents.

AFFECTING THE FUTURE: HOW CHANGES BROUGHT ABOUT BY ONE PROCESS THEN LAY THE BASIS FOR OTHER NEW PROCESSES

The process of epigenesis does not stop with the change in the family system that locomotion brings about. On the contrary, these changes bring about new emotional and social–cognitive developments in the child. Since the child is now expected to comply to parental demands, and because the child shows a new pattern of attachment to the parents, we would expect that emotions that depend heavily on approval and disapproval from significant others—emotions such as shame, pride, and guilt would have their ontogenetic roots during this period of increased intentionality by the child, and increased emotional communication from the parent. The changes in the family system can also lead to encouragement (or discouragement) of exploration and problem solving by the child, with consequent improvements in cognitive abilities. In sum, each developmental acquisition lays the basis for subsequent epigenetic acquisitions.

CONCLUSION

The onset of wariness of heights and socioemotional changes in the family following creeping onset described in this chapter highlight the importance of experience in epigenetic processes. These significant emotional changes illustrate how the emergence of a nodal skill, the onset of locomotion, can reorganize the relation of infants to their environments and set the stage for future development. New experiences gained as infants move independently through space generate a family of processes that influence subsequent development. More specifically, as infants locomote they actively generate specific patterns of correlated visual/vestibular input. Through this process infants come to expect this correlated input and react with wariness in circumstances that violate this new expectation.

The onset of locomotion affects the infants' experiences within the family through different processes than those associated with wariness of heights. As infants begin to move in their environment, parents and infants change dramatically to meet the new demands arising from the infants' mobility. This change includes parental attempts at regulation of infant behavior through distal vocal communication and physical punishment, as well as displaying new forms of affection (e.g., "tighter hugs") when their infants return from forays in the environment. A similar reorganization is seen in infants' behavior following locomotor onset, including greater expression of both positive and negative affect as a result of new experiences they encounter, and more mature displays of attachment to the primary caregiver. In sum, one significant developmental acquisition, the onset of self-produced locomotion, brings about a host of new experiences, each of which has specific effects on infants and their activities in the environment. Infants' experiences in the new settings then provide the foundation for future developmental advances.

Although it may seem surprising that changes in motoric development can have such profound emotional consequences, the new experiences generated by being able to move independently result in infants and those around them attaching new meaning and value to environmental encounters. We have theorized that such encounters become emotional by virtue of the new significance they hold for the individual—through the relation to one's goals, through the social signals of others, through their relation to hedonic stimulation, and by their evocation of schematic processes; specifically, memories of past encounters (Campos et al., 1994).

For example, decoupling of visual and vestibular information does not alone give rise to wariness of heights. The hedonic value of vestibular stimulation that accompanies visual/vestibular decoupling may be appraised as a threat involving the infant's loss of support and thereby contribute to the affective value of visual/vestibular decoupling. Similarly, new encounters infants have as they begin to locomote are not in and of themselves emotional, but gain their affective valence from the dramatic increase in opportunities for goal-congruent and goal-incongruent person–environment interactions and from equally dramatic increases in the possibilities for negative and positive social signals and communications from others. Thus, locomotor experience generates affect through a set of person–environment processes that render events personally significant.

These salient processes may arise through many domains of functioning that are not intrinsically emotional. They include perception, cognition, and motor skills. From the experiential epigenetic perspective taken here, all points of transition in the significance of person–event relations constitute fertile ground for predicting emotional development. It is at these times of transition that an individual's concerns expand to new social and environmental contexts, pacing ongoing and subsequent emotional change.

In closing, we would like to discuss the differences between developmental acquisitions that result in widespread emotional changes, and those that do not. The developmental changes that we believe will forecast major emotional changes are those that markedly influence the relation of the infant to his or her environment. These changes include phenomena like shifts in optical scanning, reaching, walking, and talking. By contrast, developmental changes such as the onset of consistent handedness or the permanent coloring of the iris of the infant's eyes do not produce developmental transitions. The degree of relational consequence of the developmental acquisition is what ultimately matters for determining times of major and widespread developmental changes.

ACKNOWLEDGMENTS

The preparation of this chapter and the research reported here were supported by grants from the National Institute of Child Health and Human Development (HD–25066), the John D. and Catherine T. MacArthur Foundation, and the MacArthur Foundation Network on Developmental Transitions.

This chapter was written while the first author was a Fellow at the Center for Advanced Study in the Behavioral Sciences. He is grateful for the support of the National Science Foundation (Grant # SBR–9022192), and from the John D. and Catherine T. MacArthur Foundation (Grant # 8900078).

REFERENCES

Ainsworth, M. D. S., Blehar, M., Waters, E., & Wall, S. (1978). *Patterns of attachment*. Hillsdale, NJ: Lawrence Erlbaum Associates.

Bertenthal, B. I., & Bai, D. L. (1989). Infants' sensitivity to optical flow for controlling posture. *Developmental Psychology, 25*, 936–945.

Bertenthal, B. I., & Campos, J. J. (1984). A reexamination of fear and its determinants on the visual cliff. *Psychophysiology, 21*, 413–417.

Bertenthal, B. I., & Campos, J. J. (1990). A systems approach to the organizing effects of self-produced locomotion during infancy. In C. Rovee-Collier & L. P. Lipsitt (Eds.), *Advances in infancy research* (Vol. 6, pp. 1–60). Norwood, NJ: Ablex.

Bertenthal, B. I., Campos, J. J., & Barrett, K. C. (1984). Self-produced locomotion: An organizer of emotional, cognitive, and social development in infancy. In R. Emde & R. Harmon (Eds.), *Continuities and discontinuities in development* (pp. 175–210). New York: Plenum.

Bowlby, J. (1969). *Attachment and loss: Vol. 1. Attachment*. New York: Basic Books.

Bowlby, J. (1973). *Attachment and loss: Vol. 2. Separation*. New York: Basic Books.

Campos, J. J. (1976). Heart rate: A sensitive tool for the study of emotional development. In L. P. Lipsitt (Ed.), *Developmental psychobiology: The significance of infancy* (pp. 1–34). Hillsdale, NJ: Lawrence Erlbaum Associates.

Campos, J. J., Bertenthal, B., & Kermoian, R. (1992). Early experience and emotional development: The emergence of wariness of heights. *Psychological Science, 3*, 61–64.

Campos, J., Campos, R., & Barrett, K. (1989). Emergent themes in the study of emotional development and emotion regulation. *Developmental Psychology, 25,* 394–402.

Campos, J., Emde, R., Gaensbauer, T. J., & Henderson, C. (1975). Cardiac and behavioral interrelationships in the reactions of infants to strangers. *Developmental Psychology, 11,* 589–601.

Campos, J., Hiatt, S., Ramsay, D., Henderson, C., & Svejda, M. (1978). The emergence of fear on the visual cliff. In M. Lewis & L. Rosenblum (Eds.), *The development of affect* (pp. 149–182). New York: Plenum.

Campos, J., Kermoian, R., & Zumbahlen, M. (1992). Socioemotional transformations in the family system following infant crawling onset. In N. Eisenberg & R. A. Fabes (Eds.), *New directions for child development: Emotion and its regulation in early development* (No. 55, pp. 25–40). San Francisco: Jossey-Bass.

Campos, J., Langer, A., & Krowitz, A. (1970). Cardiac responses on the visual cliff in pre-motor human infants. *Science, 170,* 195–196.

Campos, J., Mumme, D. L., Kermoian, R., & Campos, R. (1994). A functionalist perspective on the nature of emotion. *Monographs of the Society for Research in Child Development, 59* (2, 3, Whole No. 240).

Campos, J. J., & Stenberg, C. (1981). Perception, appraisal, and emotion: The onset of social referencing. In M. Lamb & L. Sherrod (Eds.), *Infant social cognition* (pp. 273–314). Hillsdale, NJ: Lawrence Erlbaum Associates.

Camras, L. A. (1992). Expressive development and basic emotions. *Cognition and Emotion, 6,* 269–283.

Dichgans, J., & Brandt, T. (1978). Visual–vestibular interactions: Effects on self-motion and postural control. In R. Held, H. W. Leibowitz, & H. L. Teuber (Eds.), *Handbook of sensory physiology* (Vol. 8, pp. 755–804). Heidelberg: Springer.

Emde, R. N., Gaensbauer, T. J., & Harmon, R. J. (1976). Emotional expression in infancy: A biobehavioral study. *Psychological Issues, 10*(1, Monograph 37).

Fogel, A., Nwokah, E., Dedo, J. Y., Messinger, D., Dickson, K. L., Matusov, E., & Holt, S. A. (1992). Social process theory of emotion: A dynamic systems approach. *Social Development, 1,* 122–142.

Freedman, D. (1974). *Human infancy: An evolutionary perspective.* Hillsdale, NJ: Lawrence Erlbaum Associates.

Frijda, N. (1986). *The emotions.* Cambridge: Cambridge University Press.

Gibson, J. J. (1979). *An ecological approach to visual perception.* Boston: Houghton-Mifflin.

Gibson, E. J., & Walk, R. D. (1960). The "visual cliff." *Scientific American, 202,* 64–71.

Gottlieb, G. (1983). The psychobiological approach to developmental issues. In M. Haith & J. Campos (Eds.), *Handbook of child psychology: Vol. 2. Infancy and developmental psychobiology* (pp. 1–26). New York: Wiley.

Gottlieb, G. (1991). Experiential canalization of behavioral development: Theory. *Developmental Psychology, 27,* 4–13.

Hebb, D. (1946). On the nature of fear. *Psychological Review, 53,* 259–276.

Hebb, D. (1949). *The organization of behavior.* New York: Wiley.

Hein, A. (1972). Acquiring components of visually guided behavior. In A. Pick (Ed.), *Minnesota symposia on child psychology* (Vol. 6, pp. 53–68). Minneapolis: University of Minnesota Press.

Hein, A., & Diamond, R. M. (1971). Contrasting development of visually triggered and guided movements in kittens with respect to interocular and interlimb equivalence. *Journal of Comparative and Physiological Psychology, 76,* 219–224.

Hein, A., Held, R., & Gower, E. C. (1970). Development and segmentation of visually controlled movement by selective exposure during rearing. *Journal of Comparative and Physiological Psychology, 73,* 181–187.

Held, R., & Hein, A. (1963). Movement-produced stimulation in the development of visually-guided behavior. *Journal of Comparative and Physiological Psychology, 56,* 872–876.

Higgins, C., Campos, J., & Kermoian, R. (1994). *The origins of visual proprioception.* Manuscript under review.

Hunt, J. McV. (1961). *Intelligence and experience.* New York: Ronald Press Co.

Kagan, J. (1974). Discrepancy, temperament and infant distress. In M. Lewis & L. Rosenblum (Eds.), *The origins of fear* (pp. 229–248). New York: Wiley.

Kagan, J., Kearsley, R. B., & Zelazo, P. R. (1978). *Infancy: Its place in human development.* Cambridge, MA: Harvard University Press.

Kagan, J., & Lewis, M. (1965). Studies of attention in the human infant. *Merrill–Palmer Quarterly, 11,* 95–127.

Kuo, Z.-Y. (1976). *The dynamics of behavior development* (Rev. ed.). New York: Plenum.

Lazarus, R. S. (1991). *Emotion and adaptation.* New York: Oxford University Press.

Lerner, R. (1986). *Concepts and theories of human development* (2nd ed.). New York: Random House.

Lerner, R. M. (1991). Changing organism–context relations as the basic process of development: A developmental contextual perspective. *Developmental Psychology, 27,* 27–32.

Lishman, J. R., & Lee, D. N. (1973). The autonomy of visual kinesthesis. *Perception, 2,* 287–294.

Mahler, M., Pine, F., & Bergman, A. (1975). *The psychological birth of the human infant.* New York: Basic Books.

Rader, N., Bausano, M., & Richards, J. E. (1980). On the nature of the visual-cliff avoidance response in human infants. *Child Development, 51,* 61–68.

Richards, J. E., & Rader, N. (1981). Crawling-onset age predicts visual cliff avoidance in infants. *Journal of Experimental Psychology: Human perception and performance, 7,* 382–387.

Richards, J. E., & Rader, N. (1983). Affective, behavioral, and avoidance responses on the visual cliff: Effects of crawling onset age, crawling experience, and testing age. *Psychophysiology, 20,* 633–641.

Scarr, S., & Salapatek, P. (1970). Patterns of fear development during infancy. *Merrill–Palmer Quarterly, 16,* 53–90.

Schiffman, H. R. (1970). Evidence for sensory dominance: Reactions to apparent depth in rabbits, cats, and rodents. *Journal of Comparative and Physiological Psychology, 71,* 38–41.

Seitz, V., Seitz, T., & Kaufman, L. (1973). Loss of depth avoidance in chicks as a function of early environmental influences. *Journal of Comparative and Physiological Psychology, 85,* 139–143.

Spitz, R. (1965). *The first year of life.* New York: International Universities Press.

Sroufe, L. A., & Waters, E. (1977). Heart rate as a convergent measure in clinical and developmental research. *Merrill–Palmer Quarterly, 23,* 3–27.

Walk, R. D. (1966). The development of depth perception in animals and human infants. *Monographs of the Society for Research in Child Development, 31* (5, Whole No. 5).

Walk, R. D. (1969). Two types of depth discrimination by the human infant with five inches of visual depth. *Psychonomic Science, 14,* 253–254.

Walk, R. D., & Gibson, E. J. (1961). A comparative and analytical study of visual depth perception. *Psychological Monographs, 75* (15, Whole No. 519).

Walk, R. D., Shepherd, J. D., & Miller, D. R. (1988). Attention and the depth perception of kittens. *Bulletin of the Psychonomic Society, 26,* 248–251.

Witherington, D., Campos, J., & Kermoian, R. (1995, March). *What makes a baby afraid of heights?* Paper presented at the meetings of the Society for Research in Child Development, Indianapolis, IN.

6

Gender, Emotional Expression, and Parent–Child Boundaries

Leslie R. Brody
Boston University

I first stumbled into the field of gender and emotion while doing a study exploring the use of projective stories to assess children's emotional expressiveness (Brody & Carter, 1982). Here, I told school-aged children a story and asked them to report on the intensity of how they or other, same-sex children might feel if they were in the story. An example story involved the child or a same-sex friend, such as Mary or John, eating a chocolate-chip cookie and then having someone take the cookie away for no reason. I asked children to indicate how intensely sad, angry, happy, and scared they would feel versus how they thought the other child, Mary or John, would feel. Children reported that Mary or John would experience more intense dysphoric feelings, such as sadness and fear, than they would themselves feel (Brody & Carter, 1982), thus suggesting that children censor socially unacceptable emotions when directly asked about them.

These results also revealed what to me was then an unexpected finding: School-aged girls attributed more intense sadness and fear to themselves than did boys; boys attributed more happiness to themselves than did girls (Brody, 1984). I was intrigued, and I began to focus my work on an exploration of gender differences in emotional functioning. Since that time, other researchers and I have replicated these results using different tasks and different age groups. For example, in recent research I have found that when I ask adult men and women to rate the intensity of their feelings in a situation developed to depict anger, such as *Your friend promised to mail an important letter for you and then forgot*, the adult females attribute more hurt to themselves than do the adult males (Brody, 1993).

In my years of doing research on gender differences in emotion, I have also learned that data on gender differences often generate strong feelings. I think these reactions speak to the overwhelming importance of gender in our lives and in our culture, and to how integrally our identities and our feelings are tied to issues surrounding gender. In response to such reactions, it is important to note that gender is only one of many individual difference characteristics, and contributes relatively little variance to the quality and intensity of various aspects of emotional functioning (LaFrance & Banaji, 1992). Knowing someone's sex tells you relatively little about their emotional expressiveness in contrast to knowing something about the history of the quality of their interactions with significant others. Recent research, in fact, shows that some gender-related personality characteristics, such as being nurturing, contribute more to the variance in the quality and intensity of expressed emotion than does biological gender (Brody, Hay, & Vandewater, 1990).

Nonetheless, many studies continue to document the existence of gender differences in emotional expressiveness, and others are beginning to try to unravel the puzzle of why such differences exist. "Why" is the most exciting question in the current work in gender and emotion, and the attempt to answer the question has led to explorations of gender differences in emotion socialization, in language, and in differing patterns of family relationships that may be internalized in the form of habitual emotional responses. The data that have emerged from these studies have important implications for our understanding of the nature of emotional development as emerging and developing within a cultural and family context.

In this chapter, I present data which indicate that adult females tend to be more intensely expressive of emotions using facial expressions and verbal language, whereas adult males more often tend to act behaviorally on their feelings and possibly to manage them through physiological means. In contrast to the adult literature, developmental data indicate that infant boys express emotions more intensely using facial and behavioral expressions than do infant girls. There thus seems to be a developmental shift in which males become less intensely facially expressive of emotions with age, whereas females become more so. In order to explain this shift, I present a transactional model of development which posits that the socialization of emotions by both parents and peers differs for boys and girls.

These socialization differences are influenced by several factors. First, because infant girls' expressions are less intense than those of infant boys, they may be harder for parents to recognize. This may lead to an emphasis on helping girls to amplify their emotional expressions. In contrast, infant boys' more intense emotional expressions would be easier for parents to match and recognize. This would mean that infant males would not have to work at, or amplify, their emotional expressions in order to be understood. Further, the fact that infant girls have an earlier propensity for verbal language may lead parents to use more emotion language with their infant daughters than with their infant sons. In response to these differences in parent behavior, infant girls would learn to talk increasingly about emotions whereas infant boys would not, in turn leading to more gender-differentiated parent–child interaction patterns.

I also present data to show that different patterns of parent–child boundary relationships for boys and girls, perhaps in response to early differences in expressiveness, influence gender differences in emotional expression. More specifically, I present data which indicate that adolescent mother–daughter boundaries are more permeable than are the boundaries of other dyads within the family (e.g., father–son, father–daughter, mother–son), and that the permeability of boundaries between family members systematically relates to the intensity of emotion expressed by adolescent daughters and sons.

Emotion socialization patterns within the family tend to be in accordance with prevailing cultural expectations concerning appropriate gender roles and are undoubtedly intergenerationally transmitted. For example, the gender role–emotion stereotype for males dictates that they should be emotionally inexpressive (with the possible exception of expressing anger), whereas the gender role–emotion stereotype for females dictates that they should be more intensely emotionally expressive. These stereotypes may contribute substantially to the emergence of gender differences in patterns of family interaction. Parents may interpret (either accurately or inaccurately) their children's emotional expressiveness as conforming to cultural gender stereotypes and interact with their sons and daughters accordingly, no doubt in some cases producing a self-fulfilling prophecy.

I have previously presented parts of the model that I will discuss in Brody (1993) and Brody and Hall (1993) and will present new data in this chapter to further support the model, as well as elaborate on the role that parent–child boundaries may have on gender differences in emotional expressiveness. The theoretical framework within which I work, like that of many developmental psychologists, assumes that emotions serve communicative, regulatory, and adaptive functions for both interpersonal relationships and intrapersonal processes. As recently outlined by Emde (1993), certain fundamental or basic emotions are evident in early infancy, while adult emotional functioning shows more marked individual differences, including gender differences, in the degree to which emotions are expressed and possibly experienced. The more complex emotional patterns that characterize the functioning of adults seem to be highly influenced by culture and socialization experiences.

ON GENDER DIFFERENCES AND STEREOTYPES

I begin by briefly reviewing the evidence that males' and females' emotional expressiveness differs, and that these differences are not simply due to tendencies to conform to social pressures concerning gender stereotypes. Strong stereotypes concerning emotional expressiveness have led some researchers to conclude that gender differences in emotional expressiveness may largely reflect self-presentational biases on the part of each sex in accordance with prevailing stereotypes; that is, females may report more intense emotions because that is what they believe they are expected to report. Many studies have indeed shown that females are stereotyped to express all emotions more intensely than males—especially sadness and fear. Even preschoolers believe that sadness, fear, and love or warmth are associated with females, and that anger is associated with males. Stereotypes tend to be stronger for expressiveness than for actual experience (Fabes & Martin, 1991), and for intensity rather than for the frequency of emotional expression.

The conclusion that self-presentational biases are at the heart of gender differences in emotional expression is an overly simplistic and misleading conclusion for several reasons. First, research that looks at the relations between self-presentational concerns as measured by the Marlowe–Crowne Social Desirability scale and the quality and intensity of emotions reported by each sex shows that either the patterns of emotion–social desirability relationships do not differ for the two sexes, or that individual differences in social-desirability tendencies bear no relationship to the quality and intensity of affects expressed (Brody, Lovas, & Hay, 1995; King & Emmons, 1990; Larsen & Diener, 1987).

Second, data indicate gender differences not only in the expression of emotion, but in the ability to recognize or decode the emotional expressions of others (Brody & Hall, 1993; Hall, 1978, 1984), an ability that is less likely to be affected by self-presentational concerns. Third, females tend not only to verbally self-report more embarrassment or shame, but to actively attempt more interpersonal reconciliation when such emotions occur (Gonzales, Pederson, Manning, & Wetter, 1990).

Finally, perhaps most importantly, even if men and women do experience emotions similarly, but express them differently because of stereotypes and social constraints, there is an emerging body of literature indicating that the disclosure and verbal expression of feelings has profound effects on physiological and behavioral functioning (King & Emmons, 1990; Pennebaker, Hughes, & O'Heeron, 1987). People who disclose their feelings have been found to have lower skin conductance levels (Pennebaker et al., 1987), while those who inhibit emotional expression have been found to have autonomic activity increases (i.e., King & Emmons, 1990), suggesting that the disclosure of feelings may have very complex effects on long-term health issues. I now turn to the data on adult gender differences in emotional expressiveness.

ADULT GENDER DIFFERENCES IN EMOTIONAL EXPRESSIVENESS

Let me first note that there is a large body of literature indicating that females are more accurate at recognizing emotion facial expressions than are males (i.e., Brody & Hall, 1993), which I will not review here. Concerning emotional expressiveness, I will address gender differences in four areas: verbal, facial, behavioral, and physiological.

Verbal Self-Report

Beginning with verbal report, consistent findings throughout the literature indicate that adult females report more intense emotional experiences than do males. The literature also suggests that females report more frequent (as opposed to intense) emotional experiences, but these data are less consistent. More specifically, females report more intense emotional experiences for both global positive and negative affects than do males using a self-report measure of affect intensity (the Affect Intensity Measure [AIM]; cf. Diener, Sandvik, & Larsen, 1985; Larsen & Diener, 1987). The AIM has been found to correlate with physiological and behavioral indices of emotional intensity, including measures of skin conductance, autonomic reactivity, daily records of emotional experiences, reported vicarious emotional responding (Eisenberg & Fabes, 1992; Larsen & Diener, 1987), and parent and peer ratings of participants' emotional intensity.

In other studies, females verbally report experiencing more intense specific dysphoric affects than do males, including more sadness, hurt, fear, embarrassment, shame, and guilt. The greater intensity and frequency of fear reported by females in this culture is perhaps the single most reliably documented gender difference in emotional expression (Croake, Myers, & Singh, 1987; Dillon, Wolf, & Katz, 1985; Highlen & Gilles, 1978; Highlen & Johnston, 1979; Kirkpatrick, 1984), although cross-cultural studies show that this difference does not appear among German men and women (Sommers & Kosmitzki, 1988), indicating that reported gender differences in emotional expression may be culturally specific.

In addition to fear, affects related to a negative appraisal of the self, including embarrassment, shame, guilt, sadness, and distress have been found to be expressed more intensely by females than by males across all age groups in American samples using both self-report and behavioral measures (Miller & Leary, 1992; Stapley & Haviland, 1989; Tangney, 1990; Zahn-Waxler, Cole, & Barrett, 1991). For example, Lewis, Sullivan, Stanger, and Weiss (1989) showed that 2-year-old females displayed more embarrassment in embarrassing situations than did males. Females also work harder than males to redress embarrassment (Gonzales et al., 1990). In contrast, an affect related to positive evaluation of the self—pride—has been found to be reported more by males in one study (Tangney, 1990), and feeling that you are better than most people is an item on the masculinity scale of the gender role scale (PAQ), on which males in many studies have been found to score more highly than females (Spence & Helmreich, 1978).

A recent study on the frequency (as opposed to the intensity) with which males and females report both experiencing and expressing emotions corroborates research on emotional intensity, in that love, liking, commitment, contentment, joy, depression, sadness, hurt, and loneliness were reported to be more frequently experienced by women (Sprecher & Sedikides, 1993). After controlling for which emotions were more frequently experienced, women were also found to report expressing anger, depression, hurt, insecurity, and anxiety more frequently than were males.

Although the expression of anger is stereotypically associated with males, gender differences in the intensity and frequency of anger by males and females tend to be inconsistent. For example, King and Emmons (1990) found that women scored more highly than did men on the expression of positive emotions, but there were no sex differences on the expression of emotions of entitlement, including anger. No sex differences in the intensity of experienced anger have also been described by Allen and Haccoun (1976) and Averill (1983). Other studies do report more intense anger on the part of males than of females, both in self-report studies (Gordis, Smith, & Mascio, 1991; Stapley & Haviland, 1989) as well as in a study of observed behavior in which preschool boys' and girls' expressions of anger were rated in free-play situations (Fabes & Eisenberg, 1991).

In contrast, infant girls were actually more likely to express anger toward mothers in a separation–reunion task than were boys, possibly because of stronger attachments between girls and their mothers (Malatesta, Culver, Tesman, & Shepard, 1989). Sprecher and Sedikides (1993) found that women reported expressing anger more than did men in the context of close relationships. These inconsistencies may well be due to the fact that the expression of anger, or indeed any emotion, is situationally specific. For example, in work by Wintre, Polivy, and Murray

(1990), school-age boys reported more anger than did girls in sad circumstances, but not in reponse to angry circumstances. In my own research, females in three different age groups, including school-age children, adolescents, and adults, reported being more intensely angry than did males, but only in situations that were frightening or in which males or females acted in male negative-stereotypic ways, including being coarse and cynical (Brody, Lovas, & Hay, 1995).

Facial Expressions

Turning now to facial expression, the data on gender differences in facial expressiveness indicate that females are more expressive of emotions than are males using naturalistic observational studies (Hall, 1984), slide-viewing paradigms in which participants watch affectively loaded slides and then judges rate their expressions (Buck, 1984) and judgments of deliberate or posed emotional expressions (Hall, 1984). Similar to the literature on gender differences in the intensity of verbally reported emotion, results for gender differences in the facial expression of anger have been inconsistent (Birnbaum & Croll, 1984; Brody & Hall, 1993).

Behavioral Expressions

Data are beginning to emerge which indicate that, especially where anger is concerned, males seem to use more direct, acting-out, or retaliatory strategies, such as hitting, whereas females use strategies such as avoidance, interpersonal reconciliation, turning against the self, and nonaggressive strategies (Cramer, 1991; Fabes & Eisenberg, 1991; Strayer, 1986; Whitesell, Robinson, & Harter, 1991). Females behaviorally manifest sadness more than do males in that they will weep more, whereas males will withdraw more from sad or depressing situations and engage in distracting activities, such as physical exercise (Nolen-Hoeksema, 1987). Females also use more expressive hand gestures and nod more in interpersonal situations than do males (Hall, 1984).

Physiological Expressions

Research on gender differences in the physiological manifestations of emotion have produced complex and confusing results. Across many studies, gender differences in the intensity of physiological measures, such as heart rate, skin conductance, and blood pressure, vary depending on the nature of the task used to elicit the measure. Does it, for example, involve self-disclosure? How gender-relevant is it? That is, does it concern interpersonal interaction versus erotic stimuli (LaFrance & Banaji, 1991)? Most often, this research is not theoretically driven and interprets gender differences post and ad hoc.

One theoretical perspective that has unified some physiological studies is that the two sexes may differentially use physiological and facial modes of expression. Buck (1984) found that, in reponse to a slide-viewing paradigm, males were more physiologically expressive of emotion, whereas females were more facially expressive of emotion. He termed the differing response styles of males and females as "internalizers" and "externalizers," respectively. Some work has supported this distinction (see Pennebaker et al., 1987). However, other studies have indicated that when data are analyzed within, rather than across subjects, there is a positive correlation between some physiological indices and facial modes of expressiveness (Adelmann & Zajonc, 1989). Further, since males seem to respond more behaviorally in expressing some emotions, especially anger, the word "internalizer" to capture patterns of male emotional expressiveness may be misleading.

In summary, adult females are more intensely verbally and facially expressive than are adult males in this culture, of both positive and negative affective experiences, particularly of fear and of dysphoric affects related to self-consciousness. They appear to be less expressive of affects related to self-entitlement, such as pride. Males appear to be more behaviorally expressive of anger and react to sadness by withdrawing or using distracting types of activities. Although there is some intriguing data that males express affect through physiological modes of expression more than do females, the area on gender differences in physiological expressiveness needs a great deal of further work. It is important to keep in mind that task variations in each of these expressive domains affect gender differences a great deal. For each of the modalities I have reviewed (i.e., verbal, facial, behavioral, and physiological), gender differences are always specific to the type of emotion studied and are sometimes specific to the task used to measure the emotional expressiveness (cf. LaFrance & Banaji, 1992) as well as to the culture in which the participants live (cf. Sommers & Kosmitzki, 1988). In my own research, the quality of the emotional situation and the gender of the participants in the situation has been critical in affecting the nature of gender differences in reported emotion (Brody, Lovas, & Hay, 1995).

INFANTS, GENDER, AND EMOTIONAL EXPRESSIVENESS

As is consistent with the adult literature, by 2 to 3 years of age some researchers have reported that girls talk more about emotions than do boys, especially positive emotions (Dunn, Bretherton, & Munn, 1987; Zahn-Waxler, Ridgeway, Denham, Usher, & Cole, 1993). However, compelling data on infants under the age of 1 year indicates that males are judged to be more, not less, intensely expressive of emotions. Using naive adults as judges, Cunningham and Shapiro (1984) found that infant boys were judged be more intensely emotionally expressive than were infant girls, even when the adult judges were misinformed about the infant's actual sex, thus overriding the effects of any stereotypes.

A more recent study by Weinberg (1992) indicates that 6-month-old boys showed both more frequent positive and negative emotional displays than did girls, including anger, joy, distancing, and escape/get away expressions, as judged by coders using Izard's AFFEX system. These differences were found across three different contexts as well as at two time periods separated by two weeks. Further, these gender differences were not related to the mothers' behaviors. Other data on early gender differences in expressivity similarly indicates that infant boys cry more in response to frustration than do girls, and that the frequency of negative emotional responses, including anger and crying, declines faster in infant girls than in infant boys (Kohnstamm, 1989).

These data suggest that infant boys are more emotionally expressive than are infant girls; hence, their expressions are easier for judges, and probably parents, to read. That boys' expressions may be easier to recognize and match than are girls is supported by data from Tronick and his colleagues (Tronick, 1989; Tronick & Cohn, 1989), who reported that mothers and 6- and 9-month-old sons spend 50% more time in matching, or coordinated emotional interactive states, than do mothers and daughters. Both mothers and daughters may have to work harder to read each others' emotional signals than do mothers and sons. Working harder may translate into talking more to daughters about feelings, as well as in displaying a wider range of feelings to daughters. For females, this may eventually result in both amplified facial expressiveness in order to communicate more clearly, as well as in better emotional recognition abilities.

In contrast, in adapting to their sons' higher emotional intensity, parents may respond with more constraint and a deemphasis on emotional expressiveness. These types of socialization patterns also represent a conformity to the cultural gender-role stereotype that girls should be more emotionally expressive and that boys should be more emotionally constrained. In fact, a rapidly emerging body of research indicates that parents do indeed socialize the emotional development of their sons and daughters differently, in accordance with gender-role stereotypes. I review this exciting literature next.

PARENT SOCIALIZATION OF EMOTION LANGUAGE

Consistent gender differences in the socialization of emotion emerge in three different developmental periods: infancy, preschool, and school ages. Several studies have indicated that mothers display more affect, particularly more positive affect and more smiling to their infant daughters (Malatesta, Culver, Tesman, & Shepard, 1989; Malatesta & Haviland, 1982; Parnell, 1992), use a greater variety of emotion words when talking to their preschool daughters than their preschool sons (Dunn, Bretherton, & Munn, 1987; Fivush, 1989, 1993; Zahn-Waxler et al., 1991), and emphasize different consequences for the expression of sad and angry emotions to their preschool and school-aged daughters and sons (Brock, 1993; Fuchs & Thelen, 1988; Perry, Perry, & Weiss, 1989). Day-care teachers have also been found to smile more and be more physically affectionate to girls than to boys (Botkin & Twardosz, 1988).

More specifically, several independent research groups have found either that mothers speak more about sadness or distress with daughters than with sons and more about anger with sons than with daughters, or actively attempt to minimize the extent to which their sons dwell on sadness or their daughters dwell on anger (Brock, 1993; Fivush, 1989, 1993; Greif, Alvarez, & Ulman, 1981; Kuebli & Fivush, 1992; Zahn-Waxler et al., 1993). For example, in work by Greif, Alvarez, and Ulman (1981), mothers never used the word "angry" in creating a storybook for their daughters, but did use it with their sons. Similarly, in Fivush and her colleagues' research (1989, 1993), mothers never spoke about anger with their daughters and did not attribute related dysphoric emotions to the daughters themselves, but did do so with sons. When explicitly asked to discuss angry incidents, mothers confirmed attributions and explanations of anger more frequently with sons than with daughters and focused on reestablishing harmonious relationships with their daughters when angry feelings were experienced. In contrast, they accepted retaliation as a reasonable response by their sons to angry situations.

That retaliation, a behavioral mode of expressing anger, is socialized to be more acceptable for sons than for daughters is supported by a number of studies. Fuchs and Thelen (1988) found that school-aged girls expect mothers to react more positively to the expression of sadness than to the expression of anger, whereas school-aged boys expected that both parents would be less likely to act warmly toward them after they expressed sadness. Moreover, boys were less likely to express sadness than were girls. Research by Perry, Perry, and Weiss (1989) similarly revealed that boys expect less disapproval for aggression than do girls. The socialization of responses to anger may be quite culturally specific. Fascinating case-study research on inner-city teenage mothers and their toddler daughters by Miller and Sperry (1987) reveals that mothers were very clear that their daughters' reactions of anger and ensuing aggression were acceptable only in certain situations—namely, those in which their daughters were defending themselves against attacks by others—but were not acceptable in situations in which their daughters were being demanding or self-indulgent.

That mothers may encourage sons more than daughters to retaliate when angry is consistent with the data I have reviewed that males are more apt to express anger behaviorally than are females. Similarly, Fivush (1993) found that mothers elaborated more on the causes and consequences of the feeling with sons rather than the emotional experience, emphasizing processes of control over emotions more with sons than with daughters. This research is consistent with the data that adult males express feelings less frequently and intensely than do females.

Fathers, too, socialize emotions differently for their sons and daughters. Schell and Gleason (1989) found that father–daughter dyads used the highest frequency of emotion words compared to mother–son, mother–daughter, and father–son dyads, avoiding only the word "disgust." Compared to mothers, fathers used language that included more demands, more threats, more cognitively demanding speech, and more teasing, perjorative language, such as "you dingaling." Teasing was especially more frequent in fathers' conversations with their sons (Gleason & Greif, 1983). Teasing has been viewed as a way of "toughening" up children so that they would not feel so vulnerable and of teaching children the power relations involved in the expression of anger (Crawford, Kippax, Onyx, Gault, & Benton, 1992; Miller & Sperry, 1987). School-age children reported that they would be less likely to express feelings to their fathers than to their mothers (Fuchs & Thelen, 1988). If sons, in particular, use their fathers as role models, the language their fathers use and the discomfort their fathers express with emotion may be important contributors to an intergenerational transmission of gender differences in emotional expressiveness.

THE ROLE OF VERBAL LANGUAGE
IN GENDER DIFFERENCES

The role of language may be critical in the emergence of gender differences in emotional expressiveness. Because girls are more verbally expressive at an earlier age, this would foster an interaction pattern in which parents talk more with girls about feelings than with boys. In having differential language-based experiences about emotions, males and females may develop very different abilities to understand and acknowledge emotional experiences. Stern (1985) has argued that language begins to structure experience, and enables private experiences to be shared with others. He has further argued that language enables experiences to become more conscious and understandable to the self. In a consistent vein, psychoanalytic thinkers have long hypothesized that words substitute for actions, a process Fraiberg (1959) called *word magic*. Children are thus taught to say the words "I'm angry" rather than to hit or physically hurt another person. If boys learn to verbalize emotions later, the structure of their emotional experiences and their consciousness about emotions may be quite different from that of girls, continuing to be based more in a physical, rather than in a verbal, context.

Support for this hypothesis comes from exciting recent work by Bloom and Capatides (1987), which indicates that in infancy, early talkers spend more time in neutral nonverbal affect expressions, whereas later talkers more frequently express emotionally toned nonverbal and behavioral affect. Later talkers increase their levels of nonverbal affective expression relative to earlier levels; early talkers do not. In their sample of 6 boys and 6 girls, they found no gender differences in these patterns, but it is possible that in learning to verbalize their feelings later than girls, boys show an increase in the behavioral expression of feelings relative to girls. This is consistent with the data I have reviewed that shows males tend to express both anger and sadness behaviorally more than females, while females verbally report feelings more than males.

PEER AND FAMILY INTERACTION PATTERNS

Besides the direct socialization of emotion, families and peers may play an important role in gender differences in emotional functioning simply through gender-differentiated family and peer-interaction patterns (Hall, 1987). School-age children spend the majority of their time in same-sex groups. In contrast to boys' play, girls' play tends to be in smaller rather than larger groups, is less competitive and more cooperative, and involves more turn-taking games and fewer active team games. A recent study by Crombie and DesJardins (1993) emphasizes that boys experience direct competition in their play 50% of the time, whereas girls experience it less than 1% of the time. These differences would have powerful consequences for the emotional development of the two sexes. The intimate, dyadic interaction in which girls engage would foster the recognition of social signals and require the expression and communication of feelings, as well as attempts to mimimize hostility and disagreement. Larger group competition would foster the minimization of emotions having to do with hurting others, such as guilt, shame, and fear, and would also maximize aggression. These patterns are also intergenerationally transmitted and may have powerful influences on gender differences in emotional recognition and expressive abilities.

Gender-differentiated interactions within the family may also be critical for gender differences in the development of emotion. Many theories suggest that as they develop, infants internalize dyadic and reciprocal emotional interactions, resulting in an emotional self. Repeated emotional experiences, such as abuse versus empathy, and the emotional reactions to those experiences, such as anger versus contentment, would be internalized as habitual ways of expecting the world to be, and would become internalized as part of the organization of the personality. Malatesta-Magai (formerly Malatesta) and her colleagues have elaborated a theory of emotional and personality development using these ideas (Malatesta, 1988; Malatesta & Wilson, 1988).

As the infant grows older, responses to the quality of interactions involving more than just two family participants may also be internalized. For example, families in which parents frequently argue may result in certain patterns of emotional expressiveness in the children, even though anger may not be part of the parent–child relationship, or families who are perceived to be of lower status than other families in the neighborhood may experience shame, although that feeling may not have been a response to the dyadic interactions between parents and their children. As is even more relevant to the study of gender differences, females may internalize a sense of shame because of their lower status and power relative to males in this culture (Brody, 1985; Crawford et al., 1992).

PARENT–CHILD BOUNDARIES, SHAME, AND GUILT

In the research where I am collaborating with Copeland and Sutton (Brody, Copeland, Sutton, Hsi, & Ritorto, 1993), we looked at gender differences in parent–child relationships as well as family process variables in a sample of young adult children. We theorized that gender differences in the quality of repeated interactions in the family of origin should be related to gender differences in emotional expressiveness. We were especially interested in the quality of boundary relationships between parents and their children. What we mean by boundaries is the degree to which parents and their daughters and sons are individuated or differentiated. Many theorists have posited that individuation and differentiation are intrapsychic and interpersonal processes in which a sense of individuality and self is achieved within the context of a relationship (Anderson & Sabatelli, 1990). In a highly differentiated and individuated system, behaviors, feelings, and ideas are clearly delineated as belonging to and originating with either the parent or the child, rather than with both. Boundaries between parent and child are thus less permeable and more rigid. In contrast, in a less individuated and differentiated system boundaries would be more permeable, and feelings, ideas, and thoughts would less clearly originate with or belong to only one member of the dyad.

Our interests in the relationship between parent–child boundaries and child emotional expressiveness stemmed from an integration of the work of three theorists: Chodorow (1982), Lewis (1971), and Weiss and his colleagues (Weiss, Sampson, & The Mount Zion Psychotherapy Research Group, 1986). Chodorow has theorized that since females are the primary caretakers for both sexes, girls and their primary caretakers will be more identified with each other than will boys and their caretakers, leading to less differentiation between self and other on the part of females, more permeable mother–daughter boundaries, and increased capacity for females to empathize with the feelings of others. Closer identification between mothers and their daughters might also affect the expression of emotions having to do with maintaining and restoring attachments, especially shame and guilt, which have been found to be more intensely expressed by females than by males in several studies (see Tangney, 1990).

Lewis (1971) theorized that shame is the vicarious experience of another's scorn which requires permeable boundaries between self and other. She further hypothesized that shame functions as a protection against the loss of boundaries between self and others by bringing the self into focal awareness (and thus motivating a search for identity).

Guilt has been theorized to result from the developmental task of separation between parents and their adolescent children, in which children both physically and psychologically abandon their parents as well as become potentially more powerful than their aging parents (Friedman, 1985; Zahn-Waxler, Cole, & Barrett, 1991). Due to gender differences in the parental boundary relationships of males and females, females may report more guilt than do males because separation and differentiation may be harder for females to achieve. Guilt may also be more prevalent for females in their role as family caretakers, and may be adaptive in that it helps to restore or reconnect a relationship or attachment that has been threatened or disrupted.

In summary, our research explored differing gender patterns in parent–child boundary relationships in relation to gender differences in patterns of expressed affect, especially shame and guilt. Several different theorists, including Chodorow (1982), Lewis (1971), and Weiss et al. (1986), have suggested that these relationships might be fruitful to explore in explaining different patterns in the intensity of emotions expressed by the two sexes. Our general working hypothesis was that more permeable boundaries would be related to increased affect intensity, especially more intense shame and guilt, and that boundaries between mothers and daughters would be more permeable than other types of boundaries in the family, as theorized by Chodorow (1982).

DESCRIPTION OF A STUDY ON BOUNDARIES AND EMOTIONAL EXPRESSIVENESS

Our study explored gender differences in the frequency of happiness, shame, and guilt, the intensity of warmth, shame, guilt, sadness, anger, and fear, and the intensity of more general negative and positive affective experiences. As previously discussed, shame and guilt have been reported more intensely by females than by males in the majority of previous research studies.

Our sample consisted of 64 females and 63 males, ages 18–27 years. For 62 of our subjects, we also obtained data from one of their siblings, ages 18–32 years, resulting in 31 sister–sister pairs, 21 sister–brother pairs, and 10 brother–brother pairs. At this point, we had used sibling data to confirm that some of our constructs, for example, the quality of boundaries with parents, were actually family-systems constructs and not just variables that reflect the participant's own perception. Participants and their siblings were asked to independently complete a set of measures about family functioning and about their emotional expressiveness. We measured emotional expressiveness, with a focus on shame and guilt, in several different ways, including some qualitative data that have not yet been coded. First, the frequency with which shame and guilt were experienced were measured using the Personal Feelings Questionnaire (PFQ) developed by Harder and his colleagues (Harder & Zalma, 1990). The PFQ yields self-reports of the frequency of shame, guilt, and happiness experienced, including such feelings as embarrassment, feeling ridiculous, regret, remorse, and enjoyment. These emotions are presented with no situational context.

Second, the intensity with which positive and negative, or dysphoric, emotions were experienced, including some shame and guilt emotions, were measured using the Affect Intensity Measure (AIM; Larsen & Diener, 1987), which I have previously discussed. This measure allows the subject to report the intensity of positive, negative, and total affect experienced. Participants were asked to rate the following sample items from 1 (*never*) to 6 (*always*): (a) When I accomplish something difficult I feel delighted or elated; (b) Sad movies touch me deeply; (c) I feel pretty bad when I tell a lie; (d) When I do something wrong I have strong feelings of shame and guilt. The items in this scale mostly reflect feelings related to some noninterpersonal activity in which the self is involved and do not involve interpersonal situations.

The final measure of emotion to be discussed is an Emotion Story task, which I have used in previous research (see Brody, 1993). Participants read six interpersonal situations that were previously selected and piloted to depict enraging and disappointing circumstances and were then asked to rate the intensity of 15 emotions they would experience toward the character in the story who was eliciting the emotion. I focus on six of those emotions, including shame, guilt, anger, fear, sadness, and warmth, as these are the most frequently researched in the gender-differences field. Participants were asked to rate their feelings on a 0 to 5 point scale, from "I would not at all feel ___" to "I would feel intensely ___."

Let me now turn my attention to the boundary measure we used, the Permeability of Boundaries Questionnaire developed by Olver, Aries, and

Batgos (1989). This was a self-report measure that we modified to obtain four scores: the frequency of negative, or intrusive, interactions with both mothers and fathers; and the frequency of positive, or interested and concerned, interactions with both mothers and fathers. Items included on the interested/concerned scale indicated that the parent was more respectful of the child's right to privacy than did those on the intrusiveness scale. Participants were asked to rate the frequency with which interactions such as the following occurred during the last few years: "My mother/father enters my room without knocking; reads my personal papers; goes through my bureau drawers at home" (these are negative or intrusive items); and "inquires what I am thinking and feeling; asks to read papers I have written for school" (these are interested/concerned or positive items).

Siblings' scores on the Boundaries Questionnaire were significantly correlated for each of the four variables we derived. The correlations were as follows: For intrusive boundaries with mothers, $r = .38$, $p < .001$; intrusive boundaries with fathers, $r = .36$, $p < .002$; interested/concerned boundaries with mothers: $r = .40$, $p < .001$; and for interested/concerned boundaries with fathers: $r = .42$, $p < .001$. These results suggest that the participants' boundary scores did not only reflect the individual's perception of the quality of their own parental boundaries, but also reflected a consistent style in the way mothers and fathers interacted with all of their children.

Our results revealed that females reported more intense positive, negative, and total affective experiences than did males on the AIM. This is consistent with previous literature using the AIM (see Diener, Sandvik, & Larsen, 1985). In our interpersonal story situations that asked for the intensity of anger, warmth, fear, shame, sadness, and guilt, no gender differences emerged, nor were there gender differences in the frequency of shame, happiness, and guilt reported on the PFQ. These results are depicted in Table 6.1.

TABLE 6.1
Mean Scores on Boundary and Affect Intensity
Measures for Males and Females

	Daughters		Sons		Parent Sex × Child Sex ANOVA:
	M	SD	M	SD	
Permeability scale total scores (range = 1 to 5)					
Mothers'	2.53	.56	2.33	.64	$F(1, 118) = 5.89$, $p < .02$
Fathers'	1.80	.43	1.85	.53	
AIM (range = 1 to 6)					t test (df: 118)
Positive	4.10	.60	3.74	.60	3.39*
Negative	3.85	.69	3.34	.61	4.35*
Total intensity	3.97	.50	3.58	.52	4.33*

*$p < .001$

How was affective functioning related to family functioning? Mothers had more permeable positive and negative boundaries with both sexes than fathers did, $F(1, 118) = 137.54$, $p < .001$. However, there was an interaction between parent sex and child sex, such that mother–daughter boundaries tended to be the most permeable of all of the dyads, $F(1, 118) = 5.91$, $p < .02$. Table 6.1 shows the mean scores for the dyadic boundary relationships within the family. In Tables 6.2 and 6.3, Pearson-r correlations between boundary measures and affect measures are displayed. The more permeable the negative boundaries were with mother; that is, the more intrusive mother was, the greater the intensity of negative affect reported by daughters on the AIM. Similarly for sons, the more intrusive their mothers were, the greater the intensity of the sons' negative affect on the AIM, the more intense anger, sadness, shame, fear, guilt, and warmth reported on the Interpersonal Emotion Story task, and the greater frequency of shame and guilt reported on the PFQ.

Intrusive fathers also related to increased affect intensity for sons. There were significant positive correlations between the intensity of negative affect, interpersonal anger, shame, sadness, warmth, and fathers' intrusiveness, and almost significant trends between interpersonal fear and guilt and having an intrusive father. However, for daughters, intrusive fathers seemed to mitigate emotion intensity, with significantly less in-

TABLE 6.2
Pearson r Correlations Between Emotion
and Boundary Measures for Males[a]

	Negative Boundaries		Positive Boundaries	
	Mothers	Fathers	Mothers	Fathers
Frequency(PFQ):				
Shame	.26*	.10	−.12	−.17
Guilt	.42***	.09	−.02	−.02
Happiness	−.09	−.01	.23*	.18
Intensity(AIM):				
Positive	.07	−.01	.13	.03
Negative	.21*	.24*	.01	.10
Total	.14	.08	.07	.03
Interpersonal Intensity:				
Anger	.37**	.44***	−.03	−.02
Fear	.44***	.21t	−.05	−.03
Guilt	.41***	.18t	−.02	−.01
Sadness	.35**	.27*	−.01	.09
Shame	.34**	.23*	−.09	.07
Warmth	.37**	.22*	.02	.11

[a]All data were analyzed using one-tailed Pearson-r correlations.
*$p < .05$. **$p < .01$. ***$p < .001$.

TABLE 6.3
Pearson r Correlations Between Emotion
and Boundary Measures for Females[a]

	Negative Boundaries		Positive Boundaries	
	Mothers	Fathers	Mothers	Fathers
Frequency(PFQ):				
Shame	.13	−.13	.13	−.02
Guilt	.15	−.02	.12	.01
Happiness	−.08	.08	.10	.19^t
Intensity(AIM):				
Positive	.11	.01	.07	−.16
Negative	.23*	−.13	−.03	−.22*
Total	.14	−.07	.05	−.23*
Interpersonal Intensity:				
Anger	.00	−.21^t	−.14	−.21^t
Fear	.06	−.16	−.28*	−.22^t
Guilt	.01	−.07	−.37**	−.41**
Sadness	−.10	−.26*	−.17	−.18^t
Shame	.01	−.20^t	−.24*	−.08
Warmth	−.12	−.05	.25*	.15

[a]All analyses are one-tailed Pearson-r correlations.
*$p < .05$
**$p < .01$
$^t p < .10$

terpersonal sadness reported and trends toward less intense interpersonal anger and shame as well.

Interest and concern by fathers was significantly related to less intense total and negative affect for daughters, as well as strongly related to less interpersonal guilt. Interest and concern by fathers also tended to be related to more frequent reports of happiness by daughters, and less intense interpersonal anger, fear, and sadness ($ps < .10$). Similarly, for daughters, having interested/concerned mothers related significantly negatively to the intensity of reported interpersonal shame, fear, and guilt, and positively to the intensity of reported interpersonal warmth.

For sons, interested/concerned fathers tended to relate to less frequent reports of shame and more frequent reports of happiness. More frequent reports of happiness were also reported significantly more by sons who had interested/concerned mothers.

A pattern thus emerges in which intrusive behavior on the part of mothers relates to increased negative affect intensity for both daughters and sons. More frequent negative affects and more intense negative and positive interpersonal affects for sons are also related to intrusive maternal behavior. However, intrusive behavior on the part of fathers relates in opposite directions to the intensity and frequency of reported affect for sons and daughters. For sons, having intrusive fathers relates to *more* intense negative affect and *more* intense interpersonal negative and positive emotions. In contrast, for daughters, having intrusive fathers relates to *less* intense interpersonal sadness and tends to relate to *less* intense interpersonal shame and anger. Fisher's z-tests analyzing the differences between the males' and females' correlations for the relationships between father intrusiveness and expressed emotion indicated that the correlations for the two sexes were indeed significantly different: for the relationship between the intensity of interpersonal shame and fathers' intrusiveness $(z = 2.52, p < .05)$; for the relationship between the intensity of interpersonal anger and fathers' intrusiveness $(z = 3.82, p < .01)$; for the relationship beween the intensity of interpersonal fear and fathers' intrusiveness $(z = 2.14, p < .05)$; and for the relationship beween the intensity of interpersonal sadness and fathers' intrusiveness $(z = 3.14, p < .01)$.

For both sons and daughters, having interested and concerned mothers and fathers relates to less frequently reported negative affects as well as less intense negative affects and more intense or frequent positive affects.

Two sets of stepwise multiple regression analyses were performed in order to test whether boundaries with mothers or boundaries with fathers accounted for more unique variance in sons' and daughters' emotional expressiveness. Each set consisted of 12 analyses in which the outcome variables were one of the 12 emotional expressiveness variables; for example, the frequency of reported shame or the intensity of reported interpersonal fear. In each analysis the predictor variables were the 4 variables of mothers' and fathers' intrusiveness (negative boundaries), and interest/concern (positive boundaries). In one set of analyses, the 2 variables measuring positive and negative boundaries with mothers were entered as a block first, followed by entering a block consisting of the 2 variables measuring positive and negative boundaries with fathers. In the second set of analyses, positive and negative boundaries with fathers were entered as a block first, followed by entering a block consisting of positive and negative boundaries with mothers. This procedure was followed in order to determine the unique variance in emotional expressiveness contributed by boundaries with each parent (as represented by the change in r^2) after the variance contributed by the other parent had been accounted for.

The results of these analyses are displayed in Tables 6.4 and 6.5. For daughters, the quality of boundaries with fathers contributed significantly more unique variance than did the quality of boundaries with mothers to two of the affect variables: total intensity of reported affect and the intensity of interpersonal guilt reported. For the intensity of negative affect reported, unique variance was significantly contributed by both boundaries with

TABLE 6.4
Regression Analyses for Daughters

	Fathers' Boundaries (after mothers' entered)				Mothers' Boundaries (after fathers' entered)			
	Beta pos. bound	Beta neg. bound	r^2 change	F-value	Beta pos. bound	Beta neg. bound	r^2 change	F-value
Intensity:								
Negative	−.27	−.26	.13	3.76*	.02	.30	.09	2.50[t1]
Total	−.35	−.17	.13	3.71*	.19	.16	.05	1.49
Interpersonal Intensity:								
Guilt	−.33	−.03	.10	3.01[t2]	−.26	.03	.06	1.83

*$p < .05$
[t1]$p < .10$
[t2]$p < .06$

mothers and boundaries with fathers. Thus, fathers seem especially important in affecting the intensity of their daughters' emotional functioning.

For sons, the quality of boundaries with mothers contributed significantly more unique variance than did the quality of fathers' boundaries to six of the affect variables: the frequency of guilt and shame reported, and the intensity of interpersonal shame, guilt, fear, and warmth reported. Mothers also tended to contribute significantly more unique variance than did fathers to the intensity of sadness reported. In no case did the quality of boundaries with fathers contribute significantly more unique variance than quality of boundaries with mothers. Thus, for sons, the quality of boundaries with their mothers contributes more unique variance to their emotional expressiveness than the quality of their boundaries with their fathers.

It appears that the quality of boundaries with parents clearly relates to the intensity and frequency of affect, often in ways that have been hypothesized by theorists such as Chodorow (1982). However, our work indicates that these relationships are quite complex, and that the quality of the boundary relationships; that is, whether they are experienced as positive or negative, makes a difference in emotional functioning, as does *which* family dyad is being considered, for example, mother–daughter versus father–daughter.

BOUNDARIES, GENDER, AND DEVELOPMENT

It is tempting to speculate that gender differences in the quality of mother–child boundaries play a causal role in the emergence of gender differences in expressed emotional intensity. If, as our data show, mothers are more

TABLE 6.5
Regression Analyses for Sons

	Fathers' Boundaries (after mothers' entered)				Mothers' Boundaries (after fathers' entered)			
	Beta pos. bound	Beta neg. bound	r^2 change	F-value	Beta pos. bound	Beta neg. bound	r^2 change	F-value
Frequency:								
Shame	−.14	−.04	.02	.63	−.06	.38	.09	2.53^t
Guilt	−.02	−.29	.05	1.78	−.02	.71	.30	10.66***
Interpersonal Intensity:								
Warmth	.15	−.08	.02	.60	−.06	.48	.14	4.19*
Shame	.16	−.06	.02	.69	−.16	.49	.16	4.96**
Fear	.02	−.12	.01	.28	−.06	.61	.22	7.43**
Guilt	.02	−.14	.01	.36	−.04	.57	.19	6.12**
Sadness	.13	.05	.02	.53	−.20	.37	.09	2.60^t

*$p < .05$
**$p < .01$
***$p < .001$
$^t p < .10$

intrusive with their daughters than with their sons, and if, in turn, intrusiveness relates to increased negative affect intensity, then females may be more expressive of negative affect than males because their mothers are more intrusive with them. Alternatively, it is also possible that gender differences in the permeability of mother–child (and also father–child) boundaries are a response to gender differences in the intensity of affect displayed by the child. Parents may use boundaries as a means of regulating the intensity of their childrens' expressed affect and how appropriate they feel the intensity of their child's affect is, depending on whether the child is male or female. These two alternative explanations for the relationship between boundaries and affect intensity will be discussed at length: the first, that children's affect intensity may be a response to the permeability of parent–child boundaries; the second, that the permeability of parent–child boundaries may be a response to the level of affect intensity expressed by the child. Subsequently, a model that combines the two explanations will be proposed.

Is the Intensity of Child Affect a Response to the Permeability of Parental Boundaries?

Why would children respond to permeable parent–child boundaries with more intense affect? Berscheid (1982) hypothesized that in close relationships, frequent, strong, and diverse interconnections exist between people. She has termed these interconnections *emotional time bombs*, since the more interconnections that exist between any two people, the more expectations build up and the more likely there will be interruptions in expected aspects of the relationship. It is these interruptions that result in the expression of emotion. With intrusive mothers, more frequent and more diverse interconnections exist than would otherwise, resulting in increased affect. However, this theory does not help to explain why more intrusive boundaries with fathers would relate to decreased intensity of sadness, anger, and shame among daughters.

Much of our data on boundaries and affect can also be interpreted from an object-relations perspective (Sandler & Sandler, 1986). The child is hypothesized to internalize the affective quality of parent–child relationships. If the child has a parent who is positive, interested, and concerned, that child will display increased positive affects, such as warmth and happiness, and decreased negative affects, such as shame and guilt. Conversely, if the child has a parent who is intrusive, implying a lack of respect for and empathy with the child's feelings, then the child will internalize more negative feelings, including especially anger, shame, and, possibly, guilt over feelings of anger. Many of our results fit this model, especially the findings that more interested/concerned mothers have daughters who express more intense warmth and sons who express more frequent happiness. However, once again, the results which do not fit this model are that intrusive boundaries with fathers relate to decreased, and not increased, intensity of sadness, anger, and shame among daughters.

An alternative explanation of our results is that intense affect on the part of the child may serve to reassert a sense of autonomy and separateness in the face of boundaries that are too permeable and diffuse. Intense affect may help to ward off a threatened merger with mothers, for females or with both mothers and fathers, for males. Since mothers are almost always the primary caretakers for both sexes, both males and females need to differentiate from her, possibly resulting in intense affect if she is more intrusive.

The role that fathers play in this process would be different for sons and daughters, because daughters are less identified with fathers than are sons (being dissimilar in gender). When intrusive, fathers would provide an alternative relationship for daughters (being different than mothers), and might help mothers and daughters to differentiate, thus lowering their daughters' need to assert a sense of self though intense affect expression. The suggestion that fathers act as a "wedge" in the relationship between mothers and their children, thus helping in the differentiation process, has been made by some psychoanalytic researchers (see Machtlinger, 1981). However, fathers do not seem to play this role with sons, who may be more identified with them as the same-sex parent. Sons seem to need to differentiate from involved fathers, and sons' increased emotional expressivity in the face of intrusive fathers may represent an attempt to assert a sense of self and regulate the relationship.

It is also worth noting that for sons, intrusiveness on the part of both mothers and fathers related to increased intensity of sons' interpersonal warmth. In contrast, for daughters, intrusiveness on the part of mothers and fathers did not relate to interpersonal warmth. If the quality of expressed affect is regarded as a communicative message, warmth would signal to others that the relationship should continue: Sons seem to be inviting intrusiveness more than daughters do, while at the same time asserting a separate sense of self through the intensity of their expressed affect. It may be that intrusiveness is not quite as threatening to sons' developing sense of themselves as it is to daughters' because the intrusiveness occurs at lower levels (at least on the part of mothers). Alternatively, and as discussed in the next section of this chapter, parents may feel that they have to be more intrusive, or more constraining, of sons who express more intense warmth because warmth is a socially unacceptable emotion for males.

The model I have just presented describing children's intense emotional expressions as communicative and self-differentiating responses within the context of parent–child relationships assumes that individual differences in the quality of parent–child boundaries reflect long-standing and relatively stable developmental patterns. A growing literature suggests that the quality of these relationships, particularly involving attachment patterns, is stable across development and perhaps even intergenerationally (Bartholomew, 1992). It is important to keep in mind, however, that our sample consisted of those in late adolescence, a developmental period in which it becomes more age-appropriate for increased separation to occur; when it does not, the adolescents' expectations may become violated, resulting in increased affect. That violation of expectancies results in increased affect has been hypothesized by many cognitively oriented theorists (see Fischer, Shaver, & Carnochan, 1989). However, the suggestion that the relationship between boundaries and affect in the present data may be limited to the adolescent period would still need to account for the differing patterns in the data for each sex. It would also need to explain the finding that the intense affect reported by these adolescents is not only in the context of their relationships with their parents, but in other interpersonal relationships as well.

Is the Permeability of Parent–Child Boundaries a Response to the Intensity of the Child's Affect?

The idea that maternal intrusiveness results in increased child affect has the potential to become quite mother-blaming; that is, to hold mothers responsible for the intensity of children's affect. It is important to recognize that mothers often adapt to their children's needs, as well as actively try to respond to their children in ways that are consistent with the demands of their culture (Ruddick, 1982). In particular, intrusive boundaries may be a response intended to constrain intense affect expression, whereas positive/concerned boundaries may be a response intended to encourage intense affect expression. In order to raise children who are socially acceptable to the wider culture, mothers may respond to their sons' intense affect expression with constraint, since it is socially unacceptable for males to express emotions. Further, they may respond to their daughters' positive affect expression with encouragement and to their negative affect expression with constraint since negative emotions (especially anger) are not stereotypically feminine, whereas positive emotions are.

This explanation is consistent with the data that for daughters, only negative affect intensity was significantly related to intrusive boundaries with mothers. If intrusive boundaries are attempts to constrain or discourage affect, mothers may respond to the intense expression of negative affect in their daughters by becoming intrusive. Their intent may be to discourage the expression of the affect. In contrast, mothers may respond to the intense expression of warmth with interest/concern in an attempt to encourage it. Mothers may also try to encourage less intense expressions of fear, guilt, and shame in their daughters by being less interested/concerned in daughters who intensely display these feelings and by being more interested/concerned in daughters who display less of these feelings.

Mothers may respond to the expression of almost all intense affects in their sons by being more intrusive in an attempt to discourage the expression of affect. Sons who express more intense shame, sadness, guilt, fear, anger, warmth, negative affects, and more frequent shame and guilt all have more intrusive mothers. (It is noteworthy that the expression of positive intensity and total intensity in males is also positively correlated with maternal intrusiveness, one-tailed Pearson-$rs = .19$, $p < .07$, and .24, $p < .03$, respectively, if one male outlier is eliminated from the analyses who scored 3½ standard deviations below the sample mean for the affect-intensity measure.) The expression of emotions in males, both positive and negative, is not stereotypically masculine, and mothers may actively try to constrain their sons' emotional intensity. Interestingly, only frequent expressions of happiness on the part of sons related to interested/concerned boundaries with mothers. It may be that happiness is the only expressed emotion on the part of sons that is encouraged by mothers.

The relationship between father–son boundaries and the intensity of sons' affect can also be explained well using this socialization model. Fathers, like mothers, may respond to their sons' intense affect expression with active discouragement by intruding on them. This would explain the positive relationships between father intrusiveness and sons' negative and positive affect intensity, including anger, sadness, shame, warmth, and negative affect intensity. None of the sons' affect variables related to interest/concern on the part of fathers, suggesting that fathers interest/concern in their sons is independent of their sons' expressions of affect.

The relationship between father–daughter boundaries and daughters' affect intensity is more difficult to explain using the model that the quality of fathers' boundaries may be a response to daughters' affect intensity expression. Like mothers, fathers may respond to the expression of less intense negative affects by being more interested/concerned in daughters who display less of these feelings, thus encouraging the lower intensity of these feelings. On the other hand, for daughters who display less intense anger, sadness, and shame, fathers tend to be more intrusive, and the idea that they may be trying to constrain these expressions further makes little sense. Alternatively, fathers' lower intrusiveness may be a signal that they are more comfortable when their daughters do express more intense anger, sadness, and shame, and tend not to feel the need to intrude. It may be that this is because gender-role stereotypes dictate that it is socially acceptable for daughters to express such affects. Another way of viewing this is that fathers are more responsive to their daughters when their daughters display lower intensities of affect, behavior that is consistent with the father's own stereotypically masculine emotional inexpressiveness.

A SYSTEMIC PERSPECTIVE ON BOUNDARIES

In the previous section of the chapter, I have been assuming that parental intrusiveness is a response to intense child affect, which is intended to constrain it. However, it is also possible that intrusiveness stimulates affect. This was the assumption made in the section of the chapter which theorized that children reacted to permeable or intrusive boundaries by asserting intense affect in order to differentiate a sense of self. If, in fact, intrusion is intended to constrain affect but instead stimulates it, a model develops in which parents and children reciprocally influence each other. For example, a child who displays intense affect might be responded to by a parent with intrusiveness; that child would then continue to assert intense affect in order to differentiate from the parent, or perhaps the child's intense feelings would be due to an internalization of negative feelings resulting from the lack of empathy the parent displays. In turn, the parent would respond with more intrusiveness. A cycle would thus be maintained of intense affect being associated with intrusive boundaries.

The quality of the boundaries that are initially established between parents and their children, as well as the intensity of affect that children display, may be multiply determined. These determinants would include early individual temperament differences in the intensity with which emotion is expressed (which may differ by gender), the parents' expectations regarding the appropriateness of affect expression (which may also differ by gender), and possibly the parents' own affect intensity, undoubtedly influenced by the parents' intergenerational history of boundary relationships.

Why would mothers be more intrusive and express more interest/concern in their daughters' than their sons' lives? The answers to this question are undoubtedly complex and are influenced by the cultural context in which gender is constructed. Chodorow's (1982) work and that of researchers in the Stone Center (Jordan, Kaplan, Miller, Stiver, & Surrey, 1991) suggest that mothers and daughters are more identified with each other, and that females are more focused on relationships, especially with other females. However, focusing on the role that boundaries play in regulating and maintaining affect suggests that mothers may be trying to more actively influence the expression of intense affect in their daughters through the permeability of mother–child boundaries. Because emotional expressivity is so strongly tied to stereotypically feminine gender roles, the socialization of emotional expressiveness in their daughters would be an important goal for mothers to achieve (Ruddick, 1982).

Gender differences in the quality of mother–son and mother–daughter boundaries may also reflect mothers' responses to initial temperament differences in the emotional expressiveness of their infant sons and daughters. I have presented data earlier in this chapter which indicate that girls may be less emotionally expressive than boys early in infancy. Although there are no developmental data in the present study, it is tempting to speculate that mothers may be both more intrusive and more interested/concerned in the lives of their infant girls than their infant boys in an early attempt to stimulate their expressiveness. More permeable boundaries by mothers may serve to increase the emotional expressiveness of daughters, especially their negative affect intensity, as our data indicate.

The pattern of the data is clear in suggesting that parental intrusiveness and child affect intensity are positively related, with the exception that fathers' intrusiveness and daughters' negative affect intensity are negatively related. Is intrusiveness a response to preexisting affect intensity, which is an attempt to constrain it (or possibly to initially stimulate it)? Alternatively, is the child's affect intensity an attempt to assert a separate sense of self in response to parental intrusiveness? These questions remain to be tested in future research.

CONCLUDING THOUGHTS

An analysis of the socialization and developmental patterns in emotional expressiveness suggests that gender differences emerge in a series of transactional relationships between parents and children as well as in gender-differentiated peer interactions. I am using the word "transactional" to mean a series of bidirectional interactions between parents and their children (Brody, 1993), the quality of which is determined by the original characteristics of both participants, who shape each other over time. Early gender differences in language development, emotional expressiveness, and possibly arousal level may all affect the nature and course of subsequent parent–child interactions around emotion socialization, including the quality of parent–child boundary relationships that develop. For example, if infant girls have lower arousal systems than do infant boys, Larsen and Diener's (1987) theory would suggest that a self-regulatory compensatory process would take place, in which girls would attempt to compensate for a low arousal system with increased emotional intensity, while sons would attempt to minimize an already aroused system with decreased emotional intensity. Also, for example, because girls talk earlier than boys, mothers and fathers may talk about emotions earlier with them than with boys. This would lead to a pattern in which females verbalize feelings; males act on them.

Sons and daughters may be helped in these processes by the differing quality of interactions and boundaries that their parents provide. The quality of parent–child boundaries seems to play a critical role in regulating gender differences in the intensity of affect expression. The permeability of boundaries may be a response to the intensity of affect displayed by the child, or possibly the intensity of affect displayed by the child is a self-differentiating response to the permeability of the parents' boundaries, as consistent with an object relations and self psychology perspective. The opposite-sex parent seems to play an important role in helping the child to regulate intense affect. The opposite-sex parent may help the child differentiate from the same-sex parent, and may be critical in helping the child to regulate their feelings in the face of a threatened merger with the same-sex parent. Alternatively, the opposite-sex parent may respond to the child's intense affect with different expectations regarding the appropriateness of affect expression than does the same-sex parent.

Repeated patterns of interaction and gender-differentiated relationships within the family (and undoubtedly within a larger societal context) seem to be quite important for the emergence of gender differences in the intensity of expressed emotion. Gender differences in parents' socialization patterns are quite consistent with and are probably influenced by cultural gender roles concerning emotional expressiveness. A primary goal that parents have for their children is that they be socially accepted by the culture in which they live (Ruddick, 1982). Because differing gender roles, for example, the role of child care provider versus financial provider, dictate different interpersonal goals for each sex, different emotions would be adaptive for males versus females. For example, emotions that are adaptive for being a child-care provider include minimizing anger and frustration, and maximizing warmth and intimacy. In contrast, the traditional role of financial provider requires being competitive and more autonomous, and would involve the maximization of anger and aggression. These differing sets of demands are quite consistent with the emerging evidence I have reviewed that boys are socialized to be more retaliatory when angry than are girls, whereas girls are socialized to be more appeasing. These long-standing and pervasive gender-role patterns, including power and status differences between the two sexes, provide a powerful context for family interaction patterns through which males and females learn to express and experience affect, and in which they intergenerationally transmit gender patterns in affect expression.

ACKNOWLEDGMENTS

I would like to thank the Rockefeller Foundation for their Gender Roles Grant, which laid the foundation for my work in this area, and the Boston University Graduate School for their research support (Grant # GRS–959–PSYC). I would also like to thank Anne Copeland and·Lisa Sutton for their enriching research collaboration.

REFERENCES

Adelmann, P. K., & Zajonc, R. (1989). Facial efference and the experience of emotion. *Annual Review of Psychology, 40*, 249–280.

Allen, J., & Haccoun, D. (1976). Sex differences in emotionality: A multidimensional approach. *Human Relations, 29*, 711–722.

Anderson, S., & Sabatelli, R. M. (1990). Differentiating differentiation and individuation: Conceptual and operational challenges. *American Journal of Family Therapy, 18*, 32–50.

Averill, J. (1983). Studies on anger and aggression: Implications for theories of emotion. *American Psychologist, 38*, 1145–1160.

Bartholomew, K. (1992). From childhood to adult relationships: Attachment theory and research. In S. Duck (Ed.), *Learning about relationships* (pp. 30–62). Newbury Park, CA: Sage.

Berscheid, E. (1982). Attraction and emotion in interpersonal relations. In M. Clark & S. Fiske (Eds.), *Affect & cognition* (pp. 37–55). Hillsdale, NJ: Lawrence Erlbaum Associates.

Birnbaum, D. W., & Croll, W. L. (1984). Preschoolers' stereotypes about sex differences in emotionality: A re-affirmation. *Journal of Genetic Psychology, 143*, 139–140.

Bloom, L., & Capatides, J. B. (1987). Expression of affect and the emergence of language. *Child Development, 58*, 1513–1522

Botkin, D., & Twardosz, S. (1988). Early childhood teachers' affectionate behavior: Differential expression to female children, male children, and groups of children. *Early Childhood Research Quarterly, 3*, 167–177.

Brock, S. (1993, April). *An examination of the ways in which mothers talk to their male and female children about emotions.* Poster presented at the Biennial meeting of the Society for Research in Child Development, New Orleans, LA.

Brody, L. R. (1984). Sex and age variations in the quality and intensity of children's emotional attributions to hypothetical situations. *Sex Roles, 11*, 51–59.

Brody, L. R. (1985). Gender differences in emotional development: A review of theories and research. *Journal of Personality, 53*, 102–149.

Brody, L. R. (1993). On understanding gender differences in the expression of emotion. In S. Ablon, D. Brown, J. Mack, & E. Khantzian (Eds.), *Human feelings: Explorations in affect development and meaning* (pp. 87–121). Hillsdale, NJ: Analytic Press.

Brody, L. R., Copeland, A., Sutton, L., Hsi, X., & Ritorto, B. (1993, April). *Shame, guilt and emotional intensity in relation to family structure and process in late adolescent males and females.* Poster presented at the Biennial Meeting of the Society for Research in Child Development, New Orleans, LA.

Brody, L. R., & Hall, J. A. (1993). Gender and emotion. In M. Lewis & J. Haviland (Eds.), *Handbook of emotions* (pp. 447–460). New York: Guilford Press.

Brody, L. R., Hay, D. H., & Vandewater, E. (1990). Gender, gender role identity and children's reported feelings toward the same and opposite sex. *Sex Roles, 3*, 363–387.

Brody, L. R., & Carter, A. (1982). Children's emotional attributions to self vs. other: An exploration of an assumption underlying projective techniques. *Journal of Consulting and Clinical Psychology, 50*, 665–671.

Brody, L. R., Lovas, G., & Hay, D. (1995). Sex differences in anger and fear as a function of situational context. *Sex Roles, 32*, 47–78.

Buck, R. (1984). *The communication of emotion.* New York: Guilford Press.

Buck, R., Miller, R. E., & Caul, W. F. (1974). Sex, personality, and physiological variables in the communication of affect via facial expression. *Journal of Personality and Social Psychology, 30*, 587–596.

Chodorow, N. (1982). Family structure and feminine personality. In M. Rosaldo & L. Lamphere (Eds.), *Women, culture & personality* (pp. 43–66). Stanford, CA: Stanford University Press.

Cramer, P. (1991). *The development of defense mechanisms.* New York: Springer-Verlag.

Crawford, J., Kippax, S., Onyx, J., Gault, U., & Benton, P. (1992). *Emotion and gender.* London: Sage.

Croake, J. W., Myers, K. M., & Singh, A. (1987). Demographic features of adult fears. *International Journal of Social Psychiatry, 33*, 285–293.

Crombie, G., & DesJardins, M. (1993, April). *Predictors of gender: The relative importance of children's play, games, and personality characteristics.* Poster presented at the Biennial Meeting of the Society for Research in Child Development, New Orleans, LA.

Cunningham, J., & Shapiro, L. (1984). *Infant affective expression as a function of infant and adult gender.* Unpublished manuscript, Brandeis University.

Diener, E., Sandvik, E., & Larsen, R. (1985). Age and sex effects for emotional intensity. *Developmental Psychology, 21*, 542–546.

Dillon, K. M., Wolf, E., & Katz, H. (1985). Sex roles, gender, and fear. *The Journal of Psychology, 119*, 355–359.

Dunn, J., Bretherton, I., & Munn, P. (1987). Conversations about feeling states between mothers and their children. *Developmental Psychology, 23*, 132–139.

Eisenberg, N., & Fabes, R. (1992). Emotion, regulation, and the development of social competence. In M. S. Clark (Ed.), *Emotion and social behavior, Review of Personality and Social Psychology* (Vol. 14, pp. 119–150). Newbury Park, CA: Sage.

Emde, R. (1993). A framework for viewing emotions. In R. Emde, J. Osofsky, & P. Butterfield (Eds.), *The IFEEL pictures: A new instrument for interpreting emotions, Vol. 5, Zero to Three* (pp. 217–236). Madison, CT: International Universities Press.

Fabes, R. A., & Martin, C. L. (1991). Gender and age stereotypes of emotionality. *Personality and Social Psychology Bulletin, 17*, 532–540.

Fabes, R. A., & Eisenberg, N. (1991, April). *Children's coping with interpersonal anger: Individual and situational correlates.* Poster presented at the Biennial meeting of the Society for Research in Child Development, Seattle, WA.

Fischer, K., Shaver, P., & Carnochan, P. (1989). A skill approach to emotional development: From basic to subordinate category emotions. In W. Damon (Ed.), *Child development today and tomorrow* (pp. 107–136). San Francisco: Jossey-Bass.

Fivush, R. (1989). Exploring sex differences in the emotional content of mother–child conversations about the past. *Sex Roles, 20,* 675–691.

Fivush, R. (1993). Emotional content of parent–child conversations about the past. In C. A. Nelson (Ed.), *Memory and affect in development, The Minnesota symposium on child psychology* (Vol. 26, pp. 39–78). Hillsdale, NJ: Lawrence Erlbaum Associates.

Fraiberg, S. (1959). *The magic years.* New York: Scribner's.

Friedman, M. (1985). Toward a reconceptualization of guilt. *Contemporary Psychoanalysis, 21,* 501–547.

Fuchs, D., & Thelen, M. (1988). Children's expected interpersonal consequences of communicating their affective state and reported likelihood of expression. *Child Development, 59,* 1314–1322.

Gleason, J. B., & Greif, E. G. (1983). Men's speech to young children. In B. Thorne, C. Kramarae, & N. Henley (Eds.), *Language, gender and society* (pp. 140–150). London: Newbury.

Gonzales, M., Pederson, J., Manning, D., & Wetter, D. (1990). Pardon my gaffe: Effects of sex, status, and consequence severity on accounts. *Journal of Personality and Social Psychology, 58,* 610–621.

Gordis, F., Smith, J., & Mascio, C. (1991, April). *Gender differences in attributions of sadness and anger.* Poster presented at the Biennial meeting of the Society for Research in Child Development, Seattle, WA.

Greif, E., Alvarez, M., & Ulman, K. (1981, April). *Recognizing emotions in other people: Sex differences in socialization.* Paper presented at the Biennial Meeting of the Society for Research in Child Development, Boston, MA.

Hall, J. A. (1978). Gender effects in decoding nonverbal cues. *Psychological Bulletin, 85,* 845–857.

Hall, J. A. (1984). *Nonverbal sex differences: Communication accuracy and expressive style.* Baltimore: Johns Hopkins University Press.

Hall, J. A. (1987). On explaining gender differences: The case of nonverbal communication. In P. Shavel & C. Hendrick (Eds.), *Review of personality and social psychology: Sex and gender, Vol. 7* (pp. 177–200). Newbury Park, CA: Sage.

Harder, D., & Zalma, A. (1990). Two promising shame and guilt scales: A construct validity comparison. *Journal of Personality Assessment, 53,* 729–745.

Highlen, P. S., & Gilles, S. F. (1978). Effects of situational factors, sex and attitude on affective self-disclosure with acquaintances. *Journal of Counseling Psychology, 25,* 270–276.

Highlen, P. S., & Johnston, B. (1979). Effects of situational variables on affective self-disclosure with acquaintances. *Journal of Counseling Psychology, 26,* 255–258.

Jordan, J., Kaplan, A., Miller, J. B., Stiver, I., & Surrey, J. (1991). *Women's growth in connection.* New York: Guilford.

King, L., & Emmons, R. A. (1990). Conflict over emotional expression: Psychological and physical correlates. *Journal of Personality and Social Psychology, 58,* 864–877.

Kirkpatrick, D. R. (1984). Age, gender and patterns of common intense fear among adults. *Behavior Research and Therapy, 22,* 141–150.

Kohnstamm, G. A. (1989). Temperament in childhood: Cross-cultural and sex differences. In G. A. Kohnstamm, J. E. Bates, & M. K. Rothbart (Eds.), *Temperament in childhood* (pp. 483–508). West Sussex: Wiley.

Kuebli, J., & Fivush, R. (1992). Gender differences in parent–child conversations about past emotions. *Sex Roles, 27,* 683–698.

LaFrance, M., & Banaji, M. (1992). Toward a reconsideration of the gender–emotion relationship. In M. Clark (Ed.), *Emotion and social behavior, Review of personality and social psychology* (Vol. 14, pp. 178–201). London: Sage.

Larsen, R. J., & Diener, E. (1987). Affect intensity as an individual difference characteristic: A review. *Journal of Research in Personality, 21,* 1–39.

Lewis, H. B. (1971). *Shame and guilt in neurosis.* New York: International Universities Press.

Lewis, M., Sullivan, M. W., Stanger, C., & Weiss, M. (1989). Self-development and self-conscious emotions. *Child Development, 60,* 146–156.

Machtlinger, V. J. (1981). The father in psychoanalytic theory. In M. E. Lamb (Ed.), *The role of the father in child development* (pp. 113–154). New York: Wiley.

Malatesta, C. Z. (1988). The role of emotions in the development and organization of personality. In R. Thompson (Ed.), *Nebraska symposium of motivation: Socioemotional development* (pp. 1–55). Lincoln, NE: University of Nebraska Press.

Malatesta, C. Z., Culver, C., Tesman, J., & Shepard, B. (1989). The development of emotion expression during the first two years of life. *Monographs of the Society for Research in Child Development, 54*(1–2, Serial No. 219), 1–104.

Malatesta, C. Z., & Haviland, J. M. (1982). Learning display rules: The socialization of emotion expression in infancy. *Child Development, 53,* 991–1003.

Malatesta, C., & Wilson, A. (1988). Emotion–cognition interaction in personality development: A discrete emotions, functionalist analysis. *British Journal of Social Psychology, 27,* 92–112.

Miller, R. S., & Leary, M. R. (1992). Social sources and interactive functions of emotion: The case of embarrassment. In M. Clark (Ed.), *Emotion and social behavior, Review of personality and social psychology* (Vol. 14, pp. 178–201). London: Sage.

Miller, P., & Sperry, L. L. (1987). The socialization of anger and aggression. *Merrill–Palmer Quarterly, 33,* 1–31.

Nolen-Hoeksema, S. (1987). Sex differences in unipolar depression: Evidence and theory. *Psychological Bulletin, 101,* 259–282.

Olver, R. R., Aries, E., & Batgos, J. (1989). Self–other differentiation and the mother–child relationship: The effects of sex and birth order. *Journal of Genetic Psychology, 150,* 311–321.

Parnell, K. (1992). *Mother–toddler interaction in relation to peer relations.* Unpublished doctoral dissertation, Boston University.

Pennebaker, J. W., Hughes, C., & O'Heeron, R. (1987). The psychophysiology of confession: Linking inhibitory and psychosomatic processes. *Journal of Personality and Social Psychology, 52,* 781–793.

Perry, D. G., Perry, L. C., & Weiss, R. (1989). Sex differences in the consequences that children anticipate for aggression. *Developmental Psychology, 25,* 312–319.

Ruddick, S. (1982). Maternal thinking. In B. Thorne & M. Yalom (Eds.), *Rethinking the family* (pp. 76–94). New York: Longman.

Sandler, J., & Sandler, A. (1986). On the development of object relationships and affects. In P. Buckley (Ed.), *Essential papers on objects relations* (pp. 272–292). New York: New York University Press.

Schell, A., & Gleason, J. B. (1989, December). *Gender differences in the acquisition of the vocabulary of emotion.* Paper presented at the Annual meeting of the American Association of Applied Linguistics, Washington, DC.

Sommers, S., & Kosmitzki, C. (1988). Emotion and social context: An American German comparison. *British Journal of Social Psychology, 27,* 35–49.

Spence, J. T., & Helmreich, R. L. (1978). *Masculinity and femininity: Their psychological dimensions, correlates and antecedents.* Austin: University of Texas.

Sprecher, S., & Sedikides, C. (1993). Gender differences in perceptions of emotionality: The case of close heterosexual relationships. *Sex Roles, 28*, 511–530.

Stapley, J., & Haviland, J. (1989). Beyond depression: Gender differences in normal adolescents' emotional experiences. *Sex Roles, 20*, 295–309.

Stern, D. (1985). *The interpersonal world of the infant.* New York: Basic Books.

Strayer, J. (1986). Children's attributions regarding the situational determinants of emotion in self and others. *Developmental Psychology, 22*, 649–654.

Tangney, J. P. (1990). Assessing individual differences in proneness to shame and guilt: Development of the Self Conscious Affect and Attribution Inventory. *Journal of Personality and Social Psychology, 59*, 102–111.

Tronick, E. (1989). Emotions and emotional communication in infants. *American Psychologist, 44*, 112–119.

Tronick, E., & Cohn, J. (1989). Infant–mother face-to-face interaction: Age and gender differences in coordination and the occurrence of miscoordination. *Child Development, 60*, 85–92.

Weinberg, M. K. (1992, May). Boys and girls: Sex differences in emotional expressivity and self-regulation during early infancy. Paper presented in L. J. Bridges (Chair), *Early emotional self-regulation: New approaches to understanding developmental change and individual differences.* Symposium presented at the International Conference on Infant Studies (ICIS), Miami, FL.

Weiss, J., Sampson, H., & The Mount Zion Psychotherapy Research Group (1986). *The psychoanalytic process: Theory, clinical observations, and empirical research.* New York: Guilford.

Whitesell, N. R., Robinson, N. S., & Harter, S. (1991, April). *Anger in early adolescence: Prototypical causes and gender differences in coping strategies.* Poster presented at the Biennial meeting of the Society for Research in Child Development, Seattle, WA.

Wintre, M. G., Polivy, J., & Murray, M. (1990). Self predictions of emotional response patterns: Age, sex, and situational determinants. *Child Development, 61*, 1124–1133.

Zahn-Waxler, C., Cole, P., & Barrett (1991). Guilt and empathy: Sex differences and implications for the development of depression. In J. Garber & K. Dodge (Eds.), *The development of emotion regulation and dysregulation* (pp. 243–272). Cambridge: Cambridge University Press.

Zahn-Waxler, C., Ridgeway, D., Denham, S., Usher, B., & Cole, P. (1993). Pictures of infants' emotions: A task for assessing mothers' and young children's verbal communications about affect. In R. Emde, J. Osofsky, & P. Butterfield (Eds.), *The IFEEL pictures: A new instrument for interpreting emotions, Vol. 5, Zero to Three* (pp. 217–236). Madison, CT: International Universities Press.

Personality Theory:
Birth, Death, and Transfiguration

Carol Magai
Long Island University

> *Once upon a time, we had no personalities. Is it not exciting to see their return?*
>
> —Goldberg (1993, p. 32)

In this chapter we examine the thesis that emotional traits form the core of human personality. Before we begin, it will be helpful to review some history. From the birth, death, and resurrection of personality (Allport, 1937; Mischel, 1968; and Epstein, 1983, respectively) we can trace an interesting genealogy of the concept of *trait*. Allport stressed the diversity and multitudinous nature of the trait terms that could be used to describe a personality; he and Odbert (Allport & Odbert, 1936) identified over 17,000 such terms. Later, the work of Cattell and the application of factor analysis to these personality data reduced the number to a scant 16 (Cattell, 1947, 1957; Cattell, Eber, & Tatsuoka, 1970). The work of Norman (1963; Passini & Norman, 1966) subsequently reduced the number of basic traits to five (McCrae & Costa, 1985, 1987), although an even more parsimonious approach has been advocated by Eysenck (Eysenck & Eysenck, 1985), who has offered two- and three-factor models of personality. In between Cattell and the most recent work, there was even a period during which the construct of personality took such blows from methodologists—in particular, Mischel (1968)—that it led to the premature conclusion that personality theory had died. The opening quotation indicates that the reports of its demise were greatly exaggerated.

Currently, the five-factor model of personality is enjoying a reputation as one of the most important models to rise to the surface of personality psychology in recent times. The five factors or dimensions of personality are identified as:

1. *Extraversion.* Descriptive terms are those such as fun-loving, friendly and talkative; it is generally agreed that "sociability" is central to extraversion.
2. *Neuroticism.* This dimension includes adjectives like worrying, insecure, and temperamental, and as having negative affect as a central feature.
3. *Agreeableness/antagonism.* Terms at the negative end of the pole include argumentative, mistrustful, callous, and rude.
4. *Openness to experience.* This dimension is equivalent to Norman's "culture" and is described using terms like original, imaginative, and daring.
5. *Conscientiousness.* Empirically, this dimension seems to describe a trait that includes a hard-working, persevering character (McCrae & Costa, 1987).

A series of studies have yielded similar factors across methods and across an array of questionnaires (Costa & McCrae, 1980; Digman & Takemoto-Chock, 1981; McCrae & Costa, 1985, 1987; Noller, Law, & Comrey, 1987). The five-factor model thus appears quite robust in its ability to sort the results of various personality tests into reliably identified clusters that cohere in logical ways. Despite this coherence, the five-factor model is most accurately described as a taxonomy. Although the model has the elegance of parsimony, and sufficient reliability to swell the heart of any psychometritician, it is data-driven rather than theory-driven, and rests its faith on the products of statistical compression.

Factor-analytic studies of personality are vulnerable to a variety of criticisms. In the first place, factor analysis is a linear model and assumes that factors determining behavior combine additively. Empirically, however, dimensions may behave in nonlinear ways. Anxiety, which loads on the neuroticism dimension of both the five-factor model and Eysenck's model, is well known to show a curvilinear relationship with performance. Another nonlinear relationship was detected by Allport during the course of his examination of Spranger's (1928) six ideal types, which Allport translated into the central values of the theoretic, the economic, the aesthetic, social, political and religious. The latter value was found to have a curvilinear relationship with prejudice. Another problem with factor analysis is that a statistical solution can only reflect the material that is submitted to it; thus the five factors or any other factor-analytic products may represent an aspect of personality but may not represent all the aspects or even the most important ones. Moreover, a particular rotation may yield a parsimonious solution of only two or three factors, but mask lower order factor structures, which are nested within them. For example, factor analyses of emotion terms can yield both higher order solutions of "positive" and "negative" emotion dimensions, but they can also be factored so as to reveal separability among the various negative emotions and among the various positive emotions (Izard, Libero, Putnam, & Haynes, 1993; Noller, Law, & Comrey, 1987; Watson & Clark, 1991).

Finally, the naming of factors is a high art. Statistical procedures produce lists of items that load in various ways. One reads the loading patterns, evaluates the items that contribute, and interprets them—an art that leaves considerable room for dispute. As Digman and Inouye (1986) have wryly noted, the advent of computers and computer programs have turned the task of factoring large correlation matrices into child's play, but there is still "no program that will tell us what the factors mean" (p. 120).

What is missing from these and other inductive and taxonomic approaches to personality is a larger, overarching theory that provides the motivational link between character "structure" on the one hand and predictable behavior on the other. What is required is a theory of human development and motivation.

Allport (1968), the original progenitor of American personality theory, was somewhat at a loss when it came to explaining the motivational forces behind personality. Old constructs such as the pleasure principle and tension-reduction mechanisms were invoked to describe the forces directing personality in early development. In the adult, however, behavior was said to be governed by *functionally autonomous goals* that were discontinuous from earlier motivations. That is, most adult behaviors, outside of neurophysiological-driven addictions, were seen as being derived from interests and values that no longer bore a relation to the tensions with which they may have originally been associated. However, this construct left much to be desired about the "stuff" of adult motivation. Although Allport soundly rejected the drive-reduction, reactive model of adult behavior, he could not compel himself to adopt McDougall's concept of purpose because of its association with the much-maligned instinct theory. Neither could he specify other motive forces, save to claim that the propelling force behind human behavior resides in "the present onmoving structure of personality" (p. 395).

In general, Allport's views on motivation have been seen as having more heuristic than explanatory value. Despite this, the basic tenets of his theory of personality—that personality is governed by sets of traits that are general in nature (common traits) but uniquely configured (individual traits or personal dispositions) within the individual—are assumptions that are tacitly shared by contemporary trait theories of personality. Allport (1961) described individual traits in the following way. A trait or personal disposition "is a generalized neuropsychic structure (peculiar to the individual), with the capacity to render stimuli functionally equivalent, and to initiate and guide consistent (equivalent) forms of adaptive and stylistic behavior" (p. 363).

By this, Allport meant that traits are the fundamental units of individual consistency. Traits mediate between classes of stimuli and classes of response. The trait of anxiety, for example, renders a whole class of stimuli "threatening" and produces a whole class of responses termed "defensive," including escape and avoidance behaviors. Thus, traits affect perception and behavior in broad and systematic ways. This is an important construct, and one that is implicit in contemporary theories, even in taxonomic approaches such as the five-factor model.

What trait theory, as it evolved since Allport's time, as well as the various theories of the present-day taxonomists, has failed to deal adequately with, is the *why*, the *wherefore*, and the *ontogeny* of human personality. The factor-analytic approaches evolved from an analysis of self-report and observer ratings, rather than a theory of motivation, and, we contend, a theory of personality must ultimately be rooted in a theory of motivation. Even the lofty realm of *intelligence* was seen by Piaget as deriving from the earthy impetus of biological adaptation.

Here we argue that a comprehensive theory of personality must solve the problem of motivation, map out the domains of influence, specify the occasions for the elicitation of the trait (that is, deal with the person/situation interaction effect, Pervin, 1993), and engage the central issues of human development. It must specify the origins of individual difference, and account for continuity and change over time. A number of authors have begun to tackle these problems, most notably Izard and colleagues (Izard et al., 1993). In this chapter we explore the heuristic value of a theory of personality based on discrete-emotions theory, a motivationally based account of human action and human development.

WHY?

The why of behavior is essentially the question of motivation. Why do people engage in the behaviors they do, and why does one person behave in a different fashion from someone else? The five-factor model proponents assume that we can measure the essential dimensions of personality in individuals and then characterize them in terms of the prominence of such traits in personality functioning. We expect a person who is predominantly open to experience and extroverted to behave in quite different ways from an individual who is introverted and obsessive–compulsive. Distinguishing such differences, however, fails to explain why one individual is introverted and another not, and fails to explain why these behaviors are maintained over time. Finally, why should human personality be organized along the particular dimensions of extroversion, neuroticism, agreeableness, openness, and intelligence (culture)? What is the governing principle behind these five axes? The five-factor model does not contend with such issues. A trait-analytic theory of emotions, however, which is offered in the present chapter, can. Moreover, if one accepts the central thesis of contemporary affect theory (Izard, 1977, 1991; Tomkins, 1962, 1963, 1991) that emotions constitute the primary motivational system in humans, one is moved to search beyond the labels assigned to the five factors to an emotion-based account of human personality functioning. We first pause to consider emotions as motivationally based behavior patterns.

The Role of Emotions in Motivated Behavior

Shand (1914) was perhaps the first to suggest that personality traits were organized around emotions. At the time that he was writing, the turn of the century, taxonomic approaches to personality were well-established. For example, Ribot (1903), the so-called French Wundt, claimed that there were three main types of character—sensitive, active, and apathetic—and then went on to describe a veritable hothouse of "species" and "varieties" subsumed within the three more basic "genera." Shand (1914) faulted his contemporaries for their taxonomic approaches. In his view, "Such lists of qualities do not tell us anything of their inner connection, and to what limitations they are subject, and what are the chief systems of the mind which elicit, develop, and organize them, whilst allowing other qualities to perish" (p. 26).

Shand's own approach, in *Foundations of Character*, was to tie character types to the properties and development of the affect system. As such, he considered the primary emotions as the root forces of character. Because the different emotions are associated with different activities or conduct, knowing the basic emotion in the character permitted one to predict certain kinds of behavior over others. For example, the person whose mood/temper was of Repugnance (an emotion related to, but distinct from, Disgust) would be likely to "detect the faults of its objects" (1914, p. 151) and find "satisfaction in the criticism of human nature" (1914, p. 151). Shand (1914) also understood that emotional dispositions influenced information processing: "When we are in an irascible mood we are disposed to get angry on the smallest pretexts, and to find justifications for our anger on all sides. Our sensibility to anger is increased both in range and in delicacy. Things and persons seem contrary. We are ready to blame them and to exaggerate their defects" (p. 151). Shand was less successful in delineating the origins of particular traits. He presumed that the existence of individual differences in physiology was a factor, but also experience and habit. Unfortunately, he did not elaborate on this aspect of the theory.

Shand was influenced by Darwinian theory and American functionalism. His theory was complex and quite advanced for that historical epoch. It is noteworthy in its attempts to move beyond the mere classification of character types to that of explanation and prediction. However, within the decade that Shand was writing, behaviorism would sweep America, and functionalism would be eclipsed (Beilin, 1983).

An emotions-theoretical approach to personality would not be possible again until the 1960s and 1970s, when several theories of emotion were propounded, including those of Ekman, Izard, Plutchik, and Tomkins. What all of these theories had in common was a discrete-emotions approach to understanding emotional functioning. That is, they assumed that there were a limited number of basic or primary human emotions, each of which is distinguished by a unique pattern of neurophysiology, expressive behavior, phenomenology, and motivation. There was also the suggestion, in some of the writings, that individuals could develop emotional predispositions which related to personality functioning.

Of those just mentioned, Izard (1971, 1972, 1977, 1991), in particular, has pursued the link between emotions and personality, and in addition, has tackled the developmental questions. I have also approached the problem from a discrete-emotions, functionalist, and developmental framework (Magai & Hunziker, 1993; Malatesta, 1990; Malatesta & Wilson, 1988). This chapter expands on that framework and elaborates on the data supporting such a view of human personality. Indeed, the thesis we pursue in this chapter places emotions at the core of the analysis. Elsewhere (Malatesta, 1990; Malatesta & Wilson, 1988) we have proposed that individuals are organized around emotional traits or affective biases. We contend that these biases are the developmental product of the differential activation and resolution of the fundamental emotions described by discrete emotions theory.

From this vantage point, it is interesting to examine some of the data from factor-analytic studies of personality. An examination of the data of these studies suggests that the factor labels may be masking underlying emotional traits. That is, the five factors or the two- or three-factor models of factor-analytic fame may be more coherently interpreted from within the framework of emotions theory. The factors of extraversion and neuroticism, for example, found in Eysenck's typology as well as in the five-factor theory and as assessed in empirical correlational investigations, appear to represent the superordinate categories of positive and negative affect, respectively (Izard et al., 1993; Larsen & Ketelaar, 1991). A variety of studies have demonstrated correlations between the trait of extraversion and positive affect and between neuroticism and negative affect (reviewed in Larsen & Ketelaar, 1991). Moreover, Larsen and Ketelaar (1991) found that these traits altered perception in directional ways; extroverts and introverts were differentially responsive to positive and negative emotional cuing. Subjects high on extraversion showed increased positive affect in response to positive mood induction but not greater negative affect in response to negative mood induction. Neuroticism was related to increased negative affect in response to negative mood induction but not positive affect in response to positive mood induction.

The thesis that emotion traits are at the core of personality is further supported by our analysis of how items dealing with the emotions load within the Norman Five. Although not all of the primary emotions (Izard, 1991) are represented in the item pools of the tests that have comprised the substrate of the factor analytic studies, those emotions that are well-represented tend to load on different factors. Factor 1, for example (Extroversion, Surgency), loads on items that can be construed as indexing general *happiness* and ebullience; Factor 2 (Neuroticism), as already mentioned, loads on *fearfulness*, anxiety, nervousness, and tension; Factor 3 (Agreeableness, Friendly Compliance versus Hostile Noncompliance) represents items that can be seen as biased towards *anger* and hostility; Factor 4 (Openness to experience Culture; Intelligence), in light of the fact that it taps dimensions of imaginativeness, creativity, and inquiring intellect, seems to pick up items that evaluate an individual's general *"interest"* and involvement in the world. To the extent that a low score on Factor 1 (Extraversion) implies the converse of happiness; that is, unhappiness, this factor may also be capable of identifying those individuals who might be characterized as tending toward trait *sadness*. The same factor probably also subsumes *shame/shyness* (Izard, 1977), since these tendencies would, one guesses, be features of the introversion pole of the extraversion scale; alternatively, such emotions may factor into Factor 2, since shyness has been described as a type of anxiety—social anxiety. In any case, four of the dimensions of the five-factor model could, with little violence to the data themselves, be relabeled as representing dimensions of emotion traits.

Interestingly, Izard's (1972) own factor analytic study of emotions, which used the Differential Emotions scale (DES), a state/trait emotions inventory with items representing ten emotions specified by differential-emotions theory, yielded a pattern of results validating the uniqueness of the different emotions and the possibility of identifying different personality types organized around emotion traits. In a more recent study, Izard et al. (1993) looked at the pattern of correlation between the discrete emotions identified in the DES and three other personality tests, namely Eysenck's Personality Questionnaire, Jackson's Personality Research form, and Zuckerman's Sensation Seeking Scale. Interest and Joy scales from the DES correlated positively with Eysencks' Extroversion Scale, and all the negative emotions correlated positively with neuroticism. Discrete emotions also correlated with various individual dimensions of some of the other scales. In this study shame was subsumed within the neuroticism dimension of Eysenck's scale, as were the other negative emotions. The Izard et al. study did not correlate the DES with the NEO scale of Costa and McCrae—which taps the five dimensions of personality of the five-factor model. Although the basic emotions of disgust, anger, and contempt are separable experiences, they tend to cluster together in personality as the *hostile triad* (Izard, 1972) and hence they also would be likely to load on the five factor's dimension of agreeableness–hostility.

It is dubious whether the dimension of conscientiousness would correlate with a particular emotion for two reasons: First, because this factor does not contain obviously emotional items; second, because personality traits may be organized so as to *defend* against emotions. One can easily imagine that conscientiousness may be driven by the desire to avoid anger about the consequences of incompleted tasks, or driven by the desire to avoid anxiety about others' evaluation of one's work. Thus, conscientiousness may represent a trait reflecting a defensive coping resolution of a particular emotion or pattern of emotions, and differentially so in different individuals.

Here we would like to propose that there are at least 5 higher order emotion traits (of the 10 identified by Izard) that are well represented in human personality. These are the same five emotions that emerge in different factors in the factor analytic studies mentioned previously: Happiness, Sadness, Fear, Anger, and Interest/Excitement. We do not deny that the other emotions can consolidate in personality in a trait-like way, but simply that they are less likely to be prominent aspects of personality or that they are correlated with the higher order traits. For example, Izard (1972) found that among the negative emotions, shame accounted for a large percentage of the variance in depression scores. We propose the five particular traits just mentioned for several reasons. First, as far as the negative emotions are concerned, personality and clinical psychology has long recognized traits that are organized around anger, fear, and sadness. Depression, anxiety, and hostility figure prominently as symptoms in a number of DSM-IV diagnostic categories. The most ubiquitous types of personality scales measuring emotional dimensions in personality are centered on hostility (e.g., the Cook Medley Hostility Scale, the Framingham Scale, the Anger-In/Anger-Out Scale), anxiety (the Taylor Manifest Anxiety Scale; the State–Trait Anxiety Inventory; the Zung Anxiety Scale), and sadness (Beck Depression Inventory, the Hamilton Scale; the Zung Depression Inventory). Positive emotions such as happiness and interest, in contrast, are obviously of less clinical interest and are thus less well represented in diagnostic inventories; nevertheless, we recognize that they can figure prominently in personality, as attested to by their position within the constellations that describe Factor 1 and Factor 4 of the Norman Five.

A second source of support for the contention that these five may be more "basic" and readily susceptible to the development of pronounced individual differences has to do with the basic neurophysiology of the brain. Panksepp (1990) has identified five emotion-based "neural command circuits" that appear to subserve adaptive functioning across all mammalian species. He has termed them the Rage, Panic, Exploratory, Fear, and Social-Contact circuits. When one examines the behaviors that are associated with the operation of these circuits, it would appear that they are integrally associated with the fundamental emotions of anger, sadness, interest, fear, and happiness, respectively.

In summary, the data from recent personality studies lend themselves to an emotions-based interpretation of personality—the *why* of personality dimensions; the apparent neurophysiological substrate had also been identified. At this point, we need to consider the motivational properties of particular emotions, which will take us directly to the *wherefore* question raised earlier in this chapter.

WHEREFORE

As Shand (1914) intuited, emotions are instinctually based and individual emotions activate behavior in ways that are distinct and functionally adaptive. Similarly, contemporary theories of emotion stress that *emotions* and not *drives* are the "stuff" of motivation (Izard, 1971, 1977, 1991; Tomkins, 1962, 1963, 1991). Moreover, different emotions are said to fuel different behavioral activities. The *wherefore* of personality traits has to do with the occasions that activate the emotions of emotion traits and the products of trait activation. Here we need to consider what elicits the various emotions, what functions they serve, and their domains of influence.

For this analysis, let us return to Allport's definition of traits and apply it to the emotion traits just identified. Allport maintained that traits, or personal dispositions, rendered whole classes of stimuli functionally equivalent and are predisposing for a whole pattern of responses. In less behavioristic terms, this means that traits such as anxiety affect information and behavior in a broad and pervasive way. A person organized around the emotion of anger is sensitized to the anger-cuing properties of a whole range of objects, persons, and events; it also means that the person has a low threshold to respond to these objects in a way that is consonant with the motivational qualities of anger—that is, in a sufficiently aggressive, challenging way so as to overcome obstacles posed by frustrating circumstances as well as by the "malevolent" intentions of others.

In an earlier paper (Malatesta & Wilson, 1988), we presented a framework for conceptualizing how emotions become incorporated into the structure of personality—based on their particular expressive and motivational qualities, we highlighted the signal value of emotions in cuing motivated behavior in both the self and social partners. Table 7.1 presents a synopsis of the signal properties of several of the basic emotions and their functions within the self-system and within the interpersonal system.

As indicated, each emotion is elicited by a categorically different event, and each has distinct motivational properties. *Sadness* is elicited by the general property of loss, either social or material. Within the self-system, sadness may be a reaction to personal loss or the loss of others. Loss to the self leads to motor slowing, decreased effort, and withdrawal resulting in energy conservation under conditions in which efforts to recover loss would likely be ineffectual (as in the case of death of a loved one). Sadness

TABLE 7.1
Signal Value of Emotions in Cuing Motivated Behavior

Emotion	Elicitor	Function in Self-System	Function in Interpersonal System
Sadness	Loss of valued object; lack of efficacy	At low levels promotes empathy; at higher levels serves to immobilize the individual (possibly forestalling the occasion of further trauma)	Elicits nurturance, empathy, succorance
Fear	Perception of danger	Identifies threat; promotes flight or attack	Signals submission; wards off attack
Anger	Frustration of goals; pain	Effects removal of barriers or sources of frustration towards goals	Warning of possible impending attack, aggression
Joy	Familiarity; pleasurable stimulation	Signal to self to continue the present activities	Promotes social bonding through contagion of good feeling
Interest	Novelty; discrepancy, expectancy	Opens the sensory systems for information intake	Signals receptivity

about the losses of others promotes empathic concern. As a signal within the interpersonal system, sadness cues others for the provision of nurturance and caretaking. *Fear*, in terms of its self-cuing functions, helps the individual to identify events, persons, or objects as threatening, so that emergency functions can be mobilized; in the interpersonal system it signals submission to a threatening individual and is useful in warding off attack. *Anger* tends to motivate behavior that is designed to overcome frustration and barriers to goals; as a signal to others it motivates avoidance, compliance, and submission. *Joy* insures the perpetuation of pleasurable activities; as a signal to others it promotes social bonding, reproduction, and caregiving—it makes life worth living. *Interest* opens the sensory systems for information intake and fosters continued engagement in behavioral activities; within the interpersonal system, expressions of interest signal receptivity and promote continued interchange between social partners.

As indicated earlier, the properties of emotions are functionally adaptive in the life-sphere of the individual in the context of personal as well as interpersonal goals. Over time, the repetition of particular patterns of emotion activation may result in the crystallization of recognizable personality patterns. For example, repeated activation of anger may lead to the development of a hostile personality pattern. With respect to the activation of interest, accretion over time may result in predispositions and activities that can be interpreted as the motive force behind Allport's functionally autonomous goals.

When emotions are activated they tend to have a pervasive influence on consciousness; they influence information processing (perception, judgment, interpretation, decision making) and, ultimately, behavior. Let us examine the case for anger, a particularly well-researched emotion.

Anger and the Personality Trait of Hostility

A number of writers recognize that some individuals have a predominantly angry way of engaging the world. Such persons tend to be irritable, sensitive to slights, cynical, and prone to interpret others as negatively motivated. This configuration of tendencies leads to the description of a hostile personality. There are a number of personality scales designed to measure the strength of this personality characteristic, including the Cook–Medley scale of the MMPI. In our view, when anger affect predominates in personality we say that the individual is organized around the trait of anger. The theory predicts that evidence of the central organizational nature of this emotion will be found pervasively across wide domains of information processing and behavior. Let us first examine the evidence for an anger organization. Are anger biases wide or domain-specific? What is the relation between affective state, thought, and action? How pervasive is the anger bias and how insistently and subtly does it insinuate itself into the personal lifestyle and interpersonal relationships of individuals?

The Anger Organization. Based on the properties of anger emotion described in Table 7.1, we would expect a person organized around the emotion of anger to (a) feel angry and resentful more frequently than others, (b) to have a perceptual bias that sensitizes the individual to identify occasions for anger with more than average frequency; that is, to be vigilant for hostile provocations, (c) to have a tendency to interpret ambiguous social scenes as ill-meaning; that is, to infer that others want to thwart, humiliate, or otherwise provoke the individual, and (d) to behave in an aggressive fashion more readily. There are three personality configurations that have been identified in the literature that seem prone to hostile emotion: (a) The Type A Behavior Pattern of the adult literature, (b) insecurely attached children, and (c) aggression-prone children.

Type A Behavior Pattern (TABP, or Type A) is a behavior pattern that was identified over 20 years ago, when it was called "hurry sickness" because of its association with a fast-paced, hard-driving personality and with cardiac disease. Over time the cardinal features of TABP were defined as impatience, ambitiousness, time urgency, and hostility; in fact, an irritable voice and explosive manner of speaking are the key clinical features in classifying subjects during the assessment procedure of the Structured Interview. More recently, it has become evident that it is the *hostility* component that features most prominently in the personality and is the variable most closely associated with cardiac disease.

In our own study of the emotional expressivity in Type A Behavior Pattern (TABP) (Malatesta-Magai, Jonas, Shepard, & Culver, 1992) Type A individuals scored higher on trait anger and trait aggression than did their Type B counterparts. It is important to note that Type As did not differ on other emotional dimensions; Type A and Type Bs were equivalent on measures of anxiety and depression. Another important finding was that younger Type A males (classic coronary-prone individuals) not only were angrier, but were more likely to show evidence of attempts to *suppress* anger. Clinical psychology suggests that suppressed emotion often finds an outlet in projection. Indeed, results of a subsidiary study, not yet published, provide support for this phenomenon.

Shepard and I developed and administered a test that consisted of a series of vignettes to our Type A and B subjects. These were scenes that described various emotion-charged episodes; the subject was asked to complete each scene by selecting one of two potential responses. Sixteen of the items could be resolved in favor of angry interpretations and responses, 16 in favor of sad interpretations and withdrawing responses, and 16 in favor of anxious interpretations and responses. Twenty Type As and 20 Type Bs (under the age of 50) were randomly selected from the database. (Selection was restricted to younger subjects since previous research indicated that only younger subjects conform to the classic features of TABP.) Analysis of variance applied to the anger scores showed that Type As were significantly more likely than Type Bs to resolve the stories in an angry direction.

Anger as an organizing force in personality is also found within the child developmental literature. Attachment research has identified two types of insecurely attached children, both of whom show anger organizations. *Avoidantly* attached children in general show a tendency to suppress their emotions; however, they show a disposition to engage in unprovoked attacks of aggression directed at their mothers and have been described as covertly hostile. Thus, their anger is subversive. In contrast, *ambivalent* children tend to be temperamentally irritable and to display their anger openly. This difference in the display of anger—covert versus overt—raises the issue of how anger or any emotion trait may be structured within the personality.

In an earlier paper, Wilson and I (Malatesta & Wilson, 1988) distinguished between two types of emotional bias—a deficiency bias and a surfeit bias. The surfeit condition involves the case in which a particular emotion or set of emotions monopolizes the person's repertoire—the emotions are excessively activated and expressed. In the case of the deficiency bias, emotion expression is restricted—either because the emotion is warded off due to unconscious conflict, or because the emotion is insufficiently developed. Avoidant children appear to be anger-deficient—apparently due to unconscious conflict rather than inadequate exposure to social models who express this emotion. Ambivalent children appear to be surfeited with anger in that they have a low threshold for its activation.

Berlin (1993) found that avoidant preschoolers were significantly less likely to acknowledge angry affect than ambivalent children, who had the highest scores. Working with school-age children, a student from our laboratory, Adickman (1993), found that 6–8-year-olds who were identified as insecurely attached (mainly avoidant) on the basis of the Separation Anxiety test made more errors in an emotion-decoding test that involved projected hostile emotion (anger, disgust, and contempt) than did securely attached children.

Another group of children who have been intensively studied in recent times are aggression-prone children. Although such a label describes a behavior rather than a personality type, the literature indicates that this behavior pattern is indicative of an anger organization, in that it is biased towards hostile perceptions, attributions, and unfriendly interpersonal strategies. For example, Rubin and Clark (1983) interviewed aggressive and nonaggressive preschoolers about reactions to a variety of hypothetical situations. Aggressive children offered as many solutions as nonaggressive children to problems involving the acquisition of objects or access to desired activities, but were more likely to rely on coercive strategies— agonistic and bribe strategies—and were less likely to offer prosocial strategies. Aggressive elementary children (Rubin, Moller, & Emptage, 1987) were also more likely to suggest bribe and affect manipulation strategies and less prosocial strategies than their nonaggressive counterparts across a range of scenarios. In help-seeking vignettes, aggressive children were more likely to say they would bully their targets ("You better help") and use bizarre/abnormal strategies, rather than offer prosocial strategies such as asking politely. In friendship initiation situations, aggressive children produced fewer relevant strategies and were more likely to offer bizarre/abnormal strategies and fewer invitations to potential friends. Finally, a study by Walters and Peters (1980) showed that aggressive children preferred aggressive responses as a first-choice strategy across a range of social situations.

The foregoing early studies suggested that a select group of children, at the conceptual level, have a narrower range of strategies than their nonaggressive counterparts when it comes to conflict resolution, friendship initiation, and object acquisition, and that they favor aggressive and nonnormative strategies in dealing with interpersonal situations. Subsequent research indicates that the aforementioned information-processing biases and deficiencies are causally implicated in *behavior* patterns. The work of Dodge and colleagues (Dodge, Pettit, McClaskey, & Brown, 1986) and Lochman (1987) shows that the aggressive behavior of aggressive versus nonaggressive children during real social interchanges is linked to specific perceptual and attributional biases. Dodge et al. (1986) found that aggressive children were more likely than matched nonaggressive peer controls to attribute hostile intentions to a peer provocation, to access aggressive responses to this stimulus, and to behave aggressively when provoked. Lochman (1987) assessed differences in self-perceptions, peer perceptions, and attributions of relative responsibility in aggressive and nonaggressive boys under experimental conditions of competitive dyadic discussion. The aggressive boys had distorted perceptions of their own aggressiveness; despite equivalent levels of aggression in aggressive and nonaggressive peers during the interaction, aggressive boys perceived their partners as being more aggressive than themselves.

Aggressive children also apparently have a lower threshold to anger arousal. For example, Underwood, Cole, and Herbsman (1992) found that aggressive children reported more anger in response to anger-eliciting videos than did nonaggressive children. This lower threshold apparently holds under ambiguous situations as well. In a study by Graham, Hudley, and Williams (1992), aggressive and nonaggressive adolescents were exposed to negative outcome scenarios; when the scenes were ambiguous, aggressive subjects assumed more malicious intent on the part of pictured children, reported greater anger, and said they would respond in hostile ways more often than nonaggressive subjects.

It is important to note that these effects tend to be of small magnitude under relaxed testing conditions, and tend to increase during real or simulated events that involve threat or challenge (Dodge & Somberg, 1987). Thus, we cannot expect biases to be in evidence at all times. Emotion biases may be camouflaged under ordinary circumstances and in the context of polite social intercourse. They are activated when they can assist at the performance of goal-related behavior, and are thus likely to be called into play mainly during occasions of challenge or when goals are activated.

The tendency for emotion biases to be elicited selectively and to interact with situational context is nicely illustrated by an analysis of regional differences for aggressive behavior in adult males. Nisbett's (1993) analysis focused mainly on the behavioral and attitudinal qualities of Caucasian males in different parts of the country. He showed that homicide rates for Southern-American males are substantially higher than those of their Northern counterparts. Examining a wide array of data, he systematically ruled out competing explanations and concluded that the rates are linked to regional differences in the harshness of parental disciplinary practices, and regional differences in attitudes about the legitimate and proper provocations to aggression. Specifically, Southerners report more severe beatings by parents than Northerners, and Southern men more strongly endorse spanking as an appropriate discipline policy than Midwestern subjects. In terms of attitudes, although Southerners do not endorse violence across the board, they do for selected items related to protection for self, family, and one's honor.

For example, Southerners versus non-Southerners are twice as likely to endorse killing as justifiable violence when it comes to defending the home; they are also significantly more likely to agree that a man has the right to kill a person to defend his family, and that police should shoot to kill rioters. Southern White men are also twice as likely to report having guns for protection as rural Midwestern White men. In one of the few experimental studies to test the regional disposition to aggression and violence, college students were deliberately challenged by a confederate's rude and insulting behavior; the subjects were observed during the experimental manipulation and their affective behavior was coded. The subjects also completed several projective measures. Southern versus non-Southern subjects displayed significantly greater anger in response to the provocation.

However, the anger did not affect the quality of their responses on all the projective measures. An elevation in anger content was evident in only one of the three projective media, the one involving affront and sexual challenge, with Southern versus non-Southern students being more likely to respond with violent imagery. Here it is important to note that the projective scenario resembled the experimental manipulation in that it involved an offensive insult, although the real-life insult was directed at the subject and to a protagonists' romantic partner. Thus, background variables of regional upbringing interacted with situation-specific anger priming to produce a significant bias in information processing.

In summary, an anger-prone personality configuration is well-identified in the literature. Individuals with an anger/hostility bias are likely to experience more anger on a day-to-day basis, to have a lower threshold for anger provocation, to perceive more stimuli as requiring hostile or aggressive responses, to more readily interpret other individuals as having hostile intentions or as behaving in a provocative manner, and to actually behave in a more aggressive, hostile manner. The bias thus appears to be pervasive and widely influential across psychological domains of perception, information processing, and behavior. We can also speculate that such individuals would be likely to score at the high end of Costa and McCrae's Agreeableness Factor of the NEO personality measure; that is, to be disagreeable, mistrustful, callous, and rude. The latter personality characteristics do not at first appear to have much to do with the original motivational properties described for anger—the removal of barriers to goals. An analysis of the *development* of traits will help clarify the relationship.

ONTOGENY

As indicated in the introduction to this chapter, personality theory must not only deal with differential description and prediction, but with the issue of ontogeny. That is, how do children and adults develop affective biases and how do these dispositions become consolidated or change over time? We begin with a review of some of the general developmental principles thought to be implicated in the ontogeny of emotion traits and then turn to a consideration of the specifics of anger socialization.

General Principles

As Tomkins (1962, 1963) originally suggested, children are likely to acquire emotional organizations or affective biases under conditions that involve the punitive socialization of emotion (Malatesta, Culver, Tesman, & Shepard, 1989). In contrast, under rewarding socialization of emotion the child develops a balanced repertoire, one in which no particular emotion dominates the personality; such an individual experiences and uses affects flexibly in the organization of goal-directed behavior, and possesses general socioemotional competence. It is now apparent that parental warmth and sympathy are important conditions for the rewarding socialization of emotion.

For example, Roberts and Strayer (1987) found that parental warmth was significantly related to the encouragement of expression of negative affect, and that warmth and responsiveness accounted for 61–69% of the variance seen in children's general socioemotional competence. Parental warmth is also correlated with children's empathy (Barnett, 1987), and parental sympathy is correlated with children's self-reported situational sympathy, at least for girls (Fabes, Eisenberg, & Miller, 1990).

Eisenberg et al. (1991) found that family cohesiveness, a variable assumed to provide the kind of emotional support believed to facilitate empathy and sympathetic responding, was associated with reported sympathy, as well as sadness in reaction to a sympathy-provoking film. Parents who are characterized by greater than average personal distress or anger had children with less dispositional sympathy and empathy (Fabes et al., 1990; Crockenberg, 1985, respectively).

In summary, having a warm, sympathetic parent whose own emotional organization is well-balanced and not constricted by the monopolization of any particular emotional bias will likely encourage the development of the child's full emotional repertoire, general socioemotional competence, and dispositions towards interpersonal sympathy and empathy. In contrast, the parent whose own personality favors some emotions to the exclusion of others is likely to create an emotional climate that fosters the development of emotion biases to a greater or lesser extent. Parental influence, however, is only one force in the development of emotion organizations. We turn now to a fuller consideration of the factors that may come into play in the development of an anger organization.

Ontogeny of the Hostile Personality

Although it is somewhat remarkable, the voluminous literature on Type A personality, spanning almost three decades, has only recently begun to investigate the developmental origins of the Type A personality, and some of that evidence is quite indirect. Two studies by Baer and colleagues (Baer, Vincent, Williams, Bourianoff, & Bartlett, 1980; Baer et al., 1983) suggest that there may be a "hypertensive" family style with negative verbal and nonverbal behavior (including contempt, sarcasm, and criticism) and gaze aversion as characteristic features of interaction; such features were found more frequently in families with a hypertensive father than in families with a normotensive father. In terms of developmental patterns, much of the initial work on the early antecedents of coronary-prone behavior was devoted to developing instruments to identify children who showed behavioral analogues of adult Type A behavior pattern.

More recent work has shifted to descriptive and predictive studies of Type A children. The literature indicates that TABP is relatively stable between 5 and 11 years of age, suggesting that the personality pattern may develop relatively early in life. Type A children have been found to be more aggressive in their interactions with others and to experience more frequent aversive life events than Type B children (Murray, Matthews, Blake, & Prineas, 1986). Matthews, Manuck, and Saab (1986) found that trait anger, but not Type A predicted increases in diastolic blood pressure in 15-year-olds during a natural stressor (having to give a speech in an English class), indicating that like adults, anger and hostility may be the crucial variables in the development of cardiovascular disease. In another study, McCann and Matthews (1988) found that in contrast to global Type A, one component—potential for hostility—affected children's cardiovascular response, independent of parental history of hypertension. Children with high scores on potential for hostility showed exaggerated systolic and diastolic blood pressure in one of several stress tasks.

What is clear from this earlier review is that children begin to show Type A behavior patterns early in life, that the pattern is stable over time—that TABP, and especially predisposition to anger/hostility, is associated with the kind of cardiovascular patterns seen in adult coronary-prone Type A individuals. What is not yet known is how the Type A pattern in children originates. One study (Matthews, Stoney, Rakaczky & Jamison, 1986) found that Type A boys tend to have Type A mothers and fathers. Rosenman and colleagues (Matthews, Rosenman, Dembroski, Harris, & MacDougall, 1984; Rosenman, Rahe, & Borhani, 1974) established that there was no significant heritability component of global Type A behavior as assessed by the Structured Interview, although some self-report scales did have heritable components.

A reanalysis of a subsample from the original Rosenman study using tape recorded interviews with 80 monozygotic and 80 dizygotic twin pairs (Matthews et al., 1984) suggested that certain clinical ratings—loudness of speech, competition for control of the interview, and potential for hostility (actually a measure of expressed hostility)—might have a heritable component. However, interestingly, other ratings that appeared to index the tendency to suppress or inhibit anger, were either not evaluated or did not show such a pattern. Thus, it is possible that certain aspects of emotionality—such as arousability or irritability—might have a genetic loading, but that styles of management (open expression versus controlled) introduce a source of learned variance that may be etiologically significant.

In summary, the limited children's and family literature on TABP suggests that temperamental irritability, parental modeling of Type A behavior (including, assumedly, anger and hostility), and a critical family climate may be important biological and environmental factors predisposing children to develop a hostile personality.

In terms of insecure attachments, there appear to be different sources of contribution to the angry disposition of the ambivalently and avoidantly attached children. In the first place, Kagan (1982) has suggested that children destined to be avoidantly attached may be temperamentally cool and not very reactive to stress, although this has not yet been substantiated. He has also suggested that children classed as ambivalent may simply be those who are temperamentally labile and thus more readily upset. In this case, there is some evidence for a temperamental contribution to attachment; ambivalent children are more likely to have been irritable as infants (Waters, Vaughn, & Egeland, 1980). On balance, however, most of the literature on the differential origins of attachment style implicate patterns of parenting and parental personality disposition.

Mothers of avoidant children have been described as covertly hostile, as insensitive to their infant's signals, and as overstimulating (Gaensbauer et al., 1985; Main, Tomasini, & Tolan, 1979; Belsky, Rovine, & Taylor, 1984; Malatesta, Grigoryev, Lamb, Albin, & Culver, 1986). There are thus three facets of parental behavior implicated in avoidant attachment, *and* potentially contributory to a defensive anger organization. *Covert anger*, it appears on fine-grained analysis, may not be especially well-hidden. A graduate student from our laboratory, Johanna Tesman (1992), did a detailed behavioral analysis of the vocal and facial behaviors of mothers during face-to-face play in early infancy. She found that what is typically described as covert hostility is more accurately described as conflicting signals and/or masked anger—such as the combination of a smile and irritated voice. Another graduate student, Connie Jones (1990) did a content analysis of the speech of mothers during mother–infant interactions sessions at 2½, 5, 7, and 22 months, and found that mothers of insecure infants (most of whom where avoidant) used more angry content words than did mothers of secure infants during face-to-face play. Exposure to angry words, facial expressions, and tone of voice, even when partially masked, conceivably sets the stage for negative affective contagion.

As Haviland and Lelwica have shown (1987), infants as young as 10 weeks of age are capable of differentiating sad, angry, and happy affect projected by their mothers, and, more importantly, they are differentially responsive; under the anger condition, protest and anger is recruited. In terms of *insensitivity* to infant cues, this feature of maternal behavior means that the children of these mothers will not learn the normal contingency patterns between their signals and the responses of partners. Infants as young as the first 2 to 8 months of life are capable of contingency learning, and react to *noncontingency* with anger (Lewis, Alessandri, & Sullivan, 1990). As for the exposure to *overstimulation*, it is probable that overstimulation provokes discomfort and irritation in infants, and perhaps anxiety, both of which would understandably lead to defensive strategies and avoidance.

In summary, mothers of avoidant children appear to be angrier, less sensitive, and overstimulating early in their infant's development. Later in development, the combination of avoidant attachment and exposure to maternal coercive disciplinary techniques is associated with the overattribution of hostile affect to nonhostile social stimuli (Adickman, 1993). Thus, an early anger disposition may become further consolidated in personality.

Ambivalently attached children and their mothers show a different developmental history. Ambivalently attached children express more overt anger than securely attached children during reunion in the context of the Strange Situation (Cassidy & Berlin, 1994) and under the conditions of a mastery motivation task (Frodi, Bridges, & Grolnik, 1985). According to Cassidy and Berlin's (1994) review and the work of Lyons-Ruth et al. (1982; Belsky et al., 1984) these mothers are not described as particularly angry, but rather as inconsistent or neglecting. Inconsistency of maternal behavior means that an infant's patterns of expectancy will be built up only to be dashed, producing conditions of *frustration*, a classic trigger for anger.

Comparing the behaviors of mothers of ambivalent and avoidant infants provides a clue as to the covert versus overt nature of these childrens' anger organization. The overstimulating interactive style of mothers must make them aversive partners, but if angry protest by the infant is met by anger on the part of the anger-prone mother, other defensive strategies for dealing with discomfort must be acquired—such as avoidance. Mothers of avoidant children are apparently also more controlling of their children's emotional expressions, at least according to mothers' self-report (Berlin, 1993). This constellation of behaviors may explain why avoidant children are more subversive in their anger expression.

Studies of abused children indicate that they are predominantly insecurely attached (see review by Magai & McFadden, 1995); they are typically classified as avoidant or as showing a mixed avoidant/ambivalent pattern. The literature on maltreatment is thus germane to the issue of emotion socialization for anger biases in avoidant and ambivalent children. Lyons-Ruth, Connell, Zoll, and Stahl (1987) found that maltreating mothers were more likely than nonmaltreating mothers to exhibit hostility towards their infants in subtle ways, and tended to interfere in their infants' activities. Mothers who behaved in a covertly hostile manner (e.g., exhibiting behaviors such as smiling while speaking in a sharp voice) tended to have children who were avoidantly attached, and who showed a pattern of mixed avoidant and resistent behavior in the context of the laboratory procedure of the Strange Situation.

Crittenden (1981) found that abusing mothers interfered with their infant's goal-directed behavior (i.e., frustrated them), and displayed conflicting emotional signals often involving covert hostility. During mother–infant interaction, infants of abusive mothers reacted to their intrusive, hostile, confusing signals by fussing, gaze aversion and refusing to interact. Other studies have shown that abusive mothers distort the affective value of emotion signals. For example, Kropp and Haynes (1987) found that abusive mothers tended to label negative affect as positive. In addition, Oldershaw and Walters (1989) found that abusive mothers perceived their children more negatively than controls, even when their children's behavior was similar; abusing parents and their children are also characterized by low empathy (Miller & Eisenberg, 1988).

THE ISSUE OF CONTINUITY AND CHANGE IN EMOTIONAL ORGANIZATIONS

So far we have described some of the factors that come into play in forging early emotion organizations; in this particular instance, that of anger. Here we consider the forces that act to reinforce and sustain the developing organization. In a later section we consider how such organization may come to be altered.

Continuity

Thus far in the present developmental analysis, our infants have developed their attachment styles and are well on their way to their unique emotional organizations. The fussy ambivalent child of infancy may now be the demanding toddler with a whine in her voice. The inexpressive, avoidant child of infancy now makes occasional "unprovoked" attacks against his mother, and seems to behave in a resentful way from time to time. Will these nascent tendencies continue and coalesce or will they undergo transformation? Here we consider the forces that help to maintain and consolidate early anger organizations.

From our earlier discussion, it is easy to see why infants who find their mothers insensitive and overstimulating would learn to avoid face-to-face contact. Obviously this is an adaptive strategy—at least in the short run—since it reduces the chances of further discomfort. However, it also deprives them of important social learning experiences, namely experiences contributing to knowledge about the expressive, communicative qualities of the human face. Such infants will thus develop their own kind of insensitivity.

A longitudinal study by Crockenberg (1985) supports this interpretation. In that study, mothers' attitudes and beliefs about infant care were originally assessed in the prenatal period, which yielded an index of maternal responsiveness. Infant irritability during the early postnatal period was also assessed, using the Neonatal Behavioral Assessment Scale. During the toddler period, mothers who had been trained in behavior observation and record keeping kept tape-recorded diaries of events along with detailed accounts of the emotions their children were exposed to and their reactions. These tapes were then coded for maternal emotion expression, toddler emotion expression, and their empathic, nonempathic, and transitional response to anger and other emotions whether directed toward the child or towards someone or something else.

Crockenberg found that mothers who expressed more anger during the toddler period had less responsive attitudes during the prenatal period. There was no significant degree of relationship between infant irritability and maternal anger, nor between early irritability and later toddler empathy, although all five of the less empathic children were irritable as babies.

Most importantly for our thesis, in the toddler period, maternal anger expressed towards children was found to have a unique effect on empathy. When maternal anger (versus other negative emotions) was directed towards the child, toddlers showed less concern for others, showed more concern for the self, were less compliant, and displayed more angry defiance towards others. The lack of empathy in these children is traceable to a developmental history specific to anger socialization. The link here between maternal anger and children's lack of empathy is interpretable within the framework of a discrete emotion, functionalist perspective. A child exposed to greater than average parental anger will necessarily orient to the implicit threat of physical abuse or abandonment. As such, the child's cue sensitivity will be narrowed, and defensive behaviors mobilized. There will thus be less vigilance toward cues indicative of others' needs.

Indeed, as mentioned earlier, abused children have been found to do more poorly on emotion-decoding tasks than nonabused children. Other facets of parent–child interaction promoting anger biases in this context are related to modeling factors. Parents with poor anger control ostensibly deprive their children of opportunities to observe appropriate anger modulation; moreover, given the monopolization of anger in the parents' repertoire, they also deprive their children of opportunities to observe other emotions, and to observe empathic responses to others.

We can envision how children's own anger organizations may become consolidated over time. Exposure to angry affect tends to reproduce anger in others because of the principle of affect contagion. That is, the affect of one person has a tendency to spread to that person's social partners (Izard, 1972).

The spread of *anger* among those exposed to the angry affect of others is illustrated in a series of studies by Cummings and colleagues (e.g., Cummings, 1987; Cummings, Ballard, El-Sheikh, & Lake, 1991; El-Sheikh, Cummings, & Goetsch, 1989). In these studies, children were exposed to background anger while they were alone or playing with other children. The anger occurred in the context of arguments between adults, either parents or unfamiliar individuals. What Cummings and colleagues have shown, convincingly enough, is that mere exposure to angry affect, even when it is not directed at the child, produced feelings of anger and distress in those children who overheard it; in some children, it even instigated aggressive behavior.

In terms of parent–child interactions, there will be more involved than contagion of parental anger, though this is surely a component. As Crockenberg (1985) has pointed out, there is likely a reciprocal relation between maternal attitudes and behaviors and children's behaviors that help to maintain maternal anger, such that mothers who are less responsive characterologically may set the stage for children's noncompliance, which in turn may stimulate more maternal anger and further noncompliance from children.

Development beyond early infancy will also be affected by parental child-rearing styles of discipline and conflict resolution. Parent–child conflicts are emotionally charged, salient, and repetitive; they are conceivably an important crucible for the development of emotion organizations and for learning affect management strategies and defenses (Malatesta & Wilson, 1988). Magai, Distel, and Liker (1993) found that adult subjects who reported that their parents used coercive disciplinary styles (including physical punishment) to a significant extent had emotion trait profiles organized around the hostile emotions. Adickman (1993), studying 6- to 8-year-olds, found that it was the combination of insecure attachment and coercive disciplinary styles that was associated with hostile biases in emotion projection.

Language is another vehicle for the elaboration of an anger sensitivity. As Jones (1990) has shown, the mothers of children destined to be avoidantly attached engage in more anger narrative than the mothers of those who develop secure attachments. Miller and Sperry (1987) did an ethnographic study of the socialization of anger and aggression in children from the urban, working-class neighborhood of south Baltimore; the children were 18 to 25 months old at the start of the study and they and their mothers were studied over a period of 8 months. What they found in analyzing verbatim transcripts of tape-recorded interactions between mothers and children and in interviews with mothers was that the mothers were, in effect, preparing their children for the street-tough life that characterizes south Baltimore. It was especially noteworthy that the socialization of their children included deliberate instigation of anger in their children, such as through teasing. The latter behavior was apparently designed to toughen their children; in addition, mothers' narratives were structured so as educate their children in the proper response to provocation—that is, to be angry rather than sad—and included instruction in the instrumental strategies for dealing with both one's own anger as well as the anger and aggression of others.

Dodge's (Dodge et al., 1986) analysis of the information processing strategies of aggressive children also suggests some of the reasons why angry patterns may be maintained over time and become consolidated in personality. These researchers found that aggressive versus nonaggressive children were more likely to attribute hostile intentions to a peer provocation, to access aggressive responses to this stimulus, and to behave aggressively when provoked. More importantly, they were also more likely than average children to receive negative and ignoring peer responses when they attempted to enter a group, thus probably reinforcing their sense of needing to screen the world for the hostile intentions of others.

In any case, it is clear that children can develop emotion-specific biases in their behavior at a very young age, in this case, an anger organization. In fact, such biases may develop as early as the first year of life. Shiller, Izard, and Hembree (1986), who coded the emotional response of 13-month-olds to separation from the mother, found that some high-negative emotion expressers displayed predominantly anger, whereas others showed mainly sadness. Anger biases may persist over long periods of time. Caspi, Elder, and Bem's (1987) analysis of data from the Berkeley longitudinal study, tracking development from early childhood (8–10 years of age) until 30–40 years of age, indicates that ill-tempered boys become ill-tempered men and ill-tempered girls grow up to have marriages characterized by dissention and conflict, and which tend to dissolve.

An examination of the literature on the Type A personality configuration begins to shed light on what kinds of circumstances and processes help to maintain the organization over time. The latest research indicates that a key feature of the Type A personality is not only that Type As experience anger more frequently, but that their emotion management style is one of suppression (Malatesta-Magai et al., 1992). According to clinical observation, suppression of anger should result in projection—and indeed, as indicated earlier, in our own research we were able to empirically confirm the tendency of Type As to project anger onto the protagonists of ambiguous vignettes. Projection of anger, interpersonally, is, of course, a primary vehicle for the maintenance of interpersonal friction.

The aforementioned literature sheds light on the origins and some of the factors involved in the maintenance of anger organizations over time. One factor, of course, is constitutional irritability. Other factors involve exposure to social agents who are frustrating, overly intrusive and insensitive to infant cues, who lack empathy, who display excessive anger, who use coercive disciplinary strategies, who elaborate an angry world view, and/or whose regulation of anger is poorly performed. Early emotion biases are then sustained through the mechanisms of either interpersonal avoidance or regular angry interchanges. Repetitive emotional experiences also affect cognitive function in pervasive ways, including perception and appraisal, encoding, memory, interpretation of information, and attributions. Over time, these experiences help to create the development of informational "structures" that are conditioned to process information in preferential ways. Such cognitive biases then come to sustain particular kinds of emotion. In the case of anger, perceptions, appraisals, and attributions are inclined to find the world a hostile, frustrating, and humiliating place. This in turn generates behaviors whose products confirm the hostility of the world. Emotion, cognition, and behavior thus interact in a synergistic way such that perceptions and feeling sustain one another in a recursive loop.

From the earlier discussion, we can distill some general principles of emotion socialization, but certain features will be idiosyncratic to the unique functional and signal properties of anger. General principles include constitutional predispositions, affect contagion (i.e., the spread of affect between social partners), self-regulation and defensive coping, and emotional–cognitive–behavioral loops. Anger-specific processes involve the emotion-specific properties of anger as a motivational signal to the self, and as an informational/motivational signal to others. Experiences with *frustration* will provoke anger, not fear or happiness. Interpersonally, displaying an angry face and voice will provoke aggression in others; displaying a fearful, sad, or interested face and voice will likely not, and so on. This issue is discussed in greater detail elsewhere (Magai & McFadden, 1995), in the context of a more comprehensive discussion of emotion socialization and the development of emotion biases.

Before we conclude this section, let us return to the five factor model's dimension of agreeableness/antagonism. Personality terms that load on that factor are terms like mistrustful, callous, and rude. The latter two qualities appear to relate to lack of empathy and insensitivity to the social cues of others. Mistrust seems more directly related to attribution of malevolent intentions of others. Both, it should now be clear, are conceptually assimilable to the dynamics of an anger emotional organization. Other terms that load on the agreeableness/antagonism factor—selfish, stubborn, unfair, suspicious, cold, stingy, critical, headstrong, negativistic, and jealous (Digman & Inouye, 1986; McCrae & Costa, 1985)—are interpretable within this framework as well.

Discontinuity

From the earlier discussion, it is clear what goes into the maintenance of emotional biases once they are formed. What is less clear are the factors that come in to play to produce discontinuity and behavior change. Developmental psychology, for the most part, has assumed a continuity model of human development. One such model is found in the attachment literature where the assumption is that attachment patterns established early in life inform and structure later social relationships and that these styles will endure over time. Indeed, attachment patterns have shown stability coefficients of about .60 to .80% over 1- and 2-year intervals, and one study has shown significant stability over 5 years. However, these figures also reflect the fact that some children change attachment classification over time, although this has not yet generated much research attention. What are the mutative factors behind changing attachment patterns, or change in any other aspect of personality for that matter? Because there is little research material on this question, my colleagues and I have examined biographical material, most recently the lives of Carl Rogers and Leo Tolstoy (Magai & Hunziger, 1993).

Here I conclude with a biographical account of an individual from our followup study of Type A personality. This individual, who is now 71 years old and retired, had been a career workaholic. Brilliant, determined, hard-driving, and relentless in his pursuit of success, he was the president of a large corporation by the time he was 60. During the interview he recounted how he had lost a good deal of steam after this point, and it had little to do with the approach of retirement. At 50 he had entered therapy to deal with certain issues relevant to his career; in the course of treatment, he confronted and dealt with the relationship with his parents, which had always been anger-filled and tumultuous. In gaining insight to the causes of their friction, including his conflicting needs for security and autonomy, and in altering his subsequent behavior toward them with positive results, the anger, in large part, was resolved and became dissipated. With his storehouse of anger so depleted he found that he was less inclined to challenge his subordinates or colleagues, and was less likely to get embroiled in internecine conflict. With less to be angry about at work, he lapsed into a more peaceful framework.

His gains were next consolidated in a personal relationship. Hot-tempered and domineering earlier in life, his first marriage had frayed after some 15 years. After his therapy he met and married an even-tempered, nonconfrontational woman with whom he rarely fought. Deprived of his usual sources of anger, he temporarily became depressed. In his words, he felt that all the punch had been taken out of him, that it had left a void, and that he felt disoriented. It dawned on him that the energy behind his drivenness had been largely fueled by anger, that anger had been a large source of his animation. Thus the anger had had both positive and negative consequences in his life. On the one hand, it had been the source of drive behind his accomplishments, on the other it had created friction in all his personal relationships.

There were also positive and negative consequences of the depletion of his anger. On the one hand, he was no longer constantly a jangle of nerves; on the other, he did not seem to have the aggressive energy he had had earlier, and he became less driven at work. For a while he did not know how he would replace the anger and drive, but in time found that the dissipated anger was replaced with a less frantic approach to his work, which did not actually suffer in the long run, and there was energy left for pursuits that he had given up earlier in life—reading, travel, and more sanguine social relationships.

This vignette illustrates that the same dynamic principles responsible for the establishment and maintenance of emotion organizations are drawn into play in their destablization and in the reorganization of personality. It was the emotion-specific properties of anger—hostility, defensiveness, and aggression—that when reduced in the psychic structure (i.e., motivationally), altered patterns of information processing and the propensity to behave in a confrontational way. When the social world is responsive to such changes—as it was in the case of this man's parents, partner, and work colleagues—the transformation was sustained. In this particular case, it appears that the change was initiated by a prolonged period of psychotherapy. There are, however, probably many other mutative agents in life change. The fields of developmental psychology and personality psychology have only begun to explore life change and nonconforming cases, yet it is probably true that the study of behavioral discontinuity will be essential to the development of more complex models that capture and reflect the dynamics of real human personality development (Magai & McFadden, 1995).

REFERENCES

Adickman, J. D. (1993). *Children's emotion biases: Their relation to internal representations of attachment security and to patterns of perceived maternal discipline.* Unpublished dissertation, Long Island University, Brooklyn, NY.

Allport, G. (1937). *Personality: A psychological interpretation.* New York: Henry Holt.

Allport, G. (1961). *Pattern and growth in personality.* New York: Holt, Rinehart & Winston.

Allport, G. & Odbert, H. S. (1936). Trait names: A psycho-lexical study. *Psychological Monographs, 47,* 1–171.

Baer, P. E., Reed, J., Bartlett, P. C., Vincent, J. P., Williams, B. J, & Bourianoff, G. G. (1983). Studies of gaze during induced conflict in families with a hypertensive father. *Psychosomatic Medicine, 45,* 233–241.

Baer, P. E., Vincent, J. P., Williams, B. J., Bourianoff, G. G., & Bartlett, P. C. (1980). Behavioral response to induced conflict in families with a hypertensive father. *Hypertension, 2,* 70–77.

Barnett, M. A. (1987). Empathy and related responses in children. In N. Eisenberg & J. Strayer (Eds.), *Empathy and its development* (pp. 46–162). Cambridge, England: Cambridge University Press.

Beilin, H. (1983). The new functionalism and Piaget's program. In E. K. Scholnick (Ed.), *New trends in conceptual representation* (pp. 3–40). Hillsdale, NJ: Lawrence Erlbaum Associates.

Belsky, J., Rovine, M., & Taylor, D. G. (1984). The Pennsylvania infant and family development project: III. The origins of individual differences in infant–mother attachment: Maternal and infant contributions. *Child Development, 55,* 718–728.

Berlin, L. (1993, March). Attachment and emotions in preschool children. In J. Cassidy & L. Berlin (Chairs), *Emotion and attachment.* Symposium at the biannual meeting of the Society for Research in Child Development, New Orleans, LA.

Caspi, A., Elder, G. H., & Bem, D. J. (1987). Moving against the world: Life-course patterns of explosive children. *Developmental Psychology, 23,* 308–313.

Cassidy, J. S., & Berlin, L. J. (1994). The insecure/ambivalent pattern of attachment: Theory and research. *Child Development, 65,* 971–991.

Cattell, R. B. (1947). Confirmation and clarification of primary personality traits. *Psychological Bulletin, 72,* 402–421.

Cattell, R. B. (1957). *Personality and motivation structure and measurement.* New York: World Book.

Cattell, R. B., Eber, H. W., & Tatsuoka, M. M. (1970). *Handbook for the Sixteen Personality Factor Questionnaire.* Champaign, IL: Institute for Personality and Ability Testing.

Costa, P. T., Jr., & McCrae, R. R. (1980). Still stable after all these years: Personality as a key to some issues in adulthood and old age. In P. B. Baltes & O. G. Brim, Jr. (Eds.), *Life span development and behavior* (Vol. 3, pp. 75–102). New York: Academic Press.

Crittenden, P. M. (1981). Abusing, neglecting, problematic, and adequate dyads: Differentiating by patterns of interaction. *Merrill–Palmer Quarterly, 27,* 201–218.

Crockenberg, S. (1985). Toddlers' reactions to maternal anger. *Merrill–Palmer Quarterly, 31,* 361–373.

Cummings, E. M. (1987). Coping with background anger in early childhood. *Child Development, 58,* 976–984.

Cummings, E. M., Ballard, M., El-Sheikh, M., & Lake, M. (1991). Resolution and children's responses to interadult anger. *Developmental Psychology, 27,* 462–470.

Digman, J. M., & Inouye, J. (1986). Further specification of the five robust factors of personality. *Journal of Personality and Social Psychology, 50,* 116–123.

Digman, J. M., & Takemoto-Chock, N. K. (1981). Factors in the natural language of personality: Re-analysis and comparison of six major studies. *Multivariate Behavioral Research, 16,* 149–170.

Dodge, K. A., Pettit, G. S., McClaskey, C. L., & Brown, M. M. (1986). Social competence in children. *Monographs of the Society for Research in Child Development, 51*(2), 1–80.

Dodge, K. A., & Somberg, D. R. (1987). Hostile attributional biases among aggressive boys are exacerbated under conditions of threats to the self. *Child Development, 58,* 213–224.

Eisenberg, N., Fabes, R. A., Schaller, M., Miller, P., Carlo, G., Poulin, R., Shea, C., & Shell, R. (1991). *Journal of Personality and Social Psychology, 61,* 459–470.

Epstein, S. (1983). The stability of behavior across time and situations. In R. Zucker, J. Aronoff, & A. I. Rabin (Eds.), *Personality and the prediction of behavior.* San Diego, CA: Academic Press.

El-Sheikh, M., Cummings, E. M., & Goetsch, V. L. (1989). Coping with adults' angry behavior: Behavioral, physiological, and verbal responses in preschoolers. *Developmental Psychology, 25,* 490–489.

Eysenck, H. J., & Eysenck, M. W. (1985). *Personality and individual differences: A natural science approach.* New York: Plenum.

Fabes, R. A., Eisenberg, N., & Miller, P. (1990). Maternal correlates of children's vicarious emotional responsiveness. *Developmental Psychology, 26,* 639–648.

Frodi, A., Bridges, L., & Grolnick, W. (1985). Correlates of master-related behavior: A short-term longitudinal study of infants in their second year. *Child Development, 56,* 1291–1298.

Gaensbauer, T. J., Harmon, R. J., Culp, A. M., Schultz, L. A., Van Doornick, W. J., & Dawson, P. (1985). Relationships between attachment behavior in the laboratory and the caretaking environment. *Infant Behavior and Development, 8,* 355–369.

Goldberg, L. R. (1993). The structure of phenotypic personality traits. *American Psychologist, 48,* 26–34.

Graham, S., Hudley, C., & Williams, E. (1992). Attributional and emotional determinants of aggression among African-American and Latino young adolescents. *Developmental Psychology, 28,* 731–740.

Haviland, J. M., & Lelwica, M. (1987). The induced affect response: Ten-week-old infants' responses to three emotion expressions. *Developmental Psychology, 23,* 17–104.

Izard, C. E. (1971). *The face of emotion.* New York: Appleton-Century-Crofts.

Izard, C. E. (1972). *Patterns of emotions: A new analysis of anxiety and depression.* San Diego, CA: Academic Press.

Izard, C. E. (1977). *Human emotions.* New York: Plenum.

Izard, C. E. (1991). *The psychology of emotions.* New York: Plenum.

Izard, C. E., Libero, D. Z., Putnam, P., & Haynes, O. M. (1993). Stability of emotion experiences and their relations to traits of personality. *Journal of Personality and Social Psychology, 64,* 847–860.

Jones, C. (1990). *The effects of maternal emotion word use on children's emotional development.* Unpublished doctoral dissertation, New School for Social Research, New York.

Kagan, J. (1982). *Review of research in infancy.* New York: Grant Foundation.

Kropp, J. P., & Haynes, O. M. (1987). Abusive and nonabusive mothers' ability to identify general and specific emotion signals of infants. *Child Development, 58,* 187–190.

Larsen, R. J., & Ketelaar, T. (1991). Personality and susceptibility to positive and negative emotional states. *Journal of Personality and Social Psychology, 61,* 132–140.

Lewis, M., Alessandri, S. M., & Sullivan, M. W. (1990). Violation of expectancy, loss of control, and anger expressions in young infants. *Developmental Psychology, 26,* 745–751.

Lochman, J. E. (1987). Self- and peer perceptions and attributional biases of aggressive and nonaggressive boys in dyadic interactions. *Journal of Consulting and Clinical Psychology, 55,* 404–410.

Lyons-Ruth, K., Connell, D. B., Zoll, D., & Stahl, J. (1987). Infants at social risk: Relations among infant maltreatment, maternal behavior, and infant attachment behavior. *Developmental Psychology, 23,* 223–232.

Magai, C., Distel, N., & Liker, R. (1993, March). Emotion socialization, attachment and adult personality traits. In J. Cassidy & L. Berlin (Chairs), *Attachment and emotion.* Symposium at the biennial meeting of the Society for Research in Child Development, New Orleans, LA.

Magai, C., & Hunziker, J. (1993). Tolstoy and the riddle of developmental transformation: A lifespan analysis of the role of emotions in personality development. In M. Lewis & J. Haviland (Eds.), *Handbook of emotions* (pp. 247–259). New York: Wiley.

Magai, C., & McFadden, S. (1995). *The role of emotion in social and personality development: History, theory, and research.* New York: Plenum.

Main, M., Tomasini, L., & Tolan, W. (1979). Differences among mothers of infants judged to differ in security. *Developmental Psychology, 15,* 472–473.

Malatesta, C. Z. (1990). The role of emotions in the development and organization of personality. In R. Thompson (Ed.), *Nebraska Symposium on Motivation: Socioemotional development* (pp. 1–56). Lincoln: University of Nebraska Press.

Malatesta, C. Z., Culver, C., Tesman, J. R., & Shepard, B. (1989). The development of emotion expression during the first two years of life. *Monographs of the Society for Research in Child Development, 54*(1–2).

Malatesta, C. A., Grigoryev, P., Lamb, C., Albin, M., & Culver, C. (1986). Emotion socialization and expressive development in preterm and full term infants. *Child Development, 57,* 316–330.

Malatesta, C. Z., & Wilson, A. (1988). Emotion/cognition interaction in personality development: A discrete emotions, functionalist analysis. *British Journal of Social Psychology, 27,* 91–112.

Malatesta-Magai, C. Z., Jonas, R., Shepard, B., & Culver, C. (1992). Type A personality and emotional expressivity in younger and older adults. *Psychology and Aging, 7,* 551–561.

Matthews, K. A., Manuck, S. B., & Saab, P. G. (1986). Cardiovascular responses of adolescents during a naturally occurring stressor and their behavioral and psychophysiological predictors. *Psychophysiology, 23,* 198–209.

Matthews, K. A., Rosenman, R. H., Dembroski, E. T. M., Harris, E. L., & MacDougall, J. M. (1984). Familial resemblance in components of the Type A behavior pattern: A reanalysis of the California Type A twin study. *Psychosomatic Medicine, 46,* 512–522.

Matthews, K. A., Stoney, C. M., Rakaczky, C. J., & Jamison, W. (1986). Family characteristics and school achievements of Type A children. *Health Psychology, 5,* 453–467.

McCann, B. S., & Matthews, K. A. (1988). Influences of potential for hostility, Type A behavior, and parental history of hypertension on adolescents cardiovascular responses during stress. *Psychophysiology, 25,* 503–511.

McCrae, R. R., & Costa, P. T. (1985). Updating Norman's "Adequate Taxonomy" Intelligence and personality dimensions in natural language and in questionnaires. *Journal of Personality and Social Psychology, 49,* 710–721.

McCrae, R. R., & Costa, P. T. (1987). Validation of the five-factor model of personality across instruments and observers. *Journal of Personality and Social Psychology, 52,* 82–91.

Miller, P. A., & Eisenberg, N. (1988). The relation of empathy to aggressive and externalizing/antisocial behavior. *Psychological Bulletin, 103,* 324–344.

Miller, P., & Sperry, L. L. (1987). The socialization of anger and aggression. *Merrill–Palmer Quarterly, 33,* 1–31.

Mischel, W. (1968). *Personality and assessment.* New York: Wiley.

Murray, D. M., Matthews, K. A., Blake, S. M., & Prineas, R. (1986). Type A behavior in children: Demographic, behavioral, and physiological correlates. *Health Psychology, 5,* 159–169.

Nisbett, R. E. (1993). Violence and U.S. regional culture. *American Psychologist, 48,* 441–449.

Noller, P., Law, H., & Comrey, A. L. (1987). Cattell, Comrey, and Eysenck personality factors compared: More evidence for the five robust factors? *Journal of Personality and Social Psychology, 53,* 775–782.

Norman, W. T. (1963). Toward an adequate taxonomy of personality attributes. *Journal of Abnormal and Social Psychology, 66,* 574–583.

Oldershaw, L., & Walters, G. C. (1989). A behavioral approach to the classification of different types of physically abusive mothers. *Merrill–Palmer Quarterly, 35,* 255–279.

Panksepp, J. (1990). The neurobiology of emotions: Of animal brains and human feelings. In H. Wagner & A. Manstead (Eds.), *Handbook of social psychophysiology.* New York: Wiley.

Passini, F. T., & Norman, W. T. (1966). A universal conception of personality structure. *Journal of Personality and Social Psychology, 4,* 44–49.

Pervin, L. (1993). Affect and personality. In M. Lewis & J. Haviland (Eds.), *Handbook of emotions* (pp. 301–312). New York: Wiley.

Ribot, T. (1903). *The Psychology of the emotions.* London: The Walter Scott Publishing Co.

Roberts, W., & Strayer, J. (1987). Parents' responses to emotional distress of their children: Relations of children's competence. *Developmental Psychology, 23,* 415–422.

Rosenman, R. H., Rahe, R. H., & Borhani, N. O. (1974). Heritability of personality and behavior pattern. *Acta Genetica Medica Gemollol Roma, 23,* 37–42.

Rubin, K. H., & Clark, M. L. (1983). Preschool teachers' rating of behavioral problems: Observational, sociometric, and social–cognitive correlates. *Journal of Abnormal Child Psychology, 11,* 273–285.

Rubin, K. H., Moller, L., & Emptage, A. (1987). The pre-school Behaviour Questionnaire: A useful index of behavior problems in elementary school-age children? *Canadian Journal of Behavioural Sciences, 19,* 86–100.

Shand, A. F. (1914). *The foundations of character.* London: Macmillan.

Shiller, V. M., Izard, C. E., & Hembree, E. A. (1986). Patterns of emotion expression during separation in the strange-situation procedure. *Developmental Psychology, 22,* 378–382.

Spranger, E. (1928). *Types of Men: The psychology and ethics of personality.* New York: Johnson Reprint.

Tesman, J. R. (1992). *Affective development in five-year-olds: Consequences of early exposure to incongruent messages and maternal insensitivity.* Unpublished doctoral dissertation, New School for Social Research, New York.

Tomkins, S. S. (1962). *Affect, imagery, consciousness. Vol 1: The positive affects.* New York: Springer.

Tomkins, S. S. (1963). *Affect, imagery, consciousness. Vol 2: The negative affects.* New York: Springer.

Tomkins, S. S. (1991). *Affect, imagery, consciousness. Vol 3: Anger and fear.* New York: Springer.

Underwood, M. K., Cole, J. D., & Herbsman, C. R. (1992). Display rules for anger and aggression in school-age children. *Child Development, 63,* 366–380.

Walters, J., & Peters, R. D. (June, 1980). *Social problem solving in aggressive boys.* Paper presented at the annual meeting of the Canadian Psychological Association, Calgary, Alberta.

Waters, E., Vaughn, B. E., & Egeland, B. R. (1980). Individual differences in infant–mother attachment relationships at age one: Antecedents in neonatal behavior in an urban economically disadvantaged sample. *Child Development, 51,* 208–216.

Watson, D., & Clark, L. A. (1991). Self- versus peer ratings of specific emotional traits: Evidence of convergent and discriminant validity. *Journal of Personality and Social Psychology, 60,* 927–940.

8

Emotional Experiences: The Pains and Pleasures of Distinct Regulatory Systems

E. Tory Higgins
Columbia University

My interest in emotions began with the question of why the same life event, such as the death of one's spouse or being fired from one's job, can make some people depressed but can make other people anxious. What is it about people that predisposes them to respond emotionally to events in such different ways? When the emotional experiences are chronic and intensely negative, as with depression or anxiety, these varying predispositions are usually described as emotional vulnerabilities. Although a general theory of emotional experiences must account for more than emotional vulnerabilities, any insight into the nature of such vulnerabilities should facilitate the development of such a theory. This chapter proposes that distinct self-regulatory systems underlie vulnerabilities for specific emotional experiences. By considering the nature of these distinct regulatory systems, the present chapter could increase our understanding of emotional experiences in general.

In examining emotional vulnerabilities, I began with the principle that scholars such as Weber, Durkheim, Freud, James, and Cooley developed at the turn of the century: that people derive meanings from the events in their lives and then respond to those meanings. This insight into the fundamental characteristic of people is nicely captured in Thomas and Thomas' (1928) statement, "If men define situations as real, they are real in their consequences." In social psychology as well, Asch (1952), Lewin (1935), and Mead (1934) emphasized early on the importance of the *psychological situation* in determining people's motivations and actions.

The role of psychological situations in emotional vulnerabilities was also stressed in self-discrepancy theory (see Higgins, 1987, 1989a, 1989b). According to the theory, self-regulation in relation to distinct types of personal goals and standards; that is, self-guides, produced vulnerabilities for experiencing specific psychological situations and their associated emotions.

A major aspect of self-discrepancy theory is its distinction between different types of self-guides—in particular the distinction between the *Ideal* self and the *Ought* self. The Ideal self is a representation of someone's hopes, wishes, and aspirations for a person; the Ought self is a representation of someone's beliefs about a person's duty, obligations, and responsibilities. People can regulate themselves (either chronically or momentarily) in relation to either self-guide.

Self-discrepancy theory proposes that when a self-concept attribute is represented as a mismatch to an ideal self-guide, the psychological situation involves "the absence of a positive outcome" and dejection-related emotions, such as feeling sad and disappointed, are experienced. When a self-concept attribute is represented as a match to an ideal self-guide, the psychological situation involves "the presence of a positive outcome" and cheerfulness-related emotions, such as feeling happy and satisfied, are experienced. In contrast, when a self-concept attribute is represented as a mismatch to an ought self-guide, the psychological situation involves the "presence of a negative outcome" and agitation-related emotions, such as feeling tense and restless, are experienced. When a self-concept attribute is represented as a match to an ought self-guide, the psychological situation involves "the absence of a negative outcome" and quiescence-related emotions, such as feeling calm and relaxed, are experienced.

According to this initial proposal of self-discrepancy theory, then, individuals who predominantly self-regulate in relation to an ideal self-guide, and who represent themselves as being chronically discrepant from that self-guide, should be vulnerable to suffering from dejection-related emotions, including depression in extreme cases. In contrast, individuals who predominantly self-regulate in relation to an ought self-guide, and who represent themselves as being chronically discrepant from that self-guide, should be vulnerable to suffering from agitation-related emotions, including anxiety in extreme cases.

Much of the early research that tested self-discrepancy theory was concerned with providing empirical support for these hypothesized distinct relations between possessing a specific type of self-discrepancy; that is, actual/ideal discrepancy versus actual/ought self-discrepancy, and being vulnerable to a particular kind of emotional suffering; that is, dejection-related suffering versus agitation-related suffering, respectively. The next section provides a brief review of some of this research (for fuller reviews, see Higgins, 1987, 1989a; Higgins, Tykocinski, & Vookles, 1990). It also introduces additional distinctions among types of self-discrepancies and relates these distinctions to vulnerabilities for specific kinds of emotional experiences.

SELF-DISCREPANCIES AND VULNERABILITIES FOR SPECIFIC EMOTIONAL EXPERIENCES

The psychological literature has historically distinguished among various facets of the self (see Erikson, 1963; Greenwald & Pratkanis, 1984; Markus & Wurf, 1987; Piers & Singer, 1971; Rogers, 1961; Schafer, 1967; Sullivan, 1953). Only rarely, however, have different types of self-beliefs or self-state representations been related systematically to different kinds of emotional problems (e.g., James, 1890/1948). Self-discrepancy theory assumes that just as momentary events can temporarily induce particular kinds of psychological situations in people (see Mowrer, 1960), people can possess chronic patterns of self-beliefs that cause them to be generally vulnerable to experiencing particular kinds of psychological situations.

It has been noted in the literature that belief inconsistencies reflect personal costs and problems and not simply a failure to achieve internal consistency or a "good Gestalt fit" (e.g., Abelson, 1983; Holt, 1976; Kemper, 1978; Plutchik, 1962; Schlenker, 1985). Self-discrepancy theory shares this viewpoint and proposes that different patterns of beliefs, in this case self-beliefs, have psychological significance by chronically representing particular kinds of psychological situations. Let us begin by considering the basic types of self-belief patterns and negative psychological situations discussed earlier.

Actual Self Versus Ideal Self. If a person possesses this discrepancy, actual self-attributes (from the person's own standpoint) do not match the Ideal self that he or she personally wishes or hopes to attain or believes some significant other person wishes or hopes that he or she would attain. This discrepancy represents one of the two basic kinds of negative psychological situations discussed earlier—*the absence of positive outcomes*. On the basis of various accounts in the literature concerning the kinds of emotional/motivational states associated with this type of negative psychological situation (e.g., Jacobs, 1971; Lazarus, 1968; Mowrer, 1960; Roseman, 1984; Stein & Jewett, 1982), it is hypothesized that people possessing this type of self-discrepancy are vulnerable to *dejection-related problems*, such as feeling sad and empty.

Actual Self Versus Ought Self. A person who shows this discrepancy possesses attributes (from the person's own standpoint) that violate the state that he or she, or some significant other, believes it is his or her duty or obligation to attain. Because violation of prescribed duties or obligations is associated with self- or other-administered sanctions (i.e., punishment, criticism), this discrepancy represents the other basic kind of negative psychological situation discussed earlier—*the presence of negative outcomes.* On the basis of various accounts in the literature concerning the kinds of emotional/motivational states associated with this type of psychological situation (see Jacobs, 1971; Lazarus, 1968; Mowrer, 1960; Roseman, 1984; Stein & Jewett, 1982), it is hypothesized that people possessing this type of self-discrepancy are vulnerable to *agitation-related problems,* such as fear and tension.

In addition to these two basic types of self-state relations involving two self-states, there is a third type:

Self-Guide Versus Self-Guide. A person who possesses this discrepancy has two self-guides in conflict with one another. Because a person is motivated to approach both self-guides and to avoid discrepancies from both self-guides, a self-guide:self-guide conflict represents the negative psychological situation of *a double approach–avoidance conflict.* On the basis of various descriptions of this kind of conflict (e.g., Epstein, 1978; Heilizer, 1977; Lewin, 1935; Miller, 1944, 1959), it is hypothesized that people possessing this type of self-discrepancy are vulnerable to *confusion-related problems,* such as feeling indecisive and unsure of themselves.

Self-discrepancy theory has also identified self-state patterns involving three elements (see Higgins, Tykocinski, & Vookles, 1992). These new patterns introduced two additional self-beliefs into self-discrepancy theory: (a) the *Can* self, which is your representation of someone's beliefs about your capabilities or potential (who you can be); and (b) the *Future* self, which is your representation of the attributes that someone believes you are likely to possess in the future (who you will be).

Descriptions of self-beliefs in the literature have not been restricted to the self-concept or to self-guides. Possible or potential actual selves—"self-possibilities"—have also been considered (e.g., Bandura, 1982; James, 1890/1948; Markus & Nurius, 1986; for a review, see Higgins, 1990). Markus and Nurius (1986) assessed both subjects' "now" self and "probable possible self," which are most similar to the actual self and future self, respectively. In addition, Bandura's (1982) *perceived self-efficacy* has properties of both the can self and the future self. The can and future selves in combination with other self-beliefs had not been examined as distinct vulnerability factors, however.

Each of the three-element patterns involves a relation between the actual self and either a self-guide or a self-possibility as a standard with a third element specifying the meaning of the standard. Each pattern *as a whole* has a distinct meaning because of the type of relation between the actual self and the standard, the type of standard involved, and the meaning of the standard specified by the third element. In the following description of these patterns, the "<" and ">" notations give the direction of a discrepancy, the "=" notation stands for a congruency, and the "[ ]" notation indicates the third element and its relation to the standard that specifies the meaning of the standard:

1. An actual self that is congruent with a can self as standard whose meaning is specified by its being less than the Ideal self: A = C[<I]. To begin with the standard, C[<I] signifies that the can self falls short of the Ideal self. Thus, C[<I] means limited potential. A = C signifies that one's actual self is congruent with one's can self, one is fulfilling one's potential. A = C[<I] as a whole, then, represents the psychological situation of "fulfillment of one's limited potential."

2. An actual self that is less than the can self as standard whose meaning is specified by its congruent relation with the Ideal self: A < C[=I]. To begin with the standard, C[=I] signifies that the can self matches or is congruent with the Ideal self. Thus, C[=I] means positive potential. A < C signifies that one's actual self falls short of one's can self, one is chronically failing to meet one's potential. A < C[=I] as a whole, then, represents the psychological situation of "chronic failure to meet one's positive potential."

3. An actual self that is less than the Ideal self as standard whose meaning is specified by its being greater than the future self: A < I[>F]. To begin with the standard, I[>F] signifies that the Ideal self is higher than the future self. Thus, I[>F] means that the Ideal self will not be attained in the future, it is a desired end state than one does not expect to attain, which is a "wish." A < I signifies that one's actual self falls short of one's Ideal self. A < I[>F] as a whole, then, represents the psychological situation of "nonattainment of wished for, but not expected, self."

4. An actual self that is less than the Ideal self as standard whose meaning is specified by its congruent relation with the future self: A < I[=F]. To begin with the standard, I[=F] signifies that the Ideal self is congruent with or matches the future self. Thus, I[=F] means that the Ideal self is a desired end state that one does expect to attain, which is a "hope." A < I signifies that one's actual self falls short of one's Ideal self. A < I[=F], then, represents the psychological situation of "chronically unfulfilled hopes."

Table 8.1 provides a summary of the meaning of each of these patterns.

TABLE 8.1
Notations, Descriptions, and Holistic Significance
of Different Types of Self-Belief Patterns

Significance Notation	Description	Holistic
A = C[<I]	An actual self that matches the can self as standard whose meaning is specified by its being less than the ideal self	"Fulfillment of one's limited potential"
A < C[=I]	An actual self that is less than the can self as standard whose meaning is specified by its matching the ideal self	"Chronic failure to meet one's positive potential"
A < I[>F]	An actual self that is less than the ideal self as standard whose meaning is specified by its being greater than the future self	"Nonattainment of wished for, but not expected, self"
A < I[=F]	An actual self that is less than the ideal self as standard whose meaning is specified by its matching the future self	"Chronically unfulfilled hopes for self"

Evidence Relating Self-Belief Patterns to Vulnerabilities for Distinct Emotional Experiences

In most of our studies, introductory psychology undergraduates filled out a "Selves Questionnaire" that was included in a general battery of measures handed out at the beginning of the semester, and the dependent measures were collected 4 to 8 weeks later. The Selves Questionnaire simply asks respondents to list up to 8 or 10 attributes for each of a number of different self-states. It is administered in two sections, the first involving the respondent's own standpoint and the second involving the standpoints of the respondent's significant others (e.g., mother, father, best friend).

On the first page of the questionnaire the actual, Can, Future, Ideal, and Ought self-states are defined (as described earlier). On each subsequent page there is a question about a different self-state, such as "Please list the attributes of the type of person *you* think you *actually* are" or "Please list the attributes of the type of person your *Mother* thinks you *should or ought* to be." The respondents are also asked to rate for each listed attribute the extent to which the standpoint person (self or other) believes they actually possess that attribute, ought to possess that attribute, and so on.

The basic coding procedure for calculating the magnitude of a self-discrepancy involves a two-step procedure:

1. For each self-discrepancy, the attributes in one self-state (e.g., actual self) are compared to the attributes in the other self-state (e.g., Ideal self/own standpoint) to determine which attributes are synonyms and

which are antonyms according to Roget's thesaurus. Attributes across the two self-states that are neither synonyms nor antonyms are considered to be *nonmatches*. Antonyms are considered to be *antonymous mismatches*. Synonyms for which the attributes have the same basic extent ratings are considered to be *matches*. Synonyms for which the attributes have very different extent ratings (e.g., actual self: "slightly attractive" versus Ideal/own: "extremely attractive") are considered to be *synonymous mismatches*.

2. The magnitude of self-discrepancy for the two self-states is calculated by summing the total number of mismatches and subtracting the total number of matches, with antonymous mismatches being weighted twice that of synonymous matches and mismatches.

The procedure for calculating the three-element self-state patterns described earlier differed somewhat from this basic coding procedure by being more configurational in nature (see Higgins, Vookles, & Tykocinski, 1992). The unique procedure in measuring these patterns is that the standard (i.e., the Can self or the Ideal self) is specified first by its relation to the third element (as indicated in the square brackets). Only then are the attributes in the actual self compared to the specified subset of attributes in the standard. For the A < C[=I] pattern, for instance, only those Can self attributes were selected that were matches to the attributes in the Ideal self. The attributes in the actual self were then compared to only this selected subset of Can self attributes, with the discrepancy being calculated using the basic procedure described earlier.

One of our first studies used a latent variable analysis to test the hypothesis that an actual self-discrepancy in relation to the Ideal self predicts different emotional problems than an actual self-discrepancy in relation to the Ought self (Strauman & Higgins, 1988). One month after filling out the Selves Questionnaire, undergraduates filled out a battery of measures. The battery included both measures that comprised a latent variable for depression, the Beck Depression Inventory (Beck, Ward, Mendelson, Mock, & Erbaugh, 1961) and the Hopkins Symptom Checklist, Depression subscale (Derogatis, Lipman, Rickels, Uhlenhuth, & Covi, 1974), and measures that comprised a latent variable for social anxiety, the Fear of Negative Evaluation scale, the Social Avoidance and Distress scale (for both scales, see Watson & Friend, 1969), and the Hopkins Symptom Checklist, Interpersonal Sensitivity subscale.

The only model to provide an acceptable fit to the sample data was the hypothesized causal structure. Consistent with our hypotheses, as the magnitude of subjects' actual self-discrepancy to their Ideal self increased, their suffering from depression symptoms increased. In contrast, as the magnitude of subjects' actual self-discrepancy to their Ought self increased, their suffering from social anxiety symptoms increased. Each of these relations was independent of any relation between the alternative discrepancy and symptoms. Moreover, actual self-discrepancy to the Ideal self was not related to social anxiety and actual self-discrepancy to the Ought self was not related to depression.

Another study (Higgins, Klein, & Strauman, 1987) investigated the impact on emotional suffering of people's actual self-discrepancies to their Ideal and the Ought selves combined with their *self–other contingency beliefs* concerning socialization experiences in childhood. The Socialization Questionnaire first defined parents' Ideals and Oughts for their children. It then asked the following kinds of questions: (a) "Have you ever felt unloved because you didn't live up to your parents *ideals* for you? To what extent?" (b) "Have you ever felt you would be emotionally abandoned if you didn't live up to your parents *ideals* for you? To what extent?" (c) "Did you ever believe that your parents would punish you if you didn't live up to their *oughts* for you? To what extent?" (d) "Did you ever believe that your parents would reject you if you didn't live up to their *oughts* for you? To what extent?" Each subject's scores on the Ideal questions were averaged to form an overall measure of the strength of the subject's belief that negative experiences would occur if the actual self was discrepant from the parents' Ideal for him or her—Strength of Ideal Contingency Belief. Similarly, a measure of Strength of Ought Contingency Belief was calculated.

For both of the Contingency Belief measures separately, the subjects were divided using median splits into those with strong contingency beliefs and those with weak contingency beliefs. The subjects were also divided using tertiary splits into three levels of actual self discrepancy to their Ideal selves and three levels of actual self discrepancy to their Ought selves. We then performed a Level of Actual:Ideal Discrepancy × Strength of Ideal Contingency Belief analysis of covariance (with level of actual:ought discrepancy as the covariate) on the dependent measures of emotional/motivational problems, and a Level of Actual:Ought Discrepancy × Strength of Ought Contingency Belief analysis of covariance (with level of Actual:Ideal discrepancy as the covariate) on the same dependent measures.

A squared multiple correlation (R^2) was used as a summary statistic of the amount of variance of the dependent variables that was accounted for by the main effects and interactions of the two independent variables. As predicted, higher levels of actual self discrepancy to the Ideal self combined with stronger Ideal contingency beliefs were significantly related to higher levels of depression (zero-order multiple correlations [R] ranged from .52 to .62), but were unrelated to fear/anxiety-related problems. In contrast, higher levels of actual self-discrepancy to the Ought self plus stronger Ought contingency beliefs were significantly related to higher levels of fear/anxiety-related problems (zero-order multiple correlations [R] ranged from .47 to .49), but were unrelated to depression.

In another set of studies (Van Hook & Higgins, 1988), we tested the hypothesis that *conflict between two self-guides* would be uniquely related to *confusion-related symptoms*. Undergraduates who possessed a conflict between self-guides were compared to a control group of undergraduates who did not. Subjects' levels of actual self-discrepancies to the Ideal and Ought selves were controlled both by selecting subjects so that these discrepancies would be equivalent between the two groups and by using subjects' scores on these discrepancies as covariates in our analyses. As predicted, the subjects with a conflict between self-guides reported experiencing each of the following symptoms significantly more often than subjects without this conflict—confusion, muddledness, uncertainty about self and goals, identity confusion, indecision, distractibility, and rebelliousness.

Most recently, Higgins et al. (1992) have tested hypotheses concerning the distinct vulnerabilities associated with the different three-element patterns (see Table 8.1). This study examined the relation between dejection-related suffering and different types of actual/ideal discrepancies. The study found, first, that both the A < C[=I] pattern and the A < I[=F] pattern were more strongly associated with dejection-related suffering than the A = C[<I] pattern and the A < I[>F] pattern. Indeed, partial correlations revealed that once the common properties are controlled for (e.g., the fact that all four patterns contain a discrepancy between the actual self and the Ideal self), only the A < C[=I] and A < I[=F] patterns are uniquely associated with dejection-related suffering.

Table 8.2 shows the zero-order and partial correlations for the A < C[=I] pattern and the A < I[=F] pattern. Partial correlational analyses were necessary because these two patterns were moderately correlated: $r = .54$, $p < .001$. The partial correlations indicate that these two patterns were uniquely predictive of different kinds of dejection-related suffering as measured 8 to 12 weeks later. The A < C[=I] pattern, which was hypothesized to reflect the negative psychological situation of "chronic failure to meet one's positive potential," was uniquely predictive of items such as "not satisfied with myself and my accomplishments," "have to push myself to do anything," "[not] driven," "[not] self-controlled," "listless," and "there is something wrong with me that prevents me from fulfilling my potential." Together, this set of symptoms are best described as a *"feeling weak"* kind of dejection (where "weak" means "lacking proficiency, potency, or vigor," "ineffective" according to Webster's Ninth New Collegiate Dictionary, 1989, p. 1335). In contrast, the A < I[=F] pattern, which was hypothesized to reflect the negative psychological situation of "chronically unfulfilled hopes," was uniquely predictive of

TABLE 8.2
Predictive Relations to Dejection-Related Symptoms and Beliefs
of Two Types of Actual/Ideal Discrepancy Patterns
Involving the Can Self Versus the Future Self—
the A < C[=I] Pattern and the A < F[=I] Pattern

	Zero-Order Correlations		Partial Correlations	
Symptoms and Beliefs	A < C[=I]	A < F[=I]	A < C[=I]	A < F[=I]
BDI	.36***	.41***	.18	.27**
Feel like a failure	.35***	.31**	.22*	.15
Not satisfied with myself and my accomplishments	.24*	.02	.27**	.14
Have to push myself to do anything	.43***	.33**	.31**	.13
(Not) Driven	.30**	.13	.28**	.04
(Not) Alert	.21*	.02	.24*	.12
Listless	.31**	.21*	.24*	.05
(Not) Energetic	.28**	.19*	.21*	.05
There is something wrong with me that prevents me from fulfilling my potential	.26**	.06	.36***	.26**
(Not) Self-controlled	.23*	.11	.20*	.02
Helpless	.33***	.30**	.21*	.15
Feeling sad	.17	.36***	.04	.33**
Feeling discouraged	.25*	.32**	.09	.22*
Feeling frustrated	.25*	.29**	.11	.19*
Feeling disappointed	.23*	.31**	.08	.22*
Hopeless	.19*	.33**	.02	.27**
Regretful	.13	.28**	.03	.25*

*$p < .05$. **$p < .01$. ***$p < .001$.

items such as "feeling discouraged," "feeling hopeless," "feeling sad," and "feeling regretful." Together, this set of symptoms is best described as a *"feeling despondent"* kind of dejection (where "despondent" means "feeling discouraged and hopeless," according to Webster's Ninth New Collegiate Dictionary, 1989, p. 344).

These results are generally consistent with the literature on depression. Perceiving oneself as chronically failing to meet one's positive potential or high self-perceived capability has been associated with dejection-related depression (e.g., Bandura, 1986; Blatt, D'Afflitti, & Quinlan, 1976). Disparities between hopes or future standards and current performance have been associated with dejection-related suffering as well (e.g., Bandura, 1986; Heider, 1958). The results of this study are unique in identifying two distinct patterns of self-beliefs, both of which involve an actual self-discrepancy to the Ideal self, that predict specific kinds of dejection-related suffering depending on the relation between the Ideal self and a third self-belief (i.e., matching the Can self versus the Future self).

Chronic self-discrepancies not only predict vulnerability to specific kinds of emotional problems—they also predict sensitivity to the emotional problems of others. Houston (1990) selected undergraduate subjects who possessed either a discrepancy between their actual and Ideal selves or a discrepancy between their actual and Ought selves or both types of discrepancy or neither type of discrepancy. Weeks later the subjects read about another student's affective reaction to an incident that exemplified the student's chronic difficulties in meeting new people. The description of this target's discomfort was either dejection-related or agitation-related.

Houston (1990) found, first, that subjects with a discrepancy between their actual and Ideal selves reported more dejection-related emotions in response to the target's discomfort (even when the target was agitated) than did subjects with a discrepancy between their actual and Ought selves, and subjects with a discrepancy between their actual and Ought selves reported more agitation-related emotions in response to the target's discomfort (even when the target was dejected) than did subjects with a discrepancy between their actual and Ideal selves.

Second, the subjects' empathic concern for the target's discomfort and their judgments of the appropriateness of the target's affective reaction to the incident were both higher when the specific suffering of the target matched the emotional vulnerability of the subject (i.e., target dejection matching subjects with a discrepancy between their actual and Ideal selves, and target agitation matching subjects with a discrepancy between their actual and Ought selves).

Knowledge Activation Assumptions of Self-Discrepancy Theory

Self-discrepancy theory postulates that people acquire self–other contingency knowledge as children from their interactions with significant others, and this procedural knowledge develops into representations of the significant others' desires and values for them and self-regulation in terms of these self-guides (see Higgins, 1989b, 1991). Because self-evaluation is also in relation to these self-guides, representations of actual self-attributes become associated with the attributes in these self-guides. As discussed earlier, the psychological situations represented by matches and mismatches to self-guides depend on the significance of the *relation* between the actual self and a particular self-guide (or self-guide/self-possibility unit). Thus, although actual selves and self-guides are themselves distinct constructs, chronic actual self-matches and mismatches to a self-guide necessarily involve interconnectedness between the self–state representations. As such, they would be expected to function like knowledge structures (Assumption 1).

If actual self-matches and mismatches to self-guides function like knowledge structures, then their likelihood of activation should increase as their preexposure accessibility increases, because less external stimulation of the structure would be needed for the structure to reach the threshold level of activation or utilization (see Higgins, 1989c). When the accessibility of actual self matches and mismatches to self-guides is high, even vague or ambiguous stimuli should be sufficient to activate them (Assumption 2).

If actual self-matches and mismatches to self-guides function like knowledge structures, their likelihood of activation should increase as their applicability to a considered event increases (see Higgins, 1989c). This is because less accessibility is needed to reach the threshold level of activation if the external stimulation is high (i.e., high overlap between the event attributes and the matching or mismatching attributes). Indeed, when the considered event has attributes that are sufficiently similar to those in the matches or mismatches, it may only be necessary for the matching or mismatching attributes to be available (i.e., stored in memory) in order for them to be activated (Assumption 3).

If actual self-matches and mismatches to self-guides function like knowledge structures, then the activation of one attribute should spread to other, interconnected attributes (the "spreading activation" effect; see Collins & Loftus, 1975). Indeed, if actual self-matches and mismatches to self-guides function like unitized knowledge structures, and a person has a self-discrepancy, then it should be possible to activate an entire self-discrepancy by activating only one of its major components. Such automatic spreading activation from one component of the self-discrepancy to another should also increase the likelihood that self-discrepancies would be activated. More generally, activation of one component of an actual self relation to a self-guide should increase the likelihood that the other components would be activated (Assumption 4).

Most of the research testing the implications of these assumptions has focused on actual-self mismatches to self-guides and on individuals who possess a chronic self-discrepancy. The following section reviews this research. Each of the studies experimentally manipulates the likelihood of activating specific types of self-discrepancies and predicts that such activation will produce particular kinds of emotional states. These studies, then, permit a more direct test of the central hypotheses concerning the distinct psychological situations represented by different types of self-discrepancies.

Evidence Relating Self-System Activation and Distinct Emotional Experiences

If self-discrepancies function like knowledge structures (Assumption 1), then increasing the accessibility of a self-discrepancy should increase the likelihood of its activation (Assumption 2). One method of increasing the momentary accessibility of a construct is by recently activating or priming the construct (see Higgins & King, 1981; Wyer & Srull, 1981). Thus, if a person possesses more than one type of self-discrepancy, whichever type of self-discrepancy has been recently primed should be more likely to be activated. In addition, as the likelihood of activating a particular type of self-discrepancy increases, the likelihood of a person experiencing the kind of discomfort associated with that type of self-discrepancy should increase.

This hypothesis was tested in a study by Higgins, Bond, Klein, and Strauman (1986, Study 2). Undergraduates completed the Selves Questionnaire 4 to 6 weeks before the experimental session. Two groups of subjects were recruited for the experiment—subjects who had *both* an actual self-discrepancy to their Ideal self and an actual self-discrepancy to their Ought self, and subjects who possessed neither type of self-discrepancy. The ostensible purpose of the study was to obtain the self-reflections of a youth sample for a life-span developmental study. Subjects were told that their current mood would be measured throughout the study ostensibly to check later whether the subjects' mood during the session had any influence on their self-reflections. In this way, the impact of priming subjects' self-discrepancies on mood change (to be described later) could be unobtrusively measured.

Half of the subjects in each discrepancy group were randomly assigned to an Ideal priming condition, and the other half were assigned to an Ought priming condition. In the Ideal priming condition, the subjects were asked to describe the kind of person that they and their parents would ideally like them to be and to discuss whether there had been any change over the years in these hopes and aims for them. In the Ought priming condition, the subjects were asked to describe the kind of person that they and their parents believed they Ought to be and whether there had been any change over the years in these beliefs. Both before and after this priming manipulation, subjects filled out a mood questionnaire that included both dejection-related and agitation-related emotions, and were asked to rate the extent to which they now were feeling each emotion.

As predicted, subjects high in both Ideal and Ought self-discrepancies experienced an increase in the kind of discomfort associated with the type of self-discrepancy that was recently activated by priming—an increase in dejection-related emotions when the Ideal self was primed and an increase in agitation-related emotions when the Ought self was primed (see Table 8.3). In contrast, subjects who were low in both types of self-discrepancies experienced, if anything, an opposite pattern—a slight decrease in dejection-related emotions in the Ideal priming condition and a slight decrease in agitation-related emotions in the Ought priming condition (see Table 8.3). This slight reversal for subjects who were low

TABLE 8.3
Mean Change in Dejection-Related Emotions and Agitation-Related
Emotions as a Function of Level of Self-Discrepancies and Type of Priming

Level of Actual/Ideal and Actual/Ought Discrepancies	Ideal Priming		Ought Priming	
	Dejection	Agitation	Dejection	Agitation
High in Both Discrepancies	3.2	−0.8	0.9	5.1
Low in Both Discrepancies	−1.2	0.9	0.3	−2.6

Note. The more positive the number, the greater the increase in discomfort.

in both types of self-discrepancies was probably due to the priming manipulation activating these subjects' matches (either actual self-matches to the Ideal self or actual self-matches to the Ought self), which would produce the positive emotions associated with whichever type of match had been primed.

If self-discrepancies function like knowledge structures, one would also expect that the likelihood of activating a self-discrepancy would increase as the applicability of the discrepancy to a considered event increased (Assumption 2). This prediction was tested in another study by Higgins et al. (1986, Study 1). Undergraduates were asked to imagine either a positive event in which performance matches a common standard (e.g., receiving a grade of A in a course) or a negative event in which performances fail to match a common standard (e.g., receiving a grade of D in a course that is necessary for obtaining an important job). If self-discrepancies represent negative psychological situations, they should be more applicable (i.e., have greater similarity) to negative events than to positive events. Thus, the likelihood of activating a self-discrepancy should be greater when a considered event is negative than when it is positive. We expected, therefore, that the specific kinds of discomfort associated with subjects' dominant self-discrepancies would be more likely to be induced when subjects' imagined a negative event than when they imagined a positive event.

Subjects filled out the Selves questionnaire a few weeks before the experimental session. They were divided into two groups on the basis of their questionnaire responses—one group who had relatively high discrepancy scores between their actual and Ideal selves and relatively low discrepancy scores between their actual and Ought selves (the predominant Ideal discrepant group), and another group who had relatively high discrepancy scores between their actual and Ought selves and relatively low discrepancy scores between their actual and Ideal selves (the predominant Ought discrepant group). When subjects arrived at the experimental session, they first completed a semantic differential questionnaire that assessed their general mood prior to the experimental manipulation (i.e., the guided-imagery task). They also performed a simple writing-speed task. Subjects then received the guided-imagery task, performed the writing-speed task again, and filled out an emotions questionnaire measuring their current dejection-related and agitation-related emotions.

As predicted, there was no difference in mood change between the predominant-Ideal-discrepant subjects and the predominant-Ought-discrepant subjects when they imagined a positive event. As expected, however, when subjects imagined a negative event the predominant-Ideal-discrepant subjects experienced an increase in dejection-related emotions, whereas the predominant-Ought-discrepant subjects experienced an increase in agitation-related emotions. Indeed, as shown in Table 8.4, for subjects in this condition there was a clear pattern of correlations between the magnitude and type of subjects' self-discrepancies and the specific kind of mood change they experienced *weeks later*. The same basic pattern of results was also found for the writing-speed measure, with writing speed decreasing (i.e., motor retardation) as the discrepancy between actual and Ideal selves increased, and writing speed increasing (i.e., motor agitation) as the discrepancy between actual and Ought selves increased.

If self-discrepancies function like knowledge structures, and especially if they function like unitized knowledge structures, one would also expect that activation of even a single attribute in a self-discrepancy would be sufficient to activate the whole self-discrepancy and thus induce the discomfort associated with that self-discrepancy (Assumption 3). Thus, activating a single attribute in a person's self-guide should be sufficient to activate any discrepancy that person possesses between his or her actual self and that self-guide. Moreover, since the self-guide attributes

TABLE 8.4
Partial Correlations Between Types of Self-Discrepancies
and Types of Postmanipulation Mood in the Positive Event
and Negative Event Conditions

| | Guided-Imagery Manipulation Task | | | |
| | Positive Event | | Negative Event | |
Type of Postmood	Dejection Emotions	Agitation Emotions	Dejection Emotions	Agitation Emotions
Type of Self-Discrepancy				
Actual/ideal	.17	.13	.39**	−.33*
Actual/ought	.05	.26***	.04	.46**

Note. Partial correlations shown have premanipulation mood and the alternative type of self-discrepancy partialled out of each.

$^*p < .05.$ $^{**}p < .01.$ $^{***}p < .10.$

of self-discrepancies are positive (i.e., desired and valued), it should be possible to prime a single *positive* attribute and yet produce discomfort. This prediction was tested in a number of recent studies (see Strauman, 1989; Strauman & Higgins, 1987).

In one study (Strauman & Higgins, 1987, Study 2), for example, two groups of undergraduates were selected on the basis of their responses to the Selves questionnaire obtained weeks earlier—subjects who were predominant-Ideal-discrepant and subjects who were predominant-Ought-discrepant. A covert, idiographic priming technique was used to activate self-attributes in a task supposedly investigating the "physiological effects of thinking about other people." Subjects were given phrases of the form, "An X person _____" (where X would be a trait adjective such as "friendly" or "intelligent"), and were asked to complete each sentence as quickly as possible. For each sentence, each subject's total verbalization time and skin conductance amplitude were recorded. Subjects also reported their mood on scales measuring dejection-related and agitation-related emotions both at the beginning and end of the session.

Subjects were randomly assigned to one of the following priming conditions: (a) "nonmatching" priming, where the trait adjectives were attributes in a subject's self-guide but the attributes did not appear in the subject's actual self; (b) "mismatching" priming, where the trait adjectives were attributes in a subject's self-guide and the subject's actual self was discrepant from the self-guide for those attributes; and (c) "yoked (mismatching)" priming, where the trait adjectives were attributes that did not appear in either a subject's self-guide or actual self but were the *same* attributes that were used for some other subject in the "mismatching" priming condition. These attributes defined the subject-related attributes. All subjects also received the same set of "subject-unrelated" trait adjectives, which were attributes that did not appear in any of the subjects' self-guides or actual selves.

As predicted, in the "mismatching" priming condition *only* a dejection-related syndrome (i.e., increased dejected mood, lowered standardized skin conductance amplitude, decreased total verbalization time) was produced in the predominant actual:Ideal discrepant subjects, whereas an agitation-related syndrome (i.e., increased agitated mood, raised standardized skin conductance amplitude, increased total verbalization time) was produced in the predominant actual:Ought discrepant subjects. Figures 8.1 and 8.2 show the trial-by-trial effects for the standardized skin conductance amplitude measure and the total verbalization time measure in the "mismatching" priming condition. As is evident from these figures, there was a striking shift into and out of the syndromes as subjects received (subject-related) mismatching priming versus subject-unrelated priming, respectively. Moreover, as predicted, the direction of

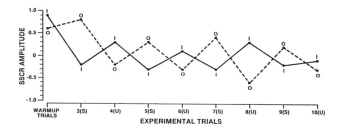

FIG. 8.1. Standardized spontaneous skin conductance response amplitude during warm-up and experimental trials for subjects in the mismatch priming condition. I = the central tendency of subjects possessing an actual(own)/ideal(own) discrepancy. O = the central tendency of subjects possessing an actual(own)/ought(other) discrepancy. S = subject-related trial in which positive attribute appeared among the subject's actual-self attributes. U = subject-unrelated trial in which positive attribute did not appear among the subject's actual-self attributes.

the shifts were opposite for the predominant actual:Ideal discrepant subjects than for the predominant actual:Ought discrepant subjects. These results are consistent with the assumption that self-discrepancies function as knowledge structures, including the assumption that activation of one attribute in a self-discrepancy (e.g., a single self-guide attribute) will automatically activate the discrepancy as a whole, thus producing its associated discomfort.

There is also evidence from recent studies by Strauman (1990; see also Strauman, 1992) that exposure to self-guide attributes will activate the self-guide and retrieve emotional memories associated with the self-guide. Subjects were told that they would be read a series of words to help them remember episodes from several years earlier. For each subject, some of

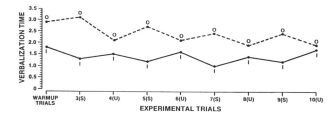

FIG. 8.2. Total verbalization time (in seconds) during warm-up and experimental trials for subjects in the mismatch priming condition. I = the central tendency of subjects possessing an actual(own)/ideal(own) discrepancy. O = the central tendency of subjects possessing an actual(own)/ought(other) discrepancy. S = subject-related trial in which positive attribute appeared among the subject's actual-self attributes. U = subject-unrelated trial in which positive attribute did not appear among the subject's actual-self attributes.

these words were attributes from the subject's Ideal self-guides and some were attributes from the subject's Ought self-guides. The subjects were not told to remember emotional episodes, but the remembered episodes did have incidental emotional content. A major aim of the study was to examine the relation between type of self-guide memory cue (i.e., Ideal-discrepant attribute, Ideal-nondiscrepant attribute, Ought-discrepant attribute, and Ought-nondiscrepant attribute) and incidental negative emotional content.

As predicted, Ideal-discrepant cues retrieved memories that had the most incidental dejection-related content, whereas Ought-discrepant cues retrieved memories that had the most incidental agitation-related content. There was also evidence that the effect of the self-guide cues on retrieving negative emotional content was not due to the chronic accessibility or self-referential nature of the cues per se. Rather, what seems to have been critical is the underlying emotional significance of the cues, the historical psychological situations they represented.

Another study reported by Houston (1990, Study 2) provides further support for the hypothesis that activating a self-guide attribute will in-fluence emotional responses, in this case, emotional responses to a target's discomfort. In this study, the target's discomfort was always described as dejection-related and subjects were either high or low in discrepancy between their actual and Ideal selves. In addition, the attribute about which the target was distressed (e.g., distressed about a failure to be "outgoing") varied for different subjects. For some subjects the attribute was not part of their self-system, for other subjects the attribute was in their Ideal self and their actual self matched it, and for the remaining subjects the attribute was in their Ideal self and their actual self was discrepant from it. The study found that subjects experienced much more dejection in response to the target's discomfort when they were high in discrepancy between their actual and Ideal selves, and the attribute about which the target was distressed was in the subjects' Ideal self and their actual self was discrepant from it.

In sum, there is considerable evidence at this point that supports the initial hypotheses of self-discrepancy theory relating specific types of self-discrepancies to particular kinds of emotional distress. These initial hypotheses were based on the proposal that different representations of relations among specific kinds of self-beliefs involve distinct psychological situations. Individuals who possess these representational patterns are predisposed to experience these distinct psychological situations and the specific emotions associated with them. Is this, however, the whole story? Our recent research suggests that underlying these varying predisposi-tions to experience specific psychological situations might be distinct self-regulatory systems. Let us now turn to this research and our current thinking about vulnerabilities and emotional experiences.

OUTCOME FOCUS AND DISTINCT
SELF-REGULATORY SYSTEMS

It is common knowledge that when people describe a glass half filled with water, it is optimists who describe it as half full and it is pessimists who describe it as half empty. This everyday example of a motivational difference exemplifies the basic assumption of motivational theories in psychology. Specifically, motivational theories, in one way or another, typically distinguish between a motivational system that concerns positive or pleasurable experiences and a motivational system that concerns negative or painful experiences. Conditioning theories distinguish between reward and punishment. Incentive theories distinguish between opportunity and threat. Achievement theories distinguish between the pride of success and the fear or shame of failure. Attitude theories distinguish between like and dislike. Consistency theories distinguish between consonance or balance and dissonance or imbalance. Cognitive therapy theories distinguish between rational or functional beliefs and irrational or dysfunctional beliefs. Theories of mood effects distinguish between good and bad moods. And so on.

If valence is such a critical motivational variable, why would only one system be involved in regulating it? Should not alternative systems regulate pain and pleasure? If this is the case, at least some emotional phenomena should reflect not so much the distinction between pain and pleasure per se, as the distinction between the pains and pleasures from different regulatory systems.

Recently, I have proposed that different systems of regulating pain and pleasure can be distinguished in terms of the variable of *outcome focus* (e.g., Higgins, in press). In his classic book, *Learning Theory and Behavior*, Mowrer (1960) distinguished between two positive or pleasurable psychological situations, the presence of positive outcomes and the absence of negative outcomes, and between two negative or painful psychological situations, the absence of positive outcomes and the presence of negative outcomes. As discussed earlier, these distinct psychological situations have been related to distinct emotions by Mowrer (1960) and others (e.g., Roseman, 1984; Stein & Jewett, 1982). These distinct emotions are organized in Table 8.5 as a function of the valence of the experience and the outcome focus of the experience.

It is clear in looking at Table 8.5 that two distinct systems for regulating pain and pleasure can be distinguished in terms of the variable of outcome focus. First, there is a *positive outcome focus* regulatory system that involves maximizing the presence of positive outcomes (pleasure) and minimizing the absence of positive outcomes (pain). Second, there is a *negative outcome focus* regulatory system that involves maximizing the absence of negative

TABLE 8.5
Types of Psychological Situations and Emotions as a Function
of Outcome Focus and Overall Valence of Experience

Outcome Focus	Positive Valence		Negative Valence	
Positive focus	Presence of positive		Absence of positive	
	Happy	Satisfied	Sad	Dissatisfied
Negative focus	Absence of negative		Presence of negative	
	Calm	Relieved	Tense	Nervous

outcomes (pleasure) and minimizing the presence of negative outcomes (pain).

In terms of Bowlby's (1969, 1973) classic account of people's fundamental survival needs, the positive-outcome focus system would be responsive to people's *nurturance* needs and the negative-outcome focus system would be responsive to people's *security* needs. Both systems for regulating pain and pleasure would be adaptive and thus all people would possess them. Nevertheless, different socialization experiences could make one system predominate in self-regulation.

Self-discrepancy theory (see Higgins, 1989b, 1991) postulates that the psychological significance of matches (i.e., congruence) and mismatches (i.e., discrepancy) between individuals' actual self (or self-concept) and their desired selves derives from distinct developmental histories of caretaker–child interactions. Parents (as the usual caretakers) who *hope or wish* that their child will possess certain types of valued attributes orient to their child in terms of positive outcomes. When the child matches their hopes, wishes, or aspirations, the parent responds in such a way as to produce positive outcomes for the child (e.g., hugging or kissing). When the child is discrepant from their hopes or wishes, the parent responds so as to remove positive outcomes for the child (e.g., love withdrawal). By 6 years of age children are capable of constructing an ideal self representing the parents' hopes or wishes for them as a self-regulatory guide. According to self-discrepancy theory, such children begin to self-regulate in terms of an *ideal self-guide* that orients them toward *positive outcomes*—to maximize the presence of positive outcomes (as a type of positive event) and to minimize the absence of positive outcomes (as a type of negative event).

In contrast, parents who believe that it is their child's *duty, obligation, or responsibility* to possess certain types of valued attributes orient to their child in terms of negative outcomes. When the child behaves in a manner that mismatches their demands or prescriptions, the parent responds so as to produce negative outcomes for the child (e.g., sanctions or punishment). When the child behaves in a manner that matches their demands or prescriptions, the parent responds so as to remove the threat of negative outcomes for the child (e.g., reassurance). By 6 years of age, such children begin to self-regulate in terms of an *ought self-guide* that orients them toward *negative outcomes*—to maximize the absence of negative outcomes (as a type of positive event) and to minimize the presence of negative outcomes (as a type of negative event).

According to self-discrepancy theory, then, self-regulation in relation to ideal self-guides involves a positive outcome focus, whereas self-regulation in relation to ought self-guides involves a negative outcome focus. If so, activating ideal self-discrepancies should produce dejection-related emotions reflecting the absence of positive outcomes, such as feeling sad and disappointed, whereas activating ought self-discrepancies should produce agitation-related emotions reflecting the presence of negative outcomes, such as feeling nervous and tense. As reviewed earlier, there is considerable evidence supporting these predictions. None of the studies reviewed thus far, however, provide direct support for the proposal that self-regulation in relation to ideal self-guides involves a positive outcome focus whereas self-regulation in relation to ought self-guides involves a negative outcome focus. Our recent studies were designed to provide such support.

Outcome Focus and Sensitivity to Distinct Psychological Situations

In a classic approach to relating personality and cognition, Kelly (1955) proposed that each individual possesses personal constructs through which he or she views the world of events. Accordingly, events should be remembered better by people whose personal constructs are related to them than by people whose personal constructs are unrelated to them— this should be true not only for events in which they are involved (i.e., autobiographical memory), but also for events in which others are involved (i.e., biographical memory). The positive-outcome focus associated with regulation in relation to an ideal self-guide can produce experiences of both positive overall valence (the presence of positive outcomes) and negative overall valence (the absence of positive outcomes). Similarly, the negative-outcome focus associated with regulation in relation to an ought self-guide can produce experiences of both positive overall valence (the absence of negative outcomes) and negative overall valence (the presence of negative outcomes).

According to self-discrepancy theory, then, the effects of chronic self-discrepancies on memory should involve differences between events in outcome focus rather than differences between events in overall valence. Higgins and Tykocinski (1992), therefore, predicted that when people read descriptions of events in another person's life, those events that reflected the presence and absence of positive outcomes would be remembered better by persons who possessed predominantly an actual/ideal discrepancy than by persons who possessed predominantly an actual/ought discrepancy, whereas the reverse would be true for those events that reflected the absence and presence of negative outcomes. Given the emphasis in the literature on memory for events varying in overall valence, such as the mood and memory literature (e.g., Gilligan & Bower, 1984; Isen, 1984), this is a rather novel prediction.

This prediction was tested by selecting subjects who were either relatively high in actual/ideal(own) discrepancy and relatively low in actual/ought(own) discrepancy (i.e., predominant actual/ideal(own) discrepancy persons) or relatively high in actual/ought(own) discrepancy and relatively low in actual/ideal(own) discrepancy (i.e., predominant actual/ought(own) discrepancy persons). A few weeks after the selection procedure, all subjects were given the same essay to read about several days in the life of a target person. Ten minutes after reading the essay (following a nonverbal filler task), the subjects were asked to reproduce the essay word-for-word.

In the essay, the different types of psychological situations described earlier were represented by different events that the target person experienced. The target person's experiences were circumstantial and not personality-related. The different types of psychological situations were represented in each day of the target person's life as follows:

1. The presence of positive outcomes [positive-outcome focus; positive overall valence]—for example, "I found a $20 bill on the pavement of Canal Street near the paint store."

2. The absence of positive outcomes [positive outcome focus; negative overall valence]—for example, "I've been wanting to see this movie at the 8th Street Theatre for some time, so this evening I went there straight after school to find out that it's not showing anymore."

3. The presence of negative outcomes [negative outcome focus; negative overall valence]—for example, "I was stuck in the subway for 35 minutes with at least 15 sweating passengers breathing down my neck."

4. The absence of negative outcomes [negative outcome focus; positive overall valence]—for example, "This is usually my worst school day. Awful schedule, class after class with no break. But today is election day—no school!"

By using these materials, we could test whether a chronic pattern of self-beliefs representing a distinct psychological situation produces sensitivity to events reflecting that psychological situation, *despite there being no overlap between the self-belief pattern and the stimulus events in either their specific content or topic.*

Because self-discrepancies can influence mood (see Higgins, 1987, 1989a) and mood can influence memory (see Gilligan & Bower, 1984; Isen, 1984), this study was designed to both control and check for any possible effects of temporary mood on memory. Previous studies of self-discrepancies have found that exposure to trait-related input can prime self-discrepancies and change subjects' mood (see Higgins, 1989a). The essay used as input in the present study minimized such priming by containing events that did not relate to personality traits. Rather, the events were clearly circumstantial factors such as finding money by chance or getting stuck in a crowded subway. In addition to attempting to control for mood in this way, subjects' moods were also measured both before and after they read the essay in order to be able to check whether individual differences in mood contributed to the findings.

A Type of Predominant Self-Discrepancy (Actual/Ideal; Actual/Ought) × Outcome Focus of Event (Positive Outcome Focus; Negative Outcome Focus) × Overall Valence of Event (Positive Overall Valence; Negative Overall Valence) analysis of variance was performed on the number of target events recalled. As shown in Table 8.6, the subjects remembered the negative overall valence events better than the positive overall valence events but remembered the positive outcome focus events better than the negative outcome focus events, which is interesting because it highlights the distinction between overall valence and outcome focus. Most importantly, however, this analysis revealed, as predicted, a significant Type of Predominant Self-Discrepancy × Outcome Focus of Event interaction.

As shown in Table 8.6, this interaction reflected the fact that, as predicted, predominant actual/ideal discrepancy subjects tended to remember target events representing the presence and absence of positive outcomes better than did predominant actual/ought discrepancy subjects, whereas predominant actual/ought discrepancy subjects tended to remember target events representing the absence and presence of negative outcomes better than did predominant actual/ideal discepancy subjects. No other interactions were significant. Thus, predominant actual/ideal discrepancy subjects and predominant actual/ought discrepancy subjects were differentially sensitive to the target events as a function of the events' outcome focus but *not* as a function of the events' overall valence.

The aforementioned 2 × 2 × 2 analysis of variance was performed again three times—once with premood as the covariate, once with postmood as the covariate, and once with change in mood as the covariate. The Type of Predominant Self-Discrepancy × Outcome Focus of Event inter-

TABLE 8.6
Mean Recall of Events Reflecting Different Types of Psychological
Situations as a Function of Outcome Focus of Event, Overall Valence
of Event, and Subject's Type of Predominant Self-Discrepancy

	Outcome Focus			
	Positive Focus		Negative Focus	
	Positive Valence (PP)	Negative Valence (AP)	Positive Valence (AN)	Negative Valence (PN)
Self-Discrepancy				
Actual:Ideal	2.7	3.5	2.2	2.3
Actual:Ought	2.3	2.8	2.4	2.6

Note. PP: Presence of positive outcomes; AP: Absence of positive outcomes; AN: Absence of negative outcomes; PN: Presence of negative outcomes.

action described earlier remained significant in every case; thus, the obtained interaction between type of predominant self-discrepancy and outcome focus of event was independent of any differences in mood.

Outcome Focus and Predilections for Distinct Self-Regulatory Strategies

The results of the Higgins and Tykocinski (1992) study provide evidence that the ideal self-regulatory system involves a positive-outcome focus, whereas the ought self-regulatory system involves a negative-outcome focus. Our subsequent studies considered further implications of such distinct regulatory systems, particulary implications for self-regulatory strategies and tactics.

Two basic distinctions regarding self-regulation have been made in the literature—one involving *the valence* of the end state that functions as the reference value for the movement (positive versus negative), and one involving the *direction* of the motivated movement (approach versus avoidance).

In regard to valence, the self-regulatory system can have either a desired end state functioning as the standard (i.e., a positive reference value), or an undesired end state functioning as the standard (i.e., a negative reference value). Both positive and negative reference values have been described in the literature (see Carver & Scheier, 1990). Various self theories have described positive selves as reference values in self-regulation, such as the type of person individuals would like to be (e.g., Cooley, 1902/1964; Higgins, 1987; James, 1890/1948; Markus & Nurius, 1986; Rogers, 1961; Schlenker & Weigold, 1989) or the type of person they believe they should be (e.g., Freud, 1923/1961; Higgins, 1987; James, 1890/1948; Schlenker & Weigold, 1989). Self theories have also described negative selves as reference values in self-regulation, such as Erikson's (1963) *evil identity*, Sullivan's (1953) *bad me*, and Markus and Nurius' (1986) *feared self*.

In regard to the direction of the motivated movement, the literature distinguishes between approaching a positive self-state and avoiding a negative self-state. Carver and Scheier (1990) proposed that when a self-regulatory system has a desired end state as a reference value, the system is discrepancy-reducing and involves attempts to move the currently perceived actual-self state as close as possible to the desired reference point. When a self-regulatory system has an undesired state as a reference value, the system is discrepancy-amplifying and involves attempts to move the currently perceived actual-self state as far away as possible from the undesired reference point. Carver and Scheier (1990) referred to the former discrepancy-reducing system as an *approach system* and the latter discrepancy-amplifying system as an *avoidance system*. In this case, the approach and avoidance concerns the direction of the movement in relation to either a desired end state or an undesired end state, respectively.

In a discrepancy-reducing system, people are motivated to move their actual self as close as possible to the desired end state. There are two alternative means to reduce the discrepancy between the actual self and a desired end state as reference point—approach self-states that match the desired end state or avoid self-states that mismatch the desired end state. For example, a person who wants to get a good grade on a quiz (a desired end state) could either study hard at the library the day before the quiz (approaching a match to the desired end state) or turn down an invitation to go out drinking with friends the night before the quiz (avoiding a mismatch to the desired end state).

In a discrepancy-amplifying system, people are motivated to move their actual self as far away as possible from the undesired end state. There are, again, two alternative means to amplify the discrepancy between the actual self and an undesired end state as reference point—approach self-states that mismatch the undesired end state or avoid self-states that match the undesired end state. For example, a person who dislikes interpersonal conflict (an undesired end state) could either arrange a meeting with his or her apartment mates to work out a schedule for cleaning the apartment (approaching a mismatch to the undesired end state) or leave the apartment when his or her two apartment mates start to argue (avoiding a match to the undesired end state).

Thus, by considering the alternative means for accomplishing discrepancy reduction in relation to desired end states and discrepancy amplification in relation to undesired end states, four different forms of self-regulation can be identified. Table 8.7 summarizes how "valence of end state as reference point" combines with "direction of means" to produce the four different regulatory forms.

One might expect that a *positive*-outcome focus would be associated with a predilection for self-regulatory forms involving *approach*, whereas a *negative*-outcome focus would be associated with a predilection for self-regulatory forms involving *avoidance*. This would also be reasonable if, as suggested earlier, the positive-outcome focus system is responsive to nurturance-like needs (e.g., obtaining nourishment), and the negative-outcome focus system is responsive to survival-like needs (e.g., escaping danger). Given that ideal self-regulation is a positive outcome focus system and ought self-regulation is a negative outcome focus system, it follows that regulation in relation to ideal self-guides would involve approach-related self-regulatory forms, whereas regulation in relation to ought self-guides would involve avoidance-related self-regulatory forms.

In one of our studies designed to test this hypothesis, we used a between-subjects manipulation of self-guide activation (see Higgins, Roney, Crowe, & Hymes, 1994). The manipulation was based on the technique used by Higgins et al. (1986, Study 2) described earlier. Subjects are asked either to report on how their hopes and goals have changed over time (activating ideal self-guides) or to report on how their sense of duty and obligation has changed over time (activating ought self-guides). A free-recall technique similar to that used in the Higgins and Tykocinski (1992) study was used to reveal subjects' predilections for different regulatory forms without requiring them to make a conscious judgment. Subjects read about 16 episodes that occurred over 4 days in the life of another student. Each of the four regulatory forms was exemplified by four different episodes. We expected that activating either the ideal or ought regulatory system would increase subject's predilection for particular regulatory forms, which in turn would make them more sensitive to, and thus more likely to recall, those episodes that exemplified those particular forms.

TABLE 8.7
Summary of Regulatory Forms as a Function of Valence
of End State as Reference Point and Direction of Means

	Valence of End State as Reference Point	
Direction of Means	Desired End State (Discrepancy-Reducing)	Undesired End State (Discrepancy-Amplifying)
Approach	Approaching matches to desired end states	Approaching mismatches to undesired end states
Avoidance	Avoiding mismatches to desired end states	Avoiding matches to undesired end states

In each of the episodes the target was trying either to experience a desired end state or not to experience an undesired end state. In order to experience a desired end state, the target either used means that would decrease the discrepancy to a desired end state (approaching matches to desired end states) or used means that would avoid increasing the discrepancy to a desired end state (avoiding mismatches to desired end states). In order not to experience an undesired end state, the target either used means that would increase the discrepancy to an undesired end state (approaching mismatches to undesired end states) or used means that would avoid decreasing the discrepancy to an undesired outcome (avoiding matches to undesired end states). Following is an example of an episode exemplifying each of the regulatory forms:

1. Approaching matches to desired end states: "Because I wanted to be at school for the beginning of my 8:30 psychology class, which is usually excellent, I woke up early this morning."
2. Avoiding mismatches to desired end states: "I wanted to take a class in photography at the community center, so I didn't register for a class in Spanish that was scheduled at the same time."
3. Approaching mismatches to undesired end states: "I dislike eating in crowded places, so at noon I picked up a sandwich from a local deli and ate outside."
4. Avoiding matches to undesired end states: "I didn't want to feel tired during my very long morning of classes, so I skipped the most strenuous part of my morning workout."

An overall Type of Self-guide Activated (Ideal; Ought) × Direction of Stated Means (Approach; Avoidance) × Valence of Stated End state (Desired end state; Undesired end state) × Story Version × Event Order analysis of variance was performed on the number of episodes subjects

TABLE 8.8
Mean Number of Episodes Recalled as a Function of Type of Self-Guide Activated, Valence of Stated End State, and Direction of Stated Means

| | Valence of Stated End State | | | |
| | Desired End State | | Undesired End State | |
Direction of Stated Means	Approach Matches	Avoid Mismatches	Approach Mismatches	Avoid Matches
Type of Activation				
Ideal guide	1.75	1.37	1.50	1.39
Ought guide	1.19	1.96	1.38	1.75

recalled for each type of episode in the story. Table 8.8 shows subjects' recall of each type of episode in the story as a function of the type of self-guide that was activated.

The overall analysis revealed a significant Type of Self-guide Activated × Direction of Stated Means interaction, reflecting the fact that there was an overall tendency for subjects to remember better episodes exemplifying an approach direction of means when ideal self-guides were activated than when ought self-guides were activated, but to remember better episodes exemplifying an avoidance direction of means when ought self-guides were activated than when ideal self-guides were activated. The specific prediction that ideal self-regulation would involve approach forms and ought self-regulation would involve avoidance forms predicts a Type of Self-guide Activated × Direction of Stated Means interaction for desired end states alone. As is evident in Table 8.8, the predicted interaction was obtained. Subjects remembered episodes exemplifying approaching matches to desired end states significantly better when ideal self-guides were activated than when ought self-guides were activated, whereas they remembered episodes exemplifying avoiding mismatches to desired end states significantly better when ought self-guides were activated than when ideal self-guides were activated. (It should be noted that the Type of Self-guide Activated × Direction of Stated Means interaction was considerably weaker and non-significant for undesired end-states.)

In this study, the predilections for different regulatory forms were measured after either ideal self-guides or ought self-guides were made temporarily more accessible through recent activation. Although this method has the advantage of enhancing experimental control, it does not permit stable predilections associated with chronic differences in ideal versus ought orientation to be examined. Our next study was designed to examine this issue by selecting subjects whose predominant orientation involved either ideal self-guides (i.e., subjects with predominant actual/ideal discrepancies) or ought self-guides (i.e, subjects with predominant actual/ought discrepancies). As a second issue, the predilections that were studied in our initial study were quite general regulatory forms, such as predilections for approaching matches or for avoiding mismatches to desired end states. Are these general predilections also revealed in specific strategies or tactics of self-regulation? Would individuals with a predominant ideal self-guide orientation versus a predominant ought self-guide orientation select different tactics for regulating an important region of their lives, such as friendship? Another aim of our next study was to begin to address this important question.

The next study consisted of three phases, the first eliciting undergraduates' spontaneous strategies for friendship as a function of outcome focus. The question about friendship that each subject answered was included as part of a half-hour battery of questions on a variety of different issues. The subjects were randomly assigned to answer one of two different questions about friendship, with half of the subjects answering each. The question framed with a *positive-outcome focus* was as follows: "Imagine that you are the kind of person who would like to be a good friend in your close relationships. What would your strategy be to meet this goal?" The question framed with a *negative-outcome focus* was as follows: "Imagine that you are the kind of person who believes you should try not to be a poor friend in your close relationships. What would your strategy be to meet this goal?"

Although a few subjects gave only one strategy, most subjects offered several strategies in response to the question they received. A rough classification system was developed, which grouped 75% of the strategies into 9 different types. Subjects in the "positive-outcome focus" framing condition responded with some of these strategy types more than subjects in the "negative-outcome focus," and vice versa. Six strategy types that most differentiated subjects in the two framing conditions, three strategy types used more by subjects in the "positive-outcome focus" framing condition and three used more by subjects in the "negative outcome focus" framing condition, were selected. For each of these six strategy types, one or more sentences that best captured the strategy were written, using the subjects' original words as much as possible.

The strategies associated more with the "positive-outcome focus" framing condition were as follows:

1. "Be generous and willing to give of yourself."
2. "Be supportive to your friends. Be emotionally supportive."
3. "Be loving and attentive."

The strategies associated more with the "negative-outcome focus" framing condition were:

4. "Stay in touch. Don't lose contact with friends."
5. "Try to make time for your friends and not neglect them."
6. "Keep the secrets friends have told you and don't gossip about friends."

On the basis of these Phase 1 results, Strategies 1–3 were selected as the "approach" strategies and Strategies 4–6 were selected as the "avoidance" strategies. The purpose of Phase 2 was to test experimentally whether the approach strategies would be selected more when friendship was framed with a positive-outcome focus versus a negative-outcome focus, whereas the avoidance strategies would be selected more when friendship was framed with a negative-outcome focus versus a positive-outcome focus. A new sample of subjects were randomly assigned to answer one of two different questions about friendship strategies, with half of the subjects answering each question. The question framed with a *positive-outcome focus* was, "When you think about strategies for *being a good friend* in your close relationships, which THREE of the following would you choose?" The question framed with a *negative-outcome focus* was: "When you think about strategies for *not being a poor friend* in your close relationship, which THREE of the following would you choose?"

There was a significant difference between the two framing conditions. Subjects in the "positive-outcome focus" framing condition chose significantly more "approach" strategies than subjects in the "negative-outcome focus" framing condition, and subjects in the "negative-outcome focus" framing condition chose significantly more "avoidance" strategies than subjects in the "positive-outcome focus" framing condition.

Using the same Phase 2 approach and avoidance strategies found to be related to outcome focus, the purpose of Phase 3 of the study was to test whether approach strategies would be spontaneously selected more by individuals with a predominant ideal versus ought self-guide orientation, whereas avoidance strategies would be selected more by individuals with a predominant ought versus ideal self-guide orientation. Using a new sample of undergraduates, median splits were performed on subjects' actual/ideal discrepancy scores and actual/ought discrepancy scores. Subjects who were high in actual/ideal discrepancy and low in actual/ought discrepancy were classified as predominant ideal discrepant subjects. Subjects who were high in actual/ought discrepancy and low in actual/ideal discrepancy were classified as predominant ought discrepant subjects.

In the experimental session held more than 2 months after measuring subjects' self-discrepancies, each subject was asked the *same, unframed* question about friendship, as follows: "When you think about strategies for *friendship*, which THREE of the following strategies would you choose?" This question was followed by the same six choices of strategies used in the Phase 2 framing study.

As predicted, a significant difference was found between the two groups. The predominant ideal-discrepant subjects chose significantly more "approach" strategies than the predominant ought discrepant subjects and the predominant ought-discrepant subjects chose significantly more "avoidance" strategies than the predominant ideal discrepant subjects. To check on whether subjects' choice of strategies might be related somehow to their self-guide attributes, the content of subjects' self-guides was compared to the content of the different strategies. The content overlap between subjects' self-guide attributes and the presented strategies was minimal, and thus did not produce the results of the study.

EMOTIONAL EXPERIENCES AS SELF-REGULATORY STATES OF PAIN AND PLEASURE

The results of our recent studies support the proposal that self-regulation in relation to ideal self-guides versus ought self-guides involves two distinct self-regulatory systems. The Ideal self-regulatory system involves a positive-outcome focus, is oriented toward maximizing the presence of positive outcomes and minimizing the absence of positive outcomes, and tends to approach matches to self-guides as its strategic means. The Ought self-regulatory system involves a negative-outcome focus, is oriented toward maximizing the absence of negative outcomes and minimizing the presence of negative outcomes, and tends to avoid mismatches to self-guides as its strategic means. These distinct self-regulatory systems are significant for theories of emotion because there is substantial empirical evidence linking them to vulnerabilities for specific kinds of emotional experiences. That is, people who possess discrepancies to ideal self-guides are predisposed to experience dejection-related emotions, whereas people who possess discrepancies to ought self-guides are predisposed to experience agitation-related emotions. What might this tell us about the nature of emotional experiences?

Perhaps the most controversial issue in the literature on emotions concerns the role of cognition as a mediator of emotions. Cognition plays a central role as mediator in some theories of emotion, such as in the theories of Schachter (e.g., Schachter & Singer, 1962), Mandler (e.g., Mandler, 1975), and Zillmann (e.g., Zillmann, 1978). In contrast, cognition plays little or no role as mediator in other theories of emotion, such as in the theories of James (1890/1948), Tomkins (e.g., Tomkins, 1962), and Zajonc (e.g., Zajonc, Murphy, & Inglehart, 1989). It is significant, however, that regardless of whether cognition is assumed to mediate emotional responses, most theories consider emotional experiences themselves to involve two attributes: pleasantness, and intensity or arousal. Moreover, this consensus among emotional theorists regarding the nature of emotional experiences has a direct parallel in the measurement literature where a consensus has developed that emotions as a whole can best be characterized in terms of the same two dimensions (see Russell, 1978; Watson & Tellegen, 1985).

Let us consider this consensus in light of the proposal that distinct self-regulatory systems underlie different emotional experiences. From the "distinct-systems" perspective, the dimension of pleasantness would continue to be critical because both self-regulatory systems attempt to maximize pleasure and minimize pain. For both the Ideal and Ought self-regulatory systems, for example, a match to a self-guide produces pleasure and a mismatch to a self-guide produces pain. The dimension of intensity or arousal, however, is not as critical from this perspective. Certainly emotions vary in intensity or arousal. However, this fact alone does not mean that intensity or arousal per se is critical for self-regulation. From the "distinct-systems" perspective, intensity or arousal accompanies emotions and can have its own psychological consequences, as in "excitation-transfer" effects (e.g., Zillmann, 1978), but it is not critical to the self-regulatory systems that constitute the motivational underpinnings of emotional experiences. The position taken here is analogous to the argument that although the state of dissonance is typically accompanied by arousal, the arousal is not critical to the motivational underpinnings of the dissonance experience. People are motivated to reduce the unpleasantness of the dissonant state rather than to reduce arousal (see Higgins, Rhodewalt, & Zanna, 1979).

If intensity or arousal is not a critical property of emotions, what is? Based on the research testing self-discrepancy theory, "outcome focus" could be considered another critical property of emotions. Our research suggests that the emotional experience of pain and pleasure varies depending on whether a positive or a negative outcome focus is involved. The pain associated with the presence of a negative outcome, such as feeling tense or nervous, is different from the pain associated with the absence of a positive outcome, such as feeling sad or discouraged. The pleasure associated with the absence of a negative outcome, such as feeling calm or quiescent, is different from the pleasure associated with the presence of a positive outcome, such as feeling cheerful or elated. From this perspective, it is the pleasantness (pain vs. pleasure) and outcome focus (positive-outcome focus vs. negative-outcome focus) entailed in distinct self-regulatory states that underlie the basic experience of these emotions rather than the combination of pleasantness and arousal. In his theory of how emotion-eliciting events are appraised, Roseman (see Roseman, 1984; Roseman, Spindel, & Jose, 1990) has also argued for the importance of a variable he calls "motivational state" that distinguishes between "appetitive" motivation (analogous to a positive-outcome focus) and "aversive" motivation (analogous to a negative-outcome focus).

The advantage of this perspective on emotions is that differences among basic types of emotional experiences can be directly related to differences among the specific states of distinct self-regulatory systems. Emotional epxeriences are considered to be neither an output of arousal plus interpretation nor the output of some separate "affective" system. Rather, emotional experiences are considered to be the direct experience of particular self-regulatory states of distinct self-regulatory systems. Each self-regulatory state is a psychological situation combining valence and outcome focus and is part of a distinct self-regulatory system. As specific psychological situations, the self-regulatory states of a distinct self-regulatory system should relate to a sensitivity to life events that reflect these psychological situations and to predilections for specific strategic means to deal with these situations. Studies supporting these predictions have been described here earlier. As part of distinct self-regulatory systems, changes in self-regulatory states should also relate to specific changes in emotional experiences and performance. Some support for this latter prediction has been provided by our recent studies, which have found that framing a task with a positive-outcome focus versus a negative-outcome focus influences both which emotions change while performing the task and the quality and persistence of the performance (see Roney, Higgins, & Shah, in press).

If the outcome focus of self-regulatory states, along with valence, underlies emotional experiences, then one might expect outcome focus to be reflected in people's emotional expressions. This is not to say that people should mention outcome focus as they might explicitly mention arousal or intensity when describing their emotions. It is not necessary for a variable to be consciously recognized in order for it to be important. One might, however, expect people's expressions of their current or recent feelings to reflect this variable; indeed, it appears that this is the case. Most studies of interassociations among emotional responses have found the following four distinct clusters: (a) a "presence of positive outcomes" cluster consisting of cheerfulness-related emotions such as happy, satisfied, elated, and enthusiastic; (b) an "absence of positive outcomes" cluster consisting of dejection-related emotions such as sad, blue, and sluggish; (c) an "absence of negative outcomes" cluster consisting of quiescence-related emotions such as calm, relaxed, and quiet; and (d) a "presence of negative outcomes" cluster consisting of agitation-related emotions such as nervous and fearful. Clusters (a) and (b), which are opposite valence on the positive-outcome focus dimension, typically fall opposite to each other in a two-factor solution, as expected. Clusters (c) and (d), which are opposite valence on the negative-outcome focus dimension, also typically fall opposite to each other in a two-factor solution, as expected. As is also expected, the bipolar "positive-outcome focus" dimension consisting of clusters (a) and (b) is typically orthogonal to the bipolar "negative-outcome focus" dimension consisting of clusters (c) and (d).

When one considers the case of people experiencing emotions over prolonged periods or across many situations, the notion that outcome focus is a critical property of emotional experiences makes a unique prediction. To the extent that individuals vary in their predispositions to respond to events with a positive versus a negative outcome focus, the bipolar ends of a particular outcome focus dimension should co-occur over time when individuals have both painful and pleasurable experiences in their lives. That is, given an approximately equal number of life events experienced as either painful or pleasurable, individuals who typically experience pleasure as the "presence of positive outcomes" should have a tendency to experience pain as the "absence of positive outcomes," and thus, over time, cluster (a) experiences should co-occur with cluster (b) experiences more than with cluster (d) experiences. Similarly, individuals who typically experience pleasure as the "absence of negative outcomes" should have a tendency to experience pain as the "presence of negative outcomes," and thus, over time, cluster (c) experiences should co-occur with cluster (d) experiences more than with cluster (b) experiences.

Emotional experiences, of course, are not restricted to the cheerfulness-related, dejection-related, quiescence-related, and agitation-related clusters. It is not the purpose of this chapter to provide a general review of emotional experiences; still, it might be useful to consider briefly the utility of the present perspective for distinguishing among emotional experiences. People feel "angry" when they experience a barrier to self-regulatory attainment. From the self-regulatory state perspective, when the barrier occurs within the positive-outcome focus people might experience "frustration" anger, whereas when the barrier occurs within the negative outcome focus they might experience "resentment" anger. Consistent with this proposal, a study by Strauman and Higgins (1988) found that frustration-related anger was uniquely associated with actual/ideal discrepancies (i.e., a positive-outcome focus), whereas resentment-related anger and anger directed toward others was uniquely associated with actual/ought discrepancies (i.e., a negative-outcome focus). To consider another example, people feel "surprised" when a state occurs that was not expected. From the self-regulatory perspective, when the surprise occurs within the positive-outcome focus people might experience "elation" for unexpected pleasure and "grief" for unexpected pain. In contrast, when the surprise occurs within the negative outcome focus people might experience "relief" for unexpected pleasure and "alarm" or "shock" for unexpected pain.

The emotional experiences considered thus far are relatively simple. As suggested by most theories of emotions, more complex emotional experiences require higher levels of mental representational capacity because additional cognitive elements are involved (e.g., Ortony, Clore, & Collins, 1988; Weiner, 1986). The self-regulatory system perspective on emotional experiences differs somewhat from previous perspectives in conceptualizing the additional cognitive elements in terms of their self-regulatory significance. As described earlier, for example, when people's beliefs about either their potential (i.e., their Can self) or the kind of person they will become (i.e., their Future self) are added to the positive-outcome focus regulatory system, it produces specific kinds of dejection for individuals possessing chronic goal discrepancies—feeling weak or "helpless" versus feeling despondent or "hopeless," respectively. To use another example, when another person's state is perceived as closer to one's goals than one's own state, one feels "disadvantaged." From the self-regulatory perspective, perhaps people are more likely to experience "envy" when the disadvantage occurs within the positive-outcome focus, whereas they are more likely to experience "jealousy" when the disadvantage occurs within the negative-outcome focus.

It should also be noted that the self-regulatory states experienced in the positive- and the negative-outcome focus regulatory systems are not the only distinct self-regulatory states that people experience. People also experience the self-regulatory state of "conflict" when they are pushed and pulled in opposite directions by incompatible goals. For example, research on discrepancies between two self-guides involving competing goals and standards was described earlier. This general self-regulatory state of conflict is experienced as "confusion" (e.g., Van Hook & Higgins, 1988). The psychodynamic literature suggests that when the conflict is between the positive- and the negative-outcome focus regulatory systems (e.g., Cameron, 1963), and thus involves a conflict between inclinations to approach and inclinations to avoid, it might be experienced more specifically as "ambivalence."

It was not the purpose of this chapter to propose a new general theory of emotional experiences. Undoubtedly, there are many different kinds of variables that underlie emotional experiences (e.g., Leventhal, 1982), and distinct self-regulatory systems are just one kind of variable. However, I believe that it is useful to consider emotional experiences as direct experiences of the specific states of distinct self-regulatory systems, states that are experienced as pleasurable when a system is working and as painful when a system is not working. Because this perspective ties emotional experiences directly to self-regulatory systems and psychological situations, the study of emotions becomes the study of motivational systems in action.

REFERENCES

Abelson, R. P. (1983). Whatever became of consistency theory? *Personality and Social Psychology Bulletin, 9,* 37–54.

Asch, S. E. (1952). *Social psychology.* Englewood Cliffs, NJ: Prentice Hall.

Bandura, A. (1982). The self and mechanisms of agency. In J. Suls (Ed.), *Psychological perspectives on the self* (Vol. 1, pp. 3–39). Hillsdale, NJ: Lawrence Erlbaum Associates.

Bandura, A. (1986). *Social foundations of thought and action: A social cognitive theory.* Englewood Cliffs, NJ: Prentice Hall.

Beck, A. T., Ward, C. H., Mendelson, M., Mock, J., & Erbaugh, J. (1961). An inventory for measuring depression. *Archives of General Psychiatry, 4,* 561–571.

Blatt, S. J., D'Afflitti, J. P., & Quinlan, D. M. (1976). Experiences of depression in normal young adults. *Journal of Abnormal Psychology, 86,* 203–223.

Bowlby, J. (1969). *Attachment and loss, Volume 1: Attachment.* New York: Basic Books.

Bowlby, J. (1973). *Attachment and loss, Volume 2: Separation: Anxiety and anger.* New York: Basic Books.

Cameron, N. (1963). *Personality development and psychopathology.* Boston: Houghton Mifflin.

Carver, C. S., & Scheier, M. F. (1990). Principles of self-regulation: Action and emotion. In E. T. Higgins & R. M. Sorrentino (Eds.), *Handbook of motivation and cognition: Foundations of social behavior, Volume 2.* New York: Guilford.

Collins, A. M., & Loftus, E. F. (1975). A spreading-activation theory of semantic processing. *Psychological Review, 82,* 407–428.

Cooley, C. H. (1964). *Human nature and the social order.* New York: Schocken Books. (Original work published 1902)

Derogatis, L. R., Lipman, R. S., Rickels, K., Uhlenhuth, E. H., & Covi, L. (1974). The Hopkins Symptom Checklist (HSCL): A self-report symptom inventory. *Behavioral Science, 19,* 1–15.

Epstein, S. (1978). Avoidance–approach: The fifth basic conflict. *Journal of Consulting and Clinical Psychology, 46,* 1016–1022.

Erikson, E. H. (1963). *Childhood and society* (Rev. ed.). New York: Norton.

Freud, S. (1961). The ego and the id. In J. Strachey (Ed. and Trans.), *Standard edition of the complete psychological works of Sigmund Freud* (Vol. 19, pp. 3–66). London: Hogarth Press. (Original work published 1923)

Gilligan, S. G., & Bower, G. H. (1984). Cognitive consequences of emotional arousal. In C. E. Izard, J. Kagan, & R. B. Zajonc (Eds.), *Emotions, cognition, and behavior* (pp. 547–588). New York: Cambridge University Press.

Greenwald, A. G., & Pratkanis, A. R. (1984). The self. In R. S. Wyer & T. K. Srull (Eds.), *Handbook of social cognition* (Vol. 3, pp. 129–178). Hillsdale, NJ: Lawrence Erlbaum Associates.

Heider, F. (1958). *The psychology of interpersonal relations.* New York: Wiley.

Heilizer, F. (1977). A review of theory and research on Miller's response competition (conflict) models. *The Journal of General Psychology, 97,* 227–280.

Higgins, E. T. (1987). Self-discrepancy: A theory relating self and affect. *Psychological Review, 94,* 319–340.

Higgins, E. T. (1989a). Self-discrepancy theory: What patterns of self-beliefs cause people to suffer? In L. Berkowitz (Ed.), *Advances in experimental social psychology* (Vol. 22, pp. 93–136). New York: Academic Press.

Higgins, E. T. (1989b). Continuities and discontinuities in self-regulatory and self-evaluative processes: A developmental theory relating self and affect. *Journal of Personality, 57,* 407–444.

Higgins, E. T. (1989c). Knowledge accessibility and activation: Subjectivity and suffering from unconscious sources. In J. S. Uleman & J. A. Bargh (Eds.), *Unintended thought* (pp. 75–123). New York: Guilford.

Higgins, E. T. (1990). Personality, social psychology, and person-situation relations: Standards and knowledge activation as a common language. In L. A. Pervin (Ed.), *Handbook of personality* (pp. 301–338). New York: Guilford Press.

Higgins, E. T. (1991). Development of self-regulatory and self-evaluative processes: Costs, benefits, and tradeoffs. In M. R. Gunnar & L. A. Sroufe (Eds.), *Self processes and* development: The Minnesota Symposia on Child Psychology (Vol. 23, pp. 125–165). Hillsdale, NJ: Lawrence Erlbaum Associates.

Higgins, E. T. (in press). Ideals, oughts, and regulatory outcome focus: Relating affect and motivation to distinct pains and pleasures. In P. M. Gollwitzer & J. A. Bargh (Eds.), *The psychology of action*. New York: Guilford.

Higgins, E. T., Bond, R. N., Klein, R., & Strauman, T. (1986). Self-discrepancies and emotional vulnerability: How magnitude, accessibility, and type of discrepancy influence affect. *Journal of Personality and Social Psychology, 51*, 5–15.

Higgins, E. T., & King, G. (1981). Accessibility of social constructs: Information processing consequences of individual and contextual variability. In N. Cantor & J. Kihlstrom (Eds.), *Personality, cognition, and social interaction* (pp. 69–121). Hillsdale, NJ: Lawrence Erlbaum Associates.

Higgins, E. T., Klein, R., & Strauman, T. (1987). Self-discrepancies: Distinguishing among self-states, self-state conflicts, and emotional vulnerabilities. In K. M. Yardley & T. M. Honess (Eds.), *Self and identity: Psychosocial perspectives* (pp. 173–186). New York: Wiley.

Higgins, E. T., Rhodewalt, F., & Zanna, M. P. (1979). Dissonance motivation: Its nature, persistence, and reinstatement. *Journal of Experimental Social Psychology, 15*, 16–34.

Higgins, E. T., Roney, C., Crowe, E., & Hymes, C. (1994). Ideal versus ought predilections for approach and avoidance: Distinct self-regulatory systems. *Journal of Personality and Social Psychology, 66*, 276–286.

Higgins, E. T., & Tykocinski, O. (1992). Self-discrepancies and biographical memory: Personality and cognition at the level of psychological situation. *Personality and Social Psychology Bulletin, 18*, 527–535.

Higgins, E. T., Tykocinski, O., & Vookles, J. (1990). Patterns of self-beliefs: The psychological significance of relations among the actual, ideal, ought, can, and future selves. In J. M. Olson & M. P. Zanna (Eds.), *Self-inference processes: The Ontario Symposium* (Vol. 6, pp. 153–190). Hillsdale, NJ: Lawrence Erlbaum Associates.

Higgins, E. T., Vookles, J., & Tykocinski, O. (1992). Self and health: How "patterns" of self-beliefs predict types of emotional and physical problems. *Social Cognition, 10*, 125–150.

Holt, R. R. (1976). Drive or wish? A reconsideration of the psychoanalytic theory of motivation. In M. M. Gill & P. S. Holzman (Eds.), Psychology versus metapsychology: Psychoanalytic essays in memory of George S. Klein. *Psychological Issues, 9*, 158–197.

Houston, D. A. (1990). Empathy and the self: Cognitive and emotional influences on the evaluation of negative affect in others. *Journal of Personality and Social Psychology, 59*, 859–868.

Isen, A. M. (1984). Toward understanding the role of affect in cognition. In R. S. Wyer & T. K. Srull (Eds.), *Handbook of social cognition* (Vol. 3, pp. 179–236). Hillsdale, NJ: Lawrence Erlbaum Associates.

Jacobs, D. (1971). Moods–emotion–affect: The nature of and manipulation of affective states with particular reference to positive affective states and emotional illness. In A. Jacobs & L. B. Sachs (Eds.), *The psychology of private events* (pp. –). New York: Academic Press.

James, W. (1948). *Psychology*. New York: The World Publishing Company. (Original work published 1890).

Kelly, G. A. (1955). *The psychology of personal constructs*. New York: W. W. Norton.

Kemper, T. D. (1978). *A social interactional theory of emotions* New York: Wiley.

Lazarus, A. A. (1968). Learning theory and the treatment of depression. *Behavior Research and Therapy, 6*, 83–89.

Leventhal, H. (1982). The integration of emotion and cognition: A view from the perceptual-motor theory of emotion. In M. S. Clark & S. T. Fiske (Eds.), *Affect and cognition* (pp. 121–156). Hillsdale, NJ: Lawrence Erlbaum Associates.

Lewin, K. (1935). *A dynamic theory of personality*. New York: McGraw-Hill.

Mandler, G. (1975). *Mind and emotion.* New York: Wiley.

Markus, H., & Nurius, P. (1986). Possible selves. *American Psychologist, 41,* 954–969.

Markus, H., & Wurf, E. (1987). The dynamic self-concept: A social psychological perspective. *Annual Review of Psychology, 38,* 299–337.

Mead, G. H. (1934). *Mind, self, and society.* Chicago: University of Chicago Press.

Miller, N. E. (1944). Experimental studies of conflict. In J. McV. Hunt (Ed.), *Personality and the behavior disorders* (Vol. 1, pp.). New York: Ronald Press.

Miller, N. E. (1959). Liberalization of basic S–R concepts: Extensions to conflict behavior, motivation, and social learning. In S. Koch (Ed.), *Psychology: A study of a science, Volume 2, General systematic formulations, learning, and special processes* (pp. 196–292). New York: McGraw-Hill.

Mowrer, O. H. (1960). *Learning theory and behavior.* New York: Wiley.

Ortony, A., Clore, G. L., & Collins, A. (1988). *The cognitive structure of emotions.* New York: Cambridge University Press.

Piers, G., & Singer, M. B. (1971). *Shame and guilt.* New York: Norton.

Plutchik, R. (1962). *The emotions: Facts, theories, and a new model.* New York: Random House.

Rogers, C. R. (1961). *On becoming a person.* Boston: Houghton Mifflin.

Roney, C. J. R., Higgins, E. T., & Shah, J. (in press). Goals and framing: How outcome focus influences motivation and emotion. *Personality and Social Psychology Bulletin.*

Roseman, I. J. (1984). Cognitive determinants of emotion: A structural theory. *Review of Personality and Social Psychology, 5,* 11–36.

Roseman, I. J., Spindel, M. S., & Jose, P. E. (1990). Appraisals of emotion-eliciting events: Testing a theory of discrete emotions. *Journal of Personality and Social Psychology, 59,* 899–915.

Russell, J. A. (1978). Evidence of convergent validity on the dimensions of affect. *Journal of Personality and Social Psychology, 36,* 1152–1168.

Schachter, S., & Singer, J. E. (1962). Cognitive, social and physiological determinants of emotional state. *Psychological Review, 69,* 379–399.

Schafer, R. (1967). Ideals, the ego ideal, and the ideal self. In R. R. Holt (Ed.), Motives and thought: Psychoanalytic essays in honor of David Rapaport. *Psychological Issues, 5*(2–3), 131–174.

Schlenker, B. R. (1985). Identity and self-identification. In B. R. Schlenker (Ed.), *The self and social life* (pp. 65–100). New York: McGraw-Hill.

Schlenker, B. R., & Weigold, M. F. (1989). Goals and the self-identification process: Constructing desired identities. In L. A. Pervin (Ed.), *Goal concepts in personality and social psychology* (pp. 243–290). Hillsdale, NJ: Lawrence Erlbaum Associates.

Stein, N. L., & Jewett, J. L. (1982). A conceptual analysis of the meaning of negative emotions: Implications for a theory of development. In C. E. Izard (Ed.), *Measuring emotions in infants and children* (pp. 401–443). New York: Cambridge University Press.

Strauman, T. J. (1989). Self-discrepancies in clinical depression and social phobia: Cognitive structures that underlie emotional disorders? *Journal of Abnormal Psychology, 98,* 14–22.

Strauman, T. J. (1990). Self-guides and emotionally significant childhood memories: A study of retrieval efficiency and incidental negative emotional content. *Journal of Personality and Social Psychology, 59,* 869–880.

Strauman, T. J. (1992). Self-guides, autobiographical memory, and anxiety and dysphoria: Toward a cognitive model of vulnerability to emotional distress. *Journal of Abnormal Psychology, 101,* 87–95.

Strauman, T. J., & Higgins, E. T. (1987). Automatic activation of self-discrepancies and emotional syndromes: When cognitive structures influence affect. *Journal of Personality and Social Psychology, 53,* 1004–1014.

Strauman, T. J., & Higgins, E. T. (1988). Self-discrepancies as predictors of vulnerability to distinct syndromes of chronic emotional distress. *Journal of Personality, 56,* 685–707.

Sullivan, H. S. (1953). *The interpersonal theory of psychiatry.* New York: Norton.

Thomas, W. I., & Thomas, D. S. (1928). *The child in America.* New York: Knopf.

Tomkins, S. (1962). *Affect, imagery and consciousness, Volume 1: The positive affects.* New York: Springer.

Van Hook, E., & Higgins, E. T. (1988). Self-related problems beyond the self-concept: The motivational consequences of discrepant self-guides. *Journal of Personality and Social Psychology, 55,* 625–633.

Watson, D., & Friend, R. (1969). Measurement of social–evaluative anxiety. *Journal of Consulting and Clinical Psychology, 33,* 448–457.

Watson, D., & Tellegen, A. (1985). Toward a consensual structure of mood. *Psychological Bulletin, 98,* 219–235.

Webster's ninth new collegiate dictionary. (1989). Springfield, MA: Merriam-Webster.

Weiner, B. (1986). Cognition, emotion, and action. In R. M. Sorrentino & E. T. Higgins (Eds.), *Handbook of motivation and cognition: Foundations of social behavior* (pp. 281–312). New York: Guilford.

Wyer, R. S., & Srull, T. K. (1981). Category accessibility: Some theoretical and empirical issues concerning the processing of social stimulus information. In E. T. Higgins, C. P. Herman, & M. P. Zanna (Eds.), *Social cognition: The Ontario symposium* (Vol. 1, pp. 161–197). Hillsdale, NJ: Lawrence Erlbaum Associates.

Zajonc, R. B., Murphy, S. T., & Inglehart, M. (1989). Feeling and facial efference: Implications of the vascular theory of emotion. *Psychological Review, 96,* 395–416.

Zillmann, D. (1978). Attribution and misattribution of excitatory reactions. In J. H. Harvey, W. J. Ickes, & R. F. Kidd (Eds.), *New directions in attribution research* (Vol. 2, pp. 335–368). Hillsdale, NJ: Lawrence Erlbaum Associates.

9

Sequential Dependencies in Emotional Experience and Behavior

Dolf Zillmann
University of Alabama

A great many scholars have proposed theories of emotion in which particular emotional experiences and behaviors are conceptualized as unique, discrete states. In contrast, few have pondered the transition from one such experience or behavior to the next and those thereafter. The lack of attention to the transition from emotion to emotion is surprising, given the fact that we move from emotion to emotion on a regular basis, often within minutes and sometimes within seconds.

To illustrate emotional transition, let us consider a personal observation. This writer once witnessed a mother with her 4-year-old son walk a crowded city sidewalk. The youngster was then attracted by something across the street. He let go of his mom's hand and stepped out into the street. An oncoming car hit the boy, who fell to the ground, face down. His mother screamed within seconds of seeing this. Holding her hands to her head, she rushed to the boy and bent down to lift him up. Actually, the boy turned around and got up on his own, reassuring his mom that "nothing happened." Upon this no-harm-done revelation, his mother went into a frenzy, grabbed her son, and started to beat his back with her fists. Bystanders had formed a circle around the couple, and as the mother looked up to them, she ceased hitting, apologized for her outburst, and started hugging the child. Eventually she cried as well and expressed contentment, if not happiness, that nothing of consequence had happened.

In terms of emotional experience and behavior, most analysts would agree that the mother went from apprehension/fear/distress to anger and aggression to remorse and joy/happiness. Irrespective of the labels used to describe her experience, however, it is clear that the mother adapted to the changing circumstances in her environment with impressive speed. The likelihood of harm to her son fostered distress. The removal of the informational basis for distress prompted anger and aggression, presumably because she found the scare she had been put through intensely annoying. Finally, cognizance of the onlookers' disapproval of her actions must have prompted the inhibition of aggression and the change to remorse, contentment, and euphoria.

However, whereas the cognitive adaptation to changing conditions was rapid, indeed, and can be considered to have led to discrete emotional states, it seemed that the excitedness triggered by, and associated with, the mother's initial distress reaction lingered throughout all subsequent emotional reactions. It seemed to intensify these subsequent reactions, possibly creating them. An anger-instigating thought like "How could you do this to me?" apparently depends on the prior experience of acute distress. Without this distress, one might surmise, anger would not have materialized. Even if it had manifested itself cognitively without prior distress, however, its experiential intensity hardly would have warranted an aggressive outburst.

It appears, then, that the intensity of all emotions subsequent to the initial distress reaction was influenced by something that is capable of affecting the intensity of acute emotions and that lingers; that is, that does not abruptly terminate with the cognitive adaptation to changed environmental conditions. A candidate for this sluggish mediation of emotional intensity is autonomic activity that is controlled by humoral, and therefore slow-acting, neuroendocrine processes.

If the proposal that cognitive adaptation is rapid and excitatory adaptation is not (or is, in fact, retarded as a rule) has merit, it should be possible to construct theories that project particular dependencies in chains of contiguous emotions. Specifically, to the extent that emotional intensity is a function of neuroendocrinologically mediated autonomic activity, any activity that outlasts the emotional experience with which it was originally associated may intensify subsequent emotional experiences and behaviors.

This chapter presents theory and research evidence concerning the indicated dependencies in emotion sequences. First, a three-factor theory of emotion is presented in brief. Compared to alternative theories, this theory is particularly sensitive to the time discrepancies between precognitive behavior evocation and guidance, cognitive elaboration, excitatory concomitants, and its experiential and behavioral consequences. On the basis of the three-factor theory of emotion, a paradigm that specifically addresses the influence of prior emotions on subsequent emotions is developed. As summaries and discussions of the research evidence pertaining to this paradigm have been published elsewhere (Mauro, 1992; Reisenzein, 1983; Zillmann, 1978, 1979, 1983, 1984, 1994), we forego a comprehensive review and, instead, focus on selected issues of theoretical significance and the status of the evidence concerning these issues. Finally, we propose clarifications and refinements for theories addressing sequential dependencies in contiguous emotions.

THREE-FACTOR THEORY OF EMOTION

The three-factor theory of emotion (Zillmann, 1978, 1979, 1984) projects emotional experience and emotional behavior as the result of the interaction of three principal components of emotional state: the dispositional, the excitatory, and the experiential component.

1. The *dispositional component* is conceived of as a response-guiding mechanism. Consistent with behavior theory (cf. Nevin, 1973), the motor aspects of behavior are considered to be either unconditionally linked to eliciting conditions or such linkages are acquired through learning. It is thus assumed that stimulus–response connections preexist or are established without the deliberate involvement of complex cognitive operations, such as reasoning and the comprehension of causal relationships. However, the preparedness for motor reactions in emotional behavior may be conceived of alternatively, at least in part, as postcognitive in the sense that reflection and contemplation have been applied previously to emotion-evoking circumstances, possibly repeatedly, and fostered neural connections that, when activated at any later time, urge specific actions without requiring further time-consuming elaboration. This neural-network conceptualization (cf. Lang, 1979, 1984) of response preparation does not preclude, however, that some response-triggering connections preexist (cf. Panksepp, 1989, this volume).[1] Essentially, then, the incipient motor reaction to the presentation of emotion-inducing stimuli is viewed as a cognitively rather unmitigated, direct response that is made without appreciable latency.

2. The *excitatory component* is conceived of as the response-energizing mechanism. It is assumed that excitatory reactions, analogous to motor

---

[1]This proposal, it should be noted, contrasts sharply with theories that make emotional behavior generally dependent on the elaborate, and thus necessarily time-consuming, contemplation of circumstances (Lazarus, 1991; Schachter, 1964). It is consistent, however, with the conceptualization of a hierarchy of action-evoking mechanisms, starting with basic "hard-wired," reflex-like sensory-motor processes and progressing to complex memory-based, "soft-wired" linkages, as posited by Leventhal and Scherer (1987).

reactions, are either unconditionally linked to eliciting conditions or that such linkages are acquired through learning. If the stimulus–response connection is established through learning, it is again assumed that this happens without the intervention of complex cognitive processes, such as the contemplation of circumstances. In accordance with Cannon's (1929, 1932) proposal of the emergency nature of emotional behavior, the excitatory reaction associated with emotional states is primarily conceived of as heightened activity in the sympathetic adrenomedullary axis that manifests itself, among other things, in transitory peripheral hyperglyce-mia and increased activity in the sympathetic nervous system. More specifically, Cannon suggested that the release of catecholamines, of epinephrine in particular, eventuates a comparatively fast-acting but short-lived increase of blood glucose, thereby readying the body for muscular exertion. The excitatory reaction is thus seen as providing the organism with the energy needed for the performance of vigorous action such as needed for fight or flight, but also for the engagement in energy-demanding gratifying behaviors, such as sexual intercourse (cf. Zillmann, 1986).

Cannon's pioneering conceptualization requires some adjustment. Re-cent research (cf. Landsberg & Young, 1992) has made it clear that in behavioral emergencies epinephrine mobilizes free fatty acids and glucose while inhibiting insulin secretion. The metabolic pattern of high fatty acid and low insulin concentration actually restricts glucose entry into skeletal muscles and tends to conserve glucose for the central nervous system. This shifts the burden of energy provision for muscular exertion from glucose to free fatty acids (cf. Cryer, 1992). Notwithstanding such modi-fication, Cannon's biological emergency model has remained the central paradigm for the involvement and function of excitation in acute emo-tions. Endangerment and threats to well-being generally, along with the prospect of essential but contested gratifications, are conditions that con-tinue to instigate heightened activity in the sympathetic adrenomedullary system with its partiality to prepare the organism for vigorous action— whether or not such action has immediate utility in warding off threats or in assisting the attainment of gratifications.

In considering the mediation of the excitatory component of emotions, it must be recognized that sympathetic adrenocortical activity interacts with activity in other neuroendocrine systems, the foremost of which being the pituitary adrenocortical system and the gonadal system. Height-ened activity in the adrenocortical axis is known to increase sympathetic excitation through the confounded release of cortisone and catechola-mines (cf. Frankenhaeuser, 1986). Similarly, testosterone release is asso-ciated with increased sympathetic activity (cf. Henry, 1986). To the extent that activity in these and yet other systems augments sympathetic excitation, they enhance emotional behavior; and to the extent that these systems impair sympathetic excitation, they diminish emotionality.

3. The *experiential component* of emotional behavior is conceptualized as the conscious experience of either the motor or the excitatory reaction or of both these aspects of the response to a stimulus condition. It is assumed that both interoception and exteroception of the motor and/or excitatory components of incipient or persistent emotional actions force awareness of the emotionality of the behavior on the individual. Cognizance of this emotionality defines *emotional experience*. Such experience is expected to instigate scrutiny of the utility of the action. Cognition now comes to serve the appraisal of emotional reactions and action in the context of circumstances. Behavior monitoring of this kind may sanction incipient reactions and foster continued action. It may, at times, give added impetus to the action and enhance emotionality. Additionally and more characteristically, however, monitoring may lead to disapproval and censure of emotional action; such censure may, in turn, foster diminished emotionality by curbing the motor and/or excitatory manifestations of the incipient or persistent emotional behavior.

The experiential component of emotions, then, is viewed as a *modifier* or a *corrective* that, within limits, controls impulsive emotional responsiveness which is governed by more fundamental, if not archaic, unlearned and learned stimulus–response connections. However, as the corrective intervention in incipient or persistent emotional behavior is also subject to response acquisition by the mechanics of learning, the modified response, if repeatedly performed, may come to dominate the original one. The elicitation of emotion thus can be postcognitive, yet controlled by subcontemplative mechanisms.

The interdependencies between the three specified components of emotion are expressed in the following propositions. In addition, these propositions further explicate the concepts of emotion monitoring and emotion appropriateness.

1. A stimulus condition that evokes a specific motor response without evoking an excitatory reaction will produce nonvigorous behavior which individuals are unlikely to experience as emotional.

2. A stimulus condition that evokes a specific motor response and an excitatory reaction will produce vigorous *emotional behavior*. As individuals become cognizant of their state of elevated excitation, they will appraise (i.e., monitor and evaluate) their reaction. If they deem their behavior appropriate, they will continue to respond emotionally. If they deem it inappropriate, they will correct their mode of reacting. Correction of motor actions and expressive concomitants, such as facial and postural

signaling, can be immediate. Correction of excitatory activity, on the other hand, depends on both appraisals and changed motor activity; it is likely, therefore, to lag behind considerably. Individuals will *perceive and experience their behavior as emotional* to the extent that it is characterized as emotional by the community whose judgmental criteria for the perception of emotion they have adopted.

3. A stimulus condition that evokes an excitatory reaction without evoking a specific motor response will produce a state of acute response ambiguity marked by motor restlessness. As individuals become aware of their aimless, excited behavior, they are likely to perform an epistemic search directed at the comprehension of the inducement of their state of elevated excitation.[2] The adopted explanation will guide further activities both at the motor and the excitatory levels. Again, individuals will perceive and experience their behavior as emotional to the extent that it is characterized as emotional by the community whose judgmental criteria for the perception of emotion they have adopted.

In these propositions, it is generally assumed that (a) most complex motor reactions are under volitional control, (b) excitatory reactions are usually *not* under volitional control, (c) linguistically mature individuals habitually appraise the effectiveness and appropriateness of their behavior, and (d) unless motor reactions are voluntarily controlled as the result of appraisals, the vigor of reactions and actions tends to be a simple function of the level of sympathetic excitation prevailing at that time. It is further assumed that (e) the intensity of the subjective experience of emotional reactions and actions tends to be proportional to the level of prevailing sympathetic excitation. However, (f) in case emotional behavior and experience is deemed inappropriate and is corrected dispositionally, whereas the excitatory response associated with the dispositionally modified emotion remains markedly elevated (as it does, for some time), a close correspondence between level of sympathetic excitation and both behavioral and experiential emotionality is unlikely.

The three-factor theory of emotional behavior and experience thus has various characteristics that distinguish it from alternative theories, especially those that rely on attributional process in the evocation of emotional behavior and experience (e.g., Lazarus, 1991; Schachter, 1964). First and foremost, the three-factor theory projects that the evocation of immediate emotional responding, in terms of both motor and excitatory reactions, is governed by basal mechanisms that require neither volition nor contemplation. The theory allows, however, that emotion-controlling re-

---

[2]This is the limited condition that Schachter (1964), in his two-factor theory of emotional experience, deemed normative.

sponse dispositions may be formed on the basis of the contemplation of frequently occurring circumstances that have been associated with emotional experiences in the past.

Second, the theory stipulates that all motor elements of emotional behavior are under volitional control, and that on recognition of inappropriate responding, any overt action can be inhibited or redirected immediately. As expressive behavior is included, immediate corrections may be applied to skeletal motor actions, to the facial and bodily expression of emotional action, or to both. In contrast, the theory posits that excitatory responding is not readily controlled by volition.[3] The incipient excitatory reaction may be modified to some degree by incoming information that proves anger, fear, or any other emotional upheaval groundless. However, the counterregulatory response tends to run its course, being primarily controlled by homeostatic regulation.

Third, three-factor theory stipulates that the behavioral and experiential intensity of emotions is determined by prevailing levels of sympathetic excitation, but only if the incipient emotional response goes uncorrected. Emotion monitoring that results in the recognition of inappropriate responding and that fosters volitional intervention in overt behaviors compromises the correspondence between sympathetic excitation and emotion intensity.

Lastly, by stipulating a correspondence between level of sympathetic excitation and acute emotional behavior and experience under the limited conditions specified, the theory implies that (a) the hyperglycemic effect of adrenomedullary activity (or more accurately, the ample supply of free fatty acids to the skeletal muscles) creates the discussed partiality toward action (also referred to as *action readiness*; Frijda, 1986, this volume) and, in case of action, *behavioral intensity*; and that (b) global interoceptive feedback of sympathetic excitation, potentially supplemented by exteroceptive feedback, provides individuals with sufficient information to grasp the *experiential intensity* of emotions.

EXCITATION TRANSFER THEORY

In contiguous emotional states, transfer of sympathetic excitation from an antecedent to a subsequent emotion is expected to produce a modification of emotionality; usually, but not necessarily, an intensification of

---

[3]It is recognized, of course, that the excitatory response is modifiable by training aimed at, among other things, enhanced interoceptive sensitivity or superior relaxation strategies (cf. Schwartz, 1977). Individuals with such training are the exception, however, and may be neglected here.

emotional behavior and experience. The discussed time discrepancy between cognitive and excitatory adjustment to changing environmental circumstances is exploited to predict that, after cognitive adjustment to a subsequent emotion-evoking condition has occurred, elements of excitation from the prior state persist and are absorbed into the response to the subsequent stimuli, modifying the intensity of this response.

For emotions associated with elevated sympathetic activity, so-called "acute" or "active" emotions (Leventhal, 1979), the prior state is expected to leave behind residual amounts of such activity. These residual amounts are expected to augment subsequently generated excitation and thereby intensify emotionality in response to subsequently prevailing conditions.

The following propositions (Zillmann, 1978, 1983) formalize and elaborate the outlined rationale:

1. Given a situation in which (a) individuals respond to emotion-inducing stimuli and assess their responses, (b) levels of sympathetic excitation are still elevated from prior, potentially unrelated stimulation, and (c) individuals are not provided with obtrusive intero- and/or exteroceptive cues that unambiguously link their excitatory state to prior stimulation, residues of excitation from prior stimulation will inseparably combine with the excitatory reaction to the present stimuli and thereby intensify both emotional behavior and emotional experience.

2. Emotional behavior and/or emotional experience will be enhanced in proportion to the magnitude of transferred residual excitation.

3. Both the period of time during which transfer can occur and the magnitude of residues for transfer are a function of (a) the magnitude of the preceding excitatory reaction and/or (b) the rate of recovery from the associated excitatory state.

4. Individuals' potential for transfer is (a) proportional to their excitatory responsiveness and (b) inversely proportional to their proficiency to recover from excitatory states.

Figure 9.1 presents a graph of the additive combination of residual excitation from prior stimulation and excitation specific to subsequent stimulation. It thus visualizes the excitatory aspects of Propositions 1, 2, and 3.

It should be recognized that the transfer paradigm is not limited to the intensification of emotional behavior or experience by residual excitation from just one prior emotion. The paradigm accommodates the integration of excitatory residues from potentially many prior emotional reactions. The number of residues that may be integrated depends, first of all, on the *rapidity of emotional instigation in a sequence*. The more

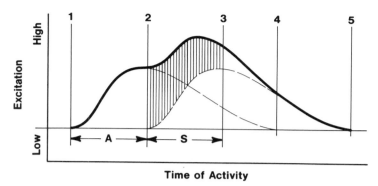

Time of Activity

FIG. 9.1. A model of excitation transfer in which residual excitation from a preceding excitatory reaction combines additively with the excitatory reaction to current stimulation. An antecedent stimulus condition (*A*), persisting from *time 1* to *time 2*, is assumed to produce excitatory activity that has entirely decayed only at *time 4*. Similarly, a subsequent stimulus condition (*S*), persisting from *time 2* to *time 3*, is assumed to produce excitatory activity that has entirely decayed only at *time 5*. Residual excitation from condition *A* and excitation specific to condition *S* combine from *time 2* to *time 4*. The extent to which the transfer of residues from condition *A* increases the excitatory activity associated with condition *S* is shown in the shaded area. From Zillmann (1979). Copyright 1979 by Lawrence Erlbaum Associates. Reprinted with permission.

proximate in time the instigations, the more likely the integration of their excitatory components. This condition is of interest in considering *emotional escalation*. From the exploration of violence among intimates, for instance, it is apparent that intensely experienced rage and impulsive aggressive outbursts grow from a series of provocations, all of which are minor and utterly incommensurate with the ultimate behavior (e.g., Gelles, 1979; Pagelow, 1984). In such and analogous emotional escalations (for instance, in a chain of comparatively minor quasi-contiguous fear inductions that leads to panic), any excitatory reaction late in the escalation sequence can be considered to ride the tails of all earlier excitatory reactions. The reaction to a minor provocation late in the escalation sequence, then, is associated with disproportionally high levels of sympathetic excitation that may be expected to foster great behavioral and experiential intensity and result in aggressive overreactions.

Second, the number of residues of excitation that may be integrated depends on the *inertia of regulation*. The longer it takes for excitation to return to basal levels, the longer persists the propensity for integration with excitation from alternative sources. Excitatory residues from multiple sources may thus combine to intensify subsequent emotional behavior and experience. An illustration of the outlined processes can again be drawn from the domain of violence among intimates. It has been reported that, independent of excitatory escalation, minimal provocation often leads to violent action that is patently incommensurate with the provocation (e.g., Gelles, 1974; Straus, Gelles, & Steinmetz, 1980). The concept of penned up frustration is commonly used to account for this phenomenon. It would appear, however, that concentration on the excitatory concomitants of frustrations and similar experiences of annoyance reveals the elements of a mechanism that is capable of explaining the effects in question more completely. The proposal is this: To the extent that frustrations, by activating the pituitary adrenocortical system, elevate sympathetic excitation, comparatively slowly decaying, persistent residues are created for transfer into acute emotions. Heightened adrenocortical activity thus may intensify numerous acute emotions that fall within the period of incomplete decay of very slowly regulated sympathetic excitation. The propensity for such emotional overreactions by transfer that adrenocortical activity produces is said to be *tonic*. The contrasting, comparatively short-lived intensification of acute emotions is said to be *phasic* or *episodic*.

The tonic versus phasic distinction concerning the time course of pituitary adrenocortical versus sympathetic adrenomedullary activity is of considerable theoretical interest. Focus on the interaction of these systems in determining emotional intensity holds promise of elucidating a variety of emotional overreactions and misreactions. Such reactions are frequently impulsive, as in destructive aggressive outbursts (cf. Zillmann, 1994), and their adaptive utility tends to be negligible or nil. In view of the social significance of these behaviors, it is surprising to find that the emotional implications of the interaction under consideration have gone unexplored. Presumably because of the great difficulty of conducting controlled behavioral experiments over longer periods of time, little is known about the consequences of adrenocortical activity as a persistent excitatory undercurrent for both the elicitation and the intensification of acute emotional behavior and experience that is primarily defined by adrenomedullary activity.

Research on excitation transfer has been limited to sequences of acute, *phasic* emotions—actually to sequences of just two such emotions. Moreover, although the excitatory response to various emotion inducements has been assessed through catecholamine release (e.g., Frankenhaeuser, 1986; Levi, 1965), transfer research has ascertained sympathetic activity in peripheral manifestations only (mostly in changes of systolic and diastolic blood pressure, vasoconstriction, and heart rate). In addition, the emotion sequences that have been explored consisted of acute, hypersympathetic reactivity, such as anger, fear, distress, or euphoria, and excluded hyposympathetic states, such as helplessness or serenity.

Given these restrictions, the intensification of subsequent emotional behavior and experience by residual sympathetic excitation from immediately preceding or somewhat delayed emotional instigations has been observed for a considerable variety of acute emotions. In the majority of these demonstrations, the hedonic valence of the prior emotion proved to be immaterial. This is to say that residual sympathetic excitation proved capable of facilitating subsequent emotions whether the prior emotion was hedonically compatible or incompatible.

Emotion facilitation by excitation transfer has been observed, for instance, from sexual arousal to anger and aggressive behavior (Donnerstein & Hallam, 1978; Zillmann, 1971; Zillmann, Bryant, Comisky, & Medoff, 1981) as well as to altruistic feelings and prosocial behavior (Jaffe, 1981; Mueller & Donnerstein, 1981). Residual sympathetic excitation from either sexual arousal or disgust has been found to facilitate such diverse experiences as the enjoyment of music (Cantor & Zillmann, 1973; Zillmann & Mundorf, 1987), the appreciation of humor (Cantor, Bryant, & Zillmann, 1974), and feelings of sadness (Zillmann, Mody, & Cantor, 1974). Residues from feelings of sadness and fear, in turn, have been found to intensify joyous reactions to fortuitous happenings (cf. Zillmann, 1980, 1991). Frustration has been observed to intensify euphoric as well as angry subsequent feelings (Fry & Ogston, 1971). Finally, hedonically neutral residual sympathetic excitation from strenuous physical exercise has been demonstrated to be capable of enhancing feelings of anger and aggressive behavior (Zillmann & Bryant, 1974; Zillmann, Katcher, & Milavsky, 1972), of intensifying sexual excitedness (Cantor, Zillmann, & Bryant, 1975), of promoting help giving (Sterling & Gaertner, 1984), of eliciting feelings of grandiosity and elation (Gollwitzer, Earle, & Stephan, 1982), of fostering favorable reactions to advertisements (Mattes & Cantor, 1982), and of facilitating heterosexual attraction (e.g., White, Fishbein, & Rutstein, 1981).

Proposition 4 applies the transfer paradigm to individual differences in excitatory responding. As sympathetic reactivity is considered to be the primary mediator of emotional intensity, focus has been on cardiovascular/cardiorespiratory fitness as a trait-like condition that exerts a considerable degree of control over sympathetic reactivity. Figure 9.2 visualizes the proposed differences in excitatory responding. Specifically, it shows that cardiorespiratory fitness (a) prevents excessive excitatory reactions and (b) fosters speedy regulation. Comparatively unfit persons, then, exhibit initially stronger reactions to challenge, and their excitatory recovery consumes substantially longer periods of time. The consequence of interest is that these cardiorespiratorily unfit individuals, compared to their fitter counterparts, are more vulnerable to excitation transfer. Because of their extended vulnerability period, they are more likely to encounter the conditions for transfer, and as they encounter these conditions, comparatively greater amounts of residual excitation may be expected to foster stronger emotional intensification. The transfer paradigm

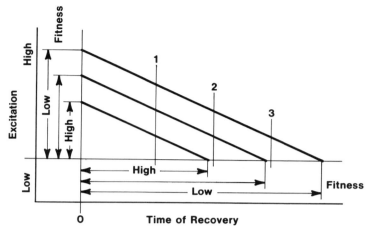

FIG. 9.2. Illustration of the inverse relationship between cardiovascular fitness and the propensity for transfer. As shown in the simplified decay gradients, the excitatory reaction to a particular stimulus (*time 0*) and the time of recovery from that reaction decrease as cardiovascular fitness increases. At *time 1*, residual excitation for transfer exists in all fitness conditions in differing amounts. At *time 2*, recovery to basal levels of excitation is complete for high fitness, but the propensity for transfer is maintained, to different degrees, for intermediate and low fitness. At *time 3*, the propensity for transfer is maintained only for low fitness. From Zillmann (1979). Copyright 1979 by Lawrence Erlbaum Associates. Reprinted with permission.

thus offers an explanation for the often-asserted emotional stability of fit persons—as well as for the tendency toward emotional lability of severely unfit persons.

Corroborative evidence comes from investigations of acute anger and aggressive behavior (Zillmann, Johnson, & Day, 1974a). Such behavior was transfer-intensified by residual excitation from physical exertion exactly as projected by the model. Specifically, fit persons showed minimal amounts of residual excitation for transfer, and they did so for only short periods of time. At the time of complete regulation (i.e., after complete decay of excitatory residues), their aggressive behavior was at control levels. At that time, unfit persons still exhibited substantial amounts of residual excitation, and their aggressive overintensity was proportional to the prevailing amounts. Research with athletes active in a nonaggressive sport, such as swimming or tennis, also suggests that fitness prevents intense anger and aggressiveness in response to provocation (Zillmann, Johnson, & Day, 1974b).

Moreover, following a 10-week aerobic exercise class, participants recorded improved frustration tolerance (Jasnoski, Holmes, Solomon, &

Aguiar, 1981). Cardiorespiratory fitness also curbed responses to a variety of psychosocial stressors (Cox, Evans, & Jamieson, 1979). Finally, in situations that rule out contamination by motor responses (i.e., sitting motionlessly while exposed to visual stimuli), cardiorespiratory fitness proved to control the excitatory reaction to medical procedures deemed disgusting and disturbing, as well as to erotica deemed pleasant (Cantor, Zillmann, & Day, 1978). There can be little doubt, then, that cardiorespiratory fitness generalizes to iconically or symbolically induced excitatory reactions that influence emotional behavior and experience.

ASSUMPTIONS, LIMITATIONS, AND EXTENSIONS

The assumptions underlying the transfer paradigm have been detailed elsewhere (Zillmann, 1979, 1983, 1984). Rather than repeat them here, we concentrate on those that have been misread, misinterpreted, or challenged. On occasion, we supplement clarification with theoretical extensions.

Limits of Excitatory Summation

It has been assumed that residual excitation combines *additively* with subsequently generated excitation. This assumption is parsimonious. It also proved useful in accommodating the pertinent research findings. To date, the measurement of the excitatory processes under consideration are marred by a degree of imprecision that renders the construction of more specific, nonadditive models premature. However, it should be clear that the prediction of the transfer-intensification of emotions cannot always be based on the additive combination of two or more excitatory reactions that are assessed against basal, regulated levels. To do so would, on occasion, result in the projection of intolerably high levels of sympathetic excitation, that is, of levels markedly above those that characterize the most intense acute emotions. The paradigm thus must, in one form or another, incorporate the so-called law of initial values (Sternbach, 1966; Wilder, 1957). It must be accepted that the magnitude of excitatory reactions is a function of prevailing levels of excitation; more specifically, that excitatory reactions tend to be inversely proportional to preexisting levels. The needed restriction is this: When preexisting excitation is at basal levels, the subsequently elicited excitatory response can manifest itself in full; when preexisting levels are at a maximum already, the subsequently elicited excitatory response cannot at all increase preexisting levels; hence, the amount of excitation contributed by the subsequent response is smaller the more elevated the preexisting levels of excitation.

A simple linear correction has been suggested for the estimation of the excitatory contribution of a subsequent response:

$$\alpha = 1 - \frac{p - b}{m - b},$$

where p is the prestimulus, b the basal, and m the maximal level of excitation. The factor α thus modifies the intensity of the subsequent excitatory response (i.e., its intensity assessed against basal levels). By definition, this intensity is maintained if $p = b$. If $p = m$, in contrast, it is reduced to zero. Intermediate values of p reduce α proportionally.

At present, little is known about the excitatory capacity of emotional instigation at subnormal preexisting levels of sympathetic activity. In extension of our rationale for proportional correction of subsequent responsiveness, an excitatory reaction of supernormal intensity may be expected. Alternatively, however, response intensity may be quite normal or even impaired. In this case, the summation model leads to projections of diminished emotionality due to "negative" excitation transfer.

Ambiguity in Subsequent States

Transfer theory stipulates that subsequent states, in order to be intensified by residual excitation from preceding states, must be emotionally unambiguous. The prevailing circumstances must elicit specific emotional reactions, and individuals must construe their reactions as a particular emotional experience. Nonemotional, ambivalent reactions, or affective responses without clear definition, are unlikely to be transfer intensified.

Support for this stipulation comes from investigations in which the subsequent state was poorly or unambiguously defined. In an experiment by Zillmann, Katcher, and Milavsky (1972), for instance, subjects were or were not aggressively instigated. Anger and retaliatory intentions were thus established or not established. Residual excitation from prior conditions facilitated anger and retaliatory aggression only when the agonistic emotion was established. When it was not, residual excitation merely produced motor restlessness. In a similar investigation on retaliatory aggression (Ramirez, Bryant, & Zillmann, 1982), subjects were mildly or severely provoked. Residues from prior sexual excitation facilitated anger and aggression only in the condition of severe provocation. The mild provocation apparently failed to establish the emotion of anger sufficiently clearly. An investigation by Sterling and Gaertner (1984) corroborates this interpretation. Residual arousal from a prior state promoted help giving in an emergency only when the conditions that required the rendering of help were unambiguous to subjects. Ambiguity in the emergency prevented facilitation of help giving. Put drastically, then, the transfer intensification of an emotion may be expected only when there is an emotion to be transfer intensified.

Ambiguity in Preceding States

No similar restrictions are placed on preceding states. This state may be a well-defined emotion, an experience of ambivalence, or an entirely ambiguous response. For transfer to be possible, it is merely stipulated that this state (a) be terminated (i.e., that it no longer preoccupies cognition) and (b) leave sufficient amounts of residual excitation behind.

This stipulation receives support from transfer studies that involved substantially different and differently intense preceding emotions (e.g., Cantor, Zillmann, & Bryant, 1975; Donnerstein & Hallam, 1978) as well as from nonemotional preconditions, such as physical exertion (e.g., Gollwitzer, Earle, & Stephan, 1982; Zillmann, Katcher, & Milavsky, 1972).

Hedonic Incompatibility

Much transfer research has found the hedonic compatibility or incompatibility of preceding and subsequent emotions in contiguous emotion chains to be immaterial for the intensification of a subsequent emotion by residual excitation from a preceding emotion. These findings are consistent with the proposal (a) that experienced hedonic valence is cognitively determined, and (b) that sympathetic excitation is hedonically impartial. On occasion, however, hedonic compatibility has been observed to enhance the effect of excitation transfer. Zillmann et al. (1980), for instance, reported that anger and aggression were facilitated to a greater degree by residual excitation from hedonically compatible, unpleasant stimulation than from similar amounts of residual excitation from hedonically incompatible, pleasant stimulation.

These and similar effects of hedonic compatibility in the intensification of anger and aggression (cf. Baron, 1983) appear to be independent of excitation transfer. In the cited investigation, for example, the compatibility effect is most parsimoniously explained as annoyance summation. Subjects in the hedonically compatible transfer condition were aggressively instigated plus exposed to extremely disgusting material, such as mutilated faces from textbooks of reconstructive surgery and mutual flagellation during sexual intercourse by an elderly couple. Such exposure treatment must have intensified annoyance, and this added annoyance must have expressed itself in the retaliatory actions. There is no reason to assume that the experienced hedonic valence qualitatively altered sympathetic activity—and thereby altered the effect of transferred excitation.

The independence of effects of hedonic compatibility and incompatibility from excitation-transfer effects is further attested to by the demonstration of influences on emotions by preceding or intervening hedonically compatible or incompatible yet entirely unexcited states (cf. Bandura, 1973; Baron, 1983; Zillmann, 1984).

The possibility of a connection between transfer effects and effects of hedonic compatibility remains, however. It concerns the cognitive adaptation to changing environmental conditions. Switching from a preceding to a subsequent emotion may require less cognitive effort, and hence be more rapidly accomplished, when these emotions are hedonically compatible than when they are incompatible. Redundancy in activated neural networks (cf. Lang, 1984) may be invoked to lend credence to such a proposal. More rapid and complete adjustment to novel yet hedonically compatible circumstances might thus be expected to create more efficiently the conditions necessary for transfer: unambiguous subsequent affect and well-defined emotional experience. Such possible differences seem to favor situational ambiguity for subsequent emotions. If emotional reactivity is devoid of ambiguity, it is difficult to see why switching to hedonically incompatible emotions, as from fear to euphoria on the abolition of the fear-inducing agents, should be less swift than switching to hedonically compatible emotions, as from fear to anger about the anger-inducing conditions. At any rate, it should be clear that these suggestions are highly speculative, and that the cognitive adjustment to hedonically and taxonomically similar or different subsequent emotion-evoking conditions still awaits empirical examination.

Attributional Considerations

Counter to persisting misinterpretations,[4] transfer theory does not make the intensification of emotional behavior and experience by residual excitation from preceding activities dependent on recognition of residual excitedness and its attribution to inducing circumstances. It is not assumed that emotional individuals routinely ponder their excitatory states and attributionally link their states to excitation-inducing conditions.[5] Such

---

[4]For instance, Mauro (1992) continues to suggest that transfer theory projects the intensification of emotional behavior as the result of the *misattribution* of residual excitation from prior states to the subsequent emotional instigation. Transfer theory explicitly denies this possibility. It actually posits (Zillmann, 1978) that awareness of residual excitation, which would seem to be a prerequisite for its causal misattribution, prevents transfer effects.

[5]This is in contrast to Schachter's (1964) two-factor theory of emotional experience in which it is assumed that individuals, as they become aware of excitatory reactions, conduct a so-called epistemic search for causes. In this theory, such searches are deemed necessary for individuals to comprehend their emotions—that is, to label them as experiences that fit consensually accepted emotional taxonomies.

pondering is presumed the rare exception, limited to excited states that occur without apparent reason. As a rule, the causal conditions for emotions are abundantly apparent and foster specific emotional behavior and experience—usually before excitatory activity, because of its latency, can force awareness of itself.

This is not to say that individuals do not reflect on their excitatory states relative to their emotions. Pronounced excitatory reactions may have come about under particular prevailing conditions, and individuals may have become cognizant of the quasi-concurrence of inducing stimuli and reaction. Obtrusive interoception and exteroception of the excitatory state may virtually force such cognizance of stimulus–response simultaneity (cf. Pennebaker, 1982; Pennebaker & Epstein, 1983). Such cognizance may be expected to prompt, in turn, the *causal attribution* of emotional reactions to time-linked stimuli.

Assumptions of transfer theory that pertain to this causal attribution of excitation are twofold. They concern (a) the interoception and exteroception of sympathetic excitation and (b) the consequences of executed attributions.

Regarding the interoception and exteroception of excitation, it is assumed that activity in the autonomic nervous system is largely, although not entirely, nonspecific to emotion. Whatever specificity may exist (e.g., Levenson, 1992; Schwartz, 1986; Schwartz, Weinberger, & Singer, 1981; Wenger, Clemens, Coleman, Cullen, & Engel, 1961) is presumed compromised by afferent structures that are either insensitive or whose sensitivity is not utilized (cf. Ádám, 1967). At any rate, minor specificity in excitatory patterns is presumed lost, essentially, and hence immaterial for emotion and excitation transfer. Transfer theory focuses on the redundancy in sympathetic reactions across emotions. In further diminishing the significance of minute patterned differences, it stipulates that "only comparatively gross excitatory changes will draw attention and produce awareness of the state of excitation" (Zillmann, 1983, p. 222). However, it is posited that these gross, global, and readily noticeable changes in sympathetic excitation provide individuals with sufficient interoceptive and exteroceptive feedback of the *intensity* of their emotional reaction.

Research by Pennebaker, Gonder-Frederick, Stewart, Elfman, and Skelton (1982), for instance, lends considerable support to the indicated processes. Systolic blood-pressure changes, a primary index of emotional intensity, were related to a host of physical symptoms, such as muscle tension, tenseness in the stomach, breathing rate, and hand sweating. Systolic blood pressure—and emotional intensity to the extent that this index closely corresponds with intensity—was predictable from various symptoms, but only in terms of response stereotypy. This is to say that individuals differ greatly in the symptoms they focus on to determine their emotional intensity. However, whatever idiosyncratic set of symptoms they rely on apparently enables them to trace nontrivial changes in their state of sympathetic excitation, and to do so reliably and with adequate accuracy.

Concerning the attribution or misattribution of residual excitation, the following assumption of transfer theory is particularly relevant:

> Individuals do not partition excitation compounded from reactions to different inducing conditions. Autonomic and/or somatic feedback permits neither the isolation of all factors that contribute to a state of excitation, nor the apportionment of excitation to the various contributing factors. As a result, individuals tend to ascribe their excitatory reaction in toto to one specific, though potentially complex inducing condition. (Zillmann, 1983, p. 225)

It is this assumption that virtually precludes the argument that residual excitation, as it combines with excitation in response to prevailing stimuli, could be causally misattributed. According to the assumption, the residual portion in confounded excitation cannot be isolated—at least not with any degree of accuracy. If there is cognizance of excitatory inducement, and this cognizance is carried into subsequent responding, a confounded excitatory state is likely to be totally attributed to the preceding stimulation. Thus, the subsequent emotional experience cannot be intensified by residual excitation because all prevailing excitation is presumed elicited by preceding stimuli and attributed to them. Moreover, the experiential component of three-factor theory should come into play and correct any tendency to overreact behaviorally to prevailing stimuli.

The prevention of transfer effects resulting from cognizance of the induction of strong excitatory reactions to preceding stimuli, as well as from the presumption of the lingering of these reactions, has been observed in various investigations. Research on the transfer intensification of anger and aggression, for instance, has shown that immediately after demanding physical exercise, when residues of excitation are extreme but presumably correctly attributed to exertion, anger and aggression lack intensity (Zillmann, Johnson, & Day, 1974a). Transfer intensification came about only after obtrusive symptoms of the prior excitation induction, such as heavy breathing and trembling hands, had vanished. Excitation transfer from strenuous exercise into sexual excitedness showed the same pattern (Cantor, Zillmann, & Bryant, 1975). As can be seen from Figure 9.3, immediately following exertion, when residual excitation was most pronounced, subjects reported the least sexual excitedness in response to sexual imagery. The fact that their sexual excitedness tended to be lower than that of subjects who saw the same imagery after residues of excitation had completely dissipated attests to the proposed in toto attribution: As

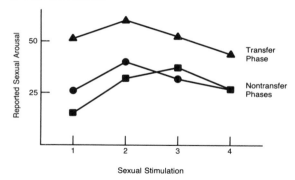

FIG. 9.3. Facilitation of sexual excitedness by excitation transfer from exertion. Sexual stimulation occurred immediately following strenuous physical exercise when subjects perceived themselves to be aroused from the exercise (squares), in the transfer phase when subjects were still aroused from exercise but failed to recognize it (triangles), or after further delay when subjects had actually recovered and believed themselves to have recovered (circles). Sexual excitedness thus was transfer-intensified only when subjects were unaware of residual excitation from exertion. Transfer intensification was not observed as long as subjects had cause to attribute their excitatory state to the preceding exertion. From Zillmann (1984). Copyright 1984 by Lawrence Erlbaum Associates. Reprinted with permission.

residual excitation from exertion and excitation in response to the images could not be partitioned, subjects underexperienced sexual excitedness, thinking that their excitatory state was still entirely determined by the preceding exertion.

These and similar findings (e.g., Cantor & Zillmann, 1973) have prompted a refinement of transfer theory. It became necessary to separate the transfer phase proper from the phase in which obtrusive feedback from preceding excitatory instigation is capable of preventing the transfer intensification of subsequent emotional behavior and experience.

Three phases were distinguished: Phase 1, in which (a) residual excitation persists, potentially in large amounts; and (b) individuals, because of lingering obtrusive feedback, are cognizant of persisting residual excitation. Phase 2, in which (a) residual excitation persists to varying degrees; and (b) individuals, because of lacking obtrusive feedback and the distraction of prevailing stimulation, are no longer cognizant of residual excitation. Phase 3, finally, constitutes a control condition in which (a) residual excitation is nil because of completed regulation, and (b) individuals have no cognizance of excitatory residues.

Excitation-transfer effects may be expected in Phase 2 only. This expectation is the direct consequence of the posited inability to partition confounded excitation.

The three postulated phases have been empirically established. Cantor, Zillmann, and Bryant (1975) used physical exertion to elevate sympathetic excitation and then ascertained subjects' excitatory recovery (a) in physiological measures and (b) in ratings. Specifically, subjects were instructed to consider their arousal immediately after exertion as 100%, and to report the portion of that amount thereafter in one-minute intervals until complete recovery at 0%. Excitatory recovery, measured in physiological indices, was essentially linear.[6] The subjective assessment of this recovery, in contrast, was rather abrupt after a short period of time. Most significantly, subjects thought to have recovered, completely so, long before their actual return to basal levels of sympathetic activity. The three conceptual phases, then, were found to exist and their duration to be determinable.

Knowledge of their time course was used to place experimental treatments into the three phases. In the investigation under consideration, this treatment was exposure to sexual imagery. The transfer intensification of sexual excitedness was predicted for Phase 2 only. The supportive findings are summarized in Figure 9.3.

The existence of the specified transfer phases, as well as their utility in preventing mispredictions (i.e., of erroneous prediction of transfer effects in Phase 1), has been further demonstrated in similar investigations by Mattes and Cantor (1982), Gollwitzer, Earle, and Stephan (1982), and Cacioppo, Tassinary, Stonebraker, and Petty (1987).

The latter study is of interest in that it refined the procedures for the estimation of the phases. Subjects in the investigation did not merely trace perceived arousal from exertion, but had to separate such arousal from generally prevailing arousal. This procedure better approximates the perception of excitatory residues from a preceding emotion when these residues are confounded with excitation from a subsequent emotion. It should be noticed, however, that research on the subjective tracing of separate contributions to confounded excitation, where these contributions come from different or similar *emotional* instigations, does not exist. Moreover, it should be clear that the procedures used to estimate the time course of the phases pertaining to transfer are marred by inaccuracy, due to the necessity of focusing the subjects' attention on excitatory residues. As a result of this attentional focus, the duration of Phase 1 is, in all probability, overestimated. Under normal circumstances, individuals are unlikely to even attempt an excitatory accounting, and if they were to attempt it, they would suffer considerable distraction from on-

---

[6]Focus is on the regulation of systolic blood pressure. Heart rate recovery is curvilinear. The rate drops sharply at first, but then stabilizes minimally above basal levels for extended periods.

going emotional instigations. The transfer phase (Phase 2) thus may be presumed to be somewhat longer than the tracing studies suggest.

Commonality in Excitation Across Emotions

As has been suggested already, minor differences in the autonomic response pattern across different acute emotions may prove inconsequential for excitation transfer. The principal reason for this is that essential elements are redundant and pose no problem for the transition from emotion to emotion. If redundancy is dominant, secondary elements that fail to match may quickly adjust to response patterns that are specific to subsequent emotions.

For instance, fear, anger, and sexual excitedness share a strong sympathetic component, but differ in specific parasympathetic aspects: Genital tumescence is primarily parasympathetically controlled, and it is closely associated with sexual excitedness rather than with anger and fear. Does this now mean that the indicated discrepancy will impair the transition from fear or anger to sexual excitedness or vice versa? Ample evidence shows that it does not (cf. Zillmann, 1984, 1986, 1989). Neither the transition nor the intensification of the subsequent behavior and experience by residual sympathetic excitation are impeded. The secondary element in an excitatory pattern, in this case genital tumescence, is drawn in when the transition is from fear or anger to sexual excitedness (e.g., Hoon, Wincze, & Hoon, 1977) and presumably phased out when the transition takes the reverse direction. Focus on the commonality in patterns of excitation, then, seems more productive than stifling emphasis of potentially irrelevant uniqueness.

The psychoneuroendocrinological analysis of emotions (cf. Zillmann & Zillmann, in press) may be called on to clarify the commonality proposal.

Smith (1973), after an exhaustive review of the research literature on the effects of adrenal hormones on emotional behavior, concluded categorically that "adrenal catecholamines and corticoids are *reliable, nonspecific*, and *insensitive*" [italics added] (p. 340). Catecholamines and corticoids are considered *reliable* because, on emotion evocation, their levels always rise markedly. These hormones are considered *nonspecific* because their levels rise on evocation of a variety of distinct emotional states, and most of them are considered *insensitive* because their levels do not reliably reflect variations in emotional intensity. According to his analysis, epinephrine is the exception, showing a reliable correspondence with emotional intensity. Smith (1973) is careful to rule out any influence in the evocation of emotion, linking epinephrine to emotional intensity specifically: "Epinephrine does not elicit specific emotions, but *epinephrine intensifies the experience of a variety of emotions*" [italics added] (p. 342).

Much of the emotionally nonspecific action of epinephrine manifests itself in the provision of energy for muscular exertion. As argued before, emotional instigation places great demands on energy mobilization. The liver releases glucose for usage in the central nervous system. Fatty acids, stored as triglycerides in adipose tissue, are converted and released as free fatty acids into blood plasma (Jeanrenaud, 1965; Scow & Chernick, 1970). Activity in the sympathetic nervous system appears to play a significant part in the necessary mobilization of triglycerides and their conversion to free fatty acids (Carlson, 1965). Increased levels of plasma catecholamines are associated with increased activity in the sympathetic nervous system, and both increased catecholamine levels and increased activity in the sympathetic nervous system are associated with increased levels of free fatty acids. These joint changes seem to occur in all acute emotions. Among other things, the pattern connected with free-fatty-acid mobilization has been observed for fear (Cardon & Gordon, 1959), sexual excitedness (Gustafson, Winokur, & Reichlin, 1963), stressful tasks (Powell, Eisdorfer, & Bogdonoff, 1964), and competition for dominance (Bogdonoff, Back, Klein, Estes, & Nichols, 1962). The anticipation of muscular exertion alone is capable of producing the response pattern under consideration (Bogdonoff & Nichols, 1965).

Linked to this energy mobilization is the shunting of blood from the skin and viscera to the muscles. Additional peripheral manifestations of the reaction are, among others, increased heart rate, blood pressure, respiration rate, and experienced muscle tension. Associated with enhanced muscle tension is a reduction in the firing threshold of the skeletal muscles (Goffard & Perry, 1951). All these changes are a function of the release of the catecholamines epinephrine and norepinephrine in the sympathetic adrenomedullary system, cortisol in the pituitary adrenocortical system, and testosterone in the gonadal–hormone axis.

Emotional intensity is most directly influenced by epinephrine action on energy provision. Afferent signals from the skeletal muscles, primarily, are considered to create the action tendency of acute emotions. The associated ample supply of free fatty acids then fuels the intensity of emotional behavior in case overt actions are taken. The intensity of emotional experience is also seen to be controlled by afferent feedback from the skeletal muscles. This feedback may be complemented, however, by a host of symptoms of sympathetic excitation (cf. Pennebaker, 1982).

The psychoneuroendocrinological analysis of emotions thus projects ample commonality between all acute emotions. Residues of sympathetic excitation should be freely transferable from emotion to emotion, at least from acute emotion to acute emotion. But not all assessments have argued for a lack of specificity in neuroendocrine response patterns across emotions. Frankenhaeuser (1986) and Henry (1986, 1992) may be considered the main proponents of the view that the degree of control that persons can exercise over challenging, threatening conditions fosters *specific* response patterns.

Henry (1986) focused on human emotions. Based on the key concept of control over challenge, he created his own emotional taxonomy: A trichotomy of three emotions, along with two counteremotions. Specifically, he proposed that (a) taking control, (b) striving/struggling, and (c) loss of control convert to (a) anger, (b) fear, and (c) depression. *Anger* is characterized as a catecholamine emotion, with norepinephrine dominance over epinephrine, with high testosterone involvement, but without appreciable involvement of cortisol. It is further associated with strongly elevated blood pressure and cardiac output. Anger is linked to fight and persistence. *Fear* is also characterized as a catecholamine emotion. In contrast to anger, however, it is deemed associated with epinephrine dominance over norepinephrine and with some involvement of cortisol. It is associated with somewhat elevated blood pressure and cardiac output. *Depression*, the state linked to loss of control, is characterized as an adrenocortical emotion. It is associated with strongly elevated cortisol and strongly depressed testosterone levels, but with negligible changes in catecholamine levels. Blood pressure and cardiac output are said to be unaffected or, if anything, at subnormal levels.

The counteremotion of anger is *serenity*, that of fear *relaxation*. These counteremotions are derived by reversing the neuroendocrine and autonomic pattern of anger and fear. The reversal of anger results in the pattern of depressed norepinephrine and epinephrine release and reduced blood pressure and cardiac output. Serenity, then, is a catecholamine emotion, with acutely diminished activity of the sympathetic adrenomedullary system. The reversal of fear is less pure. Mostly, the involvement of cortisol is removed. Pituitary adrenomedullary activity is relaxed altogether. The focus, however, is not on catecholamines, because strong catecholamine release is known to be associated with intense feelings of elation (Fredrikson, 1989; Levi, 1965, 1967). Instead, it is on testosterone. In contrast to the association between fear and low testosterone levels, elation is said to be linked to greatly elevated levels of this hormone. Table 9.1 summarizes these proposed patterned responses (see Zillmann & Zillmann, in press, for a discussion of the evidence pertaining to Henry's proposal).

Henry's (1986, 1992) model has significant implications for excitation transfer in contiguous emotions. On the premise that individuals do experience particular emotions to current stimulation prior to the complete dissipation of all elements of an excitatory pattern from a preceding emotion, they must be assumed capable of accommodating elements of excitation that are incompatible with their present emotional experience.

TABLE 9.1
Neuroendocrinological Differentiation of Emotion,
According to Henry (1986)

Response	to Challenge			in Security	
Emotion	Anger	Fear	Depression	Elation	Serenity
Limbic system mediation	Amygdalar central nucleus	Amygdalar basal nucleus	Septum, hippocampus	Hippocampus	Amygdala
Behavioral manifestation	Fight, effort	Flight, effort	Subordination, loss of control	Success, control	Relaxation, meditation
Neuroendocrine pattern:					
Norepinephrine	markedly up	slightly up	normal		markedly down
Epinephrine	slightly up	markedly up	normal		markedly down
Renin	markedly up				
Testosterone	markedly up		markedly down	markedly up	
Cortisol	normal	slightly up	markedly up	markedly down	
Endorphins			markedly up	markedly down	
Autonomic pattern:					
Blood pressure	markedly up	slightly up	normal		markedly down
Pulse	markedly up	slightly up	slightly down		slightly down

Nonetheless, such accommodation may vary in degree of difficulty and be time-consuming. Degree of difficulty would seem to be defined by the discrepancy in endocrine/autonomic pattern between preceding and subsequent emotions. For instance, the discrepancy between anger and fear, as can be seen from Table 9.1, is minimal; that between depression and anger is considerably stronger; and that between the counteremotions fear and serenity is extreme.

Transfer between the active emotions anger and fear, as well as between all other emotions associated with sympathetic dominance in the autonomic nervous system, should therefore be easy and efficient. In contrast, transfer between the counteremotions fear and serenity, as well as between other active versus passive emotions, should be comparatively inefficient and tardy.

Comparison of the neuroendocrine patterns of emotions, as pioneered by Henry (1986, 1992), thus holds promise of elucidating the mechanics of emotional transition and excitatory dependency. The task at hand is (a) to determine the degree of specificity in the excitatory pattern of primary emotions, (b) to delineate the elements in discrepant excitatory patterns that are functionally dominant, and (c) to ascertain the time course of these dominant elements under different conditions of discrepancy.

MIXED EMOTIONS

The premise of this exposition—that is, the time discrepancy between rapid cognitive and sluggish excitatory adjustment to changing, emotion-evoking environmental conditions—has two heretic implications. First, it challenges the notion that emotional behaviors and experiences depend on emotion-specific excitatory patterns. Emotion theorists have been preoccupied with the creation of emotional taxonomies in which emotions are treated as behaviors and experiences of considerable duration, and they have explicitly or implicitly assumed that a particular bodily state is connected with each and every discrete emotion they proclaimed to exist. What has been entirely neglected is that emotions may come and go, and change from one to another, within seconds, if not fractions of a second.

For instance, individuals who just survived a severe car crash may find themselves torn between laughing (because they survived it without injury) and crying (because it means the instant end of a Florida vacation and a host of related disappointments). Typologists might speak of a fluctuation between some form of euphoria and sadness—or an admixture of these emotions that calls for further classification. Irrespective of labels that analysts may attach, however, it should be clear that the fluctuation is between extremely different emotions. Does this now mean that an excitatory pattern of luck appreciation exists when laughing occurs? Likewise, that an excitatory sadness pattern exists when crying occurs? Neuroendocrine and physiological considerations speak against such possibilities. More likely is that the startle and shock of the accident generated a strong sympathetic reaction that then intensified whatever was felt at the moment.

The principal inference is that individuals are very capable of experiencing emotions when excitatory reactivity at the time is *not, or not as yet*, specific to their emotion. In the rapid transition from fearful apprehension to acute anger in our initial mother-and-son exemplification, for instance, the mother is likely to have felt anger before the minor fear/anger difference proposed by Henry (1986; see Table 9.1) could have been removed and the excitatory pattern could have turned anger-specific. In uncounted, daily-occurring, rapid emotional transitions, then, emotions will be experienced, and intensely so, despite the absence of especially fitting excitatory patterns—should such patterns exist.

Second, the rapidity of cognitive adjustments to changing emotion-evoking conditions challenges the merits of numerous taxonomies of emotion. Acute emotions can, of course, be internally consistent from beginning to end and span minutes, if not hours. Abusively treated, provoked persons, for instance, may ruminate their abuse and probe plans of corrective or retaliatory actions. Their emotional experience, as all cognitive elaborations concern the circumstances and consequences of provocation, could rightly be labeled an episode of anger. Such pure anger may be the exception, however, rather than the rule.

In all probability, acutely angry individuals will also contemplate, if only for fleeting moments, the capabilities of the abuser and fear further abuse (cf. Zillmann, 1979, 1994). These moments of fear in anger indicate a conceptual dilemma: Is the emotion still anger, as anger dominates fear in terms of time? Do we deal with a mixed emotion that calls for a new label? Or should we not simply accept the fact that anger was felt for some time, that the emotion status then momentarily but definitely changed to fear, and that anger returned thereafter?

Focus on pure, discrete, and episodically stable emotions may have prevented recognition of the fleeting nature of cognitions that define behavior and experience in states of heightened excitation. Admixtures of emotions—such as moments of anger in fear, of apprehension during elation, of pity in anger, and of disgust during sexual engagements—appear to be the rule, not the exception. Even if they were the rare exception, however, emotion theory still would have to accommodate them. One promising, constructive way of doing this is by ignoring confining emotion typologies and by embracing the conceptualization that emotional behavior and experience, although mostly evoked without great cognitive deliberation, is subjectively defined by the individual's train of thought. Whatever idiosyncratic nomenclature people habitually use when angry, fearful, disgusted, or sad, for instance, will tell them that they are angry, fearful, disgusted, or sad. And as idiosyncratic verbiage shifts in the reaction to changing emotion-evoking conditions, so will the experience of emotion and experientially mediated emotional behavior.

REFERENCES

Ádám, G. (1967). *Interoception and behavior: An experimental study.* Budapest: Publishing House of the Hungarian Academy of Sciences.

Bandura, A. (1973). *Aggression: A social learning analysis.* Englewood Cliffs, NJ: Prentice-Hall.

Baron, R. A. (1983). The control of human aggression: A strategy based on incompatible responses. In R. G. Geen & E. I. Donnerstein (Eds.), *Aggression: Theoretical and empirical reviews: Vol. 2. Issues in research* (pp. 173–190). New York: Academic Press.

Bogdonoff, M. D., Back, K. W., Klein, R. F., Estes, E. H., Jr., & Nichols, C. (1962). The physiologic response to conformity pressure in man. *Annals of Internal Medicine, 57*, 389–397.

Bogdonoff, M. D., & Nichols, C. R. (1965). Psychogenic effects on lipid mobilization. In A. E. Renold & G. F. Cahill, Jr. (Eds.), *Handbook of physiology: Section 5. Adipose tissue* (pp. 613–616). Washington, DC: American Physiological Society.

Cacioppo, J. T., Tassinary, L. G., Stonebraker, T. B., & Petty, R. E. (1987). Self-report and cardiovascular measures of arousal: Fractionation during residual arousal. *Biological Psychology, 25*, 135–151.

Cannon, W. B. (1929). *Bodily changes in pain, hunger, fear and rage: An account of researches into the function of emotional excitement* (2nd ed.). New York: Appleton–Century–Crofts.

Cannon, W. B. (1932). *The wisdom of the body.* New York: Norton.

Cantor, J. R., Bryant, J., & Zillmann, D. (1974). Enhancement of humor appreciation by transferred excitation. *Journal of Personality and Social Psychology, 30*, 812–821.

Cantor, J. R., & Zillmann, D. (1973). The effect of affective state and emotional arousal on music appreciation. *Journal of General Psychology, 89*, 97–108.

Cantor, J. R., Zillmann, D., & Bryant, J. (1975). Enhancement of experienced sexual arousal in response to erotic stimuli through misattribution of unrelated residual excitation. *Journal of Personality and Social Psychology, 32*, 69–75.

Cantor, J. R., Zillmann, D., & Day, K. D. (1978). Relationship between cardiorespiratory fitness and physiological responses to films. *Perceptual and Motor Skills, 46*, 1123–1130.

Cardon, P. V., Jr., & Gordon, R. S., Jr. (1959). Rapid increase of plasma unestrified fatty acids in man during fear. *Journal of Psychosomatic Research, 4*, 5–9.

Carlson, L. A. (1965). Inhibition of the mobilization of free fatty acids from adipose tissue: Physiological aspects of the mechanisms for the inhibition of mobilization of FFA from adipose tissue. *Annals of the New York Academy of Sciences, 131*, 119–142.

Cox, J. P., Evans, J. F., & Jamieson, J. L. (1979). Aerobic power and tonic heart rate responses to psychosocial stressors. *Personality and Social Psychology Bulletin, 5*, 160–163.

Cryer, P. E. (1992). Glucose homeostasis and hypoglycemia. In J. D. Wilson & D. W. Foster (Eds.), *Williams textbook of endocrinology* (8th ed., pp. 1223–1253). Philadelphia: Saunders.

Donnerstein, E., & Hallam, J. (1978). Facilitating effects of erotica on aggression against women. *Journal of Personality and Social Psychology, 36*, 1270–1277.

Frankenhaeuser, M. (1986). A psychobiological framework for research on human stress and coping. In M. H. Appley & R. Trumbull (Eds.), *Dynamics of stress: Physiological, psychological, and social perspectives* (pp. 101–116). New York: Plenum.

Fredrikson, M. (1989). Psychophysiological and biochemical indices in "stress" research: Applications to psychopathology and pathophysiology. In G. Turpin (Ed.), *Handbook of clinical psychophysiology* (pp. 241–279). Chichester: Wiley.

Frijda, N. H. (1986). *The emotions.* Cambridge: Cambridge University Press.

Fry, P. S., & Ogston, D. G. (1971). Emotion as a function of the labeling of interruption-produced arousal. *Psychonomic Science, 24*(4), 153–154.

Gelles, R. J. (1974). *The violent home.* Beverly Hills, CA: Sage.

Gelles, R. J. (1979). *Family violence.* Beverly Hills, CA: Sage.

Goffard, M. I., & Perry, W. L. W. (1951). The action of adrenaline on the rate of loss of potassium ions from unfatigued striated muscle. *Journal of Physiology, 112*, 95–101.

Gollwitzer, P. M., Earle, W. B., & Stephan, W. G. (1982). Affect as a determinant of egotism: Residual excitation and performance attributions. *Journal of Personality and Social Psychology, 43*, 702–709.

Gustafson, J. E., Winokur, G., & Reichlin, S. (1963). The effect of psychic-sexual stimulation on urinary and serum acid phosphatase and plasma nonestrified fatty acids. *Psychosomatic Medicine, 25,* 101–105.

Henry, J. P. (1986). Neuroendocrine patterns of emotional response. In R. Plutchik & H. Kellerman (Eds.), *Emotion: Theory, research, and experience: Vol. 3. Biological foundations of emotion* (pp. 37–60). Orlando, FL: Academic Press.

Henry, J. P. (1992). Biological basis of the stress response. *Integrative Physiological and Behavioral Science, 27*(1, Special section), 66–83.

Hoon, P. W., Wincze, J. P., & Hoon, E. F. (1977). A test of reciprocal inhibition: Are anxiety and sexual arousal in women mutually inhibitory? *Journal of Abnormal Psychology, 86,* 65–74.

Jaffe, Y. (1981). Sexual stimulation: Effects on prosocial behavior. *Psychological Reports, 48,* 75–81.

Jasnoski, M. L., Holmes, D. S., Solomon, S., & Aguiar, C. (1981). Exercise, changes in aerobic capacity, and changes in self-perceptions: An experimental investigation. *Journal of Research and Personality, 15,* 460–466.

Jeanrenaud, B. (1965). Lipid components of adipose tissue. In A. E. Renold & G. F. Cahill, Jr. (Eds.), *Handbook of physiology: Section 5. Adipose tissue* (pp. 169–177). Washington, DC: American Physiological Society.

Landsberg, L., & Young, J. B. (1992). Catecholamines and the adrenal medulla. In J. D. Wilson & D. W. Foster (Eds.), *Williams textbook of endocrinology* (8th ed., pp. 621–703). Philadelphia: Saunders.

Lang, P. J. (1979). A bio-informational theory of emotional imagery. *Psychophysiology, 16,* 495–512.

Lang, P. J. (1984). Cognition in emotion: Concept and action. In C. E. Izard, J. Kagan, & R. B. Zajonc (Eds.), *Emotions, cognition, and behavior* (pp. 192–226). Cambridge: Cambridge University Press.

Lazarus, R. S. (1991). *Emotion and adaptation.* New York: Oxford University Press.

Levenson, R. W. (1992). Autonomic nervous system differences among emotions. *Psychological Science, 3*(1), 23–27.

Leventhal, H. (1979). A perceptual-motor processing model of emotion. In P. Pliner, K. R. Blankstein, & I. M. Spigel (Eds.), *Advances in the study of communication and affect: Vol. 5. Perception of the emotion in self and others* (pp. 1–46). New York: Plenum.

Leventhal, H., & Scherer, K. (1987). The relationship of emotion to cognition: A functional approach to a semantic controversy. *Cognition and Emotion, 1*(1), 3–28.

Levi, L. (1965). The urinary output of adrenalin and noradrenalin during pleasant and unpleasant emotional states: A preliminary report. *Psychosomatic Medicine, 27,* 80–85.

Levi, L. (1967). Sympatho-adrenomedullary responses to emotional stimuli: Methodologic, physiologic and pathologic considerations. In E. Bajusz (Ed.), *An introduction to clinical neuroendocrinology* (pp. 78–105). Basel: Karger.

Mattes, J., & Cantor, J. (1982). Enhancing responses to television advertisements via the transfer of residual arousal from prior programming. *Journal of Broadcasting, 26,* 553–556.

Mauro, R. (1992). Affective dynamics: Opponent processes and excitation transfer. In M. S. Clark (Ed.), *Emotion* (pp. 150–174). Newbury Park, CA: Sage.

Mueller, C. W., & Donnerstein, E. (1981). Film-facilitated arousal and prosocial behavior. *Journal of Experimental Social Psychology, 17,* 31–41.

Nevin, J. A. (Ed.). (1973). *The study of human behavior: Learning, motivation, emotion, and instinct.* Glenview, IL: Scott, Foresman.

Pagelow, M. D. (1984). *Family violence.* New York: Praeger.

Panksepp, J. (1989). The neurobiology of emotions: Of animal brains and human feelings. In H. Wagner & A. Manstead (Eds.), *Handbook of social psychophysiology* (pp. 5–26). Chichester: Wiley.

Pennebaker, J. W. (1982). *The psychology of physical symptoms*. New York: Springer-Verlag.

Pennebaker, J. W., & Epstein, D. (1983). Implicit psychophysiology: Effects of common beliefs and idiosyncratic physiological responses on symptom reporting. *Journal of Personality, 51*(3), 468–496.

Pennebaker, J. W., Gonder-Frederick, L., Stewart, H., Elfman, L., & Skelton, J. A. (1982). Physical symptoms associated with blood pressure. *Psychophysiology, 19*, 201–210.

Powell, A. H., Jr., Eisdorfer, C., & Bogdonoff, M. D. (1964). Physiologic response patterns observed in a learning task. *Archives of General Psychiatry, 10*, 192–195.

Ramirez, J., Bryant, J., & Zillmann, D. (1982). Effects of erotica on retaliatory behavior as a function of level of prior provocation. *Journal of Personality and Social Psychology, 43*, 971–978.

Reisenzein, R. (1983). The Schachter theory of emotion: Two decades later. *Psychological Bulletin, 94*, 239–264.

Schachter, S. (1964). The interaction of cognitive and physiological determinants of emotional state. In L. Berkowitz (Ed.), *Advances in experimental social psychology* (Vol. 1, pp. 49–80). New York: Academic Press.

Schwartz, G. E. (1977). Biofeedback and patterning of autonomic and central processes: CNS–cardiovascular interactions. In G. E. Schwartz & J. Beatty (Eds.), *Biofeedback: Theory and research* (pp. 183–219). New York: Academic Press.

Schwartz, G. E. (1986). Emotion and psychophysiological organization: A systems approach. In M. G. H. Coles, E. Donchin, & S. W. Porges (Eds.), *Psychophysiology: Systems, processes, and applications* (pp. 354–377). New York: Guilford.

Schwartz, G. E., Weinberger, D. A., & Singer, J. A. (1981). Cardiovascular differentiation of happiness, sadness, anger and fear following imagery and exercise. *Psychosomatic Medicine, 43*, 343–364.

Scow, R. O., & Chernick, S. S. (1970). Mobilization, transport and utilization of free fatty acids. In M. Florkin & E. H. Stotz (Eds.), *Comprehensive chemistry* (Vol. 18, pp. 19–49). Amsterdam: Elsevier.

Smith, G. P. (1973). Adrenal hormones and emotional behavior. In E. Stellar & J. M. Sprague (Eds.), *Progress in physiological psychology* (pp. 299–351). New York: Academic Press.

Sterling, B., & Gaertner, S. L. (1984). The attribution of arousal and emergency helping: A bidirectional process. *Journal of Experimental Social Psychology, 20*, 586–596.

Sternbach, R. A. (1966). *Principles of psychophysiology: An introductory text and readings*. New York: Academic Press.

Straus, M. A., Gelles, R. J., & Steinmetz, S. K. (1980). *Behind closed doors: Violence in the American family*. Garden City, NY: Anchor.

Wenger, M. A., Clemens, T. L., Coleman, D. R., Cullen, T. D., & Engel, B. T. (1961). Autonomic response specificity. *Psychosomatic Medicine, 23*, 185–193.

White, G. L., Fishbein, S., & Rutstein, J. (1981). Passionate love and the misattribution of arousal. *Journal of Personality and Social Psychology, 41*, 56–62.

Wilder, J. (1957). The law of initial values in neurology and psychiatry: Facts and problems. *Journal of Nervous and Mental Disease, 125*, 73–86.

Zillmann, D. (1971). Excitation transfer in communication-mediated aggressive behavior. *Journal of Experimental Social Psychology, 7*, 419–434.

Zillmann, D. (1978). Attribution and misattribution of excitatory reactions. In J. H. Harvey, W. J. Ickes, & R. F. Kidd (Eds.), *New directions in attribution research* (Vol. 2, pp. 335–368). Hillsdale, NJ: Lawrence Erlbaum Associates.

Zillmann, D. (1979). *Hostility and aggression*. Hillsdale, NJ: Lawrence Erlbaum Associates.

Zillmann, D. (1980). Anatomy of suspense. In P. H. Tannenbaum (Ed.), *The entertainment functions of television* (pp. 133–163). Hillsdale, NJ: Lawrence Erlbaum Associates.

Zillmann, D. (1983). Transfer of excitation in emotional behavior. In J. T. Cacioppo & R. E. Petty (Eds.), *Social psychophysiology: A sourcebook* (pp. 215–240). New York: Guilford.

Zillmann, D. (1984). *Connections between sex and aggression.* Hillsdale, NJ: Lawrence Erlbaum Associates.

Zillmann, D. (1986). Coition as emotion. In D. Byrne & K. Kelley (Eds.), *Alternative approaches to the study of sexual behavior* (pp. 173–199). Hillsdale, NJ: Lawrence Erlbaum Associates.

Zillmann, D. (1989). Aggression and sex: Independent and joint operations. In H. Wagner & A. Manstead (Eds.), *Handbook of social psychophysiology* (pp. 229–259). Chichester: Wiley.

Zillmann, D. (1991). The logic of suspense and mystery. In J. Bryant & D. Zillmann (Eds.), *Responding to the screen: Reception and reaction processes* (pp. 281–303). Hillsdale, NJ: Lawrence Erlbaum Associates.

Zillmann, D. (1994). Cognition–excitation interdependencies in the escalation of anger and angry aggression. In M. Potegal (Ed.), *Escalation of aggression: Biological and social processes* (pp. 45–71). Hillsdale, NJ: Lawrence Erlbaum Associates.

Zillmann, D., & Bryant, J. (1974). Effect of residual excitation on the emotional response to provocation and delayed aggressive behavior. *Journal of Personality and Social Psychology, 30,* 782–791.

Zillmann, D., Bryant, J., Comisky, P. W., & Medoff, N. J. (1981). Excitation and hedonic valence in the effect of erotica on motivated intermale aggression. *European Journal of Social Psychology, 11,* 233–252.

Zillmann, D., Johnson, R. C., & Day, K. D. (1974a). Attribution of apparent arousal and proficiency of recovery from sympathetic activation affecting excitation transfer to aggressive behavior. *Journal of Experimental Social Psychology, 10,* 503–515.

Zillmann, D., Johnson, R. C., & Day, K. D. (1974b). Provoked and unprovoked aggressiveness in athletes. *Journal of Research in Personality, 8,* 139–152.

Zillmann, D., Katcher, A. H., & Milavsky, B. (1972). Excitation transfer from physical exercise to subsequent aggressive behavior. *Journal of Experimental Social Psychology, 8,* 247–259.

Zillmann, D., Mody, B., & Cantor, J. R. (1974). Empathetic perception of emotional displays in films as a function of hedonic and excitatory state prior to exposure. *Journal of Research in Personality, 8,* 335–349.

Zillmann, D., & Mundorf, N. (1987). Image effects in the appreciation of video rock. *Communication Research, 14*(3), 316–334.

Zillmann, D., & Zillmann, M. (in press). Psychoneuroendocrinology of social behavior. In E. T. Higgins & A. Kruglanski (Eds.), *Social psychology: Handbook of basic mechanisms and processes.* New York: Guilford.

10

Autistic Aloneness

Lisa Capps
Marian Sigman
University of California, Los Angeles

In 1943, child psychiatrist Leo Kanner published a paper describing 11 children who suffered from "an extreme autistic aloneness." The term *autism*, from the Greek word *autos* meaning "self," represented Kanner's observation that these children seemed isolated from people and things outside themselves, yet the "aloneness" that is attributed to autistic people is also experienced by those with whom they interact. Conveying both isolation and longing for companionship, one parent of an autistic child described two kinds of related but distinct pain: the pain of knowing of her child's social isolation, and a painful yearning for displays of understanding and empathy from the child.

In this chapter we explore autistic aloneness by considering the ways that normally developing children engage in interpersonal relationships with caregivers, peers, and other members of society. We present a perspective that grows out of the work of Mead (1934, p. 63), who stated, "Selves can only exist in definite relationships to other selves." Similarly, Taylor (1985, 1989) has suggested that we understand each other, ourselves, and objects in the world through interaction in public or common spaces: "I can only learn what anger, love and anxiety are through my and others' experience of these being objects for *us* in some common space" (1989, p. 35). The following sections examine the "common spaces" in which normally developing children connect with other people, beginning with dyadic interaction that occurs in early infancy. Identifying the forms of common space that facilitate social connection with normally developing children sheds light on the nature of emotional impairment in autism. At the same time, clarifying the ways in which autism interferes with the process of creating or engaging in common space advances understanding of normal development (Cicchetti, 1984, in press; Kanner, 1943; Sigman, 1989).

DYADIC INTERACTION, JOINT ATTENTION, AND SOCIAL REFERENCING

Several investigators have described the coordinated, dance-like quality of caregiver–infant interactions during the first year of life (e.g., Brazelton, Koslowski, & Main, 1974; Malatesta & Haviland, 1982; Stern, 1977). Children are born with patterns of social responses that are elicited by their caregivers' heartbeats, the visual configuration of their faces, and the rhythms of their voices. Soon after birth, infants begin to make eye contact with other people, smile and vocalize in response to social stimuli (Bruner, 1983; Emde & Harmon, 1972; Haith, 1977), and imitate facial and gestural expressions (Meltzoff & Moore, 1977). During the first 6 months, infants participate in dyadic interactions with caregivers, in common space created by infants' responsiveness to caregivers, and caregivers' sensitivity and attunement to infants' behaviors (Hayes, 1984). Countless repetitions of such sequences, often culminating in shared pleasure and delight, lay the groundwork for infants' ability to initiate and regulate shared or common spaces in subsequent phases of development (Sander, 1975; Sroufe, 1977; Stern, 1974).

Toward the end of the first year, children develop strong and specific attachments to their caregivers, as reflected in stranger anxiety, distress on separation, and pleasure on reunion. Gradually, caregivers take on the role of "home base" (Ainsworth, 1973; Mahler, Pine, & Bergman, 1975; Sander, 1975), serving as the center for children's exploration of the expanding world.

Infants also become less involved in dyadic exchanges and more frequently engage in triadic interactions involving caregivers and interesting objects. By 8–9 months, infants display "joint attention behaviors," allowing them to follow and direct another person's gaze with the intent to share awareness or the experience of an object or event. Infants initiate and respond to gaze with increasing accuracy (Butterworth, 1990; Scaife & Bruner, 1975), using gaze in concert with pointing, giving, and showing gestures (Harris, 1989). Emotion is central to these behaviors. Infants look up at others' faces to share emotion, in a manner that is "self-propelled and self-rewarding" (Bruner, 1983, p. 27), and usually accompanied by smiling (Bruner & Sherwood, 1983; Scanlon-Jones, Collins, & Hong, 1991).

Building on joint attention skills, 12-month-old infants engage in social referencing, which involves looking to others for clues in situations that are ambiguous or confusing, and using this information to guide behavior (see Klinnert, Campos, Sorce, Emde, & Svejda, 1983). Although it is not clear what the infant imagines of another person's knowledge or point of view, joint attention and social referencing behaviors expand the domain of common space to include attitudes and feelings about events and objects in the outside world. Together, those who inhabit this space construct a shared meaning of experience by integrating knowledge, thoughts, attitudes, and feelings.

DYADIC INTERACTION, JOINT ATTENTION, AND SOCIAL REFERENCING IN CHILDREN WITH AUTISM

First, it is important to note that the full clinical picture of autism is not manifest before age 3. Most of what is known about the social adjustment and development of very young autistic children is based on retrospective accounts from parents (Newson, Dawson, & Everard, 1984; Ornitz, Guthrie, & Farley, 1977). Although one might expect hindsight to illuminate early signs of trouble, the vast majority of parents reported that they had *not* yet suspected that "something was wrong" in their autistic child's first year. Furthermore, records of early pediatric visits among children who later became autistic rarely register abnormalities of any kind (Frith, 1989; Knobloch & Pasamanick, 1975).[1]

Research on dyadic interaction, joint attention, and social referencing in autism has been conducted with 3- to 5-year-old children. The children who participated in the studies conducted in our laboratory averaged 53.3 months of age ($SD = 11.9$ months), and many were mentally retarded (average mental age, determined by a Cattell or Stanford–Binet score, was 25.7 months, $SD = 9.1$). Studies of dyadic interaction (involving ball toss and tickling games) in this sample yielded surprising results. In contrast to clinical accounts suggesting that they would avoid eye contact, rebuff social invitations, and seem emotionally flat, autistic children appeared as responsive and playful as normal and retarded comparison children, albeit somewhat more passive (Mundy, Sigman, Ungerer, & Sherman, 1986; Sigman, Mundy, Sherman, & Ungerer, 1986). Autistic

---

[1]Determining the presence or absence of early abnormalities is central to the debate about the primacy of affective versus cognitive impairment in autism. Although undermining the theory that autism stems from an innate inability to form affective contact (Hobson, 1991; Kanner, 1943), the absence of evidence of early impairment is consistent with the "theory of mind" hypothesis, in that requisite metarepresentational abilities emerge later in development.

children also resembled comparison children in their displays of positive and negative emotion, although they showed more idiosyncratic blends of facial affect (Yirmiya, Kasari, Sigman, & Mundy, 1989), and were much less likely to smile while looking at others (Kasari, Sigman, Mundy, & Yirmiya, 1990; see also Dawson, Hill, Spencer, Galpert, & Watson, 1990).

Contrary to accounts of autism as involving "the inability to form affective contacts" (Kanner, 1943, p. 250), or "the lack of attachment behavior and relative failure of bonding" (Rutter, 1978, p. 9), considerable research suggests that children with autism do form attachment relationships (Rogers, Ozonoff, & Maslin-Cole, 1991; Shapiro, Sherman, Calamari, & Koch, 1987; Sigman & Mundy, 1989; Sigman & Ungerer, 1984). Furthermore, in a recent study we found that, despite behavioral disorganization, a significant percentage (40%) of autistic children showed signs of underlying attachment security (Capps, Sigman, & Mundy, 1994).

It appears, then, that autistic children have access to the common space of dyadic interaction, but that they are less able or likely to initiate it, and are felt to be odd or aloof, although this quality is difficult to capture. It may be that autistic children and their caregivers develop primary forms of attachment (Kraemer, 1992; Sigman & Siegel, 1992), but that their relationships are not enriched by the joint anticipatory system that converts psychobiological attachment into something more subtle and sensitive to individual idiosyncracies and to forms of cultural practice.

Studies conducted by our research group have demonstrated striking differences between young autistic and comparison children in relation to both initiation and responsiveness to joint attention behaviors, and social referencing behaviors. In contrast to normal and mentally retarded controls, autistic children rarely followed the gaze or pointing gestures of other people, and did not attempt to share positive play experiences with caregivers by making eye contact, giving, or showing toys (Mundy, Sigman, Ungerer, & Sherman, 1986; Sigman, Mundy, Sherman, & Ungerer, 1986; see also Curcio, 1978; Loveland & Landry, 1986). However, autistic children were just as likely as comparison children to look up at adults to request an object that was out of reach (Mundy, Sigman, & Kasari, 1990). Thus, children with autism frequently used gestures instrumentally, but rarely used gesture to share or comment on experience.

Similarly, in a study of pride, children with autism differed from normal and mentally retarded comparison children in that they seldom looked up at parents following completion of a puzzle (Kasari, Sigman, Baumgartener, & Stipek, 1992). Whereas all children showed pleasure in mastery, autistic children were distinct in that they neither solicited nor responded to praise; in fact, they often turned away.

The results from studies of social referencing parallel those found in studies of joint attention. When faced with an ambiguous object, the majority of autistic children did not look to the adults for information, whereas 94% of the comparison children did so (Sigman, Kasari, Kwon, & Yirmiya, 1992). Again, although they are capable of attending to objects and people at the same time, autistic children do not seem inclined to do so to share or comment on an experience.

IMPLICATIONS OF DEFICITS IN JOINT ATTENTION

Deficits in joint attention have been viewed as support for both sides of the debate about the primacy of cognitive and affective impairment in autism. Proponents of the former view suggest that joint attention deficits stem from the inability to recognize others as agents of contemplation—people with minds of their own (Leslie & Happe, 1989). In support of this view, Baron-Cohen (1989, 1990) found that although autistic children could identify what another person was looking at, they had great difficulty predicting where a person would look for an object if it was moved from its last location in the person's absence (see also Baron-Cohen, Leslie, & Frith, 1985, 1986). This result was seen as a failure to attribute different beliefs to others, or to use a "theory of mind" (Premack & Woodruff, 1978).

Those arguing for the primacy of affective impairment attribute the observed paucity of joint attention to autistic children's difficulty interpreting bodily expression of emotion (Hobson, 1989, 1993). Just as autism does not involve ubiquitous gaze avoidance or the absence of gestural communication, deficits in emotion recognition and expression are not absolute. However, individuals with autism do appear to be less accurate in labeling facial expression of emotion (Capps, Yirmiya, & Sigman, 1992; Hobson, Ouston, & Lee, 1989; Langdell, 1981; MacDonald et al., 1989; Ozonoff, Pennington, & Rogers, 1990), although the universality of such impairment has been questioned (Prior, Dahlstrom, & Squires, 1990).

Autistic children also appeared less able to match different components of a particular feeling (facial expression, vocalization, gesture, and context) than comparison children, but were just as able to match different aspects of objects, such as a picture of a bird, bird chirp, flapping wings, and nest (Hobson, 1986a, 1986b, 1989). Similarly, autistic children showed considerably more difficulty identifying pictures of various emotion items than nonemotion items on the British Picture Vocabulary Scale, whereas this discrepancy did not emerge among matched comparison children (Hobson & Lee, 1989). In addition, when Weeks and Hobson (1987) gave children the task of sorting photographs that were separable based on sex, age, facial expression, or type of hat, the majority of nonautistic children sorted first on the basis of emotional expression. In contrast, autistic children (matched on verbal IQ scores) were most inclined to sort by type of hat. Furthermore, 5 of 14 autistic people were unable to sort by facial expression when explicitly instructed to do so. Langdell's (1981) study of autistic children's ability to sort photographs by facial expression yielded consistent results.

Expression

Fewer studies have examined autistic persons' ability to produce affective expressions. Ricks (1979) reported that children with autism use intonation to express emotion idiosyncratically, rather than the common nonverbal means used by normally developing children. In addition, using a battery of facial and vocal tasks, MacDonald and her colleagues (MacDonald et al., 1989) found deficits in emotion expression among children with autism.

Most recently, Loveland, Tunali-Kotoski, Pearson, Brelsford, and Ortegon (1993, p. 2) asked autistic and nonautistic subjects to imitate five modeled expressions ("Let me see you do this"), and to produce five labeled expressions ("Show me how you look when you are . . ."). Autistic subjects produced fewer recognizable expressions than comparison subjects in both tasks, and their expressions contained many unusual, idiosyncratic features. Interestingly, imitation and expression tasks were equally difficult for autistic subjects, but expression was easier for controls. This may be due in part to normal subjects' responsiveness to display rules that prohibit imitation outside of intimate contexts (Saarni, 1979), and to autistic subjects' seemingly decontextualized or unintegrated knowledge of emotions and their expression.

THE DRIVE FOR CENTRAL COHERENCE

Meaningful systems of communication are born out of facial expression, eye gaze, and gesture, what Frith (1989) referred to as "language of the eyes and hands" (p. 153). Although demonstrating some ability to perform and understand individual expressions, people with autism seem to lack the ability or inclination to integrate and contextualize various aspects of emotional communication. This limits autistic persons' ability to convey or derive meaning from emotional expressions in the course of daily life. Nonautistic people, in contrast, possess the ability or compulsion to pull together disparate information into a coherent pattern, to give priority to understanding meaning; what Frith has called "the drive for central coherence" (p. 174). The drive for central coherence compels humans to integrate all aspects of a situation, embedding information into larger contexts. Because humans seem unable to abandon the quest for global meaning, Frith referred to the drive for central coherence as "an extension and limitation of human information processing capacity" (p. 101).

In support of the notion that individuals with autism lack a drive for central coherence, Frith (1989) cited a host of experiments that contrasted individuals' performance on tasks involving stimuli that were detached or decontextualized, and stimuli that were embedded in a larger context (e.g., memorization of unconnected and connected words, completion of puzzles made of isolated shapes, and those embedded in a recognizable design). The common denominator in the results of these studies was the high performance of autistic children on tasks requiring isolation of stimuli, and low performance on tasks requiring contextualization. Precisely the opposite trend emerged for normally developing children and mentally retarded children without autism.

COHERENCE AS INTEGRATION OF AFFECT AND COGNITION

The pattern of abilities and disabilities displayed by individuals with autism informs our understanding of the drive for central coherence. Deficits in behaviors that emerge early in normal development, specifically joint attention and social referencing, suggest that the push for coherence may begin with the drive to integrate affect and cognition in the context of social interaction. This integration is precisely what goes on in the common spaces that are only partially, if at all, accessible in interactions with autistic individuals.

Autistic aloneness is most apparent in interactions that involve experiencing events and emotions "as objects for us" (Taylor, 1989, p. 35). Taylor related the notion of common space to conversation: "In talking about something you and I make it an object for us together, that is, not just an object for me which happens also to be one for you" (p. 35). Individuals with autism seem to have great difficulty participating in such conversation, in all its forms. As is discussed in the following sections, autistic people's trouble engaging in the "language of the eyes and hands" is paralleled by a lack of participation in "rituals of interaction" (Bruner, 1991, p. 3) or "conventionalized acts" (Adamson & Bakeman, 1986, p. 215), and by difficulty mastering the pragmatics of language use. First, however, a brief account follows of what happens when development proceeds normally.

CONVENTIONALIZED ACTS: EMPATHY

Bruner (1983) explained that "language acquisition begins before the child utters lexico-grammatical speech. It begins when mother and infant create predictable formats of interaction that can serve as a microcosm for communicating and constituting a shared reality" (p. 18). Further, he suggested that normally developing infants enter the world of language and culture with a readiness to find or invent meaning-making systems, and to learn conventions for making their intentions clear and understanding the intentions of others (Bruner, 1983, 1990; see also Bretherton, 1989).

　Observational studies have shown that in the second year of life children understand actions that lead to anger or disapproval, actions that comfort, and actions that can be a shared source of amusement. Two-year-old children display evasive action, make excuses, appeal to good intentions to avoid punishment (Dunn, 1988; Dunn & Munn, 1987), and respond empathetically to others' distress (Radke-Yarrow, Zahn-Waxler, & Chapman, 1983; Zahn-Waxler, Radke-Yarrow, & King, 1979).

As Eisenberg and Strayer (1989) have pointed out, it is important to distinguish three different forms of reaction, all of which have been termed *empathy*. The first, *emotional contagion*, is a reaction in which the individual feels the same emotion as the other person without concern for the welfare of the other. The second involves reacting to the emotion of another in a way that conveys concern, or *sympathetic responding*. And the third denotes the vicarious experiencing of emotion, *feeling with* another.

During the first year of life, normally developing children generally react to another's distress by becoming upset, experiencing emotional contagion (Sagi & Hoffman, 1976; Zahn-Waxler & Radke-Yarrow, 1982). By the second year, emotional contagion is replaced by concerned attention and active attempts to alleviate distress, often accompanied by verbal expressions of sympathy (Dunn, 1988; Radke-Yarrow, Zahn-Waxler, & Chapman, 1983; Thompson, 1987). As Radke-Yarrow, Zahn-Waxler, and Chapman (1983) observed, 2-year-old children who encountered someone in distress recruited people to help, and offered cheerful and comforting objects and suggestions.

Empathy involves the integration of affective and cognitive abilities. According to Feshbach's (1982) model, for example, an empathic response requires the ability to discriminate the emotional states of other people, perspective-taking ability, and the evocation of a shared response. Showing empathy requires that one have facility with cultural conventions for conveying concern and comfort. As Dunn (1988) has pointed out, people can behave in a way that is prosocial not only because they are concerned about the feelings or needs of another, but in order to ingratiate themselves, to engage attention, to become part of a group, or to obey a rule or convention.

Thus, outward expressions of empathy, whether in the form of facial affect or comforting behavior, do not necessarily reflect internal experience. Similarly, the absence of an observable response does not necessarily mean that an individual feels nothing. In fact, children quickly pick up on social display rules (Cole, 1986; Saarni, 1979), which inhibit emotional expressiveness particularly among adolescent males (Yarczower & Daruns, 1982).

The common space that is created through ritualized interactions, such as conventional displays of empathy, facilitates many forms of connection. In addition to adopting another's perspective and "feeling with" that person, participation in displays of empathy reinforces a sense of mutual membership in a relationship that is embedded in a shared culture. For example, a young child may feel upset in response to a parents' sadness over the death of a friend, and attempt to provide comfort by offering a teddy bear. Although the child cannot adopt the adult's perspective on the experience, the meaning of the offering is clear and, because it communicates the child's intent, is undoubtedly comforting.

EMPATHY AND AUTISM

For many years, general descriptions of social impairment in autism frequently emphasize a lack of empathy, noting indifference to others' distress, and the inability to offer comfort. Fairly recently, such accounts have been investigated empirically. Members of our research group have examined empathy in two different populations of children with autism: the young, mentally retarded sample described in relation to our research on joint attention, and a sample of nonretarded adolescents. In the young sample (average age 53 months), empathy was examined through observation and analysis of children's responses to caregivers and adults who, on separate occasions, pretended to be hurt and ill. In contrast to nonautistic normal and mentally retarded children who stared attentively, sometimes attempting to provide comfort, the vast majority of autistic children did not look up; they continued to play uninterrupted (Sigman et al., 1992).

Participants in the older sample were between 9 and 14 years of age, and the majority were of average or above-average intelligence (Full Scale IQ measured by the WISC–R: 75–136). Nonautistic comparison children were matched on chronological and mental age, and on Full Scale, Verbal, and Performance IQ scores. Subjects watched videotaped vignettes in which the protagonist experienced sadness, anger, fear, pride, or happiness (Yirmiya, Sigman, Kasari, & Mundy, 1992). The segment designed to elicit sadness featured a boy looking for his lost dog. Children watched each vignette twice, at least 1 week apart, counterbalancing for order. On one occasion they were asked to label the emotion that the protagonist was feeling, and on another the emotion they were feeling. Empathy was measured as the degree of agreement between the emotion that the child attributed to the protagonist, and the emotion the child reported feeling.

Although individuals with autism performed somewhat less well than comparison children on both the labeling and empathy tasks, differences between groups were surprisingly small.

Because subjects were videotaped as they watched the vignettes, we were able to code their facial expressions while viewing (Capps, Kasari, Yirmiya, & Sigman, 1993). Again, to our surprise, individuals with autism displayed more positive affect and concentration or puzzlement than did comparison children. To determine whether this display of affect occurred at appropriate points in the vignettes, we went back to the videotapes and selected two 5-second periods within each vignette where the unambiguous, crucial information was conveyed. For example, in the happy episode, the boy learns he is being given a bike at the very end.

Results suggested that autistic children showed the most positive affect while watching happiness- and pride-engendering scenes, and more concentration than comparison children during each of the five segments. One explanation for group difference in displays of facial affect has to do with normal children's sensitivity to display rules that inhibit emotional expression, particularly in front of adults and video cameras (Yarczower & Daruns, 1982). Autistic children's facial expressiveness may reflect limited access to social channels through which display rules are learned.

These studies of empathy shed light on autistic aloneness. The contrast between older autistic children's expressiveness and young children's inattention to distressed adults may suggest that autistic people develop empathy as they get older; we are currently investigating this question. Significant issues, however, remain unresolved. Does this delayed form of empathy involve perspective taking and a shared response? Autistic children's slow and effortful responses did not evidence the smooth integration of cognitive and emotional abilities that allows nonautistic individuals to enter the psychological space of another.

A second, related question concerns the extent to which experimental measures of empathy index "real-life" behavior. Studies conducted in laboratory settings, where tasks are removed from the complex context of social interactions and participants are given unlimited time to respond, may optimize the performance of autistic people. In addition, autistic people not only seemed uninhibited by the presence of others in the room, but solicited confirmation from their parents of their own internal states. More than one autistic child, for example, turned to his mother after responding and asked, "Right, Mom?" This behavior was not characteristic of any of the normally developing children.

Loveland and Tunali (1991) reported consistent findings from their study of the use of social scripts among high-functioning verbal individuals with autism or Down syndrome. During a "tea party," the experimenter told the participant about an unhappy personal experience (sick pet, stolen wallet), to which a sympathetic or helpful response would ordinarily be expected (Fivush & Slackman, 1986; Nelson, 1986). Autistic subjects gave a significantly greater percentage of responses relating only to the tea party, whereas subjects with Down syndrome gave a significantly greater percentage of concrete suggestions and sympathetic comments.

As children grow older, engaging in common space depends on being able to shift attention, and to integrate thoughts, feelings, and cultural knowledge in increasingly sophisticated ways. The ability to empathize with another person, for example, involves understanding what the person is thinking and feeling, and knowing how to show care and concern. Each aspect of this process requires awareness of the meaning of social situations and access to the communicative conventions through which intentions and emotions are conveyed.

DEVELOPMENT OF PRAGMATICS
IN NORMAL CHILDREN

Acquiring language involves learning an array of interdependent abilities at the same time. The child learns how to handle speech sounds (phonology), to master the relations between signs and their referents (semantics), to apply the rules of grammar (syntax), and to use language for the purpose of communication in a way that is appropriate to context (pragmatics). This section extends discussion of common space and autistic aloneness through focus on pragmatics. Among these things is knowing how to use language to express emotion, achieve joint attention, and engage in joint action with other people.

Children learn names and labels through participation in a "dubbing format" (Bruner, 1983, p. 122). In these interactions, the child not only learns language but how to use it as a member of culture. As Ochs and Schieffelin (1989) have pointed out, social referencing is an integral part of language acquisition. Language learners seek out affective information from the way another uses language, just as children seek out affective information from one another's faces. Social referencing continues throughout the lifespan. Across languages and speech communities, many features of language serve to index something about the participants, their feelings, attitudes, and beliefs (see Ochs & Schieffelin, 1989). Thus, language both reflects and creates affective contexts.

Research has shown that at the earliest stages of language development, children demonstrate competent use of intonation, words, and grammatical constructions to express feelings, moods, dispositions, and attitudes (Bretherton & Beeghly, 1982; Dunn & Kendrick, 1982; Miller &

Sperry, 1987; Ochs, 1986; Schieffelin, 1986). Children as young as two can adapt their message to what listeners know or do not know, and respond to new information (Furrow, 1984; Wellman & Lempers, 1977). This range of speech acts has also been observed in studies of (nonautistic) persons who are mentally retarded (e.g., Coggins, Carpenter, & Owings, 1983; Paul & Cohen, 1985) and those with language delays (Rom & Bliss, 1981; van Kleeck & Frankel, 1981). It seems that "expressive and referential functions of language are acquired in an integrated fashion, of a piece" (Ochs & Schieffelin, 1989, p. 11). From the start, use and interpretation of language—pragmatic understanding—are not based on the literal meaning of words, but depend on context.

Language acquisition is fueled by the desire to communicate intentionally about meaningful, often emotional topics. For example, Dunn (1988) found that the issues that were most upsetting to children at 18 months were those that they communicated about most effectively at 3 years. By age 3, children also display the ability to initiate conversation, and to contribute new information to shared topics (Dunn & Shatz, 1989). Children learn to use language through social interactions in which relationships are established, (re)defined, and maintained. Perhaps the integration of emotional and cognitive understanding that occurs in the common spaces created as language develops both motivates and facilitates comprehension of the cultural expectations about how people feel, think, and believe in typical situations; in turn, such understanding qualitatively enhances communication between members of the same culture.

PRAGMATIC DIFFICULTIES IN CHILDREN WITH AUTISM

Although much has been written on many aspects of the language of autistic children (see Paul, 1987; Schopler & Mesibov, 1985, for reviews), pragmatics is of particular interest to psychologists and developmental psychopathologists (e.g., Baltaxe, 1977; Baron-Cohen, 1988; Tager-Flusberg, 1992). This interest reflects evidence that while autistic children's phonological, syntactic, and semantic development follow a fairly normal course, there are striking differences in the *use* of linguistic forms (Tager-Flusberg, 1992, 1993). The difficulties acquiring and using language that are characteristic of autism may be due to a more general problem with communication (Frith, 1989).

As mentioned earlier, language acquisition is aided by the desire to communicate intentionally about meaningful topics of shared interest. Autistic individuals' communication problems may stem in part from limited participation in the common spaces in which attention and interest are shared, or from limits in the drive or capacity to convey and interpret attitudes and emotions. Wetherby and Prutting (1984) studied four autistic children in the early stages of language development. Paralleling results from studies of joint attention, they found that autistic children frequently used language to obtain a desired object, but seldom to serve social functions, such as gaining or sharing attention.

Autistic people have great difficulty using and interpreting features of language that index something about social roles and identities, feelings, and attitudes. For example, Baltaxe (1977) found that German-speaking autistic adolescents confused the polite and familiar forms of address (Sie and Du), and seemed not to understand social norms about what is acceptable in conversation. Langdell (1981) reported that autistic children tend to ask embarrassing questions, such as "How old are you?" to adult strangers in the supermarket. In addition, autistic people often fail to grasp subtle connotations or affective attitudes that words convey, such as the difference between telling someone they look "bony," rather than "thin," or "petite," although all three words may accurately represent the person's size. The lack of sensitivity to shades of meaning displayed in autistic people's speech reveals, by contrast, the powerful role of language in constructing and socializing culturally shared understanding (Bruner, 1983; Ochs & Schieffelin, 1984; Schieffelin & Ochs, 1986)

As we have mentioned, children with autism use intonation to express emotion in an idiosyncratic manner, rather than through the common nonverbal language used by normal children (Ricks, 1979). Similarly, the speech of verbal autistic people typically includes an abundance of idiosyncratic remarks and associations, and is often accompanied by idiosyncratic gestures (Attwood, Frith, & Hermelin, 1988; Curcio, 1978; Wetherby & Prutting, 1984). Frith (1989) has interpreted idiosyncratic speech as suggesting a lack of interest or need to share with the listener a wider context of interaction, and a failure to gauge the comprehension of listeners, such that information conveyed remains a self-contained piece that is not part of an overall, coherent pattern.

The coherence that language creates is also embedded in personal relationships and in shared culture. Hence, Frith's description of detachment applies not only to pieces of information, but to one's *experience* in spoken interactions with autistic people. Idiosyncratic remarks disrupt, if not stop the flow of, conversation, which is choppy to begin with at best. Autistic individuals' tendency to perseverate on a topic has the same effect (Opitz, 1982, cited in Baron-Cohen, 1988). Autistic people have been known to interrupt other speakers inappropriately (Layton & Stutts, 1985) and to fail to use eye contact to signal turn taking (Mirenda, Donnellan, & Yoder, 1983), resulting in further discontinuity.

Despite their willingness, autistic people have trouble introducing topics for discussion and adding to existing topics of conversation (Bruner

& Feldman, 1993; Frith, 1989; Hurtig, Ensrud, & Tomblin, 1982). Hurtig et al. found that breakdowns in conversation were least likely when the autistic person was asked questions, suggesting that participants with autism could not carry the conversation on their own. Autistic people often used questions to initiate and continue conversation, but tended to repeat the same questions or ask questions they could answer. They did not seem to know where the conversation was going. These difficulties seem connected to a more pervasive lack of awareness that language in general, and conversation in particular, can be used to share information with others (Tager-Flusberg, 1993). In this sense, autistic people seem not to know that people can "go places" together in conversation by sharing experiences in a common space.

The communicative difficulties displayed by individuals with autism show, by contrast, that people speaking a common language index affiliations, roles, and identities in a way that contributes emotional continuity to interactions. This continuity is central to the construction and instantiation of cultural affiliation, interpersonal relationships, and individual identities.

By age 2 or 3, normally developing children are able to use language in a way that draws on expectations about how people feel, think, and believe in typical situations. The common space that is created through language seems to be born out of shared culture. At the same time, cultural understanding is experienced and learned in communicative interactions with people. In discussing the child's simultaneous entry into culture and language, we now turn to a central aspect of both: narrative and narrative interpretation.

NARRATIVE

Bruner (1990) has written, "While a culture must contain a set of norms, it must also contain a set of interpretive procedures for rendering departures from those norms meaningful in terms of established patterns of belief" (p. 47). This kind of meaning is achieved through narrative and narrative interpretation. The function of the story is to find a way to make sense of a deviation from a canonical cultural pattern.[2] In this way, stories alleviate the cognitive and emotional upset that can accompany unmet expectations and unexpected events and experiences. As analyses of the monologues of "Emmy," a normal 2-year-old, have shown (Nelson, 1989), such use of storytelling emerges early in the child's development (see Fivush & Hudson, 1990; McCabe & Peterson, 1991; Peterson & McCabe, 1983).

---

[2]The canons themselves are embodied and communicated in narrative form.

After being tucked into her crib for a nap or for the night, Emmy lay alone telling little stories to herself that made patterns out of the confusing events of the day. By posing puzzles to herself and putting them into problem-solving narratives or temporal narrative frames, Emmy created meaning for events and coherence out of confusion (Feldman, 1989). Pretend play provides similar opportunities for making sense of puzzling events and experiences by putting them in narratives frames.

Reciprocally, putting events and interactions into narrative form permits the child to build canonical representations of how the world of people and things work and should work. By mastering these representations, the child not only becomes able to deal with social situations, but to organize and store information in a way that is relevant to such interactions (Bruner & Feldman, 1993). Giving experience a conventional narrative form makes it more highly accessible in memory (Hudson, 1990; Mandler, 1984), and more readily available to be introduced into conversation. A failure to narrate, then, might also lead to general difficulties in encoding and communicating about experiences (Bruner & Feldman, 1993).

NARRATIVE AND AUTISM

There are many reasons to think that individuals with autism go through life without giving experience a narrative form. In comparison to normal and mentally retarded children, autistic children show deficits in pretend play (Wing & Gould, 1979), particularly with dolls (Sigman & Ungerer, 1984; Ungerer & Sigman, 1981). Further analyses revealed an association between the level of doll-directed pretend play and language ability across groups, but autistic children's deficits in symbolic play were far greater than what could be attributed to limitations in language ability (Mundy et al., 1986; Sigman & Ungerer, 1984).

Studies of high-functioning verbal persons with autism suggest that they have considerable ability to define simple emotion terms (VanLacker, Cornelius, & Needleman, 1991). Similarly, when asked to "tell about a time" when they felt various emotions (happy, sad, afraid, proud, and embarrassed), this subgroup of autistic persons related fitting examples (Capps et al., 1992). However, in comparison to normally developing children, autistic children manifested difficulty talking about their own emotional experiences, particularly socially derived emotions such as pride and embarrassment. Autistic children required more time and more prompting, and their accounts seemed tentative and "scripted." For example, a typical autistic child reported feeling proud when, "Well . . . I think . . . when I did something really good," whereas normally developing children said things like "I was proud on Saturday at my baseball game when I caught a really high good pop-up."

Autistic children also displayed limited understanding of the role of other people in eliciting embarrassment. Whereas almost all of the normally developing children referred to an audience in recounting embarrassing experiences, for example, "I was embarrassed when I threw the ball to the wrong team and everybody laughed," autistic children seldom did so, offering responses such as "feeling stupid and afraid." Because the salience of an audience in embarrassing situations is tied to awareness of others' derogatory thoughts and feelings about oneself, this finding is consistent with evidence that young autistic children have trouble monitoring and sharing the attention, attitudes, and emotions of others.

As shown in the aforementioned responses, normally developing children effortlessly recounted stories about emotional experiences, whereas autistic children did not. Further, autistic children's difficulties, at least with simple emotions, cannot be attributed to a limited understanding of the meaning of emotion terms. The ease with which comparison children related emotional experiences is not surprising given that these experiences are stored and remembered in narrative form such that they can be readily accessed and shared in conversations with others. As Bruner and Feldman (1993) have suggested, a lack of ability or inclination to narrate seems central to autistic children's difficulties in communicating about experiences.

Finally, some research has been conducted to see whether autistic people do in fact lack narrative skills. Scopinsky (1986, cited in Bruner & Feldman, 1993) compared the story-telling ability of normal and autistic children by asking each subject to make a story to go along with a short series of pictures. Analyses suggested that autistic subjects simply described the pictures, one after the next, without providing the causal and intentional features of a story. Similarly, in collaboration with Carol Feldman, we have begun a study in which we tell high-functioning adolescents with autism stories of deception, interrupting the readings with "What do you think is going to happen?" followed by "Why do you think that?" Analyses of data from 4 subjects suggests that they were quite able to answer questions about acts of deception. However, when asked to retell the story in their own words, deception did not organize the retelling. Again, the "story" resembled a description (Bruner & Feldman, 1993).

Observations of nonretarded, high-functioning individuals with autism participating in social situations suggest to us that they may use their cognitive abilities to compensate for social-affective impairment (Bruner & Feldman, 1993).[3] This view represents the sense one gets that highly intelligent autistic people struggle to understand social-affective matters

---

[3]This perspective is akin to Hermelin and O'Connor's (1985) *logico-affective hypothesis*.

as if they were solving math problems. Although they are often able to come up with "adequate," albeit strange, accounts of personal and social and personal situations, the process is laborious, operating outside of intuitive notions about how they and others ordinarily feel and think in various situations. Thus, despite diligent, genuine, and often courageous effort, even the most intelligent autistic persons cannot compensate for their limited access to common spaces that are effortlessly entered as experience is given conventional narrative form.

CONCLUSION

Stern's (1985) formulation of the "senses of self" that develop in the first few years of life offers a frame that further connects and consolidates the ideas that have been developed in this chapter. Stern (1989) defined each new sense of self as a "new organizing subjective perspective" (p. 318) that emerges in response to the development and integration of new capacities in cognitive, affective, motivational, and motor domains.

Briefly, as described in the context of dyadic interactions, a "core" sense of self emerges after the second or third month, consisting of a sense of agency, coherence, continuity, and affectivity. At about 9 months a "subjective" sense of self starts to emerge, permitting intersubjectivity and intersubjective exchange, which provide the foundation for joint attention, affective sharing, and social referencing. At 15 months, a "verbal" sense of self emerges, affording self-reflection and symbolic play. Sometime after the second year, the development of new conceptual and linguistic capacities compels another reorganization of the child's subjective perspective, this time in the domain of narrative. This reorganization involves giving narrative form to what has been sensed in different domains of experience; namely agency, coherence, continuity, affectivity, intersubjectivity, and self-reflection.

The "organizing subjective perspective" that emerges through narrative integrates and makes newly accessible the forms of connection or common spaces that the infant experiences from birth. It is this epistemological form, what Stern (1989) called the *narrative self*, that the child builds on for the rest of her life in explaining herself to herself and to others. In so doing, the child simultaneously develops a sense of who she is as an individual, in relation to others, and as part of a shared culture.

Autistic people's limited inclination or ability to narrate is not surprising if the capacity for narrative builds on the impulse to share affective experiences with others, to seek out affective information from others in making sense of ambiguous situations, and to communicate intentionally about topics of shared interest. However, as we have learned from extremely able autistic people who figure out how to interpret emotional expressions and arrive at some sort of understanding of intent, this is not enough. The capacity to experience and understand ourselves, each other, and things in the world as "objects for *us*" seems to depend on a certain predisposition, a common impulse to organize and relate experience in narrative form. The aloneness that is often experienced in interactions with autistic individuals illuminates the critical importance of the push to narrate in establishing and maintaining connections between people.

REFERENCES

Adamson, L., & Bakeman, R. (1986). Infants' conventionalized acts: Gestures and words with mothers and peers. *Infant Behavior and Development, 9*, 215–230.

Ainsworth, M. D. S. (1973). The development of infant–mother attachment. In B. Caldwell & H. Ricciuti (Eds.), *Review of child development research* (Vol. 3, pp. 1–94). Chicago: University of Chicago Press.

Attwood, A., Frith, U., & Hermelin, B. (1988). The understanding and use of interpersonal gestures by autistic and Down syndrome children. *Journal of Autism and Developmental Disorders, 18*, 241–257.

Baltaxe, C. A. M. (1977). Pragmatic deficits in the language of autistic adolescents. *Journal of Pediatric Psychology, 2*, 176–180.

Baron-Cohen, S. (1988). Social and pragmatic deficits in autism: Cognitive or affective? *Journal of Autism and Developmental Disorders, 18*, 379–402.

Baron-Cohen, S. (1989). The autistic child's theory of mind: A case of specific developmental delay. *Journal of Child Psychology and Psychiatry, 30*, 285–297.

Baron-Cohen, S. (1990). Autism: A specific cognitive disorder of "mind-blindness." *International Review of Psychiatry, 2*, 81–90.

Baron-Cohen, S., Leslie, A. M., & Frith, U. (1985). Does the autistic child have a "theory of mind"? *Cognition, 21*, 37–46.

Baron-Cohen, S., Leslie, A. M., & Frith, U. (1986). Mechanical, behavioral, and intentional understanding of picture stories in autistic children. *British Journal of Developmental Psychology, 4*, 113–125.

Brazelton, T. B., Koslowski, B., & Main, M. (1974). The origins of reciprocity: The early mother–infant interaction. In M. Lewis & L. Rosenblum (Eds.), *The effect of the infant on its caregiver* (pp. 49–76). New York: Wiley.

Bretherton, I. (1989). Intentional communication and the development of an understanding of mind. In D. Frye & C. Moore (Eds.), *Children's theories of mind: Mental states and social understanding* (pp. 49–76). Hillsdale, NJ: Lawrence Erlbaum Associates.

Bretherton, I., & Beeghly, M. (1982). Talking about internal states: The acquisition of an explicit theory of mind. *Developmental Psychology, 18*, 906–921.

Bruner, J. S. (1983). *Child's talk*. New York: Norton.

Bruner, J. S. (1990). *Acts of meaning*. Cambridge, MA: Harvard University Press.

Bruner, J. S. (1991, March). Paper presented at the Biennial Meeting of the Society for Research in Child Development, Seattle, WA.

Bruner, J. S., & Feldman, C. F. (1993). Theories of mind and the problem of autism. In S. Baron-Cohen, H. Tager-Flusberg, & D. Cohen (Eds.), *Understanding other minds: Perspectives from autism* (pp. 267–291). Oxford: Oxford University Press.

Bruner, J. S., & Sherwood, V. (1983). Thought language and interaction in infancy. In J. D. Call, E. Galenson, & R. L. Tyson (Eds.), *Frontiers in infant psychiatry* (pp. 38–52). New York: Basic Books.

Butterworth, G. (1990). The ontogeny and phylogeny of joint visual attention. In A. Whiten (Ed.), *Natural theories of mind* (pp. 202–232). Oxford: Basil Blackwell.

Capps, L., Kasari, C., Yirmiya, N., & Sigman, M. (1993). Parent perceptions of emotional expressiveness in children with autism. *Journal of Consulting and Clinical Psychology, 61*, 475–484.

Capps, L., Sigman, M., & Mundy, P. (1994). Attachment security in children with autism. *Development and Psychopathology, 6*, 249–261.

Capps, L., Yirmiya, N., & Sigman, M. (1992). Understanding of simple and complex emotions in non-retarded children with autism. *Journal of Child Psychology and Psychiatry, 33*, 1169–1182.

Cicchetti, D. (Ed.). (1984). *Developmental psychopathology*. Chicago: University of Chicago Press.

Cicchetti, D. (in press). Developmental theory: Lessons from the study of risk and psychopathology. In S. Matthysse, D. Levy, J. Kagan, & F. Benes (Eds.), *Psychopathology: The evolving science of mental disorder*. New York: Cambridge University Press.

Coggins, T. E., Carpenter, R. L., & Owings, N. O. (1983). Examining early intentional communication in Down's syndrome and non-retarded children. *British Journal of Disorders of Communication, 18*, 98–106.

Cole, P. (1986). Children's spontaneous control of facial expression. *Child Development, 57*, 1309–1321.

Curcio, F. (1978). Sensorimotor functioning and communication in mute autistic children. *Journal of Autism and Childhood Schizophrenia, 8*, 282–292.

Dawson, G., Hill, D., Spencer, A., Galpert, L., & Watson, L. (1990). Affective exchanges between young autistic children and their mothers. *Journal of Abnormal Child Psychology, 18*, 335–345.

Dunn, J. (1988). *The beginnings of social understanding*. Cambridge, MA: Harvard University Press.

Dunn, J., & Kendrick, C. (1982). The speech of two and three year olds to infant siblings. *Journal of Child Language, 9*, 579–595.

Dunn, J., & Munn, P. (1987). The development of justification in disputes with mother and with sibling. *Developmental Psychology, 23*, 791–798.

Dunn, J., & Shatz, M. (1989). Becoming a conversationalist despite (or because of) having a sibling. *Child Development, 60*, 399–410.

Eisenberg, N., & Strayer, J. (1989). Critical issues in the study of empathy. In N. Eisenberg & J. Strayer (Eds.), *Empathy and its development* (pp. 3–13). New York: Cambridge University Press.

Emde, R. N., & Harmon, R. J. (1972). Endogenous and exogenous smiling systems in early infancy. *Journal of the American Academy of Child Psychiatry, 11*, 177–200.

Feldman, C. F. (1989). Monologue as problem-solving narrative. In K. Nelson (Ed.), *Narratives from the crib* (pp. 98–122). Cambridge, MA: Harvard University Press.

Feshbach, N. (1982). Sex differences in empathy and social behavior in children. In N. Eisenberg (Ed.), *The development of prosocial behavior* (pp. 315–338). New York: Cambridge University Press.

Fivush, R., & Hudson, J. (1990). What young children remember and why. In R. Fivush & J. Hudson (Eds.), *Knowing and remembering in young children* (pp. 1–9). Cambridge: Cambridge University Press.

Fivush, R., & Slackman, E. A. (1986). The acquisition and development of scripts. In K. Nelson (Ed.), *Event knowledge: Structure and function in development* (pp. 71–96). Hillsdale, NJ: Lawrence Erlbaum Associates.

Frith, U. (1989). *Autism: Explaining the enigma*. Oxford: Blackwell.

Furrow, D. (1984). Social and private speech at 2 years. *Child Development, 55,* 355–362.

Haith, M. M. (1977). Eye contact and face scanning in early infancy. *Science, 198,* 853–855.

Harris, P. (1989). *Children and emotion*. Oxford: Basil Blackwell.

Hayes, A. (1984). Interaction, engagement and the origins of communication: Some constructive concerns. In L. Feagans, C. Garvey, & R. Golinkoff (Eds.), *The origins and growth of communications*. Norwood, NJ: Ablex.

Hermelin, B., & O'Connor, N. (1985). The logico-affective disorder in autism. In E. Schopler & G. B. Mesibov (Eds.), *Communication problems in autism* (pp. 283–310). New York: Plenum.

Hobson, R. P. (1986a). The autistic child's appraisal of expressions of emotion. *Journal of Child Psychology and Psychiatry, 27,* 321–342.

Hobson, R. P. (1986b). The autistic child's appraisal of expression of emotion: A further study. *Journal of Child Psychology and Psychiatry, 27,* 671–680.

Hobson, R. P. (1989). On sharing experiences. *Development and Psychopathology, 1,* 197–203.

Hobson, R. P. (1991). Against the theory of "Theory of Mind." *British Journal of Developmental Psychology, 9,* 33–51.

Hobson, R. P. (1993). Understanding persons: The role of affect. In S. Baron-Cohen, H. Tager-Flusberg, & D. Cohen (Eds.), *Understanding other minds: Perspectives from autism* (pp. 204–227). Oxford: Oxford University Press.

Hobson, R. P., & Lee, A. (1989). Emotion-related and abstract concepts in autistic people: Evidence from the British Picture Vocabulary Scale. *Journal of Autism and Developmental Disorders, 19,* 601–623.

Hobson, R. P., Ouston, J., & Lee, A. (1989). Naming emotions in faces and voices: Abilities and disabilities in autism and mental retardation. *British Journal of Developmental Psychology, 7,* 237–250.

Hudson, J. (1990). The emergence of autobiographical memory in mother–child conversation. In R. Fivush & J. Hudson (Eds.), *Knowing and remembering in young children* (pp. 166–196). Cambridge: Cambridge University Press.

Hurtig, R., Ensrud, S., & Tomblin, J. (1982). The communicative function of question production in autistic children. *Journal of Autism and Developmental Disorders, 12,* 57–69.

Kanner, L. (1943). Autistic disturbances of affective contact. *Nervous Child, 2,* 250.

Kasari, C., Sigman, M., Baumgartener, P., & Stipek, D. (1992). Pride and mastery in children with autism. *Journal of Child Psychology and Psychiatry, 34,* 353–362.

Kasari, C., Sigman, M., Mundy, P., & Yirmiya, N. (1990). Affective sharing in the context of joint attention interactions of normal, autistic, and mentally retarded children. *Journal of Autism and Developmental Disorders, 20,* 87–100.

Klinnert, M. D., Campos, J. J., Sorce, F. J., Emde, R. N., & Svejda, M. J. (1983). Social referencing: Emotional expressions as behavior regulators. In R. Plutchik & H. Kellerman (Eds.), *Emotion: Theory, research and experience* (Vol. 2, pp. 57–86). New York: Academic Press.

Knobloch, J., & Pasamanick, B. (1975). Some etiologic and prognostic factors in early infantile autism and psychosis. *Pediatrics, 55,* 182–191.

Kraemer, G. W. (1992). A psychobiological theory of attachment. *Behavioral and Brain Sciences, 15,* 493–511.

Langdell, T. (1981). *Face perception: An approach to the study of autism*. Unpublished doctoral dissertation, University of London.

Layton, T. L., & Stutts, N. (1985). Pragmatic usage by autistic children under different treatment modes. *Australian Journal of Human Communication Disorders, 13,* 127–142.

Leslie, A. M., & Happe, E. F. (1989). Autism and ostensive communication: The relevance of metarepresentation. *Development and Psychopathology, 1,* 205–212.

Loveland, K., & Landry, S. (1986). Joint attention and language in autism and developmental language delay. *Journal of Autism and Developmental Disorders, 16,* 335–349.

Loveland, K., & Tulani, B. (1991). Social scripts for conversational interactions in autism and Down syndrome. *Journal of Autism and Developmental Disorders, 21,* 177–186.

Loveland, K., Tunali-Kotoski, B., Pearson, D. A., Brelsford, K. A., & Ortegon, J. (1993, March). *Imitation and expression of facial affect in autism.* Paper presented at the Biennial Meeting of the Society for Research in Child Development, New Orleans, LA.

MacDonald, H., Rutter, M., Howlin, P., Rios, P., Le Conteur, A., Evered, C., & Folstein, S. (1989). Recognition and expression of emotional cues by autistic and normal adults. *Journal of Child Psychology & Psychiatry, 30,* 865–877.

Mahler, M. S., Pine, F., & Bergman, A. (1975). *The psychological birth of the infant: Symbiosis and individuation.* New York: Basic Books.

Malatesta, C. Z., & Haviland, J. M. (1982). Learning display rules: The socialization of emotional expression in infancy. *Child Development, 53,* 991–1003.

Mandler, J. (1984). *Stories, scripts, and scenes: Aspects of schema theory.* Hillsdale, NJ: Lawrence Erlbaum Associates.

McCabe, A., & Peterson, C. (Eds.). (1991). *Developing narrative structure.* Hillsdale, NJ: Lawrence Erlbaum Associates.

Mead, G. H. (1934). *Mind, self, and society.* Chicago: University of Chicago Press.

Meltzoff, A., & Moore, M. K. (1977). Imitation of facial and manual gestures by human neonates. *Science, 198,* 75–78.

Miller, P., & Sperry, L. (1987). The socialization of anger and aggression. *Merrill–Palmer Quarterly, 33,* 1–31.

Mirenda, P. L., Donnellan, A., & Yoder, D. E. (1983). Gaze behavior: A new look at an old problem. *Journal of Autism and Developmental Disorders, 13,* 397–409.

Mundy, P., & Sigman, M. (1989). The theoretical implications of joint attention deficits in autism. *Development and Psychopathology, 1,* 173–183.

Mundy, P., Sigman, M., & Kasari, C. (1990). A longitudinal study of joint attention and language development in autistic children. *Journal of Autism and Developmental Disorders, 20,* 115–123.

Mundy, P., Sigman, M., Ungerer, J. A., & Sherman, T. (1986). Defining the social deficits in autism: The contribution of non-verbal communication measures. *Journal of Child Psychology and Psychiatry, 27,* 657–669.

Nelson, K. (1986). *Event knowledge: Structure and function in development.* Hillsdale, NJ: Lawrence Erlbaum Associates.

Nelson, K. (Ed.). (1989). *Narratives from the crib.* Cambridge, MA: Harvard University Press.

Newson, E., Dawson, M., & Everard, P. (1984). The natural history of able autistic people: Their management in social context. Summary of the report to the DHSS in four parts. *Communication, 18,* 1–4.

Ochs, E. (1986). From feelings to grammar. In B. Schieffelin & E. Ochs (Eds.), *Language socialization across cultures* (pp. 251–272). Cambridge: Cambridge University Press.

Ochs, E., & Schieffelin, B. (1984). Language acquisition and socialization: Three developmental stories. In R. Schweder & R. LeVine (Eds.), *Culture theory: Essays on mind, self and emotion* (pp. 276–320). Cambridge: Cambridge University Press.

Ochs, E., & Schieffelin, B. (1989). Language has a heart. *Text, 9,* 7–25.

Ornitz, E. M., Guthrie, D., & Farley, A. H. (1977). The early development of autistic children. *Journal of Autism and Childhood Schizophrenia, 7,* 207–230.

Ozonoff, S., Pennington, B., & Rogers, S. J. (1990). Are there emotion perception deficits in young autistic children? *Journal of Child Psychology and Psychiatry, 31*(3), 343–361.

Paul, R. (1987). Communication. In D. Cohen, A. Donnellan, & R. Paul (Eds.), *Handbook of autism and pervasive developmental disorders* (pp. 117–141). New York: Wiley.

Paul, R., & Cohen, D. (1985). Comprehension of indirect requests in adults with autistic disorders and mental retardation. *Journal of Speech and Hearing Research, 28,* 475–479.

Peterson, C., & McCabe, A. (1983). *Developmental psycholinguistics: Three ways of looking at a child's narrative.* New York: Plenum.

Premack, D., & Woodruff, G. (1978). Does the chimpanzee have a "theory of mind"? *Behavior and Brain Sciences, 4,* 515–526.

Prior, M., Dahlstrom, B., & Squires, T. (1990). Autistic children's knowledge of thinking and feeling states in other people. *Journal of Child Psychology & Psychiatry, 31,* 587–601.

Radke-Yarrow, M., Zahn-Waxler, C., & Chapman, M. (1983). Children's prosocial dispositions and behavior. In P. Mussen (Series Ed.) & E. M. Hetherington (Vol. Ed.), *Handbook of child psychology: Vol. 4. Socialization, personality, and social development* (4th ed., pp. 469–546). New York: Wiley.

Ricks, D. M. (1979). Making sense of experience to make sensible sounds. In M. Bullowa (Ed.), *Before speech: The beginning of interpersonal communication* (pp. 245–268). Cambridge: Cambridge University Press.

Rogers, S. J., Ozonoff, S., & Maslin-Cole, C. (1991). A comparative study of attachment behavior in young children with autism or other psychiatric disorders. *Journal of the American Academy of Child Adolescent Psychiatry, 30,* 483–488.

Rom, A., & Bliss, L. S. (1981). A comparison of verbal communication skills of language impaired and normal speaking children. *British Journal of Communication Disorders, 14,* 133–140.

Rutter, M. (1978). Diagnosis and definition. In M. Rutter & E. Schopler (Eds.), *Autism: A reappraisal of concepts and treatment* (pp. 1–25). New York: Plenum.

Saarni, C. (1979). Children's understanding of display rules for expressive behavior. *Developmental Psychology, 15,* 424–429.

Sagi, A., & Hoffman, M. L. (1976). Empathic distress in the newborn. *Developmental Psychology, 12,* 175–176.

Sander, L. (1975). Infant and caretaking environment: Investigation and conceptualization of adaptive behavior in a system of increasing complexity. In E. J. Anthony (Ed.), *Explorations in child psychiatry* (pp. 129–166). New York: Plenum.

Scaife, M., & Bruner, J. (1975). The capacity for joint visual attention in the infant. *Nature, 253,* 265–266.

Scanlon-Jones, S., Collins, K., & Hong, H. W. (1991). An audience effect on smile production in 10-month-old infants. *Psychological Science, 2,* 45–49.

Schieffelin, B. (1986). Teasing and shaming in Kaluli children's interactions. In B. Schieffelin & E. Ochs (Eds.), *Language socialization across cultures* (pp. 165–181). Cambridge: Cambridge University Press.

Schieffelin, B., & Ochs, E. (Eds.). (1986). *Language socialization across cultures.* Cambridge: Cambridge University Press.

Schopler, E., & Mesibov, G. (Eds.). (1985). *Communication problems in autism.* New York: Plenum.

Shapiro, R., Sherman, M., Calamari, G., & Koch, D. (1987). Attachment in autism and other developmental disorders. *Journal of the American Academy of Child Adolescent Psychiatry, 26,* 485–490.

Sigman, M., Kasari, C., Kwon, J., & Yirmiya, N. (1992). Responses to the negative emotions of others by autistic, mentally retarded, and normal children. *Child Development, 63,* 796–807.

Sigman, M., & Mundy, P. (1989). Social attachments in autistic children. *Journal of the American Academy of Child Adolescent Psychiatry, 28,* 74–81.

Sigman, M., Mundy, P., Sherman, T., & Ungerer, J. (1986). Social interactions of autistic, mentally retarded, and normal children and their caregivers. *Journal of Child Psychology and Psychiatry, 27,* 647–656

Sigman, M., & Siegel, D. (1992). The interface between the psychobiological and cognitive models of attachment. *Behavioral and Brain Sciences, 15,* 523–524.

Sigman, M., & Ungerer, J. (1984). Attachment behaviors in autistic children. *Journal of Autism and Developmental Disorders, 14,* 231–244.

Sroufe, A. (1977). *Knowing and enjoying your baby.* New York: Spectrum.

Sroufe, A. (1989). Relationships, self and individual adaptation. In A. J. Sameroff & R. N. Emde (Eds.), *Relationship disturbances in early childhood* (pp. 70–96). New York: Basic Books.

Stern, D. (1974). The goal structure of mother–infant play. *Journal of the American Academy of Child Psychology, 13,* 402–421.

Stern, D. (1977). *The first relationship: Infant and mother.* Cambridge, MA: Harvard University Press.

Stern, D. (1985). *The interpersonal world of the infant: A view from psychoanalysis and developmental psychology.* New York: Basic Books.

Stern, D. (1989). Crib monologues from a psychoanalytic perspective. In K. Nelson (Ed.), *Narratives from the crib* (pp. 309–320). Cambridge, MA: Harvard University Press.

Tager-Flusberg, H. (1992). Autistic children's talk about psychological states: Deficits in the early acquisition of a theory of mind. *Child Development, 63,* 161–172.

Tager-Flusberg, H. (1993). What language reveals about the understanding of minds in children with autism. In S. Baron-Cohen, H. Tager-Flusberg, & D. Cohen (Eds.), *Understanding other minds: Perspectives from autism* (pp. 138–157). Oxford: Oxford University Press.

Taylor, C. (1985). *Human agency and language.* Cambridge: Cambridge University Press.

Taylor, C. (1989). *Sources of the self.* Cambridge, MA: Harvard University Press.

Thompson, R. A. (1987). Empathy and emotional understanding: The early development of empathy. In N. Eisenberg & J. Strayer (Eds.), *Empathy and its development* (pp. 119–145). New York: Cambridge University Press.

Ungerer, J., & Sigman, M. (1981). Symbolic play and language comprehension in autistic children. *Journal of the American Academy of Child Psychiatry, 20,* 318–327.

van Kleeck, A., & Frankel, T. L. (1981). Discourse devices by language disordered children. *Journal of Speech and Hearing Disorders, 46,* 250–257.

VanLacker, D., Cornelius, C., & Needleman, R. (1991). Comprehension of verbal terms for emotions in normal, autistic, and schizophrenic children. *Developmental Neuropsychology, 7,* 1–18.

Weeks, S. J., & Hobson, R. P. (1987). The salience of facial expression for autistic children. *Journal of Child Psychology and Psychiatry, 28,* 137–152.

Wellman, H., & Lempers, J. D. (1977). The naturalistic communicative abilities of 2-year-olds. *Child Development, 48,* 1052–1057.

Wetherby, A. M., & Prutting, C. A. (1984). Profiles of communicative and cognitive–social abilities in autistic children. *Journal of Speech and Hearing Research, 27,* 367–377.

Wing, L., & Gould, J. (1979). Severe impairments of social interaction and associated abnormalities in children: Epidemiology and classification. *Journal of Autism and Developmental Disorders, 9,* 11–29.

Yarczower, M., & Daruns, L. (1982). Social inhibition of spontaneous facial expressions in children. *Journal of Personality & Social Psychology, 43,* 831–837.

Yirmiya, N., Kasari, C., Sigman, M., & Mundy, P. (1989). Facial expression of affect in autistic, mentally retarded, and normal children. *Journal of Child Psychology & Psychiatry, 30,* 725–735.

Yirmiya, N., Sigman, M., Kasari, C., & Mundy, P. (1992). Empathy and cognition in high-functioning children with autism. *Child Development, 63,* 150–160.

Zahn-Waxler, C., & Radke-Yarrow, M. (1982). Peers and prosocial development. In K. H. Rubin & H. S. Ross (Eds.), *Peer relationships and social skills in childhood* (pp. 133–162). New York: Springer-Verlag.

Zahn-Waxler, C., Radke-Yarrow, M., & King, R. A. (1979). Child rearing and children's prosocial initiations toward victims of distress. *Child Development, 48,* 319–330.

Insights Concerning the Cerebral Basis of Emotion Based on Studies of Mood Disorders in Patients with Brain Injury

Robert G. Robinson
Sergio Paradiso
The University of Iowa College of Medicine

INTRODUCTION

Understanding the cerebral basis of emotion is an important aspect of mind–brain relationships that remains in its infancy. At the present time, we have only begun to understand which brain structures are involved in emotional activation. A recent study by Pardo, Pardo, and Raichle (1993) examined four men and three women for changes in regional cerebral blood flow (CBF) measured by 15-oxygen water technique and positron emission tomography. Subjects were asked to recall situations that would make them very sad just before measurements were taken of regional CBF. Results demonstrated that all subjects reported subjective experiences of sadness (mean visual analog scale score was 8 ± 0.9 SD on a scale of 1 [*happy*] to 10 [*most sad*]). Comparison of control resting CBF with that measured during the sad emotion condition showed increases in inferior-frontal and orbital-frontal blood flow during the sad condition bilaterally in women but predominantly left-sided in men. Although the intensity of subjective experience of emotion varied from one person to the next, it suggests an important role of inferior- and orbital-frontal cortex in normal emotional cognitive processes. Many issues, however, remain to be explained, such as whether these changes in the CBF reflect mood processing alone or mood-associated language processing, whether these metabolic changes are a cause or a consequence of emotion, and how they relate to other brain processes involved in our conscious perception of mood.

Abnormalities of blood flow in prefrontal cortex, and particularly left frontal cortex, have been reported in patients with major depression (Drevets et al., 1992; Uytdenhoef et al., 1983). Furthermore, numerous studies have also demonstrated abnormalities in metabolic activity as measured by 18-flurodeoxyglucose utilization and positron emission tomography (PET) imaging in left prefrontal cortex among patients with depressive disorders (Baxter et al., 1989; Martinot et al., 1990). Thus, previous studies examining normal emotional state or syndromic depressive disorder have demonstrated abnormalities of brain metabolic activity and blood flow particularly in left lateral and orbitofrontal cortex.

Since the pioneering work of Papez (1937) and MacLean (1952), emotional functions have been attributed to a set of neuroanatomic structures called the *limbic system*. This system is composed of several highly interconnected structures that have sometimes been divided into a medial and a ventral lateral component. The medial component (the limbic system as described by Papez) forms a circular set of structures that includes the hippocampal formation, the entorhinal cortex, the fornix, the anterior, posterior, and retrosplenial cingulate cortex, mammillary bodies, and the anterior thalamic nuclei. The ventral lateral component of the limbic system includes the olfactory and para-olfactory cortex, the amygdaloid complex, the temporal polar cortex, the anterior and posterior orbital frontal cortex, the limbic areas of the insular cortex, the ventral striatum, and the dorsal medial thalamic nuclei (see Figure 11.1). Findings from

Ventral Lateral Limbic Circuit

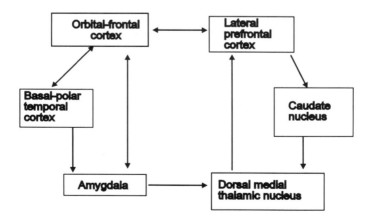

FIG. 11.1. The brain structures that have been hypothesized to play an important role in human emotion. Arrows indicate the direction of efferent connections. All pathways converge on the dorsal medial thalamic nucleus that projects to prefrontal cortex.

the studies of depressed mood or depressive disorder subjects cited here earlier have generally reported abnormalities in structures included in the ventral lateral limbic circuit, including the amygdala, thalamus, and basal ganglia (Drevets et al., 1992).

In addition to the studies of emotion in patients with primary (i.e., no known brain pathology) mood disorders and normals, studies of emotion using patients or animals with brain lesions have been traditional means of assessing the anatomic substrates of behavior and emotion. For example, lesions of the ventral anterior aspect of the temporal lobe (including the amygdala and hippocampus) in primates and humans have been associated with the Kluver–Bucy syndrome (i.e., visual agnosia, hyperorality, hypersexuality, and emotional placidity; Cummings & Duchen, 1981; Lilly, Cummings, & Benson, 1983). Studies of patients with orbitofrontal damage have demonstrated socially inappropriate behavior, poor judgment, and poor decision making in spite of preserved general intellectual ability (Eslinger & Damasio, 1985).

Over the past 10 years, we have been reporting on the use of the lesion technique to study the cerebral basis of mood disorders by examining patients with stroke or traumatic brain injury. These studies have provided insights concerning the morphological structures that play an important role in emotion. This chapter discusses some of our findings as well as implications of these findings for understanding the cerebral basis of one type of emotion, that is, mood. We examine the brain structures associated with the elevation of mood seen in mania and the decline in mood seen in depression as revealed by the study of patients with brain injury due to stroke or trauma.

POSTSTROKE DEPRESSION

Prevalence

Depression is probably the most common emotional disorder associated with focal brain injury. Investigators who have utilized structured psychiatric interviews and established diagnostic criteria have usually identified at least two forms of depressive disorder associated with brain injury. One type is major depression, which is defined by *DSM–III* or *DSM–III–R* criteria (excluding the criteria that precludes an organic factor). Under the new *DSM–IV* criteria, patients who meet the symptom criteria and the 2-week duration criteria for major depression will receive this diagnosis regardless of whether the condition is primary (i.e., without known neuropathology) or secondary (i.e., associated with and thought to be the result of some structural abnormality). The second type of depression seen in patients with brain lesions is dysthymic depression. This condition is defined by *DSM–III–R* criteria (usually excluding the 2-year duration criteria and no organic factor criteria). Under the *DSM–IV* classification, patients with brain injury may have a diagnosis of dys-thymic disorder if the condition has lasted more than 2 years. Other diagnostic categories that are appropriate for patients with structural injury and depression are adjustment disorder with depressed mood or adjustment disorder with depressed mood and anxiety.

The prevalence of these depressions varies depending on the time since brain injury, the availabity of social support, and the severity of impair-ment, as well as the nature and location of the brain lesion (Astrom, Adolfsson, & Asplund, 1993; Morris, Robinson, Raphael, & Bishop, 1991; Robinson, Bolduc, & Price, 1987). In a study of 103 consecutive patients admitted to hospital with acute cerebrovascular lesions who were capable of undergoing a verbal interview, we found that 27% met symptom criteria for major depression and 20% met symptom criteria for dysthymic (minor) depression (termed minor depression because the 2-year criteria was not met; Robinson, Starr, Kubos, & Price, 1983). Studies of patients with cerebrovascular lesions conducted by other investigators have also reported similar frequencies of major and minor depression ranging from 10–40% of the population studied (Astrom et al., 1993; Eastwood, Rifat, Nobbs, & Ruderman, 1989).

Similarly, studies of patients with brain injury produced by trauma have reported depressive disorders ranging from 10–40%. We reported among 66 patients admitted to the hospital with acute closed head injury but without significant spinal-cord or other organ-system injury that 17 (26%) met diagnostic criteria for major depression and 2 (3%) met symp-tom criteria for minor (dysthymic) depression (Fedoroff et al., 1992).

In summary, studies of patients with brain injury produced either by trauma or cerebral infarction have demonstrated frequencies of major depression of about 20–25%. There does not appear to be any significant difference in the frequency of major depression depending on whether the brain injury is due to cerebral infarction or trauma.

Relationship to Location of Brain Injury

We have conducted a series of studies examining the association between location of brain injury and frequency of major or minor depressive disorder. In a study of a consecutive series of 36 patients admitted to hospital with a first-time stroke and no risk factors for depression (i.e., no previous personal or family history of mood disorder), we found that 14 of 22 patients with left-hemisphere injury had either major or minor depression compared with only 2 of 14 patients with right-hemisphere lesions (p < .01; Robinson, Kubos, Starr, Rao, & Price, 1984). This study suggested that depressive mood may be associated with abnormality of left-hemisphere function. In another study of 45 patients with single lesions restricted to either cortical or subcortical structures in the right or left hemisphere, we reported that 44% of patients with left cortical lesions (N = 16) and 39% of patients with left subcortical lesions (N = 13) were depressed (see Figure 11.2). This contrasted with findings in patients with right-hemisphere injury in which only 11% of those with right cortical injury (N = 9) and 14% of those with right subcortical lesions (N = 7) were depressed (p < .05; Starkstein, Robinson, & Price, 1987).

When patients were further divided into those with anterior and posterior lesions, all 5 patients with left cortical anterior lesions involving the left dorsolateral frontal cortex had depression as compared to 2 of 11 patients with left cortical posterior lesions (parietal–occipital; p < .01; Starkstein, Robinson, & Price, 1987). Basal ganglia lesions (caudate and/or internal capsule and putamen) produced major depression in 7 of 8 patients with left-sided lesions and only 1 of 7 patients with right-sided lesions (see Figure 11.3). None of the patients with left (N = 6) or right (N = 4) thalamic lesions showed poststroke depression (p < .001). Similar findings have recently been reported by Astrom et al. (1993) and Herrmann, Bartles, and Wallesch (1993). These findings are consistent with the suggestion that left-hemisphere dysfunction plays an important role in depressed mood but also suggest that left frontal cortex and left

Percentage of Patients with Major and Minor Depression

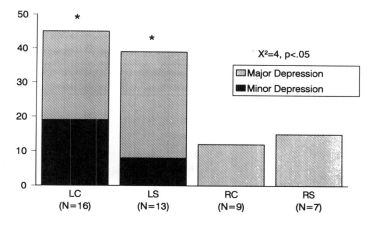

FIG. 11.2. The percent of patients with left cortical (LC), left subcortical (LS), right cortical (RC), or right subcortical (RS) stroke lesions visible on CT scan who had major or minor depression during the acute period following stroke.

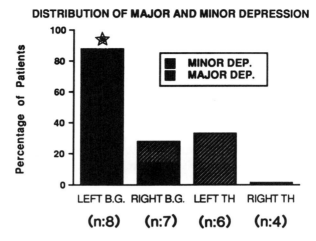

FIG. 11.3. The percent of patients with basal ganglia (BG) or thalamic (Th) stroke lesions visible on CT scan who had major or minor depression during the acute period following stroke.

basal ganglia (particularly caudate) are important structures in this mood abnormality.

Although studies of lesion location in patients with traumatic brain injury (TBI) are more difficult because of the diffuse and varied nature of the focal lesions (bleeds, shear injury, or contusion), we have also examined the relationship of depression to lesion location in these patients. Of the 66 TBI patients previously described, 42 (64%) had diffuse patterns of brain injury on their CT/MRI scans and 24 (36%) presented with focal lesions (Fedoroff et al., 1992). There were no significant differences between the major depressed and nondepressed groups in the frequency of diffuse or focal patterns of injury. In addition, no significant differences were found in the frequency of extraparenchymal hemorrhages, contusions, intracerebral or intraventricular hemorrhages, hydrocephalus or CT scan findings suggestive of brain atrophy. There was, however, a significant association between lesion location and the development of major depression. Using a logistic regression analysis to examine independent effects of each area of brain injury, the strongest correlate of major depression was left dorsolateral frontal cortex or left basal ganglia lesion location (see Figure 11.4). These results are consistent with our previously described findings in patients with stroke and suggest that left frontal cortex and left basal ganglia may play an important role in mood regulation.

Perhaps the most consistent finding related to depression and lesion location has been the correlation of depressive symptoms with distance of the lesion from the frontal pole. In 1981, we first reported that, in a

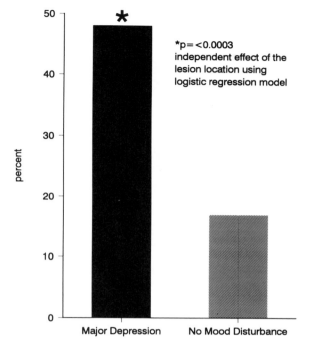

*p= <0.0003
independent effect of the
lesion location using
logistic regression model

Left Dorsal Lateral Frontal Cortex or Basal Ganglia Lesions

FIG. 11.4. The percent of patients who had major depression or no mood disturbance following traumatic brain injury who had lesions demonstrable on CT scan involving the left dorsal lateral frontal cortex or left basal ganglia. Using logistic regression, the independent effect of these lesions on the existence of major depression was significantly greater than any other lesion location. This finding is similar to the lesion locations associated with poststroke depression.

group of 29 patients with left-hemisphere lesions produced by either stroke or TBI, there was an inverse correlation between the severity of depression and distance of the anterior border of the lesion from the frontal pole measured on CT scan ($r = -.76$, $p < .001$; Robinson & Szetela, 1981) (see Figure 11.5). Since then, using CT scan imaging, we have reported the same phenomena in another group of 10 patients with single stroke lesions of the anterior left hemisphere ($r = -.92$, $p < .001$; Robinson et al., 1984) and in patients with purely cortical lesions of the left hemisphere ($N = 16$; $r = -.52$, $p < .05$; Starkstein et al., 1987) or purely subcortical lesions of the left hemisphere ($N = 13$; $r = -.68$, $p < .01$; Starkstein, Robinson, & Price, 1987; see Figure 11.3).

This phenomenon has now been replicated by 4 different groups of investigators using patients from Canada (Eastwood et al., 1989; Sinyor

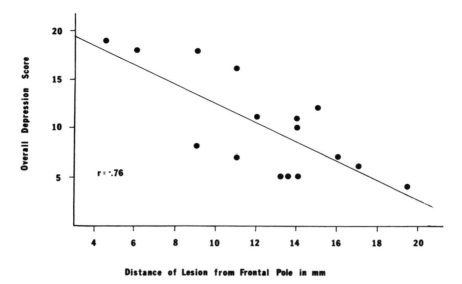

FIG. 11.5. The relationship between severity of depression as measured by combining the Zung depression, Hamilton depression, and visual analogue depression scores and the distance of the anterior border of the brain lesion (as measured on CT scan) lesion from the frontal pole. Patients had either stroke or TBI lesions. Depressive symptoms increased in severity as the lesion was closer to the frontal pole. From Robinson and Szetela (1981). Copyright 1981 by Little Brown. Reprinted with permission.

et al., 1986), England (House, Dennis, Warlow, Hawton, & Molyneux, 1990), and Australia (Morris, Robinson, & Raphael, 1992). Some of these investigators have found a significant correlation between severity of depressive symptoms and proximity of the lesion to the frontal pole in both right- and left-hemisphere lesion groups (House et al., 1990), while others have found a significant correlation only in the left-hemisphere lesion group (Eastwood et al., 1989; Morris et al., 1992). Longitudinal studies have found that this correlation between the proximity of the lesion to the frontal pole and severity of depression is strongest during the first 6 poststroke months, suggesting that this phenomenon is a dynamic one that changes over time (Parikh, Justice, Moran, & Robinson, 1988). Although there is some discrepancy between studies concerning the amount of variance in severity of depression that may be explained by lesion location, this phenomenon has emerged as one of the most consistent and robust clinical–pathological correlations ever described in neuropsychiatry.

We have suggested that this clinical–pathological correlation may be related to the underlying anatomy of the biogenic amine pathways in the cortex (Robinson et al., 1984). As lesions are closer to the frontal pole or more anterior in the basal ganglia, the ascending biogenic amine pathways, originating in the brain stem nuclei and containing norepinephrine and serotonin, are interrupted more proximal to their parent cell bodies. This hypothesis is explained in greater detail in the section on mechanism of depression.

In summary, studies of lesion location in patients with focal injury produced by brain infarction or traumatic brain injury have consistently demonstrated that left frontal cortex and left basal ganglia are associated with a high frequency of major depression. In addition, there is a provocative linear correlation between the proximity of injury to the frontal pole and severity of depressive symptoms in both cortical and subcortical lesion patients, suggesting that an underlying neurophysiological dysfunction (e.g., biogenic amine neurotransmission) important in depression is distributed in a continuous fashion across cortical and subcortical brain regions. Disruption of this function (e.g., neurotransmission) in frontal and basal ganglia structures may play an important role in the mechanism of depression.

These findings are also consistent with those reported in patients with primary depression and PET scan imaging in which blood-flow changes or glucose metabolic changes of the left prefrontal cortex have been associated with depression. These findings also support the hypothesis that the ventral lateral limbic system, including frontal cortex, basal ganglia, temporal cortex, and dorsomedial thalamus may play an important role in mediating the emotion of depression.

Longitudinal Course of Depression

The longitudinal course of major depression following stroke has been investigated by Robinson et al. (1987), Morris, Robinson, and Raphael (1990), and Astrom et al. (1993). In a 2-year follow up of 103 acute stroke patients, we reported that most of the 26% of patients with in-hospital major depression had recovered by 1 year poststroke and all of the patients had recovered by 2 years poststroke. Minor depression, however, had a more variable and less favorable prognosis. By 2 years follow-up, only 30% of the original group of acute stroke patients with minor depression had recovered. Approximately half of the original minor depression patients who remained depressed had developed major depression, whereas the rest continued to have minor depressive disorder.

Among a group of 99 patients in a stroke rehabilitation hospital, Morris et al. (1990) found that major depression had a mean duration of 40 weeks. In contrast, minor depression had a mean duration of only 12 weeks. Astrom et al. (1993) found that 8 of 14 patients with major depression at the time of the initial in-hospital evaluation had recovered by 1 year follow-up. However, among those who were still depressed at 1 year, only 1 of 6 had recovered by 3 years follow-up.

Thus, studies of the longitudinal course of major depression following stroke have identified a natural history of slightly under one year for the duration of major depression. Minor depression appears to have a more variable course with some patients developing chronic depressive disorder that may evolve into major depression, whereas others spontaneously remit and follow the course expected of a more short-term adjustment disorder.

We have recently reported on the 1-year longitudinal course of 66 patients previously described with acute traumatic brain injury (Jorge et al., 1993). Of the original 66 patients evaluated with acute TBI, 54 were reevaluated at 3 months, 43 at 6 months, and 43 at 1 year. The overall prevalence of major depression was 26% in-hospital, 30% at 3 months, 26% at 6 months, and 26% at 1 year. The mean duration of depression was 4.7 months. There were, however, patients with transient depressions ($N = 7$) lasting an average of 1.5 months, and patients with long-term depressions ($N = 9$) who had a mean duration of 7 months (Jorge et al., 1993). The patients with transient depressions were significantly more likely than prolonged depressed patients and nondepressed patients to have a left dorsolateral frontal cortical or left basal ganglia lesion location ($p = .006$), whereas patients with prolonged depression were significantly more likely than transient depressed patients and nondepressed patients to have impaired social functioning ($p = .01$).

The fact that the duration of depression was significantly longer for patients with brain infarction as compared to those with traumatic brain injury probably reflects differences in the nature of the brain injury as well as the variety of etiological disorders subsumed under the category of major depression. Traumatic brain injury produces contusions, shear injury, and hemorrhagic lesions that may lead to more axonal regeneration and recovery of function than ischemic lesions, which lead to permanent neuronal loss with less axonal sprouting and neuronal regeneration. Thus, we have hypothesized that short-term depressions associated with traumatic brain injury result from disruption of strategic brain structures that play an important role in mood regulation (Jorge et al., 1993). Major depression associated with stroke, however, may be more prolonged because of the more permanent neuronal damage produced by these vascular lesions.

Although there is a difference in the duration of major depression associated with stroke and traumatic brain injury, the association of left frontal cortical and left basal ganglia lesions with depression is a consistent finding. This suggests that left dorsolateral frontal cortex and left basal ganglia are important structures in the production or regulation of mood and that differences in the longitudinal course of these disorders may be explained by differences in the nature of the brain injury itself.

Relationship to Impairment

Although many clinicians have assumed that the most powerful determinant of depression after brain injury is the associated physical or cognitive impairment, empirical studies have consistently failed to show a strong relationship between severity of depression and severity of physical impairment (Eastwood et al., 1989; Morris et al., 1990; Robinson et al., 1983). This is not to say, however, that there is no relationship between severity of impairment and severity of depression. Numerous studies have demonstrated that severity of physical impairment is one of several factors that are correlated with depression and in some populations may be an important contributing factor (Astrom et al., 1993; Eastwood et al., 1989).

Similarly, studies of patients with traumatic brain injury have reported a weak but significant relationship between severity of physical impairment and severity of depression (Bornstein, Miller, & VanSchoor, 1989; Prigatano, 1986). In our study of 66 patients with TBI, we found no significant association between the existence of major depression and severity of intellectual impairment as measured by the Mini-Mental State Examination or physical impairment as measured by activities of daily living (Fedoroff et al., 1992).

In patients with stroke, we have found an intriguing relationship between cognitive impairment and major depression. In a study comparing patients with and without major depression who were matched for size and location of brain injury, we found that patients with major depression had significantly lower (more impaired) Mini-Mental State Examination scores than patients who did not have major depression (Starkstein, Robinson, & Price, 1988). In a subsequent study examining another group of patients and using an extensive neuropsychological test battery, we found that the neuropsychological tasks of orientation, language, visuoconstructional ability, executive motor functions, and frontal lobe tasks were significantly more impaired in patients with major depression following left-hemisphere lesions than patients with comparable-sized lesions of the left hemisphere who were not depressed (Bolla-Wilson, Robinson, Starkstein, Boston, & Price, 1989). In contrast to this significant impairment in cognitive function associated with major depression and left-hemisphere lesions, patients with right-hemisphere lesions and major depression were not significantly different in their performance on a wide-range neuropsychological battery than patients without depression and comparable lesions of the right hemisphere.

In a recent follow-up study, Downhill and Robinson (1994) found that patients with major depression had more severe intellectual impairment than nondepressed patients at 3, 6, and 12 months following stroke, but only among patients with left-hemisphere lesions. Among patients with right-hemisphere lesions, there was no significant difference in Mini-Mental State Examination scores between patients with major depression and no depression. The effect of depression on cognitive function was greatest during the acute poststroke period and declined in its effect during the 3, 6, and 12 month follow-ups (see Figure 11.6). By 2 years poststroke, there was no effect even among patients with left-hemisphere lesions.

These findings suggest that left-hemisphere lesions, particularly left dorsolateral frontal cortex and left basal ganglia lesions may provoke a different pathophysiology of depression than comparable lesions of the right hemisphere. In other words, left-hemisphere lesions may produce a dementia of depression that does not occur in patients with major depression following right-hemisphere lesions because right- and left-hemisphere lesions produce major depression through different mechanisms. Thus, this dementia of depression may result from neurophysiological or neurochemical responses to left-hemisphere injury. These findings are also

At initial evaluation

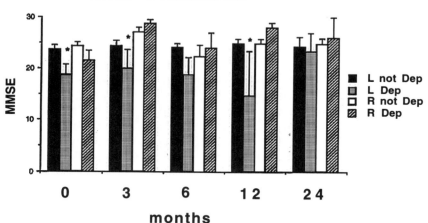

FIG. 11.6. The Mini-Mental State Exam (MMSE) scores of patients who had major depression (dep) or no mood disorder (not-dep) divided by hemisphere of stroke (R or L) in-hospital and over 2 years follow-up. Although some patients no longer had depression at follow-up, cognitive function was significantly more impaired in patients with major depression following left- but not right-hemisphere stroke. The effect lasted for about 1 year. From Downhill and Robinson (1994). Copyright 1994 by Williams and Wilkins. Reprinted with permission.

consistent with the suggestion that the left ventrolateral limbic circuit plays an important role in cognitive function as well as mood regulation.

Finally, although the relationship between severity of physical impairment and severity of depression did not appear to be closely correlated (at least during the initial in-hospital evaluation), we did find an interesting and significant influence of depression on recovery in activities of daily living (Parikh et al., 1990). Patients with a diagnosis of major or minor depression during the acute inpatient evaluation ($N = 25$) were compared with patients having no mood disorder in the hospital and no mood disorder at any time during a 2-year follow-up. Both groups, however, were comparable in their impairment of activities of daily living during the in-hospital evaluation ($N = 38$). After controlling for all variables that have been shown to influence poststroke recovery in daily activities such as acute treatment on a stroke unit, size, nature, and location of the brain injury, age, education, and duration of rehabilitation services, patients with in-hospital depression (major or minor) were found to have a significantly poorer recovery at 2 years follow-up than nondepressed stroke patients. At 2 years follow-up, however, most of the in-hospital depressions had subsided and there was no difference in severity of depression between the two groups. This suggests that even when the in-hospital depression was over, patients may have lost a "critical period" for recovery and do not catch up to their nondepressed peers. The relationship between depression and severity of physical impairment following stroke thus appears to be a complex one in which there may be some influence of severity of impairment on the severity of depression but also an important effect of the depression on the ability of the patient to recover in their daily activities following stroke.

Mechanism of Depression

Although the causes of depression following brain injury are not known, we have hypothesized that disruption of biogenic amine containing pathways by brain lesions may play an etiological role in some depressions (Robinson et al., 1984). Noradrenergic and serotonergic cell bodies located in the brain stem send ascending projections through the median forebrain bundle and basal ganglia to the frontal cortex. The ascending axons then arc posteriorly and run longitudinally through the deep layers of cortex arborizing and sending terminal projections into the superficial cortical layers (Morrison, Molliver, & Grzanna, 1979). Lesions that disrupt these pathways in the frontal cortex or basal ganglia may affect many downstream fibers. Based on the anatomy of these biogenic amine pathways and the clinical finding that severity of depression correlates with proximity of the lesion to the frontal pole, we hypothesized that depression may be a consequence of severe depletions of norepinephrine and/or serotonin produced by lesions in strategic locations of the frontal cortex or basal ganglia.

Supporting this hypothesis, some investigators have shown in rats that biogenic amines are depleted in response to cortical lesions (Finkelstein et al., 1983). Our research found that right-hemisphere lesions produced depletions of norepinephrine and accompanying increases in locomotor activity, whereas identical lesions of the left hemisphere did not produce either the biochemical or the behavioral change (Robinson, 1979). We have also reported that, in patients with stroke lesions of the right hemisphere, there was a significantly greater amount of spiperone binding (predominantly 5–HT2 receptor binding) in noninjured temporal and parietal cortex compared to patients with comparable lesions of the left hemisphere ($p < .05$; Mayberg et al., 1988). Furthermore, among patients with left-hemisphere lesions, there was a significant inverse correlation between the amount of spiperone binding in the left temporal cortex and depression scores; that is, higher depression scores were associated with lower serotonin receptor binding ($p < .05$). We have also found in rats that right-hemisphere lesions produced an increase in cortical spiperone binding (ketserin was used to show this was 5–HT2 receptor binding) that did not occur following an identical left-hemisphere lesion (Mayberg, Moran, & Robinson, 1990).

Based on these findings, we have hypothesized that brain injury produces a greater depletion of biogenic amines in patients with right-hemisphere lesions as compared to those with left-hemisphere lesions. This depletion could trigger a compensatory up-regulation of sertonin receptors that might protect against depression. On the other hand, patients with left-hemisphere lesions may have moderate depletions of biogenic amines but without a compensatory upregulation of 5HT receptors. This relative depletion could, therefore, lead to dysfunction of the serotonergic system in the left hemisphere. This dysfunction ultimately may lead to the clinical manifestations of depression. Although similar PET scan studies have not been done in patients with traumatic brain injury, the finding that short-term depressions are associated with lesions of left frontal cortex and left basal ganglia in patients with traumatic brain injury suggests that similar mechanisms may be involved in both stroke and trauma.

Mania Following Brain Injury

Mania is more common following traumatic brain injury than stroke. Although prevalence studies have not been conducted, we have found in our studies of patients hospitalized with acute stroke or traumatic brain injury that less than 1% of the 309 patients with acute stroke developed mania, whereas 9% (6 of 66) of our patients with traumatic brain injury met criteria for mania some time during the first year posttrauma. These patients have typical manic syndromes and their symptoms are similar to those found in patients with mania who do not have brain injury; that is, primary mania (Starkstein, Pearlson, & Robinson, 1987).

Relationship to Lesion Location

In a series of 17 patients with mania following stroke, trauma, or brain tumors, we reported a significantly increased frequency of right-hemisphere lesions compared with 31 patients with major depression following acute stroke and 28 non-mood-disordered controls who had also suffered an acute stroke (Robinson, Boston, Starkstein, & Price, 1988). Analysis of CT scans from these patients revealed that they had ischemic lesions involving the right orbital frontal cortex, basal temporal cortex, and subcortical areas of the right hemisphere such as the head of the caudate and the right thalamus.

In another recent study using positron emission tomography (PET; Starkstein et al., 1990), we found that three patients with right subcortical lesions (one patient had a lesion of the white matter underlying the right frontal lobe, one had lesion of the anterior arm of the right internal capsule, one had a lesion of the head of the right caudate nucleus) all had focal hypometabolism in the right polar-basotemporal cortex as measured by 18-flurodeoxyglucose utilization and PET imaging. This finding suggests that lesions may produce their behavioral or emotional changes through an effect on a brain site distant from the lesion. This phenomenon, known as *diaschisis*, may be an important phenomen in the emotional changes seen after brain injury.

Analysis of structural brain imaging in the 66 patients with acute TBI using logistic regression demonstrated that the only brain region significantly associated with mania was polar basotemporal cortex ($p = .005$). Due to the small number of patients involved and the tendency of traumatic brain lesions to be bilateral, we did not demonstrate a lateralized effect. This result is, however, consistent with our finding in patients following stroke and emphasizes the importance of polar basotemporal cortex in mood regulation.

SUMMARY AND CONCLUSIONS

Although emotion is one of the most fundamental experiences of human existence, efforts to study the cerebral basis of emotion are in relatively early stages. Studies of normal emotion as well as studies of syndromic disorders, such as major depression, have consistently implicated frontal lobe mechanisms and particularly left prefrontal and orbital frontal cortex with depressed mood. We have tried in this chapter to describe findings from our studies in patients with traumatic brain injury or stroke and how these studies may help to elucidate the anatomical basis of depressed or elevated mood.

Our studies have found a consistent association between major depression and lesions of the left frontal cortex or left basal ganglia. These findings are consistent with those of other investigators studying major depression in patients with stroke as well as the findings in patients with primary (no known neuropathology) mood disorders, and implicate the dorsal-lateral limbic structures in mood regulation. The dorsal-lateral limbic system includes the frontal cortex, basal-temporal cortex, basal ganglia and dorsal medial thalamic nucleus. Alexander, DeLong, and Strick (1986) have demonstrated topically organized neuronal loops between frontal cortex and caudate nucleus in nonhuman primates. Imput to the caudate may also project to dorsal medial thalamic nucleus and back to prefrontal cortex. Furthermore, lesions or physiological abnormalities in one part of the limbic circuit would be expected to influence neuronal activity in other areas of the circuit.

Thus, our findings that both frontal and basal ganglia lesions are associated with major depression as well as the findings of other investigators that there is abnormal metabolic activity in thalamus or amygdala are consistent with the hypothesis that the ventral-lateral limbic structures (i.e., frontal cortex, temporal cortex, amygdala, basal ganglia, and thalamus) play an important role in mediating normal mood fluctuations and pathological mood changes such as depression or mania.

Further research is needed to determine the extent to which pathological states and normal emotion may overlap in their neural substrates and what the structural or physiological differences are between these two very different mental phenomena. Ultimately, identification of the cerebral basis of emotion may lead to more specific and targeted interventions in the treatment of pathological emotional disorders.

ACKNOWLEDGMENTS

This work was supported in part by MH40355 and Research Scientist Award MH00163 (RGR).

REFERENCES

Alexander, G. E., DeLong, M. R., & Strick, P. O. (1986). Parallel organization of functionally segregated circuits linking basal ganglia and cortex. *Annual Review of Neuroscience, 9*, 357–381.

Astrom, M., Adolfsson, R., & Asplund, K. (1993). Major depression in stroke patients: A 3-year longitudinal study. *Stroke, 24*, 976–982.

Baxter, L. R., Schwartz, J. M., Phelps, M. E., Mazziotta, J. C., Guze, B. M., Selin, C. E., Gerner, R. H., & Sumida, R. M. (1989). Reduction of prefrontal cortex gluose metabolism common to three types of depression. *Archives of General Psychiatry, 46,* 243–250.

Bolla-Wilson, K., Robinson, R. G., Starkstein, S. E., Boston, J., & Price, T. R. (1989). Lateralization of dementia of depression in stroke patients. *American Journal of Psychiatry, 146,* 627–634.

Bornstein, R. A., Miller, H. B., & VanSchoor, J. T. (1989). Neuropsychological deficit and emotional disturbance in head injured patients. *Journal of Neurosurgery, 70,* 509–513.

Cummings, J. L., & Duchen, L. W. (1981). Kluver–Bucy syndrome in Pick disease: Clinical and pathological correlations. *Neurology, 31,* 1415–1422.

Downhill, J. E., Jr., & Robinson, R. G. (1994). Longitudinal assessment of depression and cognitive impairment following stroke. *Journal of Nervous and Mental Disease, 182*(8), 425–431.

Drevets, W. C., Videen, T. O., Price J. L., Preskorn, S. H., Carmichael, S. T., & Raichle, M. D. (1992). A functional anatomical study of unipolar depression. *Journal of Neuroscience, 12,* 3628–3641.

Eastwood, M. R., Rifat, S. L., Nobbs, H., & Ruderman, J. (1989). Mood disorder following cerebrovascular accident. *British Journal of Psychiatry, 154,* 195–200.

Eslinger, P. J., & Damasio, A. R. (1985). Severe bilateral disturbance of higher cognition after bilateral frontal lobe ablation: Patient EVR. *Neurology, 35,* 1731–1741.

Fedoroff, J. P., Starkstein, S. E., Forrester, A. W., Geisler, F. H., Jorge, R. E., Arndt, S. V., & Robinson, R. G. (1992). Depression in patients with acute traumatic brain injury. *American Journal of Psychiatry, 149,* 918–923.

Finklestein, S., Campbell, A., Stoll, A. L., Baldesserini, R. J., Stinus, L., Paskevitch, P. A., & Domesick, V. B. (1983). Changes in cortical and subcortical levels of monoamines and their metabolites following unilateral ventrolateral cortical lesions in the rat. *Brain Research, 271*(2), 279–288.

Herrmann, M., Bartles, C., & Wallesch, C.-W. (1993). Depression in acute and chronic aphasia: Symptoms, pathoanatomical–clinical correlations and functional implications. *Journal of Neurology, Neurosurgery, and Psychiatry, 56,* 672–678.

House, A., Dennis, M., Warlow, C., Hawton, J., & Molyneux K. (1990). Mood disorders after stroke and their relation to lesion location. A CT scan study. *Brain, 113,* 1113–1130.

Jorge, R. E., Robinson, R. G., Arndft, S. V., Starkstein, S. E., Forrester, A. W., & Geisler, F. (1993). Depression following traumatic brain injury: A 1-year longitudinal study. *Journal of Affective Disorders, 27,* 233–243.

Lilly, R., Cummings, J. L., & Benson, D. F. (1983). The human Kluver–Bucy syndrome. *Neurology, 33,* 1141–1145.

MacLean, P. D. (1952). Some psychiatric implications of physiological studies on front temporal portion of limbic system. *Psychological Review, 4,* 407–418.

Martinot, J. H., Hardy, P., Feline, A., Huret, J. D., Mazoyer, G., Attar-Levy, D., Pappata, S., & Syrota, A. (1990). Left prefrontal glucose hypometabolism in the depression state: A confirmation. *American Journal of Psychiatry, 147,* 1313–1317.

Mayberg, H. S., Robinson, R. G., Wong, D. F., Parikh, R. M., Bolduc, P., Starkstein, S. E., Price, T. R., Dannals, R. F., Links, J. M., Wilson, A. A., Ravert, H. T., & Wagner, H. N., Jr. (1988). PET imaging of cortical S2-serotonin receptors after stroke: Lateralized changes and relationship to depression. *American Journal of Psychiatry, 145,* 937–943.

Mayberg, H. S., Moran, T. H., & Robinson, R. G. (1990). Remote lateralized changes in cortical 3H-spiperone binding following focal frontal cortex lesions in the rat. *Brain Research, 516,* 127–131.

Morris, P. L. P., Robinson, R. G., Raphael, B., & Bishop, D. (1991). The relationship between the perception of social support and post-stroke depression in hospitalized patients. *Psychiatry: Interpersonal and Biological Processes, 54,* 306–316.

Morris, P. L. P., Robinson, R. G., & Raphael, B. (1990). Prevalence and course of post-stroke depression in hospitalized patients. *International Journal of Psychiatry and Medicine, 20*, 327–342.

Morris, P. L. P., Robinson, R. G., & Raphael, B. (1992). Lesion location and depression in hospitalized stroke patients: Evidence supporting a specific relationship in the left hemisphere. *Neuropsychiatry, Neuropsychology and Behavioral Neurology, 3*, 75–82.

Morrison, J. H., Molliver, M. E., & Grzanna, R. (1979). Noradrenergic innervation of the cerebral cortex: Widespread effects of local cortical lesions. *Science, 205*, 313–316.

Papez, J. W. (1937). A proposed mechanism of emotion. *Archives of Neurology and Psychiatry, 38*, 725–743.

Pardo, J. V., Pardo, P. J., & Raichle, M. D. (1993). Neural correlates of self-induced dysphoria. *American Journal of Psychiatry, 150*, 713–719.

Parikh, R. M., Justice, A., Moran, T. H., & Robinson, R. G. (1988). A two-ear longitudinal study of post-stroke mood disorders: Prognostic factors related to one and two year outcome. *International of Psychiatry and Medicine, 18*, 45–56.

Parikh, R. M., Robinson, R. G., Lipsey, J. R., Starkstein, S. E., Fedoroff, J. P., & Price, T. R. (1990). The impact of post-stroke depression on recovery in activities of daily living over two-year follow-up. *Archives of Neurology, 47*, 785–789.

Prigatano, G. P. (1986). *Psychological rehabilitation after brain injury.* Baltimore: Johns Hopkins University Press.

Robinson, R. G. (1979). Differential behavioral and biochemical effects of right and left hemispheric cerebral infarction in the rat. *Science, 205*, 707–710.

Robinson, R. G., Boston, J. D., Starkstein, S. E., & Price, T. R. (1988). Comparison of mania with depression following brain injury. Casual factors. *American Journal of Psychiatry, 145*, 172–178.

Robinson, R. G., Bolduc, P., & Price, T. R. (1987). A two year longitudinal study of post-stroke depression. Diagnosis and outcome at one and two year follow-up. *Stroke, 18*, 837–843.

Robinson, R. G., Kubos, K. L., Starr, L. B., Rao, K., & Price, T. R. (1984). Mood disorders in stroke patients: Importance of location of lesion. *Brain, 108*, 81–93.

Robinson, R. G., Starr, L. B., Kubos, K. L., & Price, T. R. (1983). A two year longitudinal study of post-stroke mood disorders: Findings during the initial evaluation. *Stroke, 14*, 736–744.

Robinson, R. G., & Szetela, B. (1981). Mood change following left hemispheric brain injury. *Annals of Neurology, 9*, 447–453.

Sinyor, D., Jacques, P., Kaloupek, D. G., Becker, R., Goldenberg, M., & Coopersmith, H. (1986). Post-stroke depression and lesion location: An attempted replication. *Brain, 109*, 539–546.

Starkstein, S. E., Mayberg, H. S., Berthier, M. L., Fedoroff, P., Price, T. R., Dannals, R. F., Wagner, H. N., Leiguarda, R., & Robinson, R. G. (1990). Mania after brain injury: Neuroradiological and metabolic findings. *Annals of Neurology, 27*, 652–659.

Starkstein, S. E., Pearlson, G. D., & Robinson, R. G. (1987). Mania after brain injury: A controlled study of etiologial factors. *Archives of Neurology, 44*, 1069–1973.

Starkstein, S. E., Robinson, R. G., & Price, T. R. (1987). Comparison of cortical and subcortical lesions in the production of post-stroke mood disorders. *Brain, 110*, 1045–1059.

Starkstein, S. E., Robinson, R. G., & Price, T. R. (1988). Comparison of patients with and without post-stroke major depression matched for size and location of lesion. *Archives of General Psychiatry, 45*, 247–252.

Uytdenhoef, P., Portelange, P., Jacquy, J., Charles, G., Linkowski, P., & Mendelwicz, J. (1983). Regional cerebral blood flow and lateralized hemispheric dysfunction in depression. *British Journal of Psychiatry, 143*, 128–132.

12

Allowing and Accepting of Emotional Experience

Leslie S. Greenberg
York University, Canada

A PROCESS CONCEPTION

Feeling involves a natural process of emergence and completion. This spontaneous process of emergence occurs because many feelings involve an automatic apprehending process over which we have little conscious control. We can control what we feel to some degree by limiting our exposure to external evoking cues or by trying to control our conscious thoughts, but we can do little to prevent the automatic evocation of many feelings. They result from complex preconscious processes of apprehension, by a sensing of things that precedes any form of conscious symbolic thought. Given that people cannot control these affective experiences, it is best that they learn to accept their feelings and learn from them.

This natural process of feeling arising and passing away can be depicted as a set of phases shown in Figure 12.1; those of emergence, awareness, owning, expressive action, and completion, followed again by the emergence of a new feeling, thereby beginning the cycle again. It is only when this process is interfered with, when awareness or owning is prevented, or when expression is interrupted or action and completion are blocked that people become mired in chronic bad feelings and become dysfunctional and chronically distressed.

It is important for people to realize that feelings are not reified "things" in themselves, that they are not static entities. Rather, they are processual in nature. They are phasic, they emerge and increase over time, and then

emergence → awareness → owning → expressive action → completion

FIG. 12.1. The emotion cycle.

decay. Change in feelings is natural. It is the blocking of the process of change that results in being stuck in certain types of bad feelings. The interference with the natural process of change in the emotion cycle is pathological and unnatural. Many people attempt to control their feelings in a variety of different ways. People entering therapy often need to learn to allow and to accept their feelings rather than trying to control them. An important therapeutic goal is the development of an open attitude toward feelings and an appreciation of their process nature; the acceptance that feelings come and go, arise and pass away.

This attitude of acceptance of process helps people learn to integrate "unwanted" feelings. In order for people to deal with unwanted feelings rather than trying to disown or control them, they need to become aware of what they themselves are doing that is making them repeat the same feelings again and again. Therapy, therefore, needs to help people become more aware not only of what is disowned but also of how they themselves interrupt the natural process of emergence and completion of emotional experience.

Painful feelings, by their nature, are difficult to endure, and therefore people attempt to avoid them or interrupt their experience of them. This strategy of disowning, however, results in preventing emotions from running their natural course to action and completion. Thus, if I squeeze back tears when I am sad, hold back my expression when I am angry, and I remain stationary when I am afraid, I prevent myself from completing and moving on. In addition, when people are unable to feel pain they numb themselves, cutting off all feeling. It is hard to deaden one emotion and to feel another in a lively manner—killing pain generally means killing love and joy as well. Because of painful feelings that cannot be endured, many people thus spend much of their lives not feeling—they go through the motions of living but do not experience emotion.

EMOTION IS ADAPTIVE

Fundamentally, our emotion system is adaptive and helps us to deal with the environment. Emotions often result from our appraisal of situations first in relation to our needs and then to our coping abilities (Frijda, 1986). Appraisals can be both rapid and automatic, making emotion a biologically adaptive rapid action response, and slow and deliberative, making emotion a culturally and socially based consequence of reflection and decision making. Emotions, be they automatic or deliberative, lead to actions designed to change the organism–environment relationship so as to make the emotion no longer necessary. Thus, when I cry I increase the probability of receiving comfort from self and other, when I am angry I increase the probability of chasing the other away, and when I am afraid I increase the probability of escaping. Once the goals of comfort, threat, or escape have been achieved the emotional response is no longer necessary and abates. The *primary* emotions are all characterized by their adaptive-action tendencies, which are designed to change the organism's relationship with the environment.

PROCESS DIAGNOSIS

We have, in earlier works, delineated a four-part, process-diagnostic scheme for assessing emotional expression in therapy (Greenberg & Safran, 1987, 1989). Here, we suggest the need to distinguish the expression in therapy of primary emotional responses, a person's fundamental, initial, emotional response to stimulus from secondary and instrumental responses. Secondary emotional responses are those reactions to more primary affective responses, such as expressing anger when feeling afraid, or more complex secondary responses to more primary cognitive processes, such as when thinking about failure leads to feeling depressed. Instrumental emotions are experienced and expressed in order to achieve some end, to influence others or manage one's image so as to appear in a desired manner, such as expressing anger to dominate or expressing dismay to impress others with one's moral virtue. Finally, primary emotion can be further subdivided into two realms: biologically adaptive and learned maladaptive. Different types of phobias and panic attacks are primary learned maladaptive responses, as is a fear of intimacy that is based on a history of neglect, abuse, or invalidation.

Having made this distinction allows us to discuss the major exceptions to our fundamental view of the adaptiveness of emotion. Thus, in addition to learned maladaptive responses, the nonprimary emotions; that is, secondary and instrumental emotions, are the cause of much of the bad press that these emotions have rightfully recieved. We all know that certain emotional responses we have are not adaptive nor desirable and they do need to be controlled. At times against our best intentions we hate our children, we rage at those we are close to, are fearfully paranoid of authority, envy our friends, feel intensely vulnerable with or jealous of our lovers, or feel disgust or anger at only the slightest provocation. These emotional overreactions stem from complex learning histories in which adaptive emotion expression and regulation has not been fully achieved.

EMOTIONAL DISORDER

Three evidently potential problems emerge for any organism with a fundamentally adaptive emotion system. The first occurs when the emotion does not achieve its aim of changing the relationship with the environment. When, as a function of an emotional response to the environment, the relationship with the environment is not successfully changed, the provoking stimulus then remains and continues to evoke the feeling. Too much ongoing feeling, especially intense negative feeling, resulting from this failure to change the organism–environment relationship produces stress and eventual breakdown. In this case recognition and removal of the source of stress is therapeutic.

Second, if the evoking source is internal rather than an environmental event, the action tendency cannot achieve its aim of changing the organism–environment relationship and the person is placed in a situation comparable to the one described earlier of not being able to leave the field, this time because the field is within. The coping style adopted in these situations is, then, often one of attempting psychologically to prevent the feeling, avoiding it by disattending, denying, or distorting. People find many ingenious ways to avoid feeling their emotions and the pain associated with them. These avoidances need to be overcome and new ways of coping must be implemented. When the painful feelings are attended to, the pain can be endured and can be utilized as information that the system has been damaged, is in disequilibrium, or is disorganized and that something needs to be done to change the situation. Emotionally focused intervention therefore promotes the *owning* of avoided or disavowed painful experience.

The third way in which emotional responses can be maladaptive is based on dysfunctional, complex meaning construction processes. Certain response sequences, such as disappointment followed by rage or feeling very insecure and afraid and worrying about being rejected, can all be highly maladaptive. However, these maladaptive responses of rage, anger and tearfulness, or worry are generally not the person's primary response to the environment. They are, rather, complex secondary reactions based on past experience and learning.

Within this category of emotional problems arising from meaning construction are those that surface as a function of faulty logic or thinking (Beck, 1976; Ellis, 1962). These are the problematic emotions with which we are least concerned in an emotionally focused approach to treatment.

It is true that faulty thinking can lead to maladaptive responses: Negative thoughts can and do lead to bad feelings as cognitive therapists claim (Beck, 1974; Ellis, 1962). This cognition–emotion link is the target of much cognitive therapy, but in our view conscious negative or irrational thinking is not the source of many psychological problems and may often be the result. It is far more often the more complex automatic functioning of the meaning construction system, including the rapid action emotion system, that is the problem in the production of enduring bad feelings. The emotion system involves preconscious appraisal of situations in relation to needs, and the primary emotional response is then subjected to subsequent automatic processing.

It is these processes of need frustration and reactions to unmet needs that require therapeutic attention, not faulty appraisals. People's appraisals are generally valid and not of primary therapeutic concern; rather, it is people's affective goals, the attainability of which the appraisals are evaluating, and people's reactions to these appraisals that is often problematic. Thus, for example, in people who are interpersonally sensitive it is not a faulty appraisal of, say, rejection or coldness by others that is problematic—the other is probably somewhat accurately perceived. Rather, what is problematic is either the intensity or desperation of the need for closeness and acceptance, or the person's subsequent construals of the emotional consequences for the self of the momentary rupture of the interpersonal bond. It is something about the affective goal or its frustration that leads the person to feel that it will be impossible to survive without the desired closeness or acceptance. It is thus not the initial appraisal that is faulty, but rather that a particular need or goal is evoked or the intensity of the reactions to the frustration of the need that is problematic.

In a further example of the importance of emotional meaning construction processes over rational process, we see in Figure 12.2 that in depression it is not the negative cognition appraising the self as worthless that *causes* depressive reactions. Rather, the process is one in which an internal structure, which we call an emotion scheme (Greenberg, Rice, & Elliott 1993), once evoked results in a felt action tendency to close down due to an experience such as discouragement/ dissappointment/sadness. This feeling state is associated with, and is a strong cue for, self-evaluative thoughts such as "you're worthless" as well as a feeling of being weak and or bad, such as, "I'm worthless." These elements, the primary sad emotion of the essential self, the harsh critical agency, and the weak/bad hopeless sense of self are all schematic outputs and aspects of emotional meaning construction that are available to consciousness when attended to.

However, as shown in Figure 12.2, the primary response and the aspect most directly linked to the depression is the emotional one. As also shown

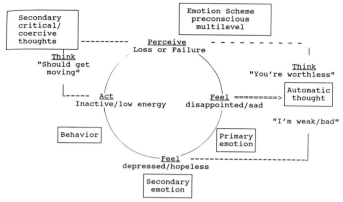

FIG. 12.2. Depressive process. Emotion is a process that unfolds dynamically over time without a definite starting point; we must apprehend the
personal meaning before we consciously appraise (checks for novelty,
pleasantness, personal significance); different kinds of cognition enter into
various stages of the emotional response; the body contributes to subjective
experience and goes hand in hand with appraisal; thinking does not have
a controlling executive role.

in the figure, the automatic felt sense of sadness and discouragement is
more strongly responsible for the activation of the negative thoughts and
the hopeless weak/bad sense of self than the other way around. The
resultant experience of depression and the feeling of hopelessness is
therefore a complex secondary response to the primary emotion and its
subsequent meaning rather than being a primary emotional response
itself. Once depressed there are also further negative self-regulatory
processes in which people become self-critical and self-coercive, thereby
creating further failure and depressive experience. It is often these
self-critical and coercive attempts at self-regulation that one first encounters when working with a depressed person. These need to be worked
through to first work through the feeling of hopelessness, then the way
it is generated, and then the more primary feeling of loss or failure.

It is also important to note that it is often far more the evocation of
emotionally laden perceptual images and scenes than of specific thoughts
that results in bad feelings. It is thus the schematically generated thought-
less images and the wordless automatic sensori-motor reponses rather than
the thought that needs to be evoked in therapy and exposed to new
information in order to modify bad feelings. Thoughts and memories that
do evoke therapeutically important emotional experience are thoughts or
memories about situations in which intense emotions were generated
without cognitive mediation.

Finally, dysfunctional regulation of emotion is a fourth possible factor
in emotional disorder. In the long run, both overregulation as well as

underregulation of emotion can be dysfunctional. Intense emotional responses that are underregulated, such as rage at a personal slight that is allowed to escalate out of control or fear or panic at being rejected that cannot be internally soothed, can be highly problematic. The inability to regulate the intensity of these emotional responses is central in certain types of emotional disorder. On the other hand, the suppression of emotion is central in other types of disorders, in that it robs the person of adaptive information and orientation. It is thus not only problems in how emotions are generated that can be problematic but also how they are regulated that may need therapeutic attention.

AVOIDANCE OF PRIMARY FEELINGS

As we have argued, feelings enhance our capacity to cope and, once accepted, can better be coped with. Their avoidance, on the other hand, leaves us doubly deficient; first the adaptive information is neglected, leaving us disoriented, and second, the avoidance unfortunately does not make the feelings or their effects disappear. Rather, it impedes our ability to cope with them effectively. Since feelings involve automatic physiological responses, their avoidance leaves the system unintegrated and in disharmony. Our physiology and sensori-motor system are in one state and our words and conscious thoughts are in another, while our intermediate consciousness-guiding, preconscious, experiencing process is caught in a struggle between guiding, or being dictated to, by conscious awareness. The spontaneous natural flow of automatically experiencing ourselves is disturbed. We no longer automatically attend to the felt referents of our experience, nor do we symbolize them in awareness, create new meanings, and promote action, thereby enabling us to carry forward our experience to a next step; rather, we remain stuck in a state of continued avoidance.

If feelings are not to be avoided are we proposing they are always to be trusted? This is a complex issue to which our answer is a definite possibly. It depends on which feelings are to be trusted, and in what way. Trusted blindly to determine action—no. Trusted as primary sources of information about our reactions and about what we experience—absolutely. After all, we are our feelings, and how we deal with them. Feeling is the process of being. Passions are so called because they capture the automaticity of feelings—we passively receive them. Our contention is that to attempt to not receive our feelings is one of the greatest follies of the active, controlling orientation of Western mind; rather, we need to live in mindful harmony with feelings, not attempt to control them. Feelings are not only received, they are an aspect of a complex construction in which we create ourselves anew every moment by a dialectical process of synthesising many elements of experience including feelings, needs, thoughts, and intentions. Rather than suggesting that we surrender and be governed only by emotions and trust them as a guide to action we are suggesting an integration of will, intellect, desire, and emotion into a holistic response of the self.

Emotions that govern goal priorities within people and communicate intentions between people are, however, survival-enhancing. It is not these emotions that are problematic or bring people into treatment; rather, it is either painful emotions or bad feelings that bring people into treatment. In working therapeutically with allowing and accepting emotions it is important to distinguish primary emotions and painful feelings from bad feelings. These will be discussed later.

PAINFUL EMOTIONAL EXPERIENCE

Emotional pain is a complex feeling state characterized by a bodily felt sense of pain that appears to be associated with trauma to the self—with the shattering of the whole. Pain is associated with the heart, often with having it broken, and is referred to as being deep and profound as well as explosive and overwhelming. People refer to feeling shattered, broken, ripped apart, having gaping wounds, and feeling empty and hopeless (Bolger, 1994). Subjective reports suggest that anger, sadness, and shame are all connected with pain. With emotional pain, people feel out of control and experience physical pain, report feeling overwhelmed, become weak and may be unable to stop crying. With such feelings comes a fear of losing control—this is extremely frightening. When pain becomes unbearable people may numb themselves and disconnect from their surroundings. Feeling pain that has been previously avoided, although initially frightening, often leads to relief, feeling alive and connected, and, ideally, letting go.

Feeling emotional pain is a primary emotional experience that, although adaptive, has only limited escape value as compared with the more anticipatory primary emotions such as fear and anger, which are designed to promote action to prevent undesirable occurrences. Pain does possess survival value, but it achieves this by teaching one to avoid things in the future that have been harmful in the past. Pain is not protectively anticipatory, as it is experienced only after the painful event has occurred. Primary emotions such as fear and anger clearly alert us to impending dangers and threats and prepare us to meet them; however, because pain is unpleasant people tend to avoid it rather than use it as a signal. Intense psychological pain results in a fear of annihilation of the self, and people therefore attempt to escape this annihilation by cutting off feeling and developing avoidance techniques. In the long run, this is not adaptive, as it cuts one off from one's primary orientation and response system.

Children who grow up in abusive environments or experience other painful trauma cope with the pain by pushing away the distress caused by the abuse or trauma by automatic or unconscious dissociation. Certain aspects of experience or parts that "contain" the traumatic feelings, memories, and thoughts are thus blocked. In unstable and abusive environments children learn that it is dangerous to be vulnerable and open about their feelings; they thus learn not to trust others and to avoid seeking comfort from or relying on others. They suppress their own feelings and become increasingly unaware of them and do not experience the fulfillment of needs that are developmentally normal and essential for development. Thus safe, supportive comfort is not experienced and autonomy and independence are not encouraged.

Painful awareness is thus split off in order to protect the self from feeling overwhelmed. Thus the rage, pain, and anguish of being abused is disassociated to protect the person from conscious awareness of the reality of the child's situation. The person may feel afraid without knowing why or feel nothing at all. These split off experiences need to be re-owned in therapy and worked through from an adult perspective. It's important too to realize that these parts were split off in order to protect their child from being overwhelmed.

BAD FEELINGS

Bad feelings, in contrast to pain (which tells us of damage and trauma), result from something not functioning properly or smoothly within— from disharmony. Either we feel torn, guilty, anxious, or depressed. This is a signal of internal problems. Bad feelings that trouble people greatly often come not from primary emotional responses to environmental contingencies, but from attempts to control those primary feelings which, if simply accepted, would themselves dissipate. It is generally disharmony within, the nonacceptance of internal experience or conflict between feelings, that often causes enduring bad feelings. It is often disaffiliative relationships between aspects of the self, not emotional responses to the environment, that cause distress.

Bad feelings, then, result from a variety of sources. Many are intrapersonal in origin, such as the overcontrol of primary emotions, internal conflict, complex cognitive/affective meaning-generating sequences, and memory. Another major source of bad feeling is interpersonal in origin— issues related to intimacy and interpersonal control as well as loss of, or disapproval by, others. Interpersonally generated bad feelings are most intense when the other person is a significant attachment figure. Sequences of despair, anger, and depression result from separation and abandonment whereas fears of abandonment, engulfment, or invalidation, result from past trauma. Dysfunctional emotional responses to others are based on prior learning in relationships and on the influence these experiences have on the way in which current situations are construed, experienced, and reacted to.

Bad feelings, then, are generally complex secondary responses, and are best understood to be the by-product of a fundamentally adaptive system rather than adaptive. Although bad feelings in themselves are disruptive, they still provide a means of regulating a complex biological/psychological/social system—the whole person. Bad feelings are a *signal*, a means of informing us that our complex system is in disharmony, disequilibrium, or hyperreactivity and needs attention. Initially the emotion system had only to deal with organism–environment interaction; with the development of the ability to reflect on ourselves to represent, imagine, and consciously remember, emotions become responses to our own process—to intraorganismic interactions as well as to responses to the environment. Emotional "disorder" thus often reflects internal disorganization or hyperreactivity—a state that, if attended to and used as a signal, is an important precusor of reorganization. Bad feelings are thus a result either of intrapersonal processes of disowning, self-control, and self-criticism, or result from interpersonal difficulties related to affiliation and control involving such things as feeling disapproved of, unsupported, or submissive. These bad feelings, rather than being purely adaptive signals about people's reactions to situations, are often signs of complex system dysfunction, of internal disorganization and disequilibrium, or of hypersensitivity and hyperreactivity to interpersonal threat or loss. They demand that people pay attention in order to facilitate system reorganization toward greater equilibrium.

Thus bad feelings, such as feeling upset, rotten, insecure, vulnerable, fearful of being unable to cope, fearful of being alone, empty, isolated, unloved, unlovable, or overly dependent or compliant are not primary, initial affective responses to situations. Rather, they are the result of complex internal affective–cognitive sequences. Feelings such as these are often secondary reactions to *underlying* intrasystemic processes. Primary feelings involve immediate and direct appraisal and reaction to situations such as anger at violation and sadness at loss and are not the same as secondary bad feelings. Rather, these bad feelings, by contrast, are the result of secondary reactions, often to primary feelings, such as reacting to primary sadness at loss with secondary panic at feeling abandoned or unlovable. Alternately, bad feelings are produced by complex intrapersonal processes of lack of self-acceptance such as self-castigation and self-denigration for feeling a certain way that is construed as unacceptable. A person thus feels guilty or contemptuous toward the self for feeling afraid or for feeling angry or envious.

Feeling upset is thus a general signal that something is amiss. Upset connotes disorder, disarray, and confusion, as well as feeling disturbed, agitated, and stirred up and generally occurs secondarily to primary anger, fear, guilt, and hurt. It tells us that some other emotion is attempting to break through. Regardless of the difference in the primary emotion, the secondary upset is the same. Often we feel upset without quite knowing why, without having registered the event or our construal of a situation that led to a response which itself went unrecognized. All we are left with is the bad, upset feeling. This feeling, then, is not the same as the primary feeling that elicits it. It is not the anger or hurt, but rather an awareness of irritability that is a sign of our increased likelihood of feeling the original feeling. It is an indication that we need to search internally for what is troubling us.

EMOTIONALLY FOCUSED INTERVENTION

The basic contention here is that personal reality and consciousness is as much a product of emotions as it is of thought and rationality. It is the high-level emotional meaning of events constructed automatically by emotion schemes (Greenberg et al., 1993) that determines both conscious emotional and cognitive responses. This high-level "sense" of things, such as feeling apprehensive or confident or powerless is deeply affective in nature. It is the emotion scheme's function to read affectively relevant patterns from the environment and guide both our emotional sense of ourselves and our orientation to the word. This guiding self-structure is only amenable to change once it has been activated—in computer terms, when it is "up and running." It is when we experience emotions that we know the scheme has been activated and is currently operating. When the emotional output of these schemes is being currently experienced and the cognitions are "hot," we know that this high-level emotional meaning structure has been activated and is amenable to change.

In emotionally focused intervention, one therefore focuses on activating the person's automatic emotional reactions in order to make these reactions available to awareness under the increased attentional allocation available in the safety of therapy, and to make the scheme amenable to change when necessary by the provision of new experience in therapy. In this framework, then, emotions are viewed either as needing to be acknowledged as adaptive responses and used as a guide to reorganization and action or as being complex responses that need to be restructured. The latter occurs when clients find that their emotional reponses, such as fear of intimacy or rage at disappointment, are maladaptive responses to current contexts as a function of past learning and trauma. As well as acknowledging primary feelings such as anger and fear for their adaptive value, the emotionally focused therapist intervenes to help people deal with and restructure the painful and bad, upset feelings for which they come into therapy.

In instances where clients are dealing with situations in which they are not fully aware of their primary feelings, the therapist attempts, by means of exploration, attentional focusing, and evocative responding, to help clients become aware of and symbolize their previously unacknowledged emotions. Here the task is one of vividly reentering the lived situation and attempting to reexperience, more fully and with more attentional allocation, the earlier experience so as to more fully acknowledge the emotional responses and the associated appraisals, needs, and action tendencies.

WORKING WITH BAD FEELINGS

Intervention with bad feelings such as hopelessness, helplessness, or vulnerability is not the same as intervention with primary affects such as anger, sadness, fear, or grief. In the latter, the goal is to acknowledge the feeling and access the action tendency resulting in, for example, feeling angry and being able to set boundaries or feeling sad and being able to grieve. In working with pain the goal is also to own the disowned, to access the pain, and live it through to completion rather than avoid it. Here the result is more of a letting go, an undoing of the avoidance, and the allowing of new experience and contact. Working with bad feelings, however, does not involve a reowning. Bad feeling, being a product of complex internal sequences of cognitive/emotional experience, requires a more complex set of interventions. There is no adaptive action tendency associated with feeling useless, worthless, helpless, or humiliated or with feeling chronic shame, guilt, or constant rejection—neither does one live a bad feeling through to completion. Rather, intervention with bad feeling involves two phases: an evocation of the bad feeling in order to make the generating process amenable to change and a restructuring that, among other things, involves the contacting of some new primary feeling or internal resource.

More than an awareness of what is felt is therefore needed in order to deal with bad feelings. The mistake in the emotionally oriented therapies has been one of not being able to clearly articulate or communicate their view on how people deal with bad feelings and not distinguishing between primary emotions, pain, and bad feelings. Simply getting in touch with bad feelings is not in and of itself helpful; one is just left feeling bad. Feeling powerless and helpless again and again is not empowering—what is needed is to enter these states in such a manner and with sufficient resources to be able to cope with them in a new way and thereby feel empowered.

The message that it is important to feel one's feelings and that this will be helpful has often been both mistakenly communicated by proponents and mistakenly interpreted by receivers of experientially oriented therapies. Proposals on the importance of feeling one's feeling have been interpreted too literally by some to mean that it is good to "get it all out." Emotion has thus been viewed mistakenly in a hydraulic fashion, as something that builds up and must be gotten rid of, cathartically. This is generally not true except in certain specific situations, and certainly not true in relation to bad feelings. Although allowing and accepting bad feelings in a supportive environment is of some help, it is not only their acceptance and expression but also the change in the manner of coping with internal experience and the generation of new meaning that is needed for the experience to be mutative. Thus working with bad feelings involves not only the allowance and acceptance of the feeling but also a process of change in which something new emerges.

In therapeutic situations in which a client experiences repeated bad feelings, the emotionally focused therapist begins by acknowledging the client's feelings and validating their appraisals and their experience. The therapist then attempts to evoke the bad feeling of, say, feeling worthless or insecure—by helping the client to attend to the feeling rather than avoid it. The person is thus encouraged to unpack, differentiate, and explore the complex internal processes *producing* the bad feeling, in order to access the dysfunctional sequences and cognitions that generate the bad feeling and finally to *access* previously unacknowledged or previously inaccessible primary adaptive feelings, action tendencies, and needs that are used to combat the dysfunctional beliefs. It may thus be that a depressed individual feels bad either as a function of being highly self-denigrating and evaluating the self as worthless, or as a function of being highly self-controlling by manipulating the self to act in ways that are inconsistent with its feelings and needs. However, the depressed individual may feel tremendously afraid of being alone and feel overly dependent on others for support, leaving him or her feeling frightened, insecure, and even angry at being abandoned, when the desperately wished-for support is not forthcoming. These are the generating processes that need to explored.

By "going into" previously avoided bad feelings such as hopelessness, helplessness, feeling like a failure, or feeling alone and abandoned in the safety- and comfort-providing presence of another, a number of things occur:

1. *The appraisals of self and situation* and *the associated action tendency* and the *needs* involved in the initial emotional reaction are identified. Thus, in exploring a feeling of powerlessness a person might identify a cognitive appraisal ("I felt so threatened by her cold unyielding stare"), identify an emotional reaction ("I felt so powerless and uncared for"), and an action tendency ("I just shrank inside and wanted to disappear").

2. The need/goal/concern involved in the situation is also identified as when one says, "I needed her to acknowledge me just to say I see you exist." Once the appraisals, the needs to which they relate, and the action tendency have been identified, the picture or meaning of client experience becomes a lot clearer.

3. Having evoked the bad feeling, the internal sequences involved in generating the feeling become accessible. Exploring these sequences finally accesses the dysfunctional beliefs that produce the bad feelings, as when the client says, "I've always been a loser, so why should it be any different now? Why should she listen to me?"

4. Finally having acknowledged the sense of resignation and hopelessness, a new sense of self emerges by a *shift* in attentional allocation or a change in perspective facilitated by the therapist's noticing the emergence of some new potential such as hope, energy, or a desire for comfort. Alternate self-organizations constituted by organismic concerns and primary adaptive emotions emerge, and are then used to combat the dysfunctional, bad-feeling producing thoughts and beliefs. This occurs when a person contacts strengths or internal resources in response to their self-castigation or negative self-evaluation, such as saying "I do have rights; I do have things to offer; if only she would listen; I want her to acknowledge me."

Thus, in working with bad feelings the process of change is brought about not by allowing and accepting the bad feeling per se but by a reorganization, a shift to some other adaptive response by gaining access to a primary emotion not previously available. This involves neither insight, a new understanding, being understood by another, nor a change in a belief, but rather a reorganization based on a newly accessed emotional response. Increased accessibility to alternate aspects of self and reorganization may be the key to change when dealing with bad feelings.

ALLOWING AND ACCEPTANCE
OF PAINFUL EXPERIENCE

Allowance and acceptance of pain, although similar to working with bad feeling in that the feeling needs to be approached rather than avoided, differs in that it is the feeling of the painful feelings, such as loss or grief, that results in the completion and relief by means of emotional processing. Facing pain does not involve nearly as much working through of the complex meanings and dysfunctional beliefs about the self as is done in working with bad feelings, but rather requires overcoming fear of the self being shattered by feeling the pain. Emotional processing, then, is a type of exposure treatment; exposure to the pain that is used in order to change elements of the pain-producing structure (Foa & Kozak, 1986; Greenberg & Safran, 1987).

Solutions to the problems of pain do not lie in understanding their sources or the losses suffered, which often are only too evident. Rather, change comes in allowing and accepting the pain that, in an attempt to protect the self has often been avoided, and in experiencing and expressing the feelings, in order to live them through to completion.

The transformation that occurs in the allowance of painful feelings has been one of the most undocumented mysteries of psychological healing—one that has been the cause of great controversy. It has been phrased thus: Does emotional release or catharsis cure or does it just provide temporary relief? As with most dichotomies, this one is false. The process of resolving pain is complex, involves a variety of processes, and can result in both relief and enduring change. Although allowing and probably accepting painful feelings relies on some organismic muscular release and neurochemical recuperative process (experienced as the ability to "go on" having suffered the pain), it is also important to recognize that it is not just the relief and release of feeling one's feelings of pain that leads to change. This experience also involves a cognitive change involving a shift in internal relations between aspects of the self, a shift in one's view that the pain will destroy the self, and, finally, a change in beliefs about the self. Feeling painful feelings, when therapeutic, involves both release and relief as well as cognitive change. The combination of all of these changes results in a strengthened sense of self.

Our (Greenberg & Safran, 1987) initial intensive analysis of a number of actual episodes of the successful therapeutic resolution of painful experience used task-analytic methods devised to study the verbal protocols and audio and video tapes of episodes of psychotherapeutic change (Greenberg, 1991). Here, we have progressively refined a model that depicts the in-therapy performance components of pain-resolution episodes. This is shown in Fig. 12.3.

As shown in the model of therapeutic resolution of painful experience, feeling pain is an early step in a stage process of change in which the previously warded-off, avoided painful feelings must first be approached and *accepted* as part of oneself. The acceptance of the pain offers a form of containment that helps create a safe distance from the feeling and allows the need or affective goal associated with the feeling to be recog-

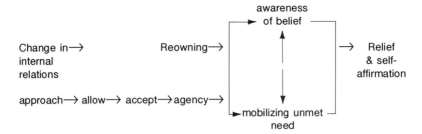

FIG. 12.3. Allowing of painful experience.

nized and mobilized, thereby empowering the organism to combat any dysfunctional appraisals that are preventing and/or causing the pain. The allowance of the pain results in an organismic sense of relief and allows the person to emerge in a new, self-affirming manner.

The critical sequence shown in Figure 12.3 of allowance and acceptance, and of increasing the sense of agency in the feeling, results in a reowning of the painful experience. This change in internal relations, which results in a reowning, helps the person to challenge the interruptive cognitions and beliefs and transform them, as well as mobilize previously unmet needs. It is this mobilization of previously inaccessible resources of the essential self, contacting the inherent exploratory curiosity and the desire to be attached to others—what can be viewed as the will to live—that helps overcome the loss and combat any dysfunctional beliefs that are involved in both causing and maintaining the pain. This process of facing pain, accessing needs, and combating dysfunctional beliefs results in both a sense of relief and the adoption of a more self-nurturing and self-affirming stance. It is thus both the tolerance of the pain and an internal reorganization that results in change.

From a phenomenological perspective, people, in coming to deal with core dreaded painful aspects of self or with bad feelings, learn that they can survive what they had previously believed to be unendurable. By living through the experience, they face their own existential death and are reborn. This is a type of exposure treatment, with three critical differences from a behavioral approach. First, the exposure in facing painful or bad feelings is exposure to previously avoided *internal* experience rather than an avoided external stimulus; second, there is a change in *meaning* rather than a change in conditioning; third, novelty is introduced by accessing new *internal* affective information and resources rather than engaging in a new behavior.

Having accepted the previously avoided feeling and survived the experience, people no longer rigidly attend to threat cues signaling the emergence of the dreaded feeling, nor do they focus solely on attempting to escape. Rather, they are now more flexible and open to new information. The conditions and opportunity for novelty, seeing new possibilities, and creating new meaning now exists.

By staying focused on their internal experience, people begin to access new resources that were previously inaccessible and look for novel ways of coping. It is the *shift* to the accessing of organismic needs and the motivation of the essential self to survive and grow that provides a basis for the novel coping. Knowing what one wants and needs empowers the individual to become an agent on one's own behalf in obtaining needed support and nurture. Nurturing and support can be obtained both internally, in the form of self-soothing and self-valuing, and through interaction, in the form of acting in the world to obtain needed support by self-assertively asking others for support or defining one's boundaries.

This process of allowing and accepting therefore requires that the pain be evoked in the session and lived through, not talked about. By experiencing the pain in its actuality, by existentially facing it, one is, in essence, in a novel situation in which, by facing the dreaded, and surviving the experience, one learns that the pain is endurable and will not destroy the self. In addition, the person is then opened to new possibilities and can attend to new information. This new experience restructures the pain-producing emotional schemes.

Two sources of new experience in the here and now that are important in dealing with the pain are (a) the safe, prizing presence of the therapist as a comforting and validating figure who is partially internalized (Greenberg et al., 1993), and (b) the development of a place to stand in which one has a view of the painful experience and how it was created (i.e., disembedding from the pain by constructive abstraction). With the help of these two aids—interpersonal support and an internal shift in perspective—one is able to access a more self-nurturing/affirming set of functions.

This move to more positive coping is in part governed by the organism's tendency to "go on" and seek more positive, comfortable, adaptive states rather than stay in pain. The paradox is that the avoidance of the aversiveness of the pain perpetuates the pain and prevents the true ability to move away from it. One needs to embrace the pain to truly move on from it by restructuring it. This is what is meant by the colloquial terms going into, and through, one's pain, in which the emergence of newness is captured by the mythic image of the phoenix rising from the ashes. In this image, organization emerges from disorganization and destruction. In working with pain, therapists therefore need to promote the aforementioned steps for resolving pain, using the emotionally focused intervention principles of attending, intensifying, and symbolizing. Therapists thus need to encourage approach and the promotion of acceptance of experience, in favor of negative evaluation of self-experience and to facilitate the taking of responsibility for the experience.

CLIENT EXPERIENCE

A further source of data for refining and validating the performance model of the allowance of painful experiences mentioned earlier are clients' subjective recall of their experience collected by means of interpersonal process recall (IPR). This method involves reviewing videotaped episodes of their in-session experiences with clients to obtain a free recall of their internal experience at important moments in the episode. Clients' IPR recalls[1] suggest that the model we have developed from observation of in-session performance is somewhat consistent with clients' internal experience. A number of categories of experience emerged from the grounded theory investigation that support the model; namely, Avoidance, Allowing, Owning, Interruptive Belief, Relief, and Self-Affirmation. Additional categories that emerged were Control and Reason/Emotion Polarity, Stuggle to Allow, and Awareness and Questioning of Interruption. The latter categories give more of a sense of the client's internal experience in this event.

Examples of recall data in each of these categories are presented here for three clients 1, 2, and 3, who engaged in an allowing of painful emotion episode while working in therapy on the resolution of emotional unfinished business with a significant other (Greenberg et al., 1993).

Avoidance

1. "I remember quite often staring at that cloth and my mind would just blank, total blank. Couldn't draw out a thought, couldn't draw out an emotion."
2. "I was afraid. It was sort of like going back 25 years and feeling the pain again, only it was stronger because at that time I didn't allow it to happen. I pretended that everything was fine."
3. "I'm avoiding, I usually avoid trying to feel it again."

Control and Reason/Emotion Polarity

1. "I can see there that my head and my emotions are not in sync with each other or something, and my logic sometimes takes over and says, 'What can you do about it? Deal with the pain and get over with it.' . . . It's like I'm too rational in my approach to things. I can't—the emotions won't come out."
2. "The restraint has been so powerful it has almost immobilized me, I guess, when I think about it, in dealing with some of this, and I

---

[1]Thanks to Ruth Rohn who designed the IPR interview and collected the data.

feel immobilized." . . . "This part of myself is saying don't feel, diminish. It's this internalized mother saying, 'Your hurt is not important.' "

3. "But I didn't know if my head was ready to let me say it. Like, I was intellectualizing, I guess, my emotions were there, yet my head was saying something different than what was here."

Struggle to Allow

1. "So I really had to struggle with bringing the emotions to the surface 'cause it's just been ground down for all these years."

2. "Should I talk about it, should I break down. The fear of that I guess was very strong, of allowing myself to, cause I knew I was going to, and I wasn't sure whether I wanted that to happen."

3. "But I feel that I still didn't get it out. It was like I've never allowed myself to do that. And I find it very difficult sitting in the chair talking to myself. Sometimes I can lose myself in it, when I get really emotional I lose myself in it. But for the most part I find that difficult." . . . "Some resistance, and also of having to build up and convince myself that it was legitimate, OK, and valid to feel. One part of me sort of wants to diminish it. So when I was crying, I didn't feel, it just seemed like a natural progression from what we had been doing."

Awareness and Questioning of Interruptive Processes

1. "What I'm doing to myself there, it drains me when I look at that. I say, 'Why are you doing that to yourself?' " (This is a somewhat current IPR reaction).

2. "And I'm looking at it now and saying, 'Is that what you do to yourself?' That's really what I was thinking. 'Is that really how you handle hurt all the time?' " (A current IPR reaction)

3. "It's like, just becoming aware of what I have done all these years. Um, accepting that that's what I did and saying, 'OK that's brought you pain so don't do it anymore.' " (Report on an in-therapy experience)

Allowing

1. "And I was feeling so much in pain that at some point that I allowed myself to feel it and it kinda took, over you know, that the emotion then took over and I did lose myself in it. But it's not often I can do that."

3. "As soon as I was feeling it it just came flooding back with such force I thought, 'Gee, there's no reason to resist this.' When I cried it just flooded into me."

Owning

1. "I said, 'It was me!' 'That was me!' That's what struck me, that don't forget that was me, because my way of coping all the way along was has been to say this almost that that wasn't me."

Dysfunctional Belief

1. "I'm afraid I'm going to, that I wouldn't stop, that I'd lose it. I'd lose it. If I let myself go there, I would lose it."
2. "My belief that I couldn't show my vulnerable side, you know, once I did do that I realized that the world doesn't change, that it's very permissible for me to do that. And how the other person takes it is not my concern, it's how I feel about it myself that's of importance."

Relief

1. "I was so completely and totally drained, but I felt like a burden had lifted, like I was carrying something here [points to chest] and it lightened, that feeling."
2. "Yes, because I can remember when it was over that it was a sense of sort of relief about having said how I felt about that situation, about him."
3. "Felt immense relief and release: don't have to keep this emotion down and away, just let it be, not suppress it."

Self-Affirmation

1. "I don't know, memories were opened up and I felt that it was OK to cry and that these feelings of mine were legitimate."

Summary Statements

1. "What shifted was I allowed myself to really feel the pain of what I went through when my husband just simply walked away. I never really dealt with that pain before, I don't think I've ever dealt with it like that. I don't think I felt it so strongly as I did. It was almost like a revelation that, 'Was I in that much pain that I would feel

that deeply and feel that hurt?' And I felt a sense of relief. That was a good feeling. That was probably the biggest change."

2. "I just feel like I've been walking around all this time with stuff buried and it's so great to release it, acknowledge it and come to terms with it. This has been invaluable, I have felt so optimistic."

CONCLUSION

Although emotion operates in different ways at different times in the therapeutic change process (Greenberg et al., 1993; Greenberg & Safran, 1987), one key aspect that operates in working with emotion is the allowing of the experience of previously disallowed emotion. The allowing of emotional experience in therapy appears to facilitate change by way of three necessary processes: a change in internal relations, a reowning and an increased sense of agency.

The change in internal relations involves a move from avoidance and negative evaluation of internal experience to an *accepting* stance. Painful, bad, and hopeless feelings are not *things* as such, but products of internal relations. The very acts of approaching, attending to, and accepting or positively evaluating one's pain lead to its transformation.

Reowning is the process of identifying with feelings and associated thoughts, memories, needs, and action tendencies that have been disowned. Disowned experiences, although not integrated into the dominant self-organization, do exert influence on behavior. People tend to deal with the unacceptable by depersonalizing their feelings and not experiencing them as their own, thus weakening their self-organization.

Therapy can be understood as not so much a process of bringing previously unconscious material into consciousness as it is one of *reclaiming disowned experience*. Gestalt therapists (Perls, Hefferline, & Goodman, 1951) use experiments of deliberate awareness to promote experiences of *"it is me who is thinking, feeling, needing, wanting, or doing this."* People can distinguish between the conceptual processing of information in an intellectual way, and the experiential linking of that information to the self (Greenberg et al., 1993). It is the latter that is important in therapeutic change.

Finally, an increased sense of agency results from the aforementioned two processes. With reowning comes an increased sense of self in relation to a domain of experience. *Hope develops*, from the sense that "It is *me* who is feeling this, it is me who is an agent in this feeling" and "It is me who can do something about this." Although a sense of agency may not yet provide a concrete plan of action, there is a feeling of confidence that action is possible and that change can occur.

REFERENCES

Beck, T. (1976). *Cognitive therapy and the emotional disorders.* New York: International Universities Press.

Bolger, L. (1994). *The subjective experience of transformation through pain in adult children of alcoholics.* Unpublished document, York University, North York.

Ellis, A. (1962). *Reason and emotion in psychotherapy.* Secaucus, NJ: Lyle Stuart.

Foa, E., & Kozak, M. (1986). Emotional processing of fear: Exposure to corrective information. *Psychological Bulletin, 99,* 20–35.

Frijda, N. (1986). *The emotions.* New York: Cambridge University Press.

Greenberg, L. (1991). Research on the process of change. *Psychotherapy Research, 1,* 3–16.

Greenberg, L., Rice, L., & Elliott, R. (1993). *Facilitating emotional change: The moment-by-moment process.* New York: Guilford Press.

Greenberg, L., & Safran, J. (1987). *Emotion in psychotherapy.* New York: Guilford Press.

Greenberg, L., & Safran, J. (1989). Emotion in psychotherapy. *American Psychologist, 44,* 19–29.

Perls, F., Hefferline, R., & Goodman, P. (1951). *Gestalt therapy.* New York: Julian Press.

Author Index

Subject Index

A

Acoustic startle reflex
  amygdala, 77–79
  cAMP, 78–79
  electrical stimulation, 77
  glutamate, 78–79
  nucleus reticularis pontis caudalis, 77–78
Acquired immunodeficiency syndrome, 100–101
Action, control precedence, 4–5
Actual/ideal discrepancy, 216, 224
  dejection-related suffering, 204–205, 211, 217–220, 233
    feeling despondent, 212
    feeling weak, 211
  frustration-related anger, 236
Actual/ought self-discrepancy, 216
  agitation-related suffering, 204, 206, 217–220, 233
  resentment-related anger, 236
Affect contagion principle, 193
Affect Intensity Measure, 143, 153–154
Affective neuroscience, 29–56, *see also* Behavioral neuroscience; Cognitive neuroscience

affective language, 34
basic emotional processes, 36
behavioral analysis, 36–39
  cross-mammalian emotions, 37
  natural behavior patterns, 38
brain analysis, 36–39
coherent psychology, 35–36
mammalian brain, 35–36
psychological analysis, 36–39
  intrinsic psychobehavioral tendencies, 38
  primitive psychic processes, 37
research program, 44
Affective valence, 45, 120
Aggression, 17, *see also* Anger
  causation of, 6
  likelihood of, 17–18
  regional disposition, 185–186
Agreeableness/antagonism, 172, 177, 195–196
Agreeableness Factor, 186
Amygdala
  acoustic startle reflex, 77–79
    cAMP, 78–79
    nucleus reticularis pontis caudalis, 77–78
  conditioned fear, 71, 74